Memoir of George Edmund Street, 1824-1881

Arthur Edmund Street

MEMOIR

OF

GEORGE EDMUND STREET, R.A.

WOODBURYTYPE

FROM A PHOTOGRAPH TAKEN FOR MEN OF MARK 1877.

MEMOIR

OF

GEORGE EDMUND STREET, R.A.

1824-1881

Frank Darling
2 Leader Lane
Toronto

July 1913

BY HIS SON

ARTHUR EDMUND STREET

WITH PORTRAIT

LONDON

JOHN MURRAY, ALBEMARLE STREET

1888

PREFACE

SOME apology is due for a book which I feel to be crude and incomplete.

Originally intended to be no more than a private record of some of my father's opinions and a few of his more important works, it suffers, I am aware, from a want of continuity and cohesion natural to such beginnings and to an inexperienced writer.

My father's home life—the more intimate side of his character—is hardly touched upon.

Such as it is, I trust the Memoir may have some interest for those whose personal acquaintance with its subject will enable them to fill up the picture.

My warm thanks are due to all the friends who have kindly helped me with their recollections.

LONDON, *March* 1888.

MEMOIR

OF

GEORGE EDMUND STREET

CHAPTER I

THE family of Street, or that branch of it from which my father traced his descent, was, at the earliest date at which it is mentioned in contemporary records, connected with the city and county of Worcester. That the Streets were people of some consideration is clear from the fact that Francis Streate was Member of Parliament for the city in 1563, while George Streete was Mayor in 1635. In the eighteenth century various members of the family seem to have migrated to Surrey; my father's great-grandfather lived in Guildford, a brother of his is spoken of as "Street of Ripley," while a niece intermarried with the family of Austen of Shalford, whose representative, Colonel Godwin Austen, now lives at Shalford House. The monument of the lady in question, on which the arms of the Streets and Austens are quartered, still exists in Shalford Church. My father's grandfather, who was settled in business in London, had three sons, of whom the youngest, Thomas, was the father of the subject of this memoir. This Thomas married, first, Mary, the widow of Thomas Brereton of Winchester, born Ridding; and secondly, in 1815, after the death of his first wife without issue, Mary Anne Millington, by whom he had three sons —Thomas Henry, Charles Lawrence, and George Edmund, born respectively in 1816, 1822, and on 20th June 1824—

B

and one daughter—Mary Anne—born in 1825. In 1784 my grandfather started business as a solicitor in Philpot Lane, living meantime in the immediate neighbourhood in Brabant Court. Some time between the birth of his second son in 1822 and that of my father in 1824 my grandfather went to live at Woodford in Essex. There he stopped till 1830, when he moved to "The Grove," Camberwell.

These first six years of my father's life offer no feature of interest : there was nothing precocious in his development, nor did he at that age display any marked aptitudes or likings ; at the same time, it may be said that the force of character and the strong moral sense which distinguished the man were, at that early age, in a degree foreshadowed to those who knew how to read the signs, and there were some who were bold enough to predict that he would be one day heard of. After the move to Camberwell in 1830, my father was sent with his elder brother Charles to a school at Mitcham, and when the collegiate school at Camberwell was opened they went there as day-boys.

In 1839 my grandfather retired, but the business was carried on in the same place till 1861, when it was transferred to Lincoln's Inn Fields. After his retirement he went to Crediton to live, and thus it came about that my father's schooling was brought to an abrupt end ; he had, however, been almost at the head of the school for some little time before leaving, so that his loss may have been more apparent than real. His behaviour at school seems to have been all that it should have been, albeit the headmaster complained of his having "too much levity;" but he seems by that time to have learnt the habit of sketching for the amusement of himself and the fellows at odd times, and probably in school hours, and on anything which came to his hand—a proceeding which, in the eyes of any well-constituted headmaster, might well have justified the use of stronger epithets. I have got now several little pen-and-ink drawings—copies, for the most part, of Cruickshank illustrations and animal subjects—done at this time. They are not absolutely without merit, and at least they show that there was already a bias in this direction, but they certainly gave no promise of any unusual powers of draughtsmanship.

In the autumn of 1839 my father's eldest brother, Thomas, who had been admitted as a partner into his father's firm in the course of that year, and lived consequently in town, came to spend his autumn holiday at Crediton ; and during his stay there took my father for an excursion of a few days to look at some of the church architecture of the neighbourhood　Had my father been an architect of a commonplace stamp, and with no special aptitude for that profession, it might very well have been said that it was to his brother that he owed being an architect at all.　Where, however, Nature had so obviously suggested a particular career, it was not likely that, even though it might be missed for a time, it should not have eventually been found.　Be that as it may, my father's brother, at this time a young man of three and twenty, had for some time been full of enthusiasm for mediæval architecture, and was in the habit, whenever he had a few spare days, of going off with his sketchbook and hunting out churches and old houses.　It was to him that my father's earliest training was due, and this, their first excursion, which was to be followed by many another, is interesting as marking an important epoch in my father's life, though unfortunately I cannot find that he put any of his impressions on paper.

Early in 1840 the boy of fifteen was sent up to town to take his place in the office, probably rather with the idea of giving him some useful employment than of actually initiating him into his real business in life.　Anyhow, the office life does not seem to have been at all to his taste, and when once broken off, was never seriously entered upon again.　The break came after a very few months, for in May 1840 my grandfather's death brought my father back to live with his mother and sister, first at Crediton, and then, after two or three months, at Exeter.　The immediate neighbourhood of the cathedral had in all probability a good deal to do with the shaping of my father's future.　The love of church architecture grew on him fast, and with it grew the love of the services which, heard under a cathedral roof, gain so much in solemnity and impressiveness.　From Exeter my father went after a time to Taunton to take

lessons in perspective from a Mr. Haseler, an uncle by
marriage, who combined teaching with the practice of his
art as a painter.   Here he seems to have worked assiduously, both at perspective and at painting in oils (begun at
a remarkably early stage one would say), but the true bent
of his mind had not yet become clear even to himself, for
he was anxious to go to college with the idea of subsequently entering the Church   Motives of economy prevented
the realisation of the first part of the programme, while the
consciousness of not feeling a sufficiently strong call for the
work induced him finally to give up the idea of taking orders.

Before going to Taunton he had made a second short
walking tour with his eldest brother to Barnstaple, Bide-
ford, Torrington, and Clovelly, and this time he put down
his impressions in a book.

This diary displays undeniable powers of observation,
and an intense enjoyment both of man's work and of
Nature's   The young enthusiast gets up before six o'clock
to make a sketch out of his bedroom window.   He describes
the towns and the features of the country through which
their road lay in funny old-fashioned phraseology, but in a
way which in a boy just turned sixteen is so uncommon as
to make one wonder that he had not even yet discovered
what his true vocation was.

After returning from Taunton he was so much at a loss
what to do as to have an idea of joining his brother Charles,
who had gone out to St. John's, New Brunswick, two years
before, with the prospect of entering some mercantile house ;
and when this plan was fortunately given up had, *faute de
mieux*, resumed his place on the office stool in Philpot Lane,
and might have continued for some time longer in that, to
him, irksome position, had not a sudden inspiration on the
part of his mother changed the whole course of his life

In the early part of 1840, while my father was in London, Mr. Haseler had sent down to Crediton a parcel of
architectural sketches made by his cousin, Mr Owen Carter
of Winchester, during a 'tour in Egypt.   My grandfather
seems to have exclaimed on seeing them, "Ah! this would
be the very thing for George!"   No more was said or

thought about it at the time, 'but six months after my
grandfather's death, when my father had for the second time
been installed in the office, the exclamation suddenly
occurred to my grandmother, and in a moment she felt
convinced that she had the solution of the problem in her
hands. She lost no time in getting Mr. Haseler to sound
his ˙cousin as to his ability or · willingness to take a · pupil.
Mr. Haseler's recommendation would seem to have been · of
so warm a character that Mr Carter was only too anxious
to secure such a paragon, for he accepted the proposition
immediately.   The preliminaries were speedily arranged,
and early in the spring of 1841 my father began work in
Winchester as Mr. Carter's aɪticled pupɪl. ˙Probably there
was not a great quantity of work going on in the office, for
my father's time seems to have been to a great extent spent
ɪn the cathedral, almost the whole of which he sketched and
measured ; once, he writes, that he has to stand on the top
of the altar-screen, rather an odd place, · âs he says, for
sketching, being only just wɪde enough for standing-room,
and fifty feet from the floor. He often worked till it was
too dark to see any longer, and he and the organist, who
was ɪn the habit of practɪsing ɪn the afternoon, were frequently the only occupants of the great church. One evening, when the strains, of the organ had made my father
quite forgetful of the present, he suddenly awoke to the
consciousness that the sound had ceased, and at the same
moment heard the door clang and the key turn in the lock.
He flew to the door, not relishing the idea of being im-
prisoned for the night, and by banging it managed to attract
the attention of the verger.   The old man seemed considerably astonɪshed that my father should have been so anxious
to attract his notice, and saɪd, " Lor' bless you, sir, if you'd
rung one of the bells, we should have come soon enough."

Besides becoming thus ɪntɪmate with the beauties of the
cathedral, my father found tɪme to make himself well
acquaɪnted wɪth almost everything oɪ interest wɪthin a
radius of twenty mɪles   During the long summer days his
brother was ˳accustomed to come down and spend the
Sundays with hɪm, and together they thoroughly ransacked

the neighbourhood for architectural treasures, besides going
farther afield when time allowed.   My father's articles
expired in two years, but Mr. Carter had by that time
become so much alive to his pupil's valuable qualities, that
he was anxious to keep him on, and their connection did
not cease for another twelve months.   This last year was
utterly irksome to my father; there was no one in the place
for whom he really cared, and his letters all express the
same longing for home and companionship.   Work was
his sole resource, and he had worked assiduously from
inclination as well as from necessity.   Three years before
he had been a mere novice, now he was an enthusiastic,
untiring, and intelligent student and ecclesiologist.   His
industry had never been called in question; it had been,
indeed, testified to time after time, but it had become
apparent now that it was united to other qualifications not
less important and of greater rarity.   In 1844 the opportunity of reunion, for which the whole family had long been
waiting, at last came.   My uncle took a house at Lee, and
was at once joined by his mother and sister   The time had
come for my father to put himself under a master of greater
pretensions and with a larger practice than Mr. Carter.   He
accordingly came up to town, and armed with a letter of
introduction from Mr Edwin Nash, and a roll of sketches
and drawings, presented himself to Messrs. Scott and Moffatt.
He was accepted at once, and such was his energy that the
third day in town saw him in his place in the office in
Spring Gardens.   Hearty in his work, he was no less hearty
in his pleasures; but it is related of him that he was frequently in the habit of foregoing an evening's enjoyment
that he might be the fresher for his work in the morning.
At the moment when he came to Scott, the drawings for
the cathedral at Hamburg were just being made, and he
was taken on provisionally at first to help till the stress of
work should be over; but so well did he acquit himself, that
the provisional engagement became a permanent one, and
was not broken till my father found he had so much coming
into his hands as to make it expedient for him to do no work
but his own.   During the years at Scott's, church-hunting was

not neglected—every day of holiday being, in fact, devoted to what they called "ecclesiologising." In company with his brother he made a tour—knapsack on back—to Chichester, Boxgrove, Cowdray, etc., during the spring of 1843 ; and the autumn of the same year found them in Lincolnshire, where they saw and sketched Langton, Tattershall, Heckington, Addlethorpe, Howden, and a multitude of other churches. In 1844 they were in Sussex. In 1845 in Northamptonshire—at Barnack and the neighbourhood. The next year they were in Northants again. And in the autumn my father made a long tour through the Lake Country, and to Lanercost, Durham, and Newcastle, and, after being joined by his brother at Richmond, to Wensleydale and the Yorkshire abbeys, missing Jervaulx however. Lanercost filled him with delight Out of much that he wrote about it I cannot forbear to quote some few sentences, because they show that his love for the church itself, and the architecture which finds its highest expression in sacred buildings, were already connected indissolubly, so that an abbey in ruins afforded him a pleasure which was little removed from pain.

"I got out," he writes, "at Milton Station, and trudged off for Lanercost Abbey, an enthusiastic ecclesiologist, with everything upon earth to make my enthusiasm higher than usual—a glorious autumn day, a beautiful walk, and an abbey in prospect, in ruins it is true, but so lovely and so admirable in its ruin that, in my admiration of it, the day, and the scenery, I had almost forgotten to be enraged with its iconoclastic destroyers ; but it was not in mortal temper, after having seen it and sketched it and studied it carefully and lovingly as I did, to ascend the hill away from it, to look at the river still rushing along as beautiful and as swift as when holy men planned its bridge of yore, to look at the sunny fields first cultivated by them, and not to feel sorrow and indignation at the thought that avarice and sin could so far have transported men as to lead them to the destruction of so fair a scene."

Again he writes : "O that the abusers of the monastic system would trouble themselves to examine this once happy valley, to watch the soothing influence of the lovely building and landscape, and would ask themselves whether they did not, in looking, feel more of reverence, more of awe and of love for the religions and for the men than they have heretofore felt.

"It is particularly characteristic of Lanercost that all is in har-mony—every portion seems designed upon the same principle, and with the same amount of reverential feeling, and all is so simple and so severe as to indicate truth and solidity and the absence of gaudy or hypocritical religion." . . . "I daresay you have smiled at the way in which I connect architecture and religion, it may perhaps be the bias of a profession which makes me do so, but I cannot but think that architecture as well as, not more than, the other fine arts is a great and most important assistant to religion Again, in the matter of abbeys, I know there will be an outcry when you read my journal against my admiration of them and of their system; but, when I lament their destruction, I lament it because I venerate the men who founded them, and preserved literature, science, and art for our use."

In the spring of 1847 my father and uncle found them-selves in Norfolk and Cambridgeshire, making the round of the magnificent fen-country churches, and in 1850 they were in Northants together for the third time My father made frequent excursions on his own account, or with other friends, and was gradually making notes of all the fine churches in the country. In these excursions the day's walk often extended to thirty miles or more, and that under the weight of a knapsack. On one occasion, while they were in Yorkshire in 1846, they arrived at Leybourne after dark, and, being obliged to leave by coach at six o'clock the next morning, borrowed a lantern and made what sketches they could of the interior of the church by its feeble light. Indeed, their enthusiasm was boundless. As my father wrote while he was still at Win-chester: "Tom and I get more fiercely architectural and antiquarian every day, and for myself, I think I attend to very little else."

It was, I think, in 1847 that my father first made acquaintance with the glorious church at West Walton. He made great friends with the vicar, Mr. Blencowe, and seems to have instructed him much as to his church This is the first time he gave distinct evidence of that power which distinguished him so much afterwards, that of reading the history of the growth of a building, and making a correct diagnosis of its anatomy. He says in a letter :—

"I ought to have said a word about delightful West Walton.

The tower, a most massive and grand fellow, stands detached from, the church at the side of the churchyard. The porch and the interior of the church are lovely in the extreme, the very *ne plus ultra* of first pointed work. The parson takes immense interest in it—scrapes off whitewash, and hopes some day to spend some thousands on a restoration. I enlightened him to a tremendous extent about the original state of the building, about which all the architects whom he has seen there have, I am sure, been making great mistakes However, he is going to dig and scratch away to find out whether I am right or not "

Mr. Blencowe, who was keenly appreciative of this enlightenment, set to work at the scraping and digging, with the result of establishing the correctness of my father's views in every particular. I believe Scott himself was to be numbered among those who had misinterpreted the building. The friendship thus commenced with Mr. Blencowe was never laid aside, and was soon rendered closer by the discovery that my father's sister and Miss Blencowe were equally interested in the question of church embroidery, Miss Blencowe being indeed at that time the best workwoman in England. My father's letters to his sister during his tours are full of descriptions of whatever mediæval embroidery he lighted upon ; he was constantly sketching it, as much for her guidance as his own pleasure, and many of his designs—numerous enough even in his early days—were worked by her, so that her name became well known as that of a skilful embroideress.

My uncle retained all his early love for architecture, and it was not till after 1849, when he married and the claims of business became more pressing, that he began to forego his expeditions. At the time they were all living together at Lee, and afterwards at Peckham, my aunt relates how the two young men used to arrive with sketchbooks full, and rolls of rubbings of brasses, and would then sit up till the small hours in all the excitement of archæological discussions and arguments. My uncle was quite untaught. His love for and appreciation of good architecture were quite spontaneous, and the proficiency which he attained with his pencil, and the knowledge he had of his subject more than considerable. That two brothers should have had similar powers of draughtsmanship (though in different degrees), and should have been so enthusiastic in the same cause, is the more remarkable because it was certainly not inherited from either parent, or, so far as is known, from any relation.

In the early part of 1846, after a stay of two years at Lee, a move was made to Peckham. Their house was only about a quarter of a mile distant from St. Giles's, Camberwell; and the church being on the way to town, my father frequently made an early breakfast, went to matins at eight o'clock or half-past with his sister, and then walked straight into town. He was now full of aspirations for the future, but doubtful how to realise them. Many were the ambitious castles in the air that he and his sister built in their walks together—how he should be made an R.A and have a great public building to design, both then seemingly most problematical, but both to be fulfilled in a score or so of years.

The first hope of getting work to do came in 1846. My uncle had at that time a pupil of the name of Barwis, whose mother was anxious to build a church, and at my uncle's instigation put herself into my father's hands. His tour to the lakes in that year, which I have already spoken of, was really undertaken primarily for the purpose of going to Langrigg in Westmoreland, where the Barwis family lived. Here my father spent a fortnight, talking the whole plan over and over, and dreaming of the fortune which the display of his capabilities should bring him; unfortunately the proverb, which warns us against over-confidence, was in this case only too strictly justified, and my father's hopes were dashed just when they seemed most certain.

The disappointment was for the moment bitter; but he had not long to wait, for it was in the same year that the much-desired opportunity came, and it was to his sister that he owed it. While staying at Bath she happened to meet a lady from Clifton, who incidentally mentioned that she was doing some work for a church which a clergyman of their acquaintance—a Mr. Prynne—intended building in Cornwall. My aunt wrote off at once to my father, suggesting that he should set to work immediately at plans for a church, and should then submit them to Mr. Prynne; while she, at the

same time, begged her friend to use her influence with Mr.
Prynne on my father's behalf. She had an interview with
Mr. Prynne about it, and his first question made her heart
sink. "Has your brother got much work going on?"
There could only be one answer. Luckily this was just the
one that was wanted ; and Mr. Prynne, finding that my
father would be able to devote all his time and attention to
this particular work, gave it him forthwith.

Thus my father secured his first commission. This was
Biscovey Church. It was finished and consecrated two years
later. Mr Prynne was transferred to St. Peter's, Plymouth,
while the work was still in progress, and a Mr. Hendy took
his place My father had all this time been working for
Scott and Moffatt, but in 1849 he felt justified in taking
chambers and starting on his own account. Of his two most
intimate office friends—Mr. William White and Mr. G. F.
Bodley—the former had settled in Truro a short time before,
and had made a considerable practice in the neighbourhood.
My father's work at Biscovey gave him a footing in the same
county, and fresh work came to him every week. Mr.
Prynne again proved himself a good friend by giving him the
restoration of St. Peter's, Plymouth. Besides these two works
he had, in 1848-49, Sticker Church, the restoration of St.
Mewan, a new church and schools in the same parish, the re-
storation of Sheviocke Church, the new church and schools
of St. Peter, Treverbyn, and restorations of St Cuthbert's, of
Lostwithiel, St. Austell, the churches at East and West
Looe, Little Petherick Church, St. Neot's, SS. Probus and
Grace at Probus, and Lanreath, all these being in Cornwall.
Besides these, he had restorations at Enfield, Hadleigh,
Heston, Sundridge, and Hawes, a new church at Bracknell,
and additions to the rectory at Peasemore, but undoubtedly
the most important events to him were the restoration of
Hadleigh Church and his introduction to Mr. Butler of
Wantage, because of the results to which they directly led.

My father's practice being at first so much in one neighbourhood led to his spending several weeks at a time in
Cornwall three or four times a year. In this way all his
works were under his immediate superintendence—a fact

which was evidently beneficial, because one work led to another in a way which could not have been the case had they not been satisfactory. He owed a great deal of his success to a Mr. Hosken—the clergyman at St. Blazey—who, having quite convinced himself that my father was the right man in the right place, went to work with the view of getting everything in Cornwall put into his hands. To this end he introduced him right and left, and many works were directly due to his advocacy.

These Cornish tours were as unlike as possible to the wearing and hurried business journeys of subsequent years. My father, indeed, did plenty of hard work while he was away ; every necessary drawing was done with his own hands, and the most careful inspection made of each and all of his works, but he seems speedily to have made friends of his Cornish clients ; and his journals and letters of those days reveal a most pleasant succession of dinners, picnics, even dances, some of them got up for his especial delectation, when the more serious work of the day was done.

Life was most enjoyable to him then ; robust of body, an enthusiastic student of nature, intensely devoted to his work, and scarcely less appreciative of the pleasures of society, he found himself on a sudden with as much work on his hands as he could manage, surrounded by good friends, and chiefly bound—for the time at least—to a part of the country where his love for nature was amply satisfied. It was about this time—in 1848—that he met the lady who was a few years later to become his wife. His employment at Hadleigh Church led to his becoming intimate with the family of the vicar, Mr. George Proctor, and at his house he first met the vicar's brother, Mr. Robert Proctor, and his children. To his second daughter, Mariquita, he seems quickly to have become something more than a mere friend, and from that time forward was a frequent visitor at her father's own house—Geys, near Maidenhead. Meantime my uncle had become engaged to the elder daughter of Mr. George Proctor, and his marriage and my father's engagement followed the year after.

My father's connection with the Ecclesiological Society,

and his restoration of Sundridge Church—only a few miles
from Brasted, where Mr. Benjamin Webb was then curate—
brought him into intimate relations with that gentleman.
Mr. Webb early recognised my father's capabilities; and
when Mr. Butler, who was then meditating building himself
a vicarage at Wantage, consulted him on the subject, he
took the opportunity of mentioning my father as a young
man of ability and originality, who, with a love for hard
work, was sure to interest himself actively and personally in
all he had to do with. Mr. Butler decided to act on Mr.
Webb's advice, and certainly never regretted having so done.
The vicarage was a great success, and speedily led to my
father's employment on new schools at Wantage and other
works. My father was now frequently there. In May 1850
he spent a week at the vicarage, and painted a compartment
of the schoolroom roof in distemper with subjects copied
from Overbeck This was by no means a solitary instance
of his setting to work to decorate a building with his own
hands. A year or two later he was engaged two or three
weeks at Sheviocke Church in painting Fra Angelico subjects in medallions; and at Boyne Hill Church, three or
four years after his marriage, to mention no other cases, he
painted a large subject in the spandrel over the chancel
arch. This was an original design, and the most serious
piece of work of the kind he had then undertaken or probably ever undertook. After the first day's work he writes
to my mother :—

"I have only been getting my hand in to-day, but I fancy I
shall be able to manage this painting tolerably well, which will be
the most satisfactory fact in my artistic life for years You know
how I long to be able to paint on church walls, but I have always
been a coward about venturing absolutely to set to work." (This
must mean on an original subject.) "The die is certainly cast at
Boyne Hill, and I *must* get out of the scrape somehow or other."

It was part of his enthusiastic creed that every architect
should be, in his degree, as Giotto was or Michael Angelo,
and should himself be able to decorate his own building
with painting and sculpture. Rapidly-increasing press of
work, which gave him little or no leisure, convinced him, I

think, of the inapplicability of such views to our modern
times, and obliged him to forego putting them into practice,
while still maintaining that such a way of working could
alone give a perfect unity of conception entirely harmonious
in all its details.

In November 1850 my father gave up his chambers in
town, and settled in Wantage—a step chiefly prompted by
his introduction to the Bishop of Oxford (Samuel Wilberforce) by Mr. Butler, and his appointment as architect to the
diocese which soon followed upon it. He was thus placed
in the middle of his work, and within easy reach of the
bishop at Cuddesdon. Success had seemed probable before ;
the patronage of the bishop practically secured it. With
his rapid power of forming a judgment, that remarkable man
had seen at once that the combination of artistic and business
faculties which my father exhibited made him unusually
well qualified for the post. The frequent intercourse with
the bishop which naturally resulted from this appointment
led to a friendship which, at least on my father's side, was
of the warmest possible kind.

The two years of hard work which were passed at
Wantage were not without their periods of relaxation, which,
if brief, were enjoyed with all the more zest on that account.
During the summer my father spent his Sundays at Geys
whenever he could. Many days were passed on the river,
but he rarely failed to combine some church seeing and
sketching with his labours at the oar. Sometimes he spent
several days running at Geys, but wherever he might be,
he might safely be trusted to do a fair share of work. And,
indeed, his mother went so far as to hint that an early
marriage would be more possible if he devoted himself
entirely to Wantage. While admitting herself that she had
no grounds for her suspicions, she yet seems to have looked
on Maidenhead as her son's Capua. Such was very far
from being the case ; if there were temptations to idleness,
he was strong enough to resist them, for he possessed in
a high degree the power of abstracting himself from
his surroundings and concentrating his attention on what
was before him, and could go on working all day, if need

were, with a bright sun and a soft breeze wooing him eloquently to the pleasures which awaited him out of doors.

Of his actual life at Wantage the present Dean of Lincoln (Dr. William Butler) writes :—

"The house which he (Mr. Street) designed was, and is, one of the most convenient and pleasant of dwellings, and it has been a subject of never-failing surprise to all who have seen it and inhabited it, that a house so bright and attractive could have been built for so small a sum of money as it actually cost. I remember that the original estimate was not exceeded by more than £25 or £30. Mr. Street, having no special ties to any locality, desired to live at Wantage, where daily service and weekly celebration had been established at a time when such were rare. He took, therefore, in conjunction with Mr. Stillingfleet,—one of the clergy of the parish,—a little house in Wallingford Street. During the time he lived there, I saw him almost daily. When not called from Wantage on business, he regularly attended every service, and took his part in the choir. He had, I remember, a baritone voice, and took a tenor part He was much interested in the improvement of services, and, although at this time far from wealthy, he offered a large annual subscription, I think it was £20, towards the payment of an organist. His religious opinions were, as all know, definitely of the High Church school; but at this, as indeed at all periods of his life, he was far from accepting the excesses of the so-called Ritualists, who at the time of which I speak had not come into existence. All that we aimed at was a hearty, loyal, and reverent setting forth of the Prayer-Book, and in this he thoroughly concurred." (A note in my father's diary of 1877 seems in point here : "Meeting of Council of English Church Union—I endeavoured in vain to get them to agree to put out a statement that they wished none to go beyond the orders in the Prayer-Book. The more violent men are, the more they seem to carry their point ; and we are driven to defend men with whom we only half agree, and to hold our tongues for their sakes when we ought to speak out.") "Never was there a man of simpler or less luxurious habits. In those two years he dined with us and the clergy of the parish, he drank no wine, and had only the plainest food. I had the privilege of mentioning his name to Bishop Wilberforce, when it was determined to appoint an architect to the diocese The other candidate was the late Mr. Ferrey, who wanted £100 per annum for his services. Fortunately for us, Mr Street was willing to take the office gratuitously, and the committee were wise enough to appoint him unanimously After he settled in Oxford I only saw him occasionally, but our intimacy never ceased "

I shall have to speak at some length later on of the importance which my father attached to the adornment of our church services. He had formed his views at an early age as to the right mode of conducting them, and several years previous to his Wantage days had written with approval of some church which he had lighted upon in the course of his wanderings, " where," he said, " the service is performed as it ought to be, with plenty of chanting and not too much sermonising."

These two years were quite uneventful, unless the gradual conversion of a small practice into a considerable one may be 'called an event. As Cornwall had been the chief theatre of his work a year before, so now was the diocese of Oxford, and he was soon engaged on quite a cluster of neighbouring churches. In September 1850 he had made his first foreign trip In ten days he saw Paris, Chartres, Alençon, Caen, Rouen, and Amiens, sketching all the time with might and main A new volume in the great book of Gothic architecture had been opened before him, and he devoured its pages with enthusiasm. The mighty fabrics themselves, the great sweeps of jewelled glass, the western porches, which seem to invite a world to enter ; the congregations, too, using the churches as they had always been meant to be used ;— all were new to him, and all struck his imagination vividly and ineffaceably. The Channel once crossed, a year rarely if ever passed without his returning to refresh and replenish his knowledge of continental architecture. He thought that the education of the Gothic architect, to be a complete one should embrace every phase of the style without exception, and where inclination and sense of duty were at one, it was not likely that there should be any slackness in doing what was right. In the summer of 1851, three weeks sufficed to make him acquainted with Mainz, Frankfurt, Wurzburg, Hamburg, Nuremberg, Ratisbon, Munich, Ulm, Freiburg, Strassburg, Heidelberg, and three or four of the best of the Belgian towns. Many of. his first impressions on this tour were to be much modified, or even reversed, afterwards. I think he would hardly have stigmatised the Cologne churches as unsketchable and not to his taste a few years later. The cathedral, in spite of its grand scale, was never among his prime favourites from first to last. Seven years later he writes . "Cologne Cathedral is more and more distasteful to me. The new work is very unpleasant in its effect externally —pretty indeed, but wanting in vigour and grandeur. Internally the effect will always be much better, owing to the simplicity of the columns, upon which almost everything depends , but the church is both short and narrow in effect." Nuremberg, too, was more modern than he had expected , its old work, that is to say, was of too late a date for the more exclusive preference of a young man Ratisbon, on the other hand, is beyond all anticipations and beyond all praise. At Constance he had his first view of the Alps, and it cost him a struggle not to make a rush to them for a few days at the expense of education. My father's enjoyment of Nature, and particularly of mountain scenery, was so intense as to make it almost a doubtful point whether or not he preferred it to the handiwork of men, as exemplified in Gothic buildings. I think, however, the human interest of the latter turned the scale ; but to work and sketch in Switzerland, or the Tyrol, or in the Bavarian Uplands, was always a source of the most real pleasure to him

For some years he had been a most active member of the Ecclesiological Society, and, besides reading papers, had at their request made a number of designs for every possible kind of church fitting and furniture. Consequently, when Mr. B P. Willis, of the enterprising firm of Newton, Jones, and Willis, of Birmingham, applied to the Society for advice as to the best man to go to for designs for church furniture for the great Exhibition, they recommended my father. "The Committee think," wrote Mr. Webb, "that these designs will be much in your way. It will be in consequence of our lecturing them upon the importance of having the guidance of an artist in these things that they will apply to you, and therefore we hope that you will accept their commission" The practice up to that time had so generally been to leave the design of the fittings of a church to chance, that my father, who always insisted on making the designs for everything without exception in any work on which he was employed,

C

60

gladly welcomed the opportunity of showing the public how much better and more congruous such work might be if it were designed by an artist. I noticed quite a short time ago that some of the altar-cloth designs still figure in Messrs. Jones and Willis's book. They are of a quite magnificent character, and it needed not the mention of the name to tell me who had been responsible for them

In December my grandmother died at a cottage which my uncle had taken at North End, Hampstead Her illness, which had been of a lingering character, was very sudden at the last, so that there was no time to summon either my father or my aunt to her bedside. The latter was away at Colton, in Staffordshire, where she was employed on some embroidery work for the church which my father had just been restoring. My father himself was at Wantage. He had been, with the exception of the four years at Lee and Peckham, very much divided from his mother since the old days at Camberwell; but the loss must, none the less, have been a very severe one to him. It is enough to read the mother's letters to see the source of the son's strength and steadfastness of character. She was one of those women who, in some indefinable way, have a powerful influence for good on all those into whose company they are thrown; who, themselves rather sparing in outward signs of affection, create in others a warm love and a perfect confidence. Her pride in her son was unbounded, but was left to be inferred rather than expressed, while her love was shown more in the demand for sacrifices, in the confidence with which she appealed to her son's sense of duty and obedience, however severe the test might be, than in its more obvious manifestations.

From the time of his going to Winchester the tone and purport of her letters to him show that, if he was still no more than a boy in years, he was fit to be treated and trusted as a man. Now and again tender words slip out, a little measure of praise and encouragement; but, as a rule, the greater compliment is paid him of taking for granted in him what would be a subject for approval in others "I knew that under the circumstances you would be philosopher enough

to give up" this or that, possibly a little holiday trip from
Winchester   That is a typical expression   It is certain
that my father had enough of the Spartan in him never to
let his mother or any one else know how utterly weary and
lonesome his life at Winchester was, or how bitter such a
disappointment must inevitably have been , but, on the
other hand, it may be guessed that the mother had no want
of appreciation of her son, and that his cheerful endurance
of deprivations, when they were necessary, did more to increase it than anything else could have done

The time had now arrived when the advisability of
having an office at some place where clients could more
conveniently come became impressed on my father   Wantage was suitable enough for his purposes as diocesan architect , but I think he felt that, as long as he practised there,
his status would be so distinctly that of a provincial architect
as to bar him from getting work of a really important
character.   It seems natural that under the circumstances
he should have looked to Oxford as the most likely place to
suit him, for he had not yet made up his mind to venture
himself in the great whirlpool into which he was to be drawn
before very long.   Mr J H. Parker, whom he consulted about
the prospects of an architect in Oxford, strongly advised him
to come, holding out the hope of his getting a good deal of
university work.   This prediction was, curiously enough, never
verified   Possibly my father's very decided adherence to the
earlier phase of Gothic, and the eagerness with which he argued
that Oxford had already enough of debased types, and should
revert to the purity of the early forms, may have frightened
the authorities   However this may have been, the rearrangement of the interior of Jesus' College Chapel was the only
university work he ever did, though he built the church of
St. Philip and James in the Parks, and another at Summertown, besides restoring, in a greater or less degree, most of
the Oxford churches.

Acting on Mr. Parker's advice, my father moved to a
house in Beaumont Street, Oxford, in May 1852, and was
married on the 17th of the following month at Bray Church
In the course of his wedding tour he saw some more

of the great French churches, visiting, among other places,
Troyes, Sens, Auxerre, and Dijon.   Till his marriage I cannot
find that he ever had any permanent help   His friend, Mr.
Bodley, used occasionally to assist him when he was much
pressed, but in general he did everything with his own hand
His working drawings were not beautifully got up, he had
neither time nor inclination for that, but they were done well,
and done rapidly.   Details were often drawn straight off in
ink, so sure was his hand.   Soon after his marriage, however,
it must have become obvious to him that he could no longer
cope single-handed with his constantly increasing work
Mr. Edmund Sedding was articled to him almost immediately on his coming to Oxford ; and soon afterwards Mr.
Philip Webb entered his office.

In April 1853 the first stone of the Theological College
at Cuddesdon was laid.   This was the most important work
which he had as yet been engaged upon.   It was not completed till five and twenty years later, but the design was
wholly made at this time.   It was bound to be simple,—
paucity of funds made that necessary,—but the absence of
enrichment is not noticed, nor is its want felt, because of the
admirable proportions and grouping of the whole building
A man of far more experience and training might well have
made a design inferior to this in the quality of self-restraint,
nor could a building be found which relies more wholly and
more successfully on legitimate means for its effect.   Just
about the same time the original design for the buildings for
the East Grinstead Sisterhood was made.   My father had
long been on terms of intimacy with Mr Neale, its founder,
and so strong were his sympathies for the welfare of the
institution that he freely gave his services then and there-
after.   This design was on somewhat the same lines as that
for Cuddesdon College, but perhaps a little more mannered
than it, and somewhat ultra-monastic and severe in character.
Cuddesdon could hardly have been improved upon, but East
Grinstead could and was, and, though the later design follows
somewhat the plan of the earlier, it is an infinitely more
beautiful and graceful conception, still simple for the most
part, but very delicate and refined in effect, with an entire

absence of the almost repellent severity of the immature effort, but without a trace of weakness.   My father's acquaintance with Mr. A M. Bennett dates from the same year Their connection as architect and client once begun was never terminated till Mr. Bennett's death.   This year— 1853—saw the commencement of various smaller works in Bournemouth and the neighbourhood, and a year or two later a start was made with some portion of what is now the very beautiful church of St. Peter's, Bournemouth, the final touch to which was not given till nearly a quarter of a century later.

This summer, having already seen something of France and the Rhineland, my father determined on an Italian tour Italy, so strange and beautiful, was a perfect revelation to him, but the enthusiasm born of such surroundings never made him for a moment disposed to place her architecture above that of his own country   In one of his letters, written while the excitement of novelty was strong upon him, he speaks of the old churches at Brescia as being " *very Italian,* and that is not so good as *very English.*"   So many notes and sketches were taken on this brief trip, that he felt justified in recording for the benefit of the public what he had seen and what his impressions were   The result was his *Brick and Marble Architecture of North Italy,* published in 1855. This book, which treated of North Italian architecture in a popular style, but none the less scientifically for that, at once made its way in public favour, and decidedly did somewhat to increase his reputation.   It was admitted on all hands to fill an obvious void, and in a way which amateurs no less than architects and archæologists could appreciate.   My father's powers of sketching, already great, served to make the book more valuable from the number, accuracy, and interest of the illustrations ; while his keenness of observation and correctness of reasoning made what seems a bewilderingly rapid journey, as one reads his accounts of it, produce the materials for a standard work

The following year his summer outing took him to North Germany,—to the brick country,—some account of which he gave in a paper on Munster and Soest, which he read before the Ecclesiological Society. He worked hard, as he always did, up early and in late. " I have got a great budget of sketches," he writes, "indeed, I have done pretty well, for in a fortnight I have mustered about fifty large sketches, besides filling a goodly memorandum book. We enjoyed Lübeck immensely, and amongst other feats astonished the natives by making rubbings of some magnificent brasses, of which Marique (my mother) did her share, to the delight of the sacristan." The zest with which my mother entered into these architectural tours was remarkable. She had quite caught the infection ; and I remember well in later years, when I participated in the summer journeys, how reluctantly she exchanged architecture for scenery, and towns for country. My father was not one of those who want driving to their work. Had such been the case, she would certainly have done so. She settled in her own mind that he ought to produce so many sketches in a day, whether landscape or architectural subjects, and did not feel quite satisfied if he fell short of his quota. The result was that every tour is chronicled in the most delightful and vivid way.

All this time he was over head and ears in work, though nothing of any special importance had as yet fallen to him. In 1855 Cuddesdon was opened, and the church and its attendant buildings at Boyne Hill begun. The summer was spent quietly at Geys, and my father got no real holiday at all. In October the writer of these pages was born at Oxford, and shortly afterwards my father began seriously to contemplate what was clearly inevitable sooner or later—the move up to London. He was strongly advised by his friends and admirers to seek a wider field for his talents than Oxford could afford him, and I think he was finally persuaded to do so by Mr. Benjamin Webb. The latter insisted that even university work would be much more likely to come into his hands if he moved, not to speak of the great churches of the land, "which," Mr. Webb said, "no one would ever think of putting into the hands of a provincial man." My uncle had already settled in Gordon Square, and after the usual amount of wearisome house-hunting, my father finally settled in Bloomsbury too, in Montagu Place.

From this date till his death, more than a quarter of a century, one important commission succeeded another in a way which would hardly have been the case had he decided to live permanently away from the great centre, so that the move was fully justified.

CHAPTER II

In 1855 it had been announced that there was to be a competition for a cathedral at Lille, for which architects throughout the world were cordially invited to enter. Ecclesiastical works on a really large scale were not so common then as they were to become from that time forward. Nothing certainly of anything like the importance of the proposed work had as yet been undertaken, the only works at all comparable being those at Marseilles, Nantes, and Cologne.

In our own country the next twenty-five years was to see the hand of the architect laid—for good or evil—on nearly every one of our cathedrals and great parish churches ; was to see complete fabrics rise out of mere ruins, and great new churches built from the very ground ; but to the English Church architect of thirty years back the possibility of having £120,000 to spend on a great church—absurdly inadequate as that sum was for such a building as the conditions specified —was almost as novel as it was attractive. So strong was the inducement that, in spite of a certain air of speculativeness which the project wore from the first, many architects of eminence were content to run the risk. My father's objection to competitions, which took deep root later in life, was at this time not sufficiently strong to deter him from taking a share in the lottery in which, as a young man with a reputation still in a great measure to make, he naturally thought that the gain would probably more than counterbalance the loss.

During the early part of his last year at Oxford he had applied himself earnestly to the plans. The conditions of the competition laid down that the design for the cathedral was to be Gothic and French in character, but my father's tours in France, short though they were, had been so well turned to account, that the latter stipulation offered no difficulty to him.

Forty-one sets of plans were sent in, of which number fifteen were eventually found to be of French, and fourteen of English origin. The authorities took the unusual course of publicly exhibiting all the drawings before they were submitted to the jury of selection, with the consequence that the criticisms passed on them were to a certain extent impartial, though it was pretty easy to see in most cases, from the way in which the drawings were got up, what their author's nationality was. My father ran over to Lille for a few days in company with Mr. William Morris, who had then lately been articled to him, and writes home jokingly about the designs :—

"We have had about three hours at the exhibition We are agreed naturally that I ought to have place No. 1 ! Mr. Clutton's (Clutton and Burges) is one of the best, but wrong in several points, and not very good The other designs are generally very inferior, and some of them are the greatest rubbish I ever saw. The perspectives are all hung, and make a good show. In other respects Clutton is as complete as I am—in the number of his plans and detail—but few others are. I really think I shall have one of the prizes. Morris says the first Clutton's church looks very small, the parts are so few and so large."

A year or two later, writing from Châlons-sur-Marne, my father speaks of the church of Nôtre Dame there as being the prototype of Mr. Burges's design for Lille Cathedral He writes :—

"I made the acquaintance of the curé at Nôtre Dame—M Champenois—a charming little enthusiast, who is busy restoring the whole church ; he has cleaned and repaired the interior completely, showing all the stone in the groining, etc , and it looks so well   .
I told him my name, and he was quite up to all about the Lille competition, the more by token that Messrs Clutton and Burges's design was to a great extent (as I saw directly, and as he told me) a copy of his church "

The letter is interesting enough to quote a little more :—

"There is only one altar in the church, the chapels round the apse being all empty   Notwithstanding a good deal of interruption from my little friend I have scored seven large sketches to-day, which I call good work : two of them tinted of old sculpture dug up in making alterations.   We had a great discussion about the arrangement of the choir, as to which he is heterodox.   How curious to find a French priest, actively engaged on church restoration, arguing in favour of singing in a western gallery, and of admitting the 'faithful' into the choir, and an Anglo-Catholic protesting against both.   Yet so it was.   However, we parted most excellent friends "

To return to Lille.   An English correspondent sent an account of the various designs to the ecclesiologist at the time, which is so minute and intelligent, and shows so much insight, that I am tempted to quote what he says about this, my father's first really important design ·—

"'Quam dilecta Tabernacula tua Domine virtutum.'   It is, we believe, neither national nor personal prejudice which leads us to detect in this English design certainly one of the best—and (we might almost say) the very best—set of drawings in the whole exhibition For here we find an unmistakable French church, rigidly observant of the strictest interpretation of the conditions of the competition, in which, however, there is, so far as we can see, little or nothing that is lifelessly copied, little or no 'bookwork' (as it would be called in a university examination), but rather a pervading unity of conception and a living instinct of design, giving proofs of originality and power in almost every detail   The artist, in short, seems to have become penetrated with his style ; or rather, the style is not merely taken up by him for the occasion, but it looks as though it were habitual to him   There is a freedom about the architectural thought which, though not absent from several other designs in the exhibition, is scarcely to be observed, as we fancy, in those nearest in merit to the one now under consideration.

"This design, instead of being a beautiful vision of the past, seems to us full of life and vigour and promise for the future   We should ourselves have preferred a more developed Pointed, and this artist would probably, though we are not sure of this, share our opinion ; but at any rate the effect of this artistic creation, as compared with some of its rivals, is, to our mind, rather that of beauty on the point of ripening into a still richer fulness than of a laboured resuscitation of the superseded details of a past and antiquated period of art.

"But to proceed to the description of this elaborate set of drawings.   The programme of the competition expressed a pre-

ference, on the score of economy, for brick over stone, as the chief
material of the proposed church; and this is one of the few designs
in the whole exhibition, and the only one among those which appear
in our first class, in which this condition has been recognised. Here,
it seems to us, brick is treated with great ability. It is made to
enter largely into the general construction, and banded with horizontal courses of stone, it gives a warm colouring to the exterior.
Inside it is used with equal boldness and effectiveness, and the
vaulting (with stone ribs and the cells constructed of red brick) is
constructionally and imperishably coloured. The plan comprises a
western narthex beween twin spires with the chapels — *des fonts*
and *des morts*—attached, a nave of seven bays, transepts of two
bays, the crossing marked by a *flèche*, choir of three bays with
seven-sided apse, a procession path and five radiating apsidal chapels.
The dependent buildings are well grouped round a cloister on the
south side. Externally the somewhat cold and heavy effect, which,
being partly the result of the severe style prescribed, we have observed
in other designs, is to be noticed in this project also; still the chevet,
with its flying buttresses and massive pinnacles, has dignity and
character, and the general massiveness and richness of detail is an
English feature most judiciously added to the French type of building. The spires, banded in colour, are by no means the most
successful part of the design   In spite of skilful gradations of stages
and much constructional merit, the result is ungraceful and ineffective.
We can believe that the architect wished to give an original and
striking contour to spires which, if erected, would be so conspicuous
a landmark in the swamps of French Flanders; and we can fancy
that in a distant view these stern, frowning, accumulated piles would
be imposing, but in a near view they lack grace. still they are true
spire compositions."

    This is of course merely an expression of individual taste,
but I think most people would allow that these spires were
amongst the best and most graceful of my father's conceptions.

    "The interior is noticeable for the good proportion of its parts,
and the proper development of arcade, triforium, and clerestory
The fittings are of great beauty   We observe an open metal rood-
screen; a *clôture de chœur* carved in subjects in relief, admirably
treated, and a ciborium which, for harmony and elegance of colour
and proportions, is surpassed by none in the whole collection   The
metalwork of this artist seems to us notably excellent, and the pavement has merits.   His woodwork also is rich and appropriate, and
the great organ at the west end, so arranged as not to interfere with

the principal western rose window, is unusually successful. This organ, we believe, does not exclude a choir organ, in a more appropriate position.

"The glass designs are a great improvement on the Bourges type (this is indeed high praise), the medallions being drawn quite free from grotesqueness, and the *grisaille* being treated in a bold floral style. A word of praise is due for some exquisite perspectives in sepia, showing the chapter-house interior and part of the cloisters.

"The crowning merit of the design is, we repeat, the proof it gives of its author's perfect mastery of the principles of Pointed design, enabling him to work up the whole of his ideas without imitation or exaggeration. We have no doubt the jury will take fully into account the unusual merits of this elaborate design, although they are of a kind which would be probably undervalued by more superficial observers."

Many of the designs are highly spoken of by the same critic, more particularly that by Messrs. Clutton and Burges,— sent in under the motto " Fœderis arca,"—which he places second to my father's ; but it is amusing to read what he has to say about some of the productions. Very probably a similar competition now would produce no better designs than the best of these ; but at least the diffusion of artistic education and the better training of to-day have made the sort of thing, which the following quotation depicts so vividly, impossible :—

"'Toute faveur insigne, tout don parfait, vient d'en haut.' This is the production of a madman. The design is one entire insanity. It is a mirage done in all sorts of colours. There are radiating jets, of coloured material apparently, spinning and twisting like a thaumatrope, green parapets, yellow tracery, sky-blue arcades, German flamboyant-twisted shafts. We can only describe the whole thing as a cauchemar, which the inventor could only have produced after diligent training on raw pork and liquid pigments. The west front is guarded by two ruffian angels, apparently of bronze, flourishing big swords, who recall the Oriental Afrits. Man of woman born could never face these monsters. They look like the angels keeping guard over paradise, and repelling the faithful from church rather than beckoning them into it. Each of them is exactly ten metres—nearly thirty-three feet—high. Above these is a whole flight of bright yellow angels, and then a covey of tender green seraphim. Above them is an open book ; then a lantern and staff ; then a large text ; then, above all, scrambling over the gable, and projected clear against the sky, the whole group of the Sistine Madonna, with the pretty little cherubs lounging with their chins on the parapet. The intersection of nave and transepts is crowned with an iron and glass spire, coloured red, blue, green, and yellow, and the whole is surmounted by a great gilded metal glory, seven metres in diameter, which, we believe, is to be illuminated, and most likely would be visible at Calais. Blasphemy, folly, and impossibility are combined in this insult to common sense and common decency."

The jury of selection began their work by eliminating for one cause or another twenty-two designs. They then selected nine designs for honourable mention, then four for silver medals, three for gold, and finally three for the prizes of 6000 frs., 4000 frs., and 3000 frs. respectively. The result was eminently complimentary to English art. The first and second prizes fell to the English representatives in Messrs. Clutton and Burges and my father, and out of the fourteen English competitors no fewer than eight got medals or honourable mention.

The critic, quoted above, says of the decision :—

"To Messrs. Clutton and Burges they have awarded the first prize, and to Mr. Street the second. As to the adjustment of the merit of these two excellent designs, it was no easy task. We pointed out—and the jury echoes our observations—that whereas the credit of bolder architectural development was due to Mr. Street, yet that for still closer adherence to the prescribed type and for unequalled hieratic skill in the *ameublement* the palm would go to his competitors. Our own sympathies perhaps rather inclined us to give the preference to the bolder and more original design, but when the jury—pledged to decide according to the rigid terms of prescribed condition—gave their verdict that, in so equally poised a balance, weight should be given to the closest fulfilment of these conditions, we can only say that their award is righteous beyond cavil or exception."

The actual adjudication of the second prize was in the following terms :—

"The second prize has been adjudged to the design 'Quam dilecta Tabernacula.' To a profound knowledge of Pointed Art, its author adds a rare power of conception which is shown as well in the details as in the ensemble. We recognise here, at first sight, the work of a great master ; in particular, we must fairly congratulate the author on having complied with all the requirements of the pro-

gramme, and on having faced more boldly than any other competitor
the difficulties of employing brick as the material of a monumental edifice. If power rather than grace is the general characteristic of this magnificent creation of art, elegance finds its due place in the ciborium,
in which it is combined with a true splendour of ornamentation.

"After a lengthened consideration we have unhesitatingly raised
this design to the second place, and little was wanting to its mounting to the first."

Mr. Burges had, with only too accurate a knowledge of
the people with whom he had to deal, disarmed opposition
by getting up his drawings in French style and on French
paper.   He triumphed for the time, and it must have been
a sore disappointment to the jury to find that after all the
victor was English ; but it soon began to be whispered
about that no plan was likely to find ultimate favour that
was not fathered by a Frenchman.

Loyal patriots refused to subscribe under conditions so
humiliating as would be the selection of a foreign architect ;
the State felt obliged to put policy before justice.   It was
evident that the religious zeal of Lille, unless stimulated by
a concession to local interests, would never produce anything
like adequate funds for the building.

The architecture of France was justly said to have met
its Agincourt at Lille, but intrigue soon snatched away from
us the fruits of victory.   It is an old story now how Mr.
Burges, after having been actually received at Lille as the
architect, was ultimately thrown over.   All the drawings of
the competitors were the property of the town ; with these
to help him, a certain well-known priest, aided by a local
architect, who was among the unsuccessful competitors, con-
cocted a new design in which many elements, much watered,
both of Mr. Burges's and of my father's design, were recog-
nisable, and this was formally accepted.   Thus it came about
that the invader was himself despoiled as well as driven out,
and the patriot prevailed.   Scarcely was my father settled
in town when, nowise damped by the unsatisfactory termination of the competition, he commenced plans for the
Crimean Memorial Church at Constantinople, to be submitted under conditions similar to those which governed

the other competition, except that the adjudication of the prizes was this time in the hands of Englishmen.

Forty-six architects from all parts of Europe competed, and the first result was similar to that which had been arrived at at Lille, viz. that Mr Burges was placed first, and my father second. Mr. Bodley gained the third prize, and Mr. Slater the fourth, while the Foreign Contingent got nothing better than an honourable mention. Mr. Burges's design was, it seems, founded on that of St. Andrea, Vercelli, a Southern church, whose architect was certainly influenced by French, possibly by English, examples. My father's design was less Southern in its primary form; but essentially so in its treatment. I find from contemporary criticism that his design was held generally to have at least fulfilled more completely what would seem to have been an all-important requirement, for he was more successful than his fortunate rival in realising the conception of a great architectural monument, and one unmistakably erected to the memory of English dead,—though modified so as to harmonise with the surroundings. He may not have been so well qualified as others to judge of the merits of his own design, as compared with that of Mr Burges, but he certainly felt very strongly about the decision, he writes in that sense to his sister .—

"You saw in *The Guardian*, I daresay, that I am second in the Constantinople competition I believe the opinion among architects who have seen the plans is unanimous that I ought to have been first However, it is too late to grumble about it now. I am working night and day, and shall not have a minute's holiday for the next three weeks."

My father's design showed a church, cruciform, aisleless, and groined throughout, the nave being of five bays, and the chancel beyond the transepts of two bays, with a five-sided apse The great vault was supported by very large external buttresses, which were pierced to form a cloister The windows were of three lights, with an external fenestration of only two lights—a feature which both produced a charming effect, and was calculated to be of great value in so hot a climate The interval between the two planes of tracery was roofed between the buttresses, and gave an external passage like that at Marburg A minaret-like turret rose on either side in the angle formed by the chancel and transepts

When a site had been given by the Sultan, it was at once found that Mr Burges's design would need serious alterations. The nave was accordingly shortened by two bays, the transepts were thrust back so as to range with the aisle walls, and the groining was much modified. This was done in 1857. Next year fresh alterations were decided upon, and the history of the church for many months reveals nothing but a succession of little changes and petty delays. Fresh members joined the Committee, and eventually the unsuitability of Mr. Burges's design having become more and more obvious, the commission was finally transferred from him to my father. It was not till many years later, in May 1864, that the work was really commenced The consecration took place in 1865, and the actual completion in 1869. The church as it now stands is of just the same character and general design as that which I have just described, but the plan was considerably modified. The east end is square instead of being apsidal. The transepts are omitted The external cloister is curtailed There is only one bell turret instead of two, and the nave is covered with a wooden-panelled roof in place of a vault The beauty of the design is great, while the system of protection from heat and glare has been made to yield features which are at once practical and picturesque The deep and wide-spanned western porch, the double fenestration, the great projecting eaves of the nave carried on the buttresses, the unusual and grand bulk of the buttresses themselves, and the arrangement by which the spaces between them are made to form inside a series of arched recesses, which intercept and modify the intense light of an eastern sun, give a marked and a suitable character to the work.

My father had managed to get a short holiday before starting work on the Constantinople drawings, and had visited for the first time Étampes, Bourges, Tours, le Mans, Poitiers, Angers, Laval, and the Loire district The three short weeks were to brace him up, not only for his ordinary work and for the Constantinople competition, but for a greater effort than that, for no sooner were the drawings for it complete than he threw himself with energy into the competition for the new Government offices. This gave him an opportunity which he would on no account have foregone,—that of making the attempt to show that the style of his choice was adaptable, not only to ecclesiastical but to any and every secular purpose.

Gothic had by this time, before this indeed, established itself firmly as *the* style for church work, but—at any rate so far as the general public was concerned—it had not made good its ground as a suitable medium for satisfying the requirements of a great public building The palace at Westminster is indeed Gothic in detail, though of a late character, and has much beauty ; but the Gothic is little more than skin deep, while its massing is so distinctly classic as to make it generally looked upon as hardly more than a compromise

The competition in question produced several veritable Gothic designs ; of the favour with which they were looked upon, the late Sir Gilbert Scott says in his *Recollections* —

"When my designs for the public offices were exhibited, they excited much attention ; indeed, they were, by those who favoured Gothic, considered generally the best, though opinions were divided to some extent between them and the designs by Mr. Street and Mr. Woodward . . . The judges, who knew amazingly little about the subject, were not well disposed towards our style, and, though they awarded premiums to all the best Gothic designs, they took care not to put any of them high enough to have much chance "

The verdict of the judges was of an undecided character, and it is well known how Sir Gilbert Scott, though not placed first in the competition, was eventually chosen. Selected as the author of a Gothic design, he fought manfully for a time on behalf of that style only to surrender unconditionally in the end to Lord Palmerston—an abnega-.tion of his early principles which many were never able to forgive There were 219 competitors, to seventeen of whom premiums were awarded, my father being among them.

He was not on the whole dissatisfied with the result. The bias against the Gothicists in the minds of the judges was so obvious as to excuse their position, and he reflected that his £100 would pay for a tour in Italy, while the exhibition of his drawings would no doubt be of service to him. "It makes one savage," he writes, "to think of nothing but Renaissance going down, but we must bide our time." To have designed in any other style would have been impossible to him, feeling, as he did, that no architect could conscientiously be a man of many styles, but in a pamphlet which accompanied his design, he gave his reasons for thinking that Gothic is naturally the right style for our national buildings, and more particularly for one which it was proposed to place on the river front, divided only from the Houses of Parliament by Westminster Bridge—which it was then intended to make a veritable Gothic structure—and in the immediate neighbourhood of the Abbey. He showed how well the picturesque towers of Westminster would group with a building of a kindred style, and how, seen from a distance above the horizontal lines of a classical building, they would not only make an incongruous medley, but would lose much of their own beauty from the unsuitability of the surroundings. He went on to show that Gothic, as such, may utilise to the full all the most modern improvements; nay, that it has a plasticity which makes it able to subserve our modern needs, with an ease which cannot be predicated of some other forms of building.

With Westminster Abbey before his eyes, itself the work of a man who had evidently studied foreign examples diligently, he felt that the English style, pure and simple, need not be adhered to scrupulously. Insularity of style, devotedly as he admired our English Gothic, was always repugnant to him, for he felt strongly that Gothic architecture throughout Europe, however great its local peculiarities and distinctions, was none the less bound together by a great unity of principle underlying all

The conditions of the competition laid down, among other things, that the buildings should be not more than three stories high. This made the use of a steep roof

essential.   My father adopted hipped roofs in preference to
gables—an arrangement for which there is not much precedent in England, but one amply justified by its adoption
in some of the most beautiful buildings in Europe, as the
Ducal palace at Venice, and the Cloth Hall at Ypres.   Another feature which is uncommon in English work he used
freely, viz. the detached shaft as a mullion ; of the use of
this he says : " There cannot, except in the narrowest view of
our insular tradition, be any rational objection to the adoption of noble features, common elsewhere in the Middle
Ages, but ordinarily neglected here."   The detached shaft,
he saw, greatly facilitated the use of ordinary sash windows,
and offered, further, a good opportunity for the introduction
of colour.

The use of two different-coloured stones—a feature with
which his tours in North Italy had more particularly familiar-
ised him—was conspicuous in various parts of the building ;
and in some places there was a considerable amount of
inlaid work in coloured material.   The entire design, indeed,
including the fine tower, showed considerable evidence of
Italian studies, but without any slavish adherence to its
forms.

Every summer was now adding somewhat to my father's
knowledge of continental architecture.   In 1857 he was
able to return to what he had reluctantly left only half seen
before, viz. North Italy.   This time he went farther south,
and fared even better than before.   Starting with Genoa, he
went on to Pisa, Lucca, and Siena.   Thence he drove across
country to Cortona and Arezzo, and from there to Perugia,
Assisi, and Florence.   Devoted as he was to each and all
of the sister arts, their systematic conjunction here, and in
so perfect a form, filled him with enthusiasm, while it made
him hope, even more ardently than before, that the return
to such a state of things might be to some extent possible
in his own country.

In 1858, tired out by long days of incessant work, he
went to France for a three-weeks' holiday without my mother.
His letters to her form not only a complete and vivid
account of all he did and saw, but are full of the most

suggestive hints and comments on the architectural features of the places he visited. He went first to Fécamp and Rouen— seeing the latter place not for the first time—Nantes, Beauvais, Soissons, Rheims, Laon, Châlons-sur-Marne, Metz, Trèves, Cologne, Liège, besides seeing many things off the road which he flattered himself few, if any, tourists but himself had ever reached. The account he gives of the sketches he has made and the note-books he has filled makes it hard of belief that he was really engaged in recruiting exhausted nature, but he certainly did all he could to falsify the saying of the old Roman poet ; for change of scene was everything to him, the cares of professional life once put aside were as if they had never existed, and the harder he worked at his self-imposed tasks, the more thoroughly he enjoyed himself, and the more complete was his refreshment

The next year was given chiefly to the cultivation of mountain scenery and hard exercise. His old habit of carrying his knapsack on his back during his architectural rambles, and doing everything on foot, made him still a very fair performer among the mountains, though he walked for the sake of enjoyment and not for mere walking's sake, and never attempted any notable ascent   The Zermatt Mountains were the main object this year, while a year later the Oberland was worked through, and a move was then made by Lyons to St Etienne, Le Puy, Brioude, Clermont-Ferrand, Nevers, and Bourges.

These two or three years saw much hard work, and among it a good deal that was of interest and importance. That which was perhaps most interesting to my father himself, because of the beauty of the design and detail, and the conclusion to which his examination of it led him, was the rehabilitation of Stone Church, near Dartford. This work, to which I shall refer again, he proved pretty conclusively to have been by the same architect and some of the same masons as Westminster Abbey, the village church being superior in delicacy of detail and in quality of workmanship.

The most important of his original works during the same period was the church of St James the Less, Garden

Street, Westminster, with its schools, because it was his first opportunity of showing what he could do in London itself. The whole group is one of the most picturesque character. The campanile, with its unusual roofing, stands on the street apart from the church. The church itself forms the north side of a little quadrangle, of which the campanile is the western, and a part of the school buildings the eastern, boundary, the side next the street being bounded by a low wall with a lofty iron railing. Looking at my father's subsequent work, it is not possible to put this church in the first rank, but, at the time it was built, it marked a great step in advance of the ordinary run of church work. Its originality and spirit are beyond all question, the massing and outline of the whole block of building are most satisfactory, and much of the detail is very good, as, for instance, in the woodwork of the stalls and the decoration of the chancel generally, while the ironwork in the screen on the street and the canopy over the font is very hard to match, but at the same time there is in some of the masonry and brickwork details, in the carving, and in the proportion of the nave arcade, a want of that grace which was so characteristic of all his work, subsequent to this date at any rate— something a little *outré* and over bold, which seems to speak of a strong and masterful imagination not as yet adequately restrained by a sense of purity and beauty of form. The evidences of Italian travel, visible, as I have said, in my father's design for the Foreign and Colonial Offices, are again to be found pervading the design for this church, but in passing through the furnace what is Italian has become so entirely absorbed in what belongs to the architect's own inspiration, that it is hard to put the finger on any actual features which recall Italian examples, the influence being traceable rather in the choice and management of materials, and the general massing of the block of buildings, than in any more specific points.

CHAPTER III

My father's comprehensive love for art, as manifested not
only in his own sphere of architecture, but not less in that of
her sisters painting and sculpture, led naturally to his seek-
ing out and associating not with architects alone, but perhaps even more with artists in general. The pre-Raphaelite
movement found in him a hearty and earnest adherent, and
one who on many occasions, by writing and speaking,
impressed on his brethren the importance and propriety of
their giving it all the moral support in their power. He
felt truly that the aim of the young enthusiasts, who were
striving for truth before everything, was in their particular
field identical with the aim of the leaders of the Gothic
Revival in the field of architecture. His known views
speedily brought him into relations of friendship with many
of those who belonged to the pre-Raphaelite group, or were
in sympathy with it. Among those with whom he had
become acquainted at the time I am speaking of may be
named the brothers Dante G. and William Rossetti, W.
Holman-Hunt, George P. Boyce, J. W. Inchbold, F. Madox-
Brown, William Morris, W. Bell Scott, and E. Burne Jones.

Living much in the world of pictures, and loving them
not less nearly, it may easily be conceived that my father
was not wanting in the desire to see them on his walls. I
think the first modern picture he bought was a small oil-
painting by Millais, which he secured at a sale in 1858.
From that time on a year rarely or never passed without
his adding one or more to his store ; a succession of pictures
by Mr. G. P. Boyce and Mr. Burne Jones being bought in the
course of the next few years. His confidence in his own

future is pretty well vouched for by the readiness with which he became a buyer of pictures, albeit in a humble way, at a time when his fortune, if fated ever to be made, was at any rate still in the future. It says a good deal for his inherent good taste that, untrained as he was, and unaided, except by the light of his own likes and dislikes when he first began buying, he still got no picture which in later life he was otherwise than glad to see on his walls.

When, many years after, Frederick Walker appeared like a meteor and ran his brief course, in no one did he excite a more sincere admiration and appreciation than in my father; and indeed, the tribute which was given to his work was given, in its degree, to others also who, with originality of their own, still owed much of the beauty of their conception and workmanship to Walker's example. My father, indeed, became the owner of pictures by both Pinwell and J. W. North before he could attain what was the summit of his ambition in this line—the possession of one of Walker's great oil pictures.

Once, when the "Harbour of Refuge" came into the market, he went down to Christie's and bid bravely for it, but against the most mighty of picture-dealers his case was hopeless, and he naturally had to return home empty-handed. When he found that the "Old Gate" was to be included in the Benzon Sale in 1874, he profited by experience and put himself in the hands of his quondam competitor, with the result that the picture became his. It was his most cherished possession, and I think it added permanently and distinctly to his sense of wellbeing and happiness.

His taste in the matter of pictures was just as decided as it was in architecture; but as the latter, strictly as he confined himself to one style in his own work, was nevertheless catholic, so also was the former. On his walls were hung not only contemporary works, but also many panels belonging to the early schools of Christian Art. These early schools, and the Italian more particularly, appealed to him in a special way, apart from whatever merits they might possess as works of art, because he read in many of them (though history records many exceptions), as he did in the pure form and detail of our old abbey churches, the devotional spirit and personal piety of the men who had given them to the world.

Foremost among those whose works breathe a spirit of purity and devotion stands Fra Angelico, and so strongly did my father feel the exalted nature of his work, that he made a proper appreciation of it a test of his own moral state. Towards the end of his life, when he was in low spirits and failing health, he visited Paris alone, and writes how he went, according to his usual habit, to feast his eyes on Fra Angelico's "Coronation of the Virgin" in the Louvre. He is fain to think that it must have been touched in some way, because it does not appeal to him quite so forcibly as it has been wont to do, and he refuses to believe that the fault is in himself, because he would attach so special a meaning to such a want. I suppose that every lover of pictures must be well content with what Florence has to offer him, whether the earlier or the later schools be his special object of admiration ; but I doubt if there be many who, while fully appreciating the other almost matchless collection, have studied so carefully or extracted so much pleasure and profit from the collection of early works in the Accademia as did my father.

To return to the friendships of his early years in town ; one to which he owed no small degree of pleasure was that with Mr. Crabb Robinson, who all his life had known everybody who was worth knowing, and at whose Sunday breakfasts, which my father frequently attended, there was a certainty of interesting company and good conversation. High Churchman and high Tory, my father was all that was naturally repugnant to Mr. Robinson's own views, but in spite of that he was a prime favourite with him, and partly too because of it. Mr. Robinson respected sincerity and strength of conviction, however decidedly their possessor might run counter to his own pet predilections, but this did not prevent his hurling all sorts of opprobrious epithets, half-meant and wholly good-humoured, at my father's head. His friendship was extended equally to my mother, and I can remember, as a boy, that he frequently came in the evening for a quiet cup of tea and a bout of arguing that was not so quiet.

Among other notices of my father in Mr. Robinson's diary I find the following :—

"Dined with the Streets Our amusement was three-handed whist. Both Mr and Mrs. Street very kind On every point of public interest he and I differ, but it does not affect our apparent esteem for one another. I hold him in very great respect—indeed, admiration He has first-rate talent in his profession as architect. He will be a great man in act—he is so in character already."

A High Churchman and high Tory my father had been by conviction from the very first, but he appreciated none the less warmly those who were opposed to him, nor did it prevent his having an intense personal admiration for one great man, Mr. Gladstone, with whose political career he could not feel any sympathy. It was in 1858 that he was first introduced to him, and received there and then to his great satisfaction an invitation to breakfast at a near date, of which he did not fail to take advantage. This privilege was afterwards extended to him on many occasions. On this occasion he naturally went in some fear and trembling of his elders and betters, but he wrote :—

"Gladstone was very friendly, and the whole party quite in-formal. Lord Lyttelton was there, the Bishop of Exeter, Mr Bulwer Lytton, and a Lord Something, whose name has run away from me in an unceremonious manner, though after breakfast he got Gladstone to introduce him to me in order to talk about my Italian book, and to thank me for the help it had been to him; and he introduced me to another man whose name I did not catch, but who knew who I was The unknown lord asked me when he might write to me, so I gave him my card; and if I don't recollect in five minutes what his name was, as I most probably shall, I shall at any rate hear from him. . . . Lord Dunraven is my friend's name."

My father had always been fond of music, and this was a taste which the wisdom of not trying his eyes too much by working every night enabled him to gratify with a clear conscience. It will be remembered that when he lived at Wantage he figured in the choir there, and was most active

in trying to promote good singing and good playing,
Wherever he spent his Sundays, he always took his place in
the choir if possible, and he was much in request in those
days at plain-song meetings.

The time for this was over now, but he and my mother
used to attend the rehearsals and concerts of the Old
Philharmonic Society with the greatest regularity. The
opera, which had not then fallen on its bad days, never
failed to attract him   Many a time, when he had just come
off a long and tiring railway journey, he went off after
snatching a hasty meal to get his brain cleared at the opera
or at a concert of chamber music.   This was a form of
relaxation which stress of work obliged him more and more
to forego, but if he heard music more rarely and gave up
his singing almost entirely, it was not because they had lost
their attraction for him.   I remember well how moved he
was the first time he ever heard Wagner's music   It was at
an open-air concert at Leipsig, and the piece was the overture to *Tannhauser*, then comparatively strange to English ears.   It was a revelation to him, and he went away
determined to make opportunities for hearing more

No one could have escaped more completely being
fossilised into one groove by constant hard work than did
my father.   His power of enjoyment continued as keen as
in his early days, and its objects became more diverse.
From his first year in London till his dying day he
was always in the habit of snatching an hour at Lord's
three or four times in the season if he could contrive, which
generally happened, to make his business lead him in that
direction.   The river had lost none of its attractions for
him, and Saturday afternoons spent on the river, with dinner
at the old " Star and Garter " at Richmond, are among my
earliest boyish recollections   As soon as I was old enough
to stick on a pony's back, he made me a present of one,
and a horse on his own account was the natural consequence
in a year or so.   In those days the whole country around
London became familiar to us.   Through all the summer
months we used to get a two hours' ride and a whiff of
country air before breakfast.   In the winter an hour in the

Row was all that was possible. Sometimes we rode to Stanmore or Harrow to lunch, or took a tour on horseback in which business was combined with pleasure. Without these hours of strong exercise and mental rest, I think even so strong a constitution as my father's would have by this time begun to show signs of wear and tear Before the days of riding, and very often too after we had a horse, the mornings before breakfast, an hour and a half or two hours were devoted to letter-writing. After a day which was always a struggle to get work done amid and in spite of the constant interruption of calls from clients, builders, clerks of works, and all the host of people with whom his large practice brought him into business relations, the evening found him at his drawing-board for three or more hours, happy in the knowledge that he was not liable to be called away at any minute. "You can hardly fancy how busy I am this year," he writes in 1859, "work seems to press in on all sides, and it is as much as I can do to keep it in hand at all." It is very difficult at all times to gauge the amount of work which has been got through in a day, because the conditions under which the work is done have to be taken into consideration, and my father did not by any means enter all he did in his diary ; but I notice three succeeding days, several years later than the date with which I am now dealing, which are a fair sample of the sort of way in which he kept himself from getting into arrears. The entries are as follows :—

"*January* 5.—Design for reredos for York Minster. Ground-plan for new church at Barnsley. Wrote to Mr. Roe with estimate for the completion of Christ Church, Dublin. Altered design for altar-cloth, St Paul's, Rome. Drew large gates and railings, Marlborough College.

"*January* 6.—Plans for the restoration of Cotterstock Church. Plans for new English church at Lausanne.

"*January* 7.—Design for high screen, Colebrooke Church. Details for York Minster reredos. Plans for reredos and organ, Warfield. Second design for ground-plan, St. Peter, Barnsley. Several sheets of details for Dunster Church. Several sheets of details for Kildare Cathedral. Wrote report on Milton parsonage, and another evening directly after produced 'seven sheets of details for restoration of Bignor Church.'"

But if the days at home were wearing, what shall I say
of the business journeys, which were almost perpetual? It
makes one feel perfectly dazed to read his descriptions of
them.   Up early, in late; getting meals piecemeal and at
all sorts of hours; driving forty miles across country to
intercept a train; fitting in the visits to different places
like a complicated puzzle—so many minutes here, so many
there; so many letters, or specifications, or reports to be
written in transit.   Letter-writing in trains was constant.
"I have written nineteen letters between Bletchley and
Moreton," he writes,—in the train, of course.   Not unfrequently he wrote his letters in cabs.   On one occasion an
old gentleman, on getting out of the train, complimented him
on being the most industrious person he had ever met.
Such a life, in which even minutes were of value, one would
hardly have thought likely to excite fresh literary aspirations; yet my father decided to add to his other labours
by doing for the unvisited parts of Spain what he had to
some extent done for North Italy.   His reason for undertaking so serious a task was, he tells us, the conviction that
the fuller and wider the study of ancient examples, and the
more intimate the knowledge of all the different developments of Gothic architecture, the more likely is the student
to become the great architect.   Unlike those who deprecated
the study of foreign examples for an English architect, my
father, whose preference for our own national type increased
rather than diminished on better acquaintance with foreign
types, thought nothing could be gained by obstinately
ignoring the existence of all Gothic other than English, and
that much might be lost.   Andalusia my father purposely
left unvisited: firstly, because it was much better known
than the other parts; and secondly, because for his particular
object it was likely to be less generally interesting and
useful; but of Leon, the Castiles, and Aragon he saw a
considerable part.   Three tours, taken respectively in the
autumn of 1861, the early summer of 1862, and the
autumn of 1863, enabled him, by dint of utilising his time
to the utmost, to see sufficient to answer his purpose, though
he was necessarily unable to do it in an exhaustive way in

so short a time as twelve weeks, which was what the three tours amounted to, and where such large tracts of country were in question. In the first tour they (for my mother had the courage to venture) entered Spain from Bayonne by San Sebastian, and so on to Burgos, which was reached after thirty-three hours in a diligence, not a very inspiriting commencement, particularly for my mother! From Burgos they visited La Cartuca and Las Huelgas, and then went on to Palencia, Valladolid, Madrid,—where my father, intent on studying the manners and customs of the people, went to a bull-fight,—from Madrid to Alcalá, Toledo, Valencia ; by sea to Barcelona, Lérida, Tarragona, Gerona, Perpiñan. In the second tour my father visited Gerona, Barcelona, Tarragona, Manresa, Lérida, Huesca, Zaragoza, Toledo, and Pampluna ; and in the third and last, Pampluna, Tudela, Tarragona, Siguenza, Guadalajara, Madrid, Toledo, Segovia, Avila, Salamanca, Zamora, Benavente, Leon, Astorga, Lugo, Santiago, La Coruña, and thence back by Valladolid and Burgos to San Sebastian and Bayonne.

The experiences of the first tour made it evident that it would be wiser in the future to travel without a lady. Adventures there were none, but inconveniences were without number, and the physical strain was great. In the last of the three tours, which took my father into quite unbeaten tracks, the perpetual travelling, and that often under conditions not the most favourable, would have been enough to knock up any one not endowed with great physical strength and proportionate energy.

Two nights' travelling in rickety diligences to one in bed was something like the proportion throughout the greater part of the tour. Many expeditions had to be made on mule-back, with the legs stretched to the utmost capacity by an enormous saddle covered with a thick manta ; reins and whip were economically combined in a single-handed rope, and with the aid of this primitive contrivance and a muleteer who ran behind and occasionally climbed up to rest himself, the ground was got over somehow. On one occasion, in an out-of-the-way district, when the diligence was slowly climbing a hill, my father, following the example of his fellow-

travellers, began to pick the grapes which hung temptingly
by the roadside, when the sudden appearance of a man with
a musket put them to a disgraceful flight. The diligence
was whipped up, and, pursued by the man, they managed to
reach and drive through a town which was near before he
could summon the authorities to stop them. What they
would have been liable to in the event of having been
stopped my father never discovered.   Ignorance of the
language proved much less of a hindrance than might have
been expected.   Intelligent good-nature on the part of the
natives, and an industrious use of a dictionary on that of the
traveller, served to get over most difficulties; occasionally my
father got help from unexpected sources. On one of his
railway journeys, for instance, he found the engine-driver to
be an Englishman, and succeeded in striking up a not wholly
disinterested acquaintance with him.   At their stopping-
place, where my father was anxious to make some notes of
the castle, the engine-driver, under the influence of a glass
of rum, introduced my father to the chief of the station, and
got him to undertake to obtain a sketching order from
the commandant   This was duly sent soon afterwards.
Sacristans all over the world are proud of the particular
churches which are under their wing ; and the Spanish ones,
at least, generally appreciated my father's diligence in
sketching their charges as a delicate attention to themselves.
His second visit to a church generally produced a hearty
hand-shake from the sacristan, and even from the priests,
though some of the less liberal-minded of the latter occasionally objected to his proceedings.   At Avila, I think it
was, a priest came up to him while he was at work and insisted on his stopping.   However, he gave my father one
last chance   " Do you reverence el Santissimo ? "—" Certainly ! "—" Ah, then you are a Christian ! " and no more
objection was made   Many of his sketches were of a most
elaborate and comprehensive character, but he did not spare
himself the drier work of noting and measuring   The plan
of every important church visited is given to scale in his
book   This was a piece of work which my father seldom if
ever failed to do, and one at which constant practice had

made him a great adept. "My favourite weakness," he calls it.

It was not till 1865 that the book appeared. Besides the large amount of letterpress which had to be got through, my father had done all the drawing on the wood himself, so as to secure the accuracy and artistic quality of the illustrations; and all this required much time, which he could ill spare. The number and character of the illustrations, the accurately-drawn plans, and the ingenious system of comparative analysis to which he subjected all he saw—tracing the work of a man or a body of workmen here, and the influence of a country there—lifted the book out of the ordinary run of such works, and made it of incalculable value to the professional man; while it was written in such a way, and was so full of information of every kind, as to make it the best possible travelling companion for the ordinary tourist. It gained for my father the credit of having practically discovered the Gothic style in Spain, and of being the first author who had not ignored or shown the greatest indifference to her heroic times. In Spain itself the book was appreciated as a most gratifying and learned tribute to the beauty of their mediæval monuments, and probably did a good deal towards opening the eyes of the people themselves to the value of their possessions. A second edition was brought out five years later; but my father never made another visit to Spain, and added nothing to what he had written.

He brought the same zeal to bear as a churchman which characterised him as an architect; for the Church, and the art which is its handmaid, were equally dear to him. Of the cause of free and open seats he had been always an untiring advocate, and his services, during the long time he was on the Council of the Free and Open Church Association, to that body were of a lasting kind; and at a time when a crisis in their affairs threatened to be fatal to the existence of the society, his tact and perseverance brought about a union which resulted in a greatly-increased sphere and power of activity. He was also on the Council of the English Church Union, and was one of its most active lay members;

speedily taking his place among that comparatively small
group of laymen who, by speech or paper at public meetings or church congresses, and by their work in church
societies, try zealously to promote the wellbeing of their
church

At All Saints, Margaret Street, he had long been Mr.
Upton Richards's right-hand man, though the thoroughness
with which he insisted on every single seat being kept free,
absolutely without exception, was at one time not wholly
acceptable to those who had to provide the ways and means
for the services of the church   This fear of shortness of funds,
however, proved groundless.   And if personal liberality were
requisite, no one could have been readier or more generous
than my father many a time and oft showed himself
to be.

In 1866 a committee was formed, of which he was one,
to present vestments to the church.   This was wholly in
accordance with his views; indeed, I believe I am right
in saying that he was the chief promoter of the movement,
as he certainly was the most energetic in getting the idea
carried out, as well as himself giving all the designs.

The next spring Mr. Richards wrote: " I know your deep
attachment to All Saints; would you allow me to nominate
you as my representative?   I do not think it will add much
to your duties or labours, and it will be a very great pleasure
to me personally if you consent."   My father accepted, and
held the churchwardenship for a considerable number of
years   He was thus able to carry out to the full and with
the best possible effect his strong views as to the right use of
a free church.   Perhaps the most striking effect which his
strong rule produced was the greatly-increased attendance of
men, due to a firmness in keeping the ladies to their own
seats, which was a task so disagreeable, and for some little
time apparently thankless, that it was only the exceeding
strength of his convictions which enabled him to fight the
battle out

Two or three years previously he had received a pleasant
proof of the widespread influence of his work in a letter
from a New York architect   This gentleman wrote to him ·——

WOODBURYTYPE

FROM A DAGUERREOTYPE TAKEN ABOUT 1850.

"I have for some years been thinking of writing to you. It seemed to me that if God had given to me a great gift, it would give me pleasure to know that one more recognised it ; but even if this is not the case with you, still I may thank you for the pleasure your works have given me, and yet I know of your designs only through a few illustrations in the *Builder.* I have your book on *Brick and Marble in North Italy.* It is a charming work, both on account of its graceful, easy style, its earnestness, and the interest of its subject. But your own designs show me that God meant you to be an architect, to exercise a creative power which was to make men happier and better. They have made me happier and, I hope, better. Their originality is wonderful ; yet I prize them most because they touch, I know not why, my heart. Strange that a print of a building in a magazine should speak to me of reverence and awe and tender love towards God, and make me anew consecrate my life to Him !"

A few years later, the writer of the letter visited Europe, and one day called on my father with a bouquet of varied and beautiful flowers, each of which had been chosen as expressing to him in some attribute one of, my father's churches. A little later, another American architect dedicated to him—as one " who is as illustrious in this country as in Europe "—a book on Church Architecture.

The influence of the Gothic school of architects had indeed become very widespread now, and was every day becoming more so. In 1860 my father speaks hopefully of the greatly-increased strength of their party in the Institute :—

"I went to the Institute last night," he writes, " hoping that the Goths would muster strongly and elect some fresh men on the Council. If they had come, they might have done what they liked, as the meeting was not largely attended. As it was, we had some fun. I objected to their sending out the balloting lists only a few days before the election, and protested against the composition of the Council ; and when it came to voting, several men scratched out every name on the House list and substituted Goths for them ; of course a considerable majority were for the House list, but I had nine votes, which was more than any other of the minority ; Scott has about seven, and so on. It was only a piece of amusement for us ; but the Dons were considerably disgusted, as I believe they have never before had such a selection of names substituted for their own.

"After the meeting Cockerell came to me in a markedly kind

manner, shook hands, and so on, and hoped I was satisfied to have him for President for another year, and that I should come frequently to the meetings."

In 1864 he writes: " I believe I am to be elected a Vice-President of the Institute of Architects this year, or rather I am to be nominated, but perhaps Mr. Tite and his friends may come down and pay me in ' my own coin by blackballing me.' I shan't be grieved if they do; it will save me much time and trouble. . . The Memorial Church at Constantinople is just being commenced, and will be finished in two years, and in that time I shall have, I suppose, to make a couple of journeys there. I have also a church to build at Genoa, which will afford a very pleasant excuse for a visit to dear Italy. As to my works in England, they are only too numerous, and I really have great difficulty in getting them all done. I must not grumble at being so prosperous   I suppose, really, that now there is no other architect among the Gothic men, save Scott, who has anything like as much as I have to do."

The election of Mr. Scott as an Associate of the Academy was a most important recognition of the Gothic architects This was followed, in the early part of 1866, by my father's election by the Committee of the Athenæum at the head of the poll, and a little later in the year he himself was made an Associate of the Academy.

A great many large and important works were now either in progress or shortly to be put in hand   The new nave of Bristol Cathedral; All Saints Church, Clifton; St. John's, Torquay, the chapel and schoolrooms at Uppingham, St Mary Magdalen, Paddington; Longmead, Bishopstoke; St. Margaret's Convent, East Grinstead; the restoration of Hedon Church, and, a little later, St. Saviour's, Eastbourne; St. Margaret's, Liverpool; the church for Lord Sudeley at Toddington, Dunecht House and Chapel for Lord Crawford; and a whole group of churches, parsonages, and schools for Sir Tatton Sykes. But these were all quite overshadowed by the two great competitions to which every one's attention was now turned,—those for the National Gallery and the New Courts of Law. These two took place almost simultaneously, but the former attracted less public attention than it would naturally have done, partly owing to the comparative smallness of the outlay proposed, but chiefly because nothing definite ever came of it, Mr. Edward Barry being merely commissioned to patch up the existing building My father was naturally much gratified at his selection as one of the limited number of competitors in both cases. He writes to his sister to tell her that he is going abroad to look at the great foreign galleries ·——

" The Government have asked me to make a design for the New National Gallery, and I want to collect all necessary information on the subject To-day also, I see by the *Times*, that it was announced in the House of Commons last night that I was one of the six architects selected to make plans for the New Courts of Law. In both cases it is a great distinction, I consider, to be asked to make a design, and though the chances of competitions are always doubtful, still, of course, there is a fair chance of success in one or other of them It is the more gratifying because I had never moved in the matter at all, and they pay enough to each architect to make it no loss of money to make the designs. Also another piece of news, which I don't think I have told you, is that the Archbishop of York has made me Diocesan Architect, so the year opens very brightly for me, and I hope I shall deserve my good fortune "

Ten sets of plans were submitted in the National Gallery competition, their authors being Messrs Owen Jones, C Brodrick, Banks and Barry, F. P. Cockerell, Digby Wyatt, Edward Barry, Somers Clarke, Penrose, Murray, and my father. It is remarkable that while so many Gothic designs were submitted for the other great building, in this case only two were sent in, one by my father and the other by Mr. Somers Clarke, the latter design also appearing, with modifications, in an Italian dress It seemed to be assumed either that Gothic was not suitable for the particular purpose, or that the surroundings in Trafalgar Square made the adoption of a style so different unadvisable. The first of these assumptions, if it existed, was quite unreasonable. A range of picture galleries offers a simplicity of plan, indeed, which makes any style possible, but does not for that reason make Gothic any less suitable, unless it were never to be used except as a *dernier ressort*. Gothic is not, to be sure, bound down to parallelograms, as some styles are, but some of its simplest examples are among the best we have

With regard to the second objection, a writer in the

Spectator at that date rightly insisted that too much stress should not be laid upon it :—

"Except St. Martin's Church," the letter ran, "there is nothing in or near the Square of any architectural value, and it would be better to secure one good building, however little in harmony with what encumbers the neighbouring ground, than choose an inferior plan merely because it suited and added one more to the many abortions that disgrace a capable site. . . Mr. Street's is the only respectable design in any style, and therefore it is, and not because it is Gothic, that its claims are urged"

My father himself did not rate the surrounding buildings very highly. The College of Physicians he thought quite unworthy to set the style to a building of much greater importance than itself, and of St Martin's Church he said : " The spire of St. Martin's-in-the-Fields takes it so completely out of the category of really classical buildings that a Gothic building would harmonise with it quite as well as one of really classic design."

Early in 1866, with the view of making himself better acquainted with the various ways of arranging picture galleries, the system of lighting, etc, he went first to Munich, then to Vienna, Prague, Dresden, Berlin, Hanover, and Hildesheim, managing to combine a great deal of interesting sight-seeing with his more special study. In the course of this tour he practically settled pretty much in his own mind what his design was to be, and made a considerable number of pen-and-ink notes and sketches of the building generally and of details, all adhered to pretty closely in the finished design.

My father gives a brief outline of this tour in a letter which is interesting as showing how much he managed to make of his time, and in what way he spent it :—

" Of course I must have told you that I had been asked to make designs for the National Gallery and the New Law Courts. Mr. Scott and myself are the only two architects asked for both, so I consider it no slight honour I made my journey to Germany mainly for the purpose of looking at picture galleries. We really enjoyed our journey very much indeed. Marique (my mother) went with me and did not knock up, and as we travelled seven nights out of the fourteen we were away, she did very well. First of all we went

by night to Antwerp; there we spent the day looking about the old
town and seeing the picture gallery Then on the next night to
Cologne, and, after an hour for breakfast, on again by the railway
along the Rhine to Mainz and thence to Munich, where we arrived
at ten o'clock at night. We were glad to get two nights there seeing all the sights. Everything is modern. Picture and sculpture
galleries, palaces, and new churches, all very gorgeously decorated.
But still it is a *triste* sort of city. Its public buildings seem too
large for the population.

"From Munich we went by night to Vienna. This is a very
different sort of place—smart, crowded, and lively. There is a fine
collection of pictures, a magnificent cathedral, and a good many
smaller churches We spent three days here, and came back by
night to Prague—a most quaint and picturesque old city, full of
interest for me. The bridge is one of the most striking in Europe,
with gateways at each end, and statues of saints all along on either
side The Jews' quarter is most remarkable. The oldest synagogue
is a curious building of the thirteenth century, singularly interesting, and nearly as it was first built. From Prague, after a day
spent there, we went by night to Dresden, where we had two days
Here the picture gallery is well arranged, and the pictures very fine. I
have seldom seen a nobler collection The town is very pleasantly
situated on the Elbe, with a charming country near it. Then from
Dresden we went to Berlin, where we had both been before, but I
wanted to look at the picture gallery again It has a fine collection
of pictures, but is abominably planned. Then from Berlin we made
our way to Hanover, a nice old town, from which we made an excursion to Hildesheim, which is famous for its cathedral and churches,
and thence by night to Cologne, arriving there on Sunday morning,
and then on to Brussels, where we dined, and on by night to London So you see we lost no time, having been only thirteen days
away. We went to a concert at Hanover, and had some good
music. At Dresden we heard a poor opera, and at Vienna saw a
very elaborate ballet. The music is always extremely good; and I
think I never heard anything so beautiful as the way the band played
the overture to *Leonora* at Hanover. At Berlin also we went to hear
Strauss's band play. They confined themselves of course to dance
music.

" I got a great deal of valuable information as to picture galleries,
and made the acquaintance of the directors of those at Munich and
Dresden, who allowed me to go over every part of them, so that my
journey was not fruitless."

To describe briefly my father's design, the Trafalgar
Square front showed a long line of roof, broken only by a

central dome over the entrance hall, with a projecting porch.
The angles between the porch and the wings of the south
façade were filled by circular engaged towers, with loggie
and dome-capped turrets   The whole front was arcaded
with two tiers in each bay, the north-east and south-east
angles of the building being treated with great richness and
originality

Of the great unbroken roof one prominent critic was
very intolerant, professing that it reminded him of nothing so
much as the long roof of a barn , otherwise the design met
with favourable comment at his hands.   In strange contra-
diction to this strongly expressed opinion, the same gentleman, in his criticisms on my father's Law Court design,
recommended him to study the Cloth Hall at Ypres as a suitable model for his Strand front.   My father's idea was that
the Ypres type was more suitable for a building with simple,
straightforward uses, like a picture gallery, rather than for
one which was to answer all sorts of different purposes, and
contain within it a most complicated system of rooms of
varied size and character; and common sense assuredly
favours his view of the matter.

The plan was generally well spoken of   The *Athenæum*
said :—

"Mr Street has secured perfect communication, easy exit from
and entrance to any part of the building without going through all
the galleries.   These latter are not too large for exhibition purposes.
. . It would be hard to find a more beautiful or better adapted
work than this."   And the *Times* said that " Mr. Street's plans, so
far as they relate to convenience, will commend themselves to
common sense."

The building, as my father proposed it, was to have been entirely of stone—externally, and was to have an area of nearly
90,000 feet for pictures, at an estimated outlay of £374,000.
It was about the cheapest of all the designs sent in, and
indeed was calculated to be as cheap again as the only other
Gothic design.   The interest in the result of this competition
was, as I have said, rather languid.   It was probably suspected
at an early stage that little would be done.   Mr. Edward
Barry's appointment as architect was notified at the same time

as was my father's to the Law Courts.   All that was done
in his day was to add several new galleries, which, while
they are in themselves a great improvement on the little
insignificant rooms of which they form the centre, still preclude the hope of a radical rearrangement or reconstruction of the whole building, which would have been the most
satisfactory course.

CHAPTER IV

THE revival of the study and practice of Gothic architecture
in this country had been coincidental with a new growth of
that devotional spirit which finds its outward expression in
the more frequent and more seemly observance of the services and ordinances of the Church. It was this spirit
which had illumined the Middle Ages, which, in times
nearer our own, had shone with a less kindly light, and, half
a century since, had seemed within a little of being ex-
tinguished. The one revival was both a cause and an effect
of the other, and their object was practically identical.

This being so, it was no more than natural that the
young men who had thrown themselves with enthusiasm
into the one revival—the rising school of Gothic architects
should have been strongly affected by the other. Such
was at any rate the case with my father

With the view of establishing more firmly the connection
between their art and the religion, in the glorification of
which it was chiefly concerned, he and others of his own
age and temper were, I find, in the year 1848, engaged in
the attempt to formulate a scheme which should bring about
this result This took the form of a society or college
where students should not only be instructed in religious art
by competent masters,—who were themselves to be members
of the college,—but should also be under certain religious
ordinances and live a life in strict accord with the lofty
character of their work.

In those days when enthusiasm was at its highest, when
each man felt, as it were, the fervour of a convert, anything
for which the Middle Ages furnished a precedent was likely

to be welcomed without further recommendation ; and the mediæval guilds and schools of architects, so far as their nature is known, may be taken to have represented pretty accurately what my father and his associates aimed at doing. The dissimilarity of conditions was, however, such as to make what had been success in the one case almost certain failure in the other. In the first place, what was in the time of the mediæval architectural guilds practically a trade secret, handed down from one generation to another—the art of design—was necessarily forty years ago no more a secret than it is now, or at most was a secret which patience and intelligence would disclose ; there would have been no possibility of keeping every architect who was engaged in church work in the college or amenable to its rules. Again, there could have been no certainty that the architects outside the pale might not have produced better work than the associates of the society , and, lastly, as the masters were not likely to be infallible, it might very well have happened that the rules laid down by them, which were to be stringently enforced, and their teaching itself might not have been the best for the attainment of the object in view. These objections and many others were no doubt raised by those of greater age and experience to whom the project was broached. However that may have been, certain it is that the scheme came to nothing, and is only worth mentioning here because it serves to throw into bold relief an all-important feature in my father's artistic life

His religion, not an acrid one nor ostentatiously worn, was intimately bound up with his work, and exerted a very real and very appreciable influence on its character It follows naturally that he should have looked for the highest development of his own and the sister arts of painting and sculpture where they were used in the service of religion and the glorification of her truths.

This was the secret of his love for the men of the Middle Ages and their handiwork. He saw that those glorious monuments, which are the boast of Europe, owe their pure and exalted type of beauty to the devotional and self-obliterating faith of the men who built them , while in their creation man's noblest qualities were called into request and developed.

Work so inspired never failed of being honest, unpretentious, and full of a beautiful symbolism ; but as the Church grew more corrupt, so did the arts which were its handmaids.

My father thought it not too fanciful to see in the passing of the stern and dignified Romanesque into the more delicate and refined Early English, of that again into the growing luxuriance of decorated work, and of that once more into the monotonous uniformity of perpendicular, with its personal conceits and displays of individual whims and cleverness, an accurate reflection of the various stages of corruption through which the Church was passing till a great convulsion of the religious and political world should bring forth the English Reformation.

It is then against the spirit of self-assertion in his work —mere attempts to display his own powers—that my father would have bid the architect steel his heart.

"This great truth must be grasped," he said, "that Christian Art is never properly developed except by an essentially Christian intention on the part of the artist, as well as on the part of those who employ his talents." And again, "The church architect must thoroughly believe the doctrines of the church for which he builds, and must lead a life of—to say the least—fair conformity to her rules and discipline. He must also be fairly acquainted with her ritual and usages "

Much of the beauty of old churches is due to the natural habit of man to express himself through symbolism, whether simply in his own person, as in bowing the head or bending the knee, or in a larger way, as in the forms of a building. This symbolism was of two kinds : firstly, that which followed the general teaching of the Church, and became in time crystallised into a regular system, being always adhered to in many features ; and, secondly, the symbolism of the individual, a factor of incalculable value the latter,—in my father's opinion,—and one to which the most strange and piquant beauties of a building are often due. Symbolism gave us first the church shaped in the form of a cross to

impress on us the Doctrine of the Atonement. To it we owe
the orientation of our churches. The choir, which tends
northwards, typifies the inclination of our Lord's head on
the Cross, and has a certain architectural value Churches
were built long and narrow in the form of a ship The
chancel was in some degree divided from the nave as a type
of the difference between the Church militant on earth and
the Church triumphant in heaven. The elevation and ornamentation of the chancel, its partial separation from the rest
of the church, the arrangement of the stalls with their
western return, the steps rising to the altar, all came undeniably from a belief in the doctrine of a real Presence in
the Sacrament, and, to use my father's words—

"Had our churches been mere halls, I cannot think that the
revival of religion would have been accomplished with so steady a
forward march ; and so if the form of our old churches has saved
us from eccentricities of belief in the past, the combination of the
same style in new buildings will do the same in the future ; whilst he
is no oversanguine man who believes that dissenters, who on all
hands nowadays seem to desire to assimilate the architecture of
their places of worship to that of our churches and chapels, will in
time be led, partly in this way, to that restoration to the Church's
fold which all who long for unity so earnestly pray to see"

Thirty years ago my father wrote . "The English architect of to-
day has opportunities as great as those of any of his predecessors,
if he will but use them ; but he must use his art as one who respects both himself and it There is no real respect for an art when
it is treated, as it always has been by the Renaissance architects
and their followers, as a mere affair of display ; no good building was
ever yet erected in which the architect designed the front and left
the flanks or the internal courts to take care of themselves So also
no good building was ever seen in which the exterior only was
thought of, and the internal decoration or design neglected. In such
treatment of art as this there is an ingrained falseness which is as
demoralising as it is ruinous. If architecture is only an affair of outside display no one will take any real interest in it ; for, from the first,
it is the evidence of the architect's love for his work which has given
the human interest which is all in all to it. It is this truthfulness
only, in every line and every detail of every part of a building, which
can ever make great architecture. It is this only which one would
wish to extract from the works of our forefathers."

It would of course be idle to deny that in every country

shams may be found, put up during the very best period
How many of the great Italian fronts are mere screens,
which explain nothing of what is behind them, and, indeed, suggest what is false! Lincoln and Ely have their
screens, St. Albans, too, has lately been endowed with
one. My father, in laying down the law of truth so
strongly, was by no means oblivious to these examples;
but he was, on the contrary, consistent and thoroughgoing
in his opinions, and could never bring himself to forgive
this unreal and unnatural arrangement even where, as at
Lincoln, it is associated with almost the best work we have
got.

This love of truthfulness for its own sake, this sympathetic cultivation of the spirit which, in spite of the
exceptions noted above, most certainly did animate the
mediæval builders, had doubtless a great and salutary influence on my father's work. It was perhaps to this quality
that his buildings owe their kinship with old work, which
was closer by far than anything which his predecessors had
been able to achieve. He felt—none more strongly—
how paramount the beauty of usefulness is, and how much
more effective a building is which is marked by a certain
dignity and restraint and obviousness of purpose than one
which is larded over with unmeaning ornament which
gives no emphasis; where parts which have insignificant
uses are promoted to the same degree of prominence, and
treated just as elaborately, as others which are of the first
importance; where the grouping of the windows conveys
nothing of the internal arrangement: a hall in one wing of
a building being balanced by a façade at the other end,
which only serves to mask a group of offices or a number of
small rooms; where, in fine, the architect is visible everywhere, controverting the natural laws which should govern
design, and intent apparently on putting into the front of a
single building a little of all he knows.

I remember hearing how Sir Gilbert Scott had mistaken
a church of my father's for one of the fourteenth century,
not from any archaism or inconvenience of plan or arrangement, but simply from the presence of that subtle quality

which I have attributed to the spirit which animated him in
his work

Somewhat akin to his love for truth in building was
the consistency with which he worked in one style—a consistency which sprang just as much from conviction as did
his other quality   Gothic was in his eyes the best of all
styles, the most flexible, the most national,—and therefore
the best adapted for our climate,—the most richly endowed
with the capacity for adopting any and every improvement,
and bending itself to satisfy our newest tastes ; and, lastly,
the most skilful in its construction.   On this head he
says :—

"The pointed arch is not only the most beautiful, but it is at
the same time incomparably the most convenient feature in construction which has ever been, or, I firmly believe, ever can be
invented, and we should not be true artists if we neglected to use
it."   And again, "The *elements* of Gothic architecture in the Middle
Ages are the adoption of the best principles of construction, and a
natural and proper treatment of ornamentation without concealment
of construction.   The *accidents* are, as it appears to me, the particular character which individual minds may have given to their
work—the savageness or grotesqueness, as it has been called, which
is mainly to be seen in the elaboration of some particular feature by
some particular sculptor or architect, of which, in the noblest work,
one sees no trace."

Here, then, was a style which was, to him, at once the
most beautiful both absolutely and also as being the most
useful.   To have worked in another would have been distasteful to him, and would have constituted to his mind a
dereliction of duty.

Sir Gilbert Scott bore witness to the general sentiment
when he said, in presenting to my father the gold medal
of the Institute of Architects ·—

"I will rather dwell on the moral side of Mr. Street's artistic
character, his steady pertinacity in following on the great movement to which he from the first attached himself   I will not say
that he has been wholly unmoved by the passing fluctuations of
taste which ever and anon float over us   that would be to convert
steadfastness into dull immobility, but he has adhered to the great
revival, and that in its best form—the revival of the earlier and more

perfect type of mediæval art . . I envy and revere this unbending steadfastness, and earnestly wish that it may prevail."

These qualities—truthfulness, abnegation of self, consistency—should, in my father's view, animate at least every church architect ; in a word, the man who works in a high cause should be actuated by high and Christian motives It should be for honest conviction to determine the choice of style in the first instance, and that choice once made, no promptings of personal interest should avail to turn the steps of the conscientious architect into strange paths.

An architect, be he, religiously speaking, ever so callous, or ever so indifferent to particular forms of worship, must at the same time, to take the lowest grounds, feel a certain interest in the proper planning, and even in the proper use of a church, for a wrong or inadequate use of it stultifies the plan and its maker ; but for the church architect in the real sense of the word, as my father was—the man who has the welfare of the church for which he builds near his heart, whose truths he has the power to emphasise by skill in arrangement—for him the whole planning of a church must ever be a work fraught with deep interest, the subject of deep thought ; while, at least in my father's case, the whole use of the church, its power to promote and foster belief, its availability for rich and poor alike, the due and fitting performance of its ritual and ceremonials, were all the subject of anxious consideration and the text of many a speech and paper.   On this point he asks :—

"How far are architects bound to go in their attempt to combine their art with a religious object and intention? It is certain that if all church architects would firmly refuse to plan churches except on certain conditions as to arrangement, and if again they would endeavour to understand the real uses and objects of churches and their arrangements, we should have far less to deplore at the present day than we have. I say, and I say positively, that the influence of some men at the present time might enable them to secure invariably in the churches which they build such arrangements of the interior as would make it difficult, if not impossible, for people long to ignore those truths which the building is intended to teach."

Much is required of the architect, but there is another thing necessary even when he has done his work well,

that the well-planned and well-designed church should be
well used   My father continues :—

"What is to be said of those whose office it is to use churches ?
I speak now alike of priest and people.   Nothing can be more disheartening than to see the building on which one has spent all
one's zeal and art misused or half-used.   The architect who
connects religion with architecture dreams to himself of church
doors open day after day and all day, of altars properly and rever-
ently decked, etc."

My father's interest perhaps was most strong in the use
of our cathedrals—the mother churches of our dioceses,
which, rightly, should be a pattern for all the daughter
churches, leading the zealous, encouraging the timid, awaken-
ing the slothful.   The mother church, as it is in all like-
lihood the most beautiful in form of all the churches in the
diocese, and the richest in capabilities for good arrangement,
should similarly excel them in the perfection of its ritual
and the completeness of its ceremonial.

He compared, and the comparison could not be a
flattering one, the state of our cathedrals a few years since,
their use, and the number of ministers and canons engaged
in carrying on the work of the services, with what had
obtained in early times and in post-Reformation days, for
even at the Reformation the old rules were not relaxed.
Cranmer proposed that in every cathedral provision should
be made for readers or lecturers in divinity as well as in
Greek and Hebrew ! that a large number of students should
be exercised in the daily worship of God, and trained in a
course of study and devotion, whom the bishop might trans-
plant out of this nursery into all parts of the diocese.   It
was the recollection of such facts as these which made
my father and others of a like mind feel with how just
a censure the cathedral commissioners had said in 1854.
"We desire to draw attention to the fact that a great part
of the fabrics of our cathedrals is at present unused for
public worship."   There were, it appears, at that time
seventeen cathedrals where the Holy Eucharist was only
celebrated monthly, in twelve others it was held weekly, and
not in a single one daily   One cathedral, Ripon, had only

one service a day.   The number of ministers had dwindled
in proportion to the services ; instead of the great establish-
ments of the Middle Ages, when it was possible to satisfy
the needs of one large congregation after another, there
were few resident canons,—in some places all residing in
one house,—the services, as we have seen, had nearly ceased,
and the congregations had dwindled even more sadly.   In
fact, the cathedral had become—as my father said with strict
justice—for people generally little more than a museum of
antiquities, wherein, in some places, was provided an enjoyable sacred concert on Sunday afternoons.

What my father earnestly desired to see in our cathedrals was a reversion to something of the old grandeur of
ceremonial.   He cordially agreed with Bishop Hamilton,
when the latter said —

"The giving of greater musical powers to the choir seems to me
so essential to the realising the primary object of our foundation
that I could even strongly recommend that one of the four existing
canonries should be suppressed, and its share of the corporate
property appropriated to the improvement of the stipends of the
present lay-vicars, and the increase of their members, if funds cannot
be obtained for this object without such a sacrifice "

His wish was to see a service of a more stately and
dignified character, such as should impress and rivet the
attention of an indifferent people ; further, he held it to be
all-important to elevate the Holy Communion again into the
great office which it still was theoretically, but had long
ceased to be in fact, celebrating it not only in the chilly
hours of early morning, but also at the later service, with
choral accompaniment of an appropriate character.

The use to which our cathedral choirs had generally
been put, choked up with chairs facing now north, now
south, now west, like an ill-arranged auditorium, offered,
and indeed offers now in some places, the first obstacle to
a proper use of the church, and to such a state of things my
father would have had a stop put instantly and peremptorily,
while he would have had the choir divided from the body of
the church by the lightest open screens, so that a large congregation in the nave might have participated in the service

in a real way. On the point of ancient close screens, he
even went so far as to affirm that he would favour their
absolute removal to some other part of the church, in the
last resort, if they proved to be an insuperable bar to a
satisfactory congregational arrangement.   Here are his own
words ·—

> "Here I would say that though I should always regret having
> to remove any old screen, I am painfully conscious that by insisting
> on its retention, together with the present use of choirs, I should
> not be doing a really conservative work.   For it cannot be denied
> that the choirs suffer much more in effect by the introduction of
> additional seats and pews, than they could suffer by the removal of
> the choir screens, if this be accompanied by the removal of the
> additional seats."

My father felt that the use of the choir and nave conjointly very frequently offered difficulties of a real kind,
because the choir had been built for a monastic or semi-
monastic use ; but even putting aside the use of the two
parts of the church conjointly, he still felt that a satisfactory
solution of the difficulty might nearly always be found without any great trouble. · In some cases the right way to go
to work seemed quite obvious.   It will be seen later how he
proposed to treat St. Paul's, and our other great London
Church seemed to him adaptable to the needs of a large
congregation with the least possible alteration.   His suggestion for dealing with the Abbey was that the choir should
simply be shifted up to the crossing, thus at one stroke
enabling the entire congregation in the transepts to hear
and see in a satisfactory way, instead of being encouraged
to be indifferent and disrespectful, as they may almost be said
to be by the present strangely mistaken arrangement.   As
a general rule, at any rate wherever an ancient close screen
was to be preserved, my father would have proposed treating
the choir almost in the light of a morning chapel—using it,
that is, for all services which were wont to attract only a
moderate congregation, whereas all the more important functions, and those which it might be hoped would be attended
by throngs of people, would have been held in the nave
These nave services, however, which, rightly conducted,

should have a certain magnificence and impressiveness, were, it is needless to say, in my father's view, to have nothing mean or temporary about them. The stalls for the choir he would have had of a permanent character, and sufficiently sumptuous ; while, as a matter of course, there would have been a second altar, not treated, as our altars were, in a cheap and unimpressive way, for in this respect we might have sat at the feet of even the Lutherans with advantage to ourselves, but elevated and enriched so as to be obviously *the* important feature, and even rendered more conspicuous by a canopy or baldachin. At the same time the eastern altar, which has very generally been shifted down west of its original position, would have been restored to its old place.

Thus would the church have been restored as nearly as might be to its early uses, for, as my father pointed out, its functions to-day are very much those of one of the great religious houses ; at one time it has to reach the hearts of thousands, at another to satisfy the needs of the two or three faithful who daily approach the altar.

A last suggestion he made, more especially with reference to impressiveness of ceremonial, and that was as to the use of the aisles. These were never meant by their builders to be anything more than passages—procession paths—and are not fitted for congregational purposes. Why, then, he asked, should we not turn them to their original use? for stateliness and richness both of ceremonial and structure, so that there be nothing meretricious, are important factors in attuning the mind to the contemplation of higher things—a consideration which, so far as the services are concerned, is too much ignored in our cathedrals. Had my father been asked for a model, worthy of imitation in all points both of structure and ceremonial, he would have pointed unhesitatingly to those Puritans of the Middle Ages—the order of Cistercians. What he felt so strongly of the use of the mother, he naturally felt also in regard to the daughter churches, though here there were fewer cobwebs to sweep away. At All Saints, Margaret Street, where he was for many years one of the most influential and energetic members of the congregation, we have seen how heartily he co-operated with Mr. Upton Richards in the introduction of vestments at Holy Communion—a step which he warmly applauded as giving practical effect to what he was always preaching, viz "That in the direction of ornament we should put a liberal interpretation on the Prayer-Book," and one which, having a legal sanction, he could, as an earnest and devoted son of the Church of England, conscientiously take. "I am," he says about the same time, "I suppose, what you call a Ritualist, for I belong to the party which for twenty years has been striving with no small success to raise the whole tone of Church opinion and practice both in architecture, music, ritual, and doctrine Every one knows how much the tone has been raised not only among churchmen, but even more remarkably among dissenters."

A High Churchman essentially he was of the best type, one who thought that no effort should be spared to make the services of the Church a real act of wórship, but who, in his own person, abstained from that extremity of prostration and genuflection which, with all its sincerity of purpose, yet seems, and it did so to him, to make the worshipper conspicuous rather than to reflect honour on the object of his worship

At All Saints my father, as I have said, was able as churchwarden to carry out to the fullest extent what were, so far as the formation of a congregation is concerned, his leading principles. Firstly, that the Church of England belongs to all classes of the community equally; and secondly, that the Church belongs as much to the man as to the woman, and that punctual attendance on her services is as incumbent on the one as on the other.

As regards free seats, I cannot express better what he felt than by quoting a letter on the subject, written some five and twenty years ago, in which he combines his experiences with certain suggestions :—

"As it happens, few men have so many opportunities as I of learning what is the real feeling of people in regard to free churches, and I am certain that, great as have been the changes which we have witnessed in Church matters during the last few years, none

has been more obvious than the way in which educated men regard
their right to the appropriation of seats in churches.   In church
building and restoration, where one used to have twenty obstinate
parishioners to convert, there is now only one to convince, and it
has become a common thing to find tradesmen and farmers zealous
in approval, who till a few years ago would have been earnest in
their opposition.   The experience of those who really know the
working of our town churches is entirely opposed to the conclusion
which you draw 'from an erroneous report of a sermon preached last
year by the incumbent of All Saints, Margaret Street.   The people
in that parish have no difficulty in getting seats in their church ; it
is but a slight hardship for them that, in return for a noble church
(built without cost to them) and frequent and beautiful services,
they must be in their places, for one or two of the Sunday services,
some ten or fifteen minutes before the service begins.   This is the
entire extent of the grievance invented for them by others   On the
other hand, if you knew the class which really fills such a church to
overflowing, you would find that it consists very largely of people
who seem to be unthought of and uncared for by those who argue
for the appropriation of pews—all that large class of decently-dressed,
well-behaved, but poor people, our domestic servants, our clerks, our
shopmen and shopwomen, sempstresses, and the like.

"For many years I have had most practical evidence of the
enormous benefits which free churches confer on those classes, and
of the fruits which the Church is reaping in London, in the enthusiastic attachment to her services on the part of those who, under the
old system, were undoubtedly repelled from her ranks.   How could
it have been otherwise ?   Did it often or ever happen that the pro-
prietors of those great London shops, which count their assistants
by the score or the hundred, secured pews for their use ?   And was
it likely that in default they—the assistants—would go, save in rare
instances, into any of those bare, dreary, and markedly inferior seats
which, in small proportions and bad positions, were ticketed 'free' ?
The thing was so unlikely that one's only surprise is that it should
have been possible to allow the system so long a life as it has
had

"It is to beg the whole question to say that the admission of
the poor is the exclusion of the rich from the churches which they
have built.   If the crowds which throng a free church are so great,
then clearly the way to meet the difficulty is to multiply the services
The additional services might easily be made to pay their expenses ;
while those who have most attentively watched the change in men's
views on this question are satisfied that there is no reason for the
way in which we confine our services to the same hours everywhere,
and that, if crowds of worshippers come to church, they will come

as well at ten o'clock as at eleven o'clock, and so make it possible to repeat the morning service to a second congregation.

"Nothing amazes me more than the waste of money which is involved by our system of appropriation of seats. If you appropriate, you make it useless for the clergyman to give more services in the day than one devout man can endure; and so our bishop has to draw a startling picture of spiritual destitution in regard to the structural provision for worshippers, which is to a large extent the result not of lack of buildings, but of lack of common sense in our way of using them."

This letter is of course rather out of date nowadays, many of its suggestions have been followed, and in churches where the seats are appropriated at the principal Sunday services, provision is frequently made by services at half-past nine or ten for those who are not seatholders; but at the time my father wrote, no such arrangement for the convenience of the poorer classes was known, and what had been done in that direction was due to the exertions of a small body of energetic workers like himself.

Even in a church like All Saints, which belonged so completely to the new order of things, my father found much to do. I have already spoken of the way in which he insisted on making the church free and open in fact as well as in name, not allowing one single pew to prove the rule by the exception, and putting a stop to the usurpation of men's seats by the other sex. Many years after, in his own church, he was able to carry out the same principle of absolute freedom of seats in the most complete way. There the church is a leveller of classes, as it should be, and serves to throw at least one plank over the gulf which separates rich from poor.

After his death the *Free and Open Church Advocate* bore testimony to his work in that cause in those words :—

"He was an earnest churchman and an ardent friend of our own cause, he worked both as actual warden of one free church, founder of another, and vindicator of all by tongue and pen. In 1872 he rendered valuable service to the cause by the tact and decision with which he helped to bring about the union of the (then two) 'London Councils,' and he was only constrained by the pressure of his many duties to resign the office of treasurer in 1874

As a counsellor and ally, he was always ready, and in both characters his genius and high authority gave a value to his co-operation which we recall with gratitude."

Perhaps, if there is one sign more than another which is suggestive of the changes which have taken place in the last half-century, it is to be found in the treatment of our altars, and the special character of such part of the service as takes place before them.   The altar and the office of Holy Communion are nowadays recognised as the sign and seal of the personal nearness of God to us, and the altar, as being the visible token of His presence, has been re-elevated to the place of honour which once belonged to it, but had been gradually usurped by the pulpit.

It is probably true that where five people listened to a sermon a couple of score of years ago fifty do so now.   The sermon has ceased to be a discourse or a mere piece of reading aloud.   It is often vivid and heart-stirring : it deals with points of doctrine, it grapples with the needs and questions of the hour, but in spite of this, the pulpit has sunk, and rightly, and the altar has risen.

Where can we find to-day what twenty years since was common enough, what might have been seen within the last five years, that concentric arrangement of seats in the form of an auditorium all looking to and converging on the imposing three-decker? or where is that mean and pitiful altar to be found which Pugin illustrates, with no exaggeration, in his book of *Contrasts ?*   It belongs to an era which is happily almost forgotten now ; but such was not the case when my father was a young man   Much still remained to be done, and among the willing hearts and hands which laboured in the cause none did so more abundantly than his.

The very excellence of the frontals with which our altars are now generally vested, and of the dossal hangings. which serve to make their surroundings rich, must, in some measure, be put down to my father's own individual work. From the very commencement of his career as an architect, or a student of architecture, he had taken a special interest in old church embroidery work, and had devoted himself with a remarkable success to designing embroidery patterns, aided greatly at first by the exertions of his sister, whose skill in reproducing his designs was well known, and did much to make them appreciated Besides advocating strongly the enrichment of the altar itself, my father held it to be a *sine quâ non* that it should be raised well above the body of the church—an arrangement which is at once valuable architecturally, and makes the altar a conspicuous object. This he did by raising it not on one great flight of steps, such as that at St. Leonard, Hythe, but on a succession of pairs or single steps (called by *The Record* "a series of terraces"), the effect of the latter arrangement being that the appearance of a convex ascent is obtained, whereas one great flight, though in theory it is more magnificent, in practice tends to look concave and weak.

There is, however, one crowning glory of the altar— using the epithet in its fullest sense—which, familiar as it is to the student of Italy, still has its footing to make good here I allude of course to the baldachin or canopy In speaking of my father's views on the right treatment of St Paul's, I shall have something further to say on the subject, because he proposed there to carry out Sir Christopher Wren's known views in that respect I merely quote now a letter written on the subject in 1873, in which he gives his reasons for his predilections. The letter, I should say, was specially directed against a suggestion which had been thrown out in the case of St Barnabas that a baldachin was not suitable for a square-ended church. He writes :—

"If people are so senseless as to condemn a thing on account of its name, without knowing what it is they are protesting against, I fear no appeal to common sense will be of much avail. . . . The question as to whether there is a sufficiency of space for a canopied altar in the small sanctuary of St. Barnabas is one which depends for its answer on the size of the proposed erection. If it were a large, heavy erection at all like the Renaissance examples, it might well be too big and clumsy for such a church. If, on the other hand, it were to be a delicate and elegant canopy, such as those in the churches of Santa Maria in Cosmedin and Santa Cecilia at Rome, I deny altogether that the chancel of St Barnabas is at all too small for it. If part of the scheme were the erection of an altar of exaggerated length, an exaggerated canopy might have followed But as this is no part of the scheme, and as a canopy or baldachin may be very delicate in its treatment and moderate in its dimensions, I entirely dissent from broad and positive assertion to the contrary I dissent also from the assertion of a necessary connection of a baldachin with an apse   Your correspondent can think of nothing but the earliest treatment of an apse, and describes the planning of almost every apse built in Europe since A D. 1250 as 'the modern false way' in which architects treat such forms ; and he goes on to allow that unless the earliest use of an apse, with seats for bishop and clergy round it behind the altar, can be revived, he sees no reason for attempting to revive the 'real' apse, and with it the canopy over the altar.   It will be quite sufficient for my purpose to show that mediæval architects saw no such difficulty as your correspondent (embarrassed by archæological recollections) assumes, in placing a baldachin somewhere else than in the centre of the apse.   In Italy, where the apse was used by the clergy, the altar and baldachin were of necessity advanced into the choir; and the examples of San Lorenzo, Rome (a square-ended church, by the way), Toscanella, Grado, St. Ambrogio (Milan), and St Mark's (Venice), are all good illustrations of the practice.   But in the last-mentioned church one of the most exquisite features is certainly the small baldachin placed against one of the piers on the north side in happy defiance of your correspondent's rule.   If we leave Italy and come to countries where the Italian use of the apse did not obtain, we shall find that the 'rule' was not obeyed.   In the fine cathedral at Regensburg, for instance, there are some very beautifully-designed Gothic baldachins standing close to the side walls of the aisles, and perfectly suitable, therefore, to a square-ended chancel.   Equally to the point is the charmingly-designed baldachin against a side wall of the Liebfrau Kirche at Eslingen, and an almost equally strong case is that of the famous canopy over the altar in the 'false apse' of the Sainte Chapelle at Paris.   Your correspondent has properly said that baldachins are commonly allowed over other features (other than altars, that is) and in other materials   The old velvet tester over the altar in San Juan de los Reyes at Toledo is an almost unique mediæval example of such a feature, and this is in a square-ended church.   The old canopy over the font at Luton, which I had the pleasure of restoring to its proper place some years ago, is the finest example of a baldachin over a font , but I need hardly say that there are others, as *e g.* in the church of St. Peter Mancroft, Norwich, and what else is the galled canopy over a high tomb but a baldachin, and who can pretend to object to such a feature as that, on architectural grounds, in an English church ?

"'To me the whole question seems a purely architectural one. Can a canopy over an altar be constructed without damage to the character of a Gothic church? To this I should unhesitatingly say 'Yes,' and I should maintain also that the scale of the church had but little to do with the question.

"If, however, it is to be regarded from the religious side, I would ask whether the Church which can tolerate and admire the rich and gorgeous reredoses now so common, is not straining at a gnat and swallowing a camel, if it accepts them and refuses the baldachin, whose whole character is of necessity simple and comparatively unadorned? Loving hands are allowed to decorate our altars, in happy antagonism to the old spirit of carelessness which left them dirty, neglected, and repulsive in their appearance, and it is sad that, while the carelessness is too often more than tolerated in high places, only too great readiness is shown to thwart its reform when, as in this case, it is possible to make capital out of the use of a word which to most people, even to those of fair education, is so meaningless, as the terrible word 'baldacchino'

"Were there less prejudice to contend with, I should say that many of our square-ended churches would be more satisfactorily treated if their altars were under canopies than if they were adorned in any other way I have myself had the satisfaction of restoring to its old use, with the bishop's consent, an altar under a wooden tester under an arch on the north side of the nave of Burford Church, Oxfordshire. This is really a baldacchino supported on oak posts, almost every part of it being old. And every one who has looked closely into the question knows that in very many square-ended chancels or choirs in England the altar was never intended to be put against the east wall. Carlisle Cathedral is a good example of this, and Ripon was until the recent unfortunately destructive alteration of its choir arrangements Furness Abbey, Arundel Church, Stone Church, and Warfield Church, Berks, are other examples, and all of them are square-ended, without chapels to the east of the choir. And in my judgment it would not unfrequently cause less interference with old work behind the altar to erect such a canopy as I propose for St. Barnabas than it would to erect the usual reredos It is self-contained, does not necessarily touch or interfere with the wall, and consequently never need conceal any old feature— aumbry, arcade, or whatever it may be.

"As to the comparative innocence in the eyes of a suspicious or extreme Protestant of a baldachin founded on any old model, and a reredos, such as has been erected in churches and cathedrals without end with full legal and episcopal consent, I cannot conceive of a question being raised. The one is of necessity confined in the scope it affords for decoration, is pure and simple in its form, and has little, if any, space for colour or sculpture. The latter may be, and often is, gorgeous in colour, covered with sculpture which, to some eyes, is more or less objectionable, and altogether much more demonstrative. A man may object to the latter, because he thinks it may be attended with some risk of image-worship; but I conceive if he objects to the former, he may just as well object to the canopy over the font, the canopy over the bishop or over the preacher, and, finally, to the dome of St Paul's itself, which (as has been well pointed out) is in itself the supreme example of a baldachin."

The extent to which the subdivision of our parishes is carried, and its consequences to our buildings, was a matter of regret to my father.

It is well to keep always in view the strong moral effect which is produced, even on the unimpressionable, by a great interior, such as we might have if we were content to have one great building instead of several of lesser size. It is a feeling with which we are all familiar, that sense of awe which a noble church inspires It probably does as much for the average man or woman as any service, however solemn or touching. Mr. R. L. Stevenson, in one of his delightful records of a holiday ramble, says :—

"I could never fathom how a man dares to lift up his voice to preach in a cathedral. What is he to say that will not be an anti-climax? For though I have heard a considerable variety of sermons, I never yet heard one that was so expressive as a cathedral 'Tis the best preacher itself, and preaches day and night, not only telling you of man's art and aspirations in the past, but convincing your own soul of ardent sympathies, or rather, like all good preachers, it sets you preaching to yourself, and every man is his own doctor of divinity in the last resort."

My father himself, treating the subject from a different point of view, writes :—

"Who among preachers can hope to preach as the gifted artist does? It is not only that the sermons are in stones or on walls or canvas, but that they are read and believed by generation after generation of the faithful. The greatest orator has no thought so comforting as this. How short is the popularity and how fleeting the influence of all but the very greatest among us. The preacher may feel well rewarded if his greatest effort save one soul "

The great church, again, is not only impressive in itself,

but it is also accompanied by a corresponding dignity in the services. Concentration of the mere bricks and mortar will involve concentration in everything else connected with the church. Each building could in such a case be served by a much more considerable staff of clergy than is ever found at present. Services could then be multiplied to suit all classes and accommodate any numbers, and the very numbers of the ministry would give that possibility of variety, especially in the matter of sermons, which is always grateful to human nature. In the earlier days of the Revival, the great mistake was made of building town churches not deficient in scale only, but, so far as any peculiar fitness or accordance with their surroundings was concerned, churches which might simply have been transferred from some quiet country village. The form was picturesque rather than dignified, and the material rough in character and rustic in appearance. My father took the greatest exception to such a misuse and misplacing of material.

"It is a shame and a misery indeed," he said, "that it should ever have been possible in such a city as London for architects to attempt to execute copies of country work. Had there only been fair Christian liberality, we should, instead of Kentish rag, have had hewn ashlar, and for plaster, gorgeous fresco or marble." And again : "I maintain that most of our churches are guilty of very flagrant unreality in their use of unsuitable, inconvenient, and (under the circumstances of London buildings) unsightly materials, and such as none of us would wish to use in any other kind of building. . Where man abounds, there his work should be made most of, and any affectation of rusticity, whether in material, design, or execution, be most carefully avoided."

These designs, in which nothing beyond prettiness was aimed at, ran counter to all my father's strongest convictions as to the proper form of a town church, and the effect which it should produce. He saw that in the country a simplicity which is in harmony with Nature should be aimed at, and could hardly fail of being effective in its own way ; but the conditions in a town are as unlike as possible, and the town church should be strong and simple in its lines, made up of few parts, and those, if possible, large, it should also be symmetrical in its massing. In the town, the forces which it is the function of the Church to combat and counteract have their own magnificence of a kind, and, to be met at all adequately, must be met somewhat on their own ground.

Those who relied on a mere rustic picturesqueness of general effect showed, to my father's mind, not merely a want of appreciation of what the special surroundings of a large town call for, but failed at the same time to supply to those who enter the church door that stimulus towards higher things which a noble architecture may be made to give.

Going more into detail, my father would have said : " If possible, build a tower or a tower and spire." Norwich alone is enough to show one how noble a feature a tower in a town may be, while, if a spire be added, it should not rely on simple broaches, but should at least have a parapet of some richness, if not pinnacles. That a spire might, however, be made effective without these adjuncts, if cleverly treated, is sufficiently clear from the successful example of All Saints, Margaret Street, and my father's own beautiful work at St. Mary Magdalen, Paddington ; still, a man who had spent his earlier years under the shadow of St. Mary's, Oxford, would naturally feel a predilection for the more ornate type so perfectly illustrated there

It is interesting to find that my father, in comparing the merits of various important town churches, was inclined to put the tower of St. Dunstan's, and still more that of Wren's church of St. Michael's, Cornhill, above most later examples, much though there was in their detail with which he could feel no sympathy. For Wren's work, however, Goth though he was, he always had a cordial admiration and respect

CHAPTER V

I HAVE already said that my father claimed for Gothic a power of adapting itself to modern uses unsurpassed by any other style, for there seemed to him to be no forms of architecture which leave the hands of the designer so practically free and untrammelled to use or to put aside "It is not," he said, "necessary to have uniformity to the sacrifice of convenience, but it is possible to have uniformity when it is desirable." To those admirers of classic who twit their Gothic brethren with practising a style which loves irregularity for itself, my father would have answered by pointing to the endless succession of similar compartments in the arcades of Exeter, or Wells, or York, or to the magnificent uniformity of the front of the Cloth Hall at Ypres. The widespread notion that Gothic is a style which is like a mummy, and must be taken exactly as it is, for fear it should crumble away before the eyes of the man who would lay a finger on it, was combated in the pamphlet which he issued in explanation of his design for the Foreign and War Office. In this, ridiculous as his task seemed to him, he had gravely to argue that it is not true that Gothic forms will allow nothing but narrow slits, high above the floor, for the admission of light, or that the arrangements for glazing are bound to be of the most primitive character, that, in a word, nothing which was not known in the thirteenth century can be accepted now.

The use of Gothic forms may indeed be readily and indefinitely extended, and, if that is so, then no less may the form itself be amended or modified. This was my father's view, for he held, and held most strongly, that Gothic as it

was laid aside and as we took it up had not necessarily
reached the limits of its possibilities in the spheres of usefulness or beauty ; but that, far from having been fossilised into
one unalterable form by the lapse of years, it had really been
rather in a state of suspended animation, and offered itself
to skilful handling rather as a model in clay than one hewn
out of a block of granite.

He saw that Gothic as it is found in every part of Europe,
different as are its forms, is but the development under
different conditions and among varying tastes of the style of
the pointed arch.   This being so, are we, he asked, bound
absolutely to adhere without any modification to the particular
style of our own country, or to any one particular style ? or
ought we not rather to consider first of all how far the differences, to take one example, between the Gothic of England
and that of Italy are the result of accident, and how far of
necessity, and whether we may not perchance get some useful
hint, or be put on the track of some useful principle, by the
study of such features as are really due to accident, and not
dictated by the peculiar conditions of climate ?   He held
the opinion, it may seem paradoxical at first, that the differences in development due to the conditions and surroundings
among which any particular style grew, are after all of a minor
kind, such, for example, as the variation in the roof-pitch, in the
depth of mouldings, in the use of materials and colour ; while
the more important features in Italian Gothic, or in German or
Spanish, might just as well have had their birth and growth
on English soil and under English skies.

What more natural, then, such being his opinion, than
that he should have turned to the continental styles with an
idea of seeing whether they offered any hope of supplementing
deficiencies in our own national branch of the universal style ?
Nor did he even stop at Gothic, for no architect, however
strongly he may be prepossessed in favour of mediæval work
as being more suited to our needs, can wilfully shut his eyes to
the merits of the masterpieces of Greek art, and my father had
no suspicion of bigotry in his honest preference.   To Greece,
then, he turned for enlightenment and instruction.   There
he found much which, as belonging exclusively to the

architecture which had not yet learnt the use of the arch, was quite useless to him   The Greek column, standing passively under a direct weight, is naturally very different in form from the column which supports an arch.   The fixity of the one is shown by the way in which it spreads to its base ; the other is only a part of one continuous growth : it carries and spreads itself into that arched form which is truly said never to sleep.   Sometimes the arch mouldings are gathered on to the cap and run down to the base in a different form ; at other times they run down without, or almost without, a break.

The Greek column, or any other which supports a dead weight, is, in consequence of it, monolithic in character, while that which bears a weight which is always straining is built in the form of masonry.   Though my father found nothing in the column itself which could be of any possible use, on raising his eye a little he became aware of the presence of a quality, the want of which he always held to be a distinct failing in our own Gothic,—and in French no less,—going far to mar even the finest work, the quality of horizontality.   Now if Gothic errs in its want of accentuation of the horizontal line, Greek work, with its heavy cornice, which frustrates any attempt at getting a vertical effect, may be said to err in the other direction.   Still my father felt that it taught a valuable lesson in spite of the exaggeration, or even by reason of it, for there is in these buildings a magnificent spirit of repose, which should affect all who are not afraid to learn a truth from an alien style

It is not necessary, however, to go so far back as Greek work for a proof of the value of the horizontal line, for Italian Gothic, if it teaches us anything, must teach us this · there indeed the effect is produced almost invariably by colour and not by shadow , but the result is really identical, and most worthy of imitation.

In our own country, even so near home as Westminster Abbey, as my father noticed, there are a good many examples of work in two different-coloured stones, which is perhaps none the less beautiful for not being so strongly contrasted, as is frequently the case in Italian work ; but these examples are, after all, few and far between. The use of flint and stone in conjunction, common enough in some counties, can hardly be classed in the same category. The horizontal effect, if given, is for the most part accidental in character, and the regular and simple coursing of the two materials, though it does occur, is still not a common feature in such work. There is another serious want in Northern Gothic, where again my father was able to refer to Greek work for the corrective, and that is in the matter of ornamentation which it is within the power of the ordinary workman to carry out. Now the decoration of a Greek building was, as he said, both beautiful to the eye and true in principle Their sculpture, when they made use of it, was, of course, of fine, often of the highest character, the work of a real sculptor, while the surface ornament generally was such that nothing was required for its execution but the ordinary manual dexterity of a fair workman. Nearer our own day we find an abundance of genuine workman's enrichment in Romanesque work, and the pointed arch, as it is frequently treated in transitional work, has a beauty which makes one wonder how it was that this form of enrichment was allowed to lapse, for there was certainly nothing in it alien to the spirit of the style which rejected it, or, at least, systematically neglected it.

In Northern Europe, from the days of the transition onwards, men worked as if all might be sculptors. Of workman's ornamentation—rightly so called—there was literally hardly anything but dog-tooth, nailhead, and ball-flower for the enrichment of mouldings, and the varieties of diapers for flat surfaces. In one of the greatest and most successful ecclesiastical works, the restoration—or reconstruction, I might almost say—of the choir of Christ Church Cathedral, Dublin, my father, who had to work on transitional lines, made the freest use of all the beautiful and varied forms of chevron for the enrichment of the arch mouldings with the happiest effect It was a chance such as men rarely have, and one which he would not have missed on any account, for he probably hoped that the example might lead to imitation. It was a matter of surprise to him,

as it was also one of regret, that even in the latter part of
his life, when Gothic had been so long and often so skilfully
handled, men were still content to ring the changes on
those few familiar forms of ornament which became so
monotonous by repetition, and should turn, for variety of
effect, rather to second-rate and lifeless carving than to that
easily-worked type of ornament, with its almost inexhaustible
changes which Romanesque affords

My father complained in his early days of "labouring in
some quarters under the entirely undeserved imputation of
being a blind admirer of everything Italian." We have seen
that it was not so. "*Very* Italian is not so good as *very*
English," he wrote while in the midst of the best Italian
work　In truth, an English Gothic had no warmer or more
loyal adherent than he. He expresses his devotion to it in
words which are sufficiently explicit .——

"Who, indeed, that has studied on the spot, as I have done, not
only a vast number of buildings in England, but also nearly all the
best examples in France, Spain, and Germany, could do otherwise
than profess his truest allegiance to be due to the truthful beauties
of his own national variety of the style "

But he was no blind admirer, and he saw that on some
points we may learn a lesson to whatever part of the Continent we may look. Firstly, in the matter of height. Here,
indeed, we have Westminster Abbey, and we do well to be
proud of its beautiful proportions ; but putting this one noble
church aside, where shall we find another with any approach
to that mysterious and thrilling effect of height which is
almost *the* feature in so many of the continental examples ?
Nothing is more impressive or more unearthly than this.
Of such building my father said that it seems to be "entirely
for the glory of God, while length (our feature *par excellence*),
on the other hand, suggests the nicely calculated less or
more,"——the building which will accommodate so many worshippers, not the willing sacrifice of a people. We have, at
least, one other great failing which no one could possibly
ignore, viz. the meanness of our doors, more especially those
in the west front　The great continental western doors

tell us at once that the building of which they are a part is
free to the world, and should be entered by all alike They
invite, while ours repel ; they seem to preach forgiveness
to all ; ours, how hardly we shall enter the kingdom of
heaven.

If examples were wanted of the salutary nature of the
doctrine that, without actually grafting one style upon another,
we should at least not be ashamed to learn from others, they are
to be found in every country.   Take as an example the west
front of Genoa Cathedral, which my father declared to be,
in his eyes, the finest Gothic front in Italy, and fit to vie with
its Northern rivals.   He describes it thus .—

"Unlike any other Italian example, the façade was apparently
intended to have been finished with two steeples.   This fact, added
to the mixed French and Italian character of the sculpture, and to
the distinctly French treatment of the mouldings, which are arranged
and undercut in a way I have never seen in other Italian works,
lead me to believe that this is not to be classed with pure Italian
work.   Either it was erected by a Frenchman, or, more probably, by
an Italian who was well acquainted with the architecture of the
north of France."

He might have referred again to the interior of St. Andrea,
Vercelli, with its evident French and possible English influences, or to the glorious Italo-German interior of Milan.   Of
the effects of foreign study and training, visible in so many of
the Spanish cathedrals, he says a great deal in his book ,
where the foreign style has been transplanted directly and
without modification, the result, it need not be said, is never
wholly good ; but where discretion has been used, the effect
is completely satisfactory.

It naturally follows from my father's objection to the
use in a town of a design or of materials only fitted for the
country, that he should have been equally opposed to a
habitual and rigid use of one type of design, whatever its
character, when materials are so varied in different parts
of the country, and types, by a natural consequence, so
different and so marked.

He travelled far afield, and, wherever he went, his eyes
were always open and his attention on the alert ; allied to

great powers of observation was a faculty of, as it were, rapidly sifting the evidence which came before him, and drawing wide and rapid conclusions with remarkable correctness and precision. The result of his observations was that, as our predecessors had formed their style from the materials which they found to their hand, and generally made use of only such materials so to obtain a really truthful and fitting style, we should make our own works conform, when there were no special reasons to the contrary, to the style of the district in which they were to be erected. He saw, of course, that with our altered conditions to-day, with our rapidity and ease of communication and transport, it would be unnatural to ignore in one place improvements which we admitted in another ; and he realised equally well that our forefathers, had they had anything like our advantages, would never have been responsible for so many different or such widely divergent styles as have been preserved to us from their times. But, allowing these considerations their full weight, he still had no doubt that the balance in favour of the conformity of style which he advocated was a considerable one. Local peculiarities, he held, should at least be respected, and not outraged, as they sometimes are or were by the introduction of strange forms and incongruous materials.

"It is impossible to look at our new buildings," he said in 1869, "without feeling that they are too often the result not of original study, but of thoughtless acquiescence in the laws which have been laid down by common custom, or by the practice of some one popular man. Our new churches consist almost always of a building planned within very close limits as to variety, and with as few evidences as possible of the personal feeling of the artist ; whereas, if we look carefully and largely at old buildings, we shall find that they show much greater variety than ours, and that their architects were much less hampered and restrained by self-imposed rules than we are."

He insists that much of the glory of our national style consists in the variety of its development, and that we should do right to study every phase of it.

"It has been very much the custom to assume that local varieties

indicate divergence of principle, so that it is not safe for a man to
study more than one of them   This is simple nonsense, for it may
much more truly be said that no one does understand Gothic art
who has not studied that of more than one country, and it is
undoubtedly true that there is as much difference in the style of old
buildings in the various-counties, districts, or provinces of one
country, as there is between any one of these and some one variety
of the work of another country."

The causes of the variety in different districts and of
the general likeness between buildings in the same district
were various, as my father showed.   In the first place, the
material at disposal was a factor of great importance, (2)
the influence exerted in particular districts by some excep-
tionally gifted man; (3) the spread of art knowledge by
Freemasons, or by religious orders, by conquest, or by the
employment of foreign architects.   He pointed out how few
the exceptions are comparatively to the rule of using the
materials to hand.   Caen stone was indeed imported at an
early date; Portland stone was taken to Cornwall; south
of England stone to Hedon in Yorkshire, Isle of Wight
stone to Winchester; Purbeck nearly all over the country;
but in spite of a certain number of such cases, the one local
style was never formed except to suit the material most
easily come by.   We owe Wells and Glastonbury to the
Doulting quarries, Peterborough to Barnack; Lincoln to
those at Haydor; the best art being found near the best
quarries   In granite countries the churches are long and
narrow, with very thick walls, and arched granite roofs
supporting the outer roof without the use of any timber.
Such buildings are to be found in Guernsey, in Wales, in
Cumberland, at Cormack's Chapel on the Rock of Cashel,
and in many continental examples timber was dispensed
with, as in the churches of Auvergne and Périgord.
The presence of flint and the absence of other stone
gives us a completely different style, and one which led to
the display of much ingenuity, as, for instance, in the round
towers of Norfolk, which were built in that form in order to
avoid having any quoin stones
The absence of stone has given us brick architecture in

North Italy, in the north-east of Germany, in the west of France, and in some parts of Spain Its development was very diverse in these different countries, but the special properties and capabilities of brick were discovered and made full use of in every case. My father noticed the affinity, visible through great dissimilarity, between such fronts as that of the Town Hall at Lubeck, the gables of the Toulouse churches, and the transepts of Cremona Cathedral ; and he noticed too, what is more remarkable, that in every one of these cases the nearest stone architecture was sensibly affected by the example of the brick buildings, so that it in some degree adopted the forms. Finally, the abundance or scarcity of timber and its size controlled to a great extent the designs for roofs, and led in many cases to the erection of wooden or half-wooden churches.

One short quotation will make it clear what my father's feelings were about the employment of brick in good work .—

"The use of brick in place of stone in connection with good architectural design is a subject of much interest. In all countries, from the earliest period, brick has been used more or less freely to supplement stone, but not often in early times—with a view to architectural effect—in place of it. It may be said, and very rightly, that on the whole Nature's materials, when she affords them, are those which will best harmonise with the highest art. But where granite or marble or stone or even flint are not to be had, it becomes the clear duty of the architect to avail himself of the aid of the brickmaker.

"Brick was of course used very largely in all Roman constructions, but it was used solely to build simple walls, and usually with no view to the effect which they might produce. Indeed, they were chiefly used as a basis for the plasterer. In one respect,—that of hardness,—however, Roman brickwork has never been surpassed."

What my father saw when he looked to old work for a guidance was quite enough to justify his contention that, unless there were special reasons to the contrary, the general lines of the local style should be adhered to in new work, modified, however, and endowed with a special character by the individuality of the artist—a necessary feature in the work of a man of power, and never, under any circumstances, absent

" I can admire what is called 'mannerism,'" my father said on one occasion, and he would have added that in a certain sense the architect should be allowed to exercise his powers of invention   Very cautiously must we use the word, however, for no style has ever yet been invented ; either it has come by growth or by decay, the process in either case being as gradual and as equal as it is in Nature itself.   The field of discovery in architecture is exhausted. It is undeniable, as Ruskin tells us, that no principle of construction has been discovered for centuries.   My father thought that Gothic architects had left nothing to be found out worth the finding in construction, and he scoffed at the idea, which some have been bold enough to entertain, that a brand-new Victorian style might be invented, whose birth should rival that of Athene—springing fully armed from the brain of some king of architects.

The tendency towards decentralisation, if it may be so called, seems to be strong in the architectural world to-day. Every morning the architect gets a notice from some manufacturer or other—whether he produces tiles or ironwork or even embroidery—who expresses his willingness to supply not only the materials but the design . a sufficient proof that among many members of the profession — whatever their status may be—such a state of things is endured if it is not fostered.   While things are allowed to go on in this way, architects cannot complain if they find, as they often do, that their work has been marred by the introduction, unknown to them, of fittings or decoration or glass of an unsuitable character.   The completeness of the artistic whole is gone for good and all directly the services of others besides the originator of the complete design are called into requisition.   It often seems, indeed it is certainly the case, that those who contribute the special designs have not so much as seen the building in which their works are to be placed   It is not their business to keep in subordination the particular features for which they are responsible, but rather to make them a conspicuous object, and this is generally attained with much success   Further than this, the manufacturer can hardly be expected to vary the type of design in the same way as the man who approaches his work from the artistic and not the business side, and certainly does not do so

Such work as this is quite alien in spirit to anything done in the Middle Ages. In them one seems to see one impress throughout. The work may not have been designed by one man, it may not have been inspired by one man, but at any rate the same spirit, the same love of pure and beautiful form infected all—masters and men. There are churches which we know to have been all the work of one man, and all executed during his lifetime, and these examples have a peculiar value of their own.

There is no reason nowadays why the architect should not design or inspire every little part which goes to make up a great design, except that it entails much training, great thoroughness, and much hard work. The architect should be able, and it should be his business to settle, the general arrangement of the stained glass, the general scheme of colour, the nature of the subjects, their setting, and their proportion to the background; and precisely the same may be said of the decoration generally—whether in marbles, mosaics, or simple colour; whether in subjects or in conventional forms of foliage, architectural patterns and ornaments, and so forth

I think I may claim for my father, without hesitation, that thoroughness of training and that love for every single part of his work which should enable the architect to deal successfully with every phase of it; and it was one of the articles of his architectural faith, which he held most unfalteringly, that a work entrusted to an architect should be done so literally, to be dealt with not in parts but as a whole, and that nothing should be inserted without having been at least submitted for his approval and acquiesced in by him.

"Three-fourths of the poetry of a building," he says, "lies in its minor details, and it is easier to design a cathedral with academical accuracy than to devise and work out a really fine idea in stained glass, or a true, vigorous, and beautiful treatment of a story, or even of foliage, in the tympanum of a doorway."

It is no uncommon thing for the architect now to see the architectural lines of his windows set at naught, and broken up by the arrangement of the colour and form in glass over which he has no control, or to find a window, which he had reckoned on as giving its quota of light, made practically useless.   My father thought that even where the best artists in glass-painting were concerned, the architect should decidedly have his say.

Painted glass he classified under architectural decoration strictly so called, and he was able to show by reference to old work that it had always been so treated in its halcyon days.

The practice which is so common nowadays, not only of spreading a subject over several lights,—that, unfortunately, must be sometimes unavoidable,—but of enclosing such subjects in a framework of ornament with canopies or what not, which run through the mullion at any angle, seem to break what is a fundamental rule in such matters, and damages the architecture as much as it might benefit it What can be less like this than the way in which the architecture in stone and glass were in many cases so evidently worked together in ancient examples! This is obviously the case in the choir of Cologne, where window tracery, which would have looked weak by itself, is corrected to the eye by a deep band of colour in the glass which follows the stonework round.   At Ratisbon my father noticed how beautifully the glass is graduated—the white background being more and more extended from aisle to triforium, and from triforium to clerestory.   He also called attention to the difference which is made by the position in which the glass is fixed.   In the great foreign clerestories it is generally found to be as near as possible to the inside face of the stonework so as to be in no way obscured ; while in many old windows, as in the east window of Merton College Chapel, the glass is fixed nearer the external face of the stonework in the tracery of the head than in the lower lights, the result being that the stonework of the tracery seems more delicate than the rest

As to the right character of glass, I cannot do better than give his own words :—

"The medium does not allow of an accurate copy being made of natural objects. The conventional treatment must therefore be boldly adopted, and this the middle-pointed designers in glass did. Conventional representations of natural forms are usually the absolute forms which Nature has produced, taken from the best maple leaves or best lilies to be found, not twisted about in the wild luxuriance of active life, but still represented in their individual shape and with their fibres and their petals just as they are. These forms, so obtained, are genuine ornamental forms; they do not require an artist to paint each leaf (cp. the advantages of workmen's ornament in wood and stone), but a patient, humble workman may do them even more effectually than the most brilliant of painters.

"In further development of the value of conventionalism, let me ask whether, for example, any representation in oak or brass of a real eagle for a book-desk ever approached in real grandeur or fitness those quaint and magnificent birds with outstretched wings, stiff feathers, and upturned heads, which we call 'eagles,' which symbolise those birds, but are really best when least like them? Or, again, is not the stiff, conventional mediæval angel infinitely more solemn and more beautiful than the wretched attempts at natural representations of heavenly beings which for three hundred years have been the fashion?"

It is worth while to compare this explanation of conventionalism with what Ruskin says on the same subject in the first volume of *Stones of Venice* :—

"In most Romanesque churches of Italy the porches are guarded by gigantic animals—lions or griffins—of admirable severity of design, yet in many cases of so rude workmanship that it can hardly be determined how much of their severity was intentional, how much involuntary. In the cathedral of Genoa two modern lions have, in imitation of this ancient custom, been placed on the steps of the west front, and the Italian sculptor, thinking himself a marvellous great man because he knew what lions were really like, has copied them, in the menagerie, with great success, and produced two hairy and well-whiskered beasts, as like to real lions as he could possibly cut them. One wishes them back in the menagerie for his pains, but it is impossible to say how far the offence of their presence is owing to the mere stupidity and vulgarity of the sculpture, and how far we might have been delighted with a realisation carried to nearly the same length by Ghiberti or Michael Angelo (I say *nearly*, because neither Ghiberti nor Michael Angelo would ever have attempted, or permitted, entire realisation, even in independent sculpture)"

Ruskin goes on to speak of the splendid conventionalism of the Egyptian and Ninevite sculptors.

My father had studied most of the early glass in Europe, and had sketched much and made many notes of it. On the experience so gained he bases certain conclusions as to the right and the wrong in glass painting :—

"No shading in glass can be good which is not transparent, and that glass is best which trusts most to outline and least to shading. . . . The absence of shading involves not only the loss of ordinary pictorial effect, or chiaro-oscuro, but also the absence of perspective, and this on grounds additional to the incompatability of perspective with the straight lines of the constructional parts of the window. If you have linear you must have aerial perspective."

In his own church at Holmbury he had his ideas admirably carried out by Messrs. Clayton and Bell. The windows there are remarkable, as compared with the ordinary run of modern windows, for the amount of light background in proportion to the deeper colour of the subjects, and for the beauty of the treatment of the background. They also are a standing proof of the excellent effect obtained by following the architectural lines and not running counter to them. There is an important advantage, too, in glass of such a kind, that it is as cheap as it is effective. I remember my father saying, on first seeing the glass in the windows of the chancel : "If I came on glass like that in old work I should set to work at once and sketch it."

What is true of glass is not less so of every other form of architectural decoration, or decoration of a building, *i.e.* that it should have an architectural and formal character, and that it should form an integral part of the design.

Whether it is proposed to use simple colour or marble, it is equally necessary that there should be a framework of a suitable character and a general symmetry of arrangement ; nor is it right to do what is frequently done, viz to convert stonework directly into marble A design which is suitable for the one may be, and probably is, quite unfitted for the other ; and this fact should be recognised, that where you reproduce in marble a design which the architect made for execution in stone, you are not carrying out his ideas, and would do better to adopt the spirit and not the letter of his work

Such, briefly, was my father's opinion. The subject of decoration generally engaged much of his attention. Feeling as strongly as he did the propriety, from every point of view, of making the chancel distinct from and richer in character than the rest of the church, he naturally turned to colour as one of the best means of doing so. In his younger days he confidently hoped that it would be possible to enlist the aid of artists of recognised eminence in church decoration, and he trusted to the work which Mr. Dyce was doing at All Saints, Margaret Street, to give the necessary stimulus to church decoration.

Speaking of himself and the other enthusiastic promoters of the Gothic revival, he said:—

"We found a dominant school of art, eaten up by eclecticism, forgetful to an extraordinary degree of natural laws, of the law of reality without which no great work of art has ever been done. Our movement has aided greatly in the revival of colour decoration, whether by stained glass, by painted decoration on walls, or by ornamental coloured pavements. We have very distinctly proclaimed from the first that we must have colour in our buildings We know that colour was to some extent applied almost invariably by the Greeks and Romans. The same is true of the Syrians, the Jews, the Indians, the Chinese, and the Phœnicians, while, when we come to Christian schools, we find even a stronger and more strongly-expressed adherence to the same principle."

He looked to Italy and saw the Arena Chapel at Padua, San Francesco at Assisi, St Mark's, Venice, the Riccardi Palace Chapel at Florence—all buildings where the decoration is all in all, and the architecture of a simple kind.

"Need I say," he continues, "how St. Louis, in the palmiest days of the French kingdom, covered the walls and windows of his votive chapel with gold and colour and mosaic; or how, in England, our monarch's wish to rival the zeal of St. Louis gave the world St. Stephen's Chapel, now, alas, gone! an example equally splendid in richness of colour

"Let us then not rest satisfied simply with colour, but let it be the most beautiful, the most glowing, and the most poetical we can obtain. We have made, as yet, but few attempts at painting on walls, and these have been almost without exception, simply decorative, and not of any high artistic merit. I shall be met by the complaint of the cost of employing artists of real skill, yet large sums of money are now very often spent on other decorative work which might at least as well be spent on good wall-painting. What immense sums are spent annually on stained glass of third-rate character, on carving and decoration of the fabric which might well be dispensed with "

I have said that my father held the opinion, quixotic as it may seem now, that to get work with real unity of character, we must have the product of one brain, and not of several working together, and that it would be well if the day should come when the great artist should stem the tide of subdivision which is setting so strongly, and once more unite in his own person the arts of architecture, sculpture, and painting ; much later on in life he still is able to say :—

"Let me tell our brethren that we rejoice when we see the brush of the painter and the chisel of the sculptor engaged in decorating and adorning public buildings, for we feel then that the work will be at its best. . . . For myself, I hope that the time may come when we may again see that the great painter and sculptor may also be the great architect. Of old we know that this was so. Giotto was not only a painter but an architect. Niccola Pisano was in the same way both sculptor and architect. Those were the palmy days of art upon which one looks back with a hope that in course of time they may be revived "

My father, as has been seen, made an attempt to practise what he preached, but was doubtless convinced of the impracticability of such a course. He was also doomed to some disappointment in his efforts to get church decoration done by artists of eminence. In the matter of sculpture he was more successful ; but he complained that the painter was expensive, and at the same time, with some notable exceptions, rather inefficient for the particular work. The fault lay to a great extent in ignorance of architectural decoration, and in the attempt to transfer easel pictures direct to the walls of a building without trying to make them at one with their framework.

He did not consider that stained glass militated at all

against decoration. In vindication of this he was able to point to many frescoes of Orcagna, Taddeo Gaddi, and others, which get all their lighting through stained glass of the most brilliant character without losing their effect.

In such circumstances, however, the painter must be content to confine himself to simple colours. My father asked pertinently whether some recurrence could not be made to the custom—well-known to have existed in the Middle Ages—as at Norwich, of producing works, relying chiefly on outline, which might be copied accurately, and without much loss, by inferior and less highly-paid artists.

The villages round Norwich bore witness to the existence of such a custom there, and a certain mediocrity of execution would be accepted gratefully nowadays, if the design were but good and original.

He found himself face to face with much the same difficulty with regard to glass mosaic. It is a material article which, rightly used, cannot be surpassed, but may easily look tawdry and distressing. What is it, my father used to ask himself, which makes the difference between old and new? Is it merely the mellowing effect of years, or is there possibly a virtue in the more haphazard way in which the tesseræ were then fixed, one edge projecting a hair's-breadth above its neighbour, till the surface became insensibly relieved of its garishness, and made richer by thousands of minute shadows and reflections? The simplicity and the magnificence of the early Ravenna mosaics makes it clear that this material too, or perhaps above all, demands a conventional form of design, and a dignified and restrained style of drawing. One great mosaic there is, in a church of my father's, which shows that there is no insuperable bar to success now. I mean the design by Mr. E. Burne Jones which fills the semidome of the apse of the American Church in Rome. This my father unfortunately did not live to see. It would have atoned for much disappointment, for, even in Rome, it holds its own, and without being affectedly archaic, has all the dignity of early examples, and much of their fine colour.

There is fortunately another kind of mosaic—marble mosaic—which, if it does not lend itself to any very striking

effects, is at any rate satisfactory in its results and quite
safe My father used a great deal of this on the aisle walls
of the Wellington Barracks Chapel, the cartoons being done
by Messrs. Clayton and Bell. The colouring is sober, but
there is plenty of variety and contrast. These mosaics were
the subject of a good deal of disparagement when they were
first put up, and they did indubitably look rather cold and
poor in colour, but my father always maintained that time
and exposure would do wonders for them, and it soon became obvious that his words would be completely verified—a
consummation which has now been long reached.

True constructional decoration, where the decorative
materials are absolutely part and parcel of the work,—the
system on which, to take a well-known instance, the cathedral and baptistery at Pisa are built,—seemed to my father
to come scarcely within the range of practical architecture
in England, except by the use of different-coloured bricks
together, or brick and stone in conjunction There are no
doubt a good many mediæval instances of such a mode of
building, and my father himself used two different-coloured
stones on several occasions , but for all that, if a contrast is
wanted, brick must usually be accepted as a substitute for
the darker stone Much has been built in this way in the
last quarter of a century ; but I am here speaking of my
father's views of many years back, when much that we take
for granted now was looked upon as almost revolutionary.

All Saints, Margaret Street, as it was one of the earliest, so
was it also one of the most successful examples of this kind of
work, to be followed many years later by a more magnificent
and more dubious example from the same hand in Keble
College, Oxford. The same architect is also responsible for
the charming chapel at Balliol, which is constructed in two
different stones.

There is another type of constructive decoration, hardly
legitimately to be so called—a type which has produced the
most splendid results. St. Mark's at Venice is the best-
known example perhaps ; other examples occur, out of Italy,
among the churches of Poitou, at Clermont-Ferrand, at St
Etienne, Nevers, where the marble is applied in thin veneers.

We may perhaps class under constructive decoration the more fantastic treatment of buildings, of which there are many instances in Northern Europe, such as the combination of brick steeples and copper spires in Germany, and the various-coloured roofing tiles on the cathedral at Bâle

But my father felt that for us the system of veneering was the most feasible, and the one to which we should naturally turn, offering, as it does, even if economy confines us to native materials, an opportunity for a rich treatment of wall spaces in a permanent way. There is, however, in such decoration, a danger which he was not slow to point out, viz. that of concealing the true construction. He would have limited veneering strictly to such walls or such parts of walls as were without any particular strain. Much ingenuity has been displayed in old work in the veneering of arches, but against this he set his face resolutely. Even St. Mark's could not reconcile him to the inherent falseness of such work.

True constructional decoration is open to the objection, as he saw, of being too stripy, but I think the truthfulness of such an effect reduced the failing to a minimum in his eyes, even if he did not quite come to regard it as a virtue

With respect to both forms of constructional decoration, it may be said that we must not follow the old models too closely or literally. " Probably they are mainly useful now as showing us certain principles which we may work out and apply to our own rather different circumstances " (*Brick and Marble*)

Bands of ornament, such as those which are not unfrequently seen on church spires, result from precisely the same principle as colour decoration pure and simple ; so, to take an instance from my father's own work, the broad band of carved enrichment, which runs nearly all round the four sides of the Courts of Justice, is intended to produce an effect almost identical with that of the use of a light and dark stone.

Lastly, there remains decoration in the form of hangings, in which my father did much beautiful and original work. Of such a mode of enrichment he says : " The old men omitted nothing. In some churches they even covered their doors with crimson linen (as at Halberstadt) or leather, or they spread rich carpets on the floor, or hung the walls with sumptuous and elaborate hangings, as you may see in Nuremberg now." Finally, he asks, " Is it right to treat sculpture, especially that of the human figure, upon those principles (of decoration) ? I think, generally speaking, it is, for every old authority favours such a treatment in some degree." Before quitting the subject of church architecture, I ought to say something further as to my father's ideas on planning. I think it will have been evident from what I have already said, that one great object in his eyes, perhaps I should say the great object, was that, if possible, every member of the congregation should be able to see the altar, or should at least be so placed as to be able to take an intelligent part, not only in those portions of the service which are conducted from the reading-desk, but also in those more solemn portions which take place before the altar itself

Such being the case, we need not be surprised to find that he had no actual objection to a western gallery as such, always providing that the amount of accommodation required absolutely demanded it, and providing also that it was not architecturally incongruous. Now, I need not say that this last qualification made the use of a gallery in ancient churches almost an impossibility; while in a new church he would have naturally provided all the seats required on the floor of the church. But in some few cases, where he had to deal with a blank west end, as at the Wellington Barracks Chapel, he found no violation of principle involved in its use. Galleries along the north and south walls he held to be architecturally indefensible ; and he condemns them further, because their arrangement, with tiers of seats facing north and south, turn what should be a place of worship into the semblance of a theatre for the display of pulpit oratory. " Those churches," he said, " which were built between the Reformation and 1830, can usually be well adapted, but the galleries must be swept away. They are always a mere auditorium arranged round the pulpit."

In the treatment of old churches built, as so many were, on the cruciform plan, with deep chancel and transepts and narrow naves, and ill adapted, consequently, for congregational purposes, he pursued various courses, according to the special circumstances of a case ; either simply putting the choir under the tower, giving those who occupied the transepts the power of joining in the service, but at a sacrifice of accommodation, or putting a second altar under the crossing, and using the chancel for early celebrations ; or, as he says, in the most extreme cases, he would have taken a leaf out of the mediæval architect's book and done what they would have done in similar circumstances, viz sacrifice antiquity to convenience and remove the tower. "If we do so, it must only be after the gravest consideration" This, I think, must be taken as the expression of the principle, which he held so strongly, that the needs of the service are paramount, and that, in the last resort, architectural history and beauty may have to be sacrificed to them, and may be put side by side with another expression of opinion already quoted, viz. the propriety under some conditions of removing an ancient close screen. This possibility is again touched on in the report which he wrote on the adaptation of Southwell Minster for a cathedral service, where he hints, or, indeed, more than hints, that though the knot admitted of being untied in that particular case, it might sometimes have to be cut. A letter which he wrote on Stewkley Church throws considerable light on his views in this respect as to the extent to which old work may be allowed, on account of its intrinsic worth, to interfere with the due performance of the services of the church :—

"As I am the architect entrusted with the restoration of Stewkley Church, will you allow me to say a few words on the subject ? It is perfectly true that, being applied to for plans for the enlargement of the church to meet the want of accommodation for the poor, I consented to undertake the work. It is one of a very distinct class of Romanesque churches, consisting of nave, central tower, and chancel, but without transepts Iffley, Kempsford, and Castle Rising churches are examples of the same type. If the church was to be enlarged (and about this I had no option, having in vain suggested a second church, which was at once found to be impossible), obviously the enlargement ought to be one which should as little as

H

possible affect the most marked characteristics of the plan. The addition of a transept or of an aisle to the nave would unquestionably have completely altered it, and neither of them was to be thought of. I fell back therefore on the lengthening of the nave, only making it a condition with my client that if the interesting and valuable west front were to be rebuilt, it should not be done by contract, but by workmen employed by me, under the direction of one of my clerks of the works, and in the most cautious way. Every stone was to be arranged in its proper order, under shelter, and re-erected in its old place again, and no scraping or redressing of the stonework was to be allowed. The question is, no doubt, a very important one, whether such work is allowable or possible? Of the latter I feel no doubt. I believe that one of our finest sculptured doorways—that of Higham Ferrers Church—was taken down and rebuilt in Archbishop Laud's time, and has in no degree lost thereby any of its former interest or value. So, too, I have seen in some of the French restorations of recent years old work taken down and reconstructed without any damage to the work in any way.

" If I mistake not, the west front of Laon Cathedral is an illustration of this, unless, *since* its reconstruction, it has been scraped and redressed in the popular fashion, in which case its interest has of course been to a great extent destroyed, though not by rebuilding. In the case of Stewkley Church, I believe I could have guaranteed the replacing of every carved stone throughout the west front in its old position, and without any alteration of its colour or surface, and so that no one should have known whether or not it had been rebuilt.

" But ought this to be allowed? Honestly, I think it ought. It may indeed be argued that the lengthening of the nave would destroy the proportions; unquestionably it would alter them, but so does the erection or retention of a western gallery; and since the nave of Stewkley Church is very short, I do not believe that any one who knows the proportions of Kempsford and Castle Rising Churches would doubt that it would at any rate not be spoilt, or its interest be in any way destroyed by being altered to something like their much more impressive size and shape. We all know perfectly well how our ancestors would have dealt with such a question. They certainly would not have allowed anything in the building to stand in the way of the greatest good of the people who were to use the church, and would probably have dealt with the church at Stewkley in a way by very far less conservative than mine.

" However, I was extremely glad not to have to alter the fabric at all. I said myself that I would infinitely rather not have to do so, because, among other reasons, I knew how easy it would be to misrepresent the kind of work I was doing, and to class it with those destructive works of church restoration which I suspect I deplore more than my critics, and of which an instance carried out under my direction will be looked for in vain It is no secret that many of our larger churches have been, or are in the course of being, restored in a mode which involves, at least, as complete an alteration of the character of the old work as would have been effected had I proposed not only to rebuild one wall of Stewkley Church stone for stone, but to rework and scrape and clean every old stone in it I yield to no one in my conviction of the extreme importance of preserving our old monuments, and rescuing them from anything like 'destructive' restoration. I have restored so many churches that perhaps it seems hardly needful to say this, for all those who have consulted me know well how anxious I am at all times to preserve every feature and fragment of antiquity with the most jealous care. . . . One word more as to the suggestion of galleries. I suppose no architect of any sense would any more shrink from making a gallery, on the ground that he could not make it look well, than he would from any other piece of work. The question of 'authority' or 'no authority' is quite beside the matter, and fit for a discussion of twenty years ago rather than for one of to-day The English school of Gothic architects has at any rate shown of late years a determination to prove that Gothic architecture is applicable to every possible purpose. This no one can deny, and the objection to galleries is not an architectural one, or it would never have become so universal "

Now I have said that it was a matter of principle with my father that churches, old or new, should before all things serve their true purpose, even at, some sacrifice of interest and beauty. It was one which he believed in fully, and when he speaks of the possibility of having to destroy old work, he speaks in all sincerity. Yet, as it happened, he never actually was forced to put this rule into practice, and I take the liberty of doubting whether he ever could have done so. Some loophole he would have found at the last moment, some expedient which would have served the purpose without obliging him to take a course so grievous to him as the obliteration and destruction of mediæval work. Of his views as to the loss of interest involved in the mere shifting of old work without alteration, I shall have something to say in another chapter.

To return to church plans. There are several which my father regarded as almost equally serviceable for large congregations

Firstly, the broad nave with narrow aisles, these being used either for chairs or simply as passages. With a nave of great width, which would necessarily result from the sacrifice of all accommodation in the aisles, the chancel would naturally be a good deal narrower, and might either be the width of the eastern wall of an apsidal termination to the nave, or the last bay of the nave might simply be inclined inwards to the desired degree. This arrangement was adopted both at St. Saviour's, Eastbourne, and St. John the Divine, Kennington; though in both these churches the aisles are used for congregational purposes. In All Saints, Clifton, my father has produced a true congregational church. There the nave is of noble width, with a lofty clerestory and a low arcade, outside which there is nothing but a passage, and the junction of the broad nave and narrower chancel with its aisles is ingenious and picturesque.

Next there is the domical plan, one which my father, however, never made use of. He regretted much, even for purely artistic reasons, that with us at least Gothic has not made the dome her own. It is a form which she might make glorious use of.

The lantern at Ely and a group of circular churches are about the only attempts to touch the problem at all; they cannot be said to be serious efforts to solve it. As to the suitability of a dome for a large congregation, who that knows St. Paul's on a Sunday afternoon, when there is a great preacher in the pulpit, can doubt it? The vast size of the dome there does, indeed, under the present conditions, make it difficult for those who are far away from the choir to join in the service in any but an unsatisfactory way, and in speaking more fully of St. Paul's, I shall show how my father would have proposed meeting that difficulty, but with a dome of moderate dimensions no such drawback would exist.

My father was able to carry out at Bolton Abbey another arrangement very much on the lines of San Clemente at Rome, which is both simple and good. The structural chancel may, if necessary, be dispensed with altogether, or in any case its proportions may be greatly reduced. The choir itself is brought down into the body of the church, surrounded by a low screen, with the pulpit and ambon attached to it. This economises space, and is, architecturally speaking, fresh and piquant.

Not long ago I saw a suggestion in a paper on church planning which amounts to much the same in effect, viz. that we should make our chancels shallower than we are accustomed to do, and that the choir should project out somewhat into the nave.

All these schemes have the great merit of enabling the congregation to join as well in that part of the service which is conducted before the altar as in the other less solemn portions.

One word on the subject of chancel screens. My father, as a strong advocate of open churches, was naturally in favour of screens and gates round the chancel. It is obvious that if a church is to be left unprotected, it must at least have the chancel fenced in, even if the barrier is of a light character. The lightest form of screen compatible with a certain measure of protection would then have been his choice.

In his own church there is an open wooden screen, but provision is made for leaving the church open at all hours without risk by means of a sort of internal narthex, the small bay at the west end of the nave being divided from the rest by an open screen which hides nothing, while it effectually bars the entrance to the body of the church. On other grounds he favoured chancel screens, and his reasons generally were given in answer to the outcry which the ultra-Protestants of Dublin raised over his screen there. In that instance at any rate—and his arguments would apply equally to other cases—he considered it to be acoustically valuable, besides being so architecturally, and, so far as there is symbolism in the division between nave and chancel, symbolically so too.

CHAPTER VI

MORALITY in architecture shows itself in many ways which are too obvious to need being insisted on. But there is one form of it, and an essential one, which is perhaps not generally recognised as being so, and that is the fixed and definite character which the true artist will stamp on his work, however varied the form into which it is thrown. Style must necessarily vary with climatic and other conditions. It would be a piece of insanity to plant the literal reproduction of an English country church on the shores of the Bosphorus. It is at least questionable whether Italian Gothic admits of being transferred as exactly as it sometimes has been to our sunless and boisterous climate. The architectural forms in which the buildings of a country or county or district are cast, must dictate in a greater or less degree the forms of a work of which they are to be the setting. It is easy enough to produce a bizarre, if not a striking, effect by the bold introduction of a style which is strange and incongruous. Some of the less instructed of the public probably mistake this for originality. I remember on one occasion finding myself in a railway carriage with several people who were going, as I myself was, to the reopening of a church which my father had just been restoring in Devonshire. One of them, a clergyman, was giving his opinion, favourable, so far as I recollect, on the restoration generally, and on the chancel screen in particular, which he did *not* like. He objected to it because, he said, it was like a Norfolk screen, but " Mr. Street is determined to be original, and that is why he has put it there." The criticism of the screen was as incorrect as the definition of originality which it implied.

Youth is as enthusiastic as it is inexperienced, and it is the young man—to whom the beauties of some style, new to him, have only just been revealed—who runs the greatest risk of perpetrating these—miscalled original—crimes. His moral character as an artist is at best only half formed. He has not yet learnt to be individual, perhaps has not the power of ever becoming so. His fancy is seized by some feature in foreign work, and he transplants it boldly to uncongenial quarters, where, to the trained eye, it disturbs its surroundings and surrenders its own beauty of propriety.

My father's individuality was not slow to express itself, though it may be said possibly that in his earlier works the man is somewhat secondary to the style, while in the maturity the converse was certainly true. Foreign study had an influence on his work throughout his career, but it is more apparent in the earlier days before the process of digestion and assimilation were thoroughly accomplished. This, however, is really true of some three or four designs only ; chiefly, perhaps, of that submitted in the competition for the Government offices. This design had much beauty, but the influence of Italian travel was perhaps too obvious to make it wholly appropriate for a national building. The same may be said in a lesser degree of the church of St. James the Less, Westminster. There, however, the process of assimilation was clearly more advanced and the man more to the fore. Of the church of St. Philip and St. James, Oxford, it may be said, though my father disclaimed it, that it is in some sort a reminiscence of Normandy, but the similarity was one of a very qualified kind, and the church is probably as strongly marked with the special characteristics of my father's early years as any other.

Men do not attain so rapidly to the fulness of their powers as to preclude the possibility of faults in the work of a young man—to be rectified possibly in after years. I can see, when I compare my father's earlier and later works, the proofs of immaturity which might reasonably be looked for in the former. There is something too uncompromising in their character—an excess of boldness or bluntness, a tinge of eccentricity, a truthfulness in displaying construction, which is too much like that of the candid friend. But if excuse is wanted, it will be found in the intention with which such work was done. It was the strongest form of protest against that dull and meaningless symmetry which had long been the leading characteristic of church architecture before the Revival, and if my father laid himself open to the charge of exaggeration, he did so in good company. The feeling which moved him and others had its exact counterpart in that which then actuated the pre-Raphaelite painters. The same exaggeration is visible in their drawings; but we forgive it and welcome it because of the purity and loftiness of the conceptions with which it was associated and the great results which it achieved.

Granting that in his first enthusiasm my father was occasionally betrayed into a somewhat over-emphasised honesty, or into too close an adherence to foreign forms, still the designs of which this is true may almost be counted on the fingers of one hand. Putting aside these early examples, his work is strong without being overbold, while it emphatically speaks of the man first and of the vehicle afterwards. It does not occur to one to ask whether this detail may or may not have been suggested by French reminiscences, or whether that one is the outcome of Italian studies. I have already said that my father thought it right to gather a hint here and a principle there rather than to blind himself to everything but what his own country presented to his eyes; but there is a difference, and a great one, between embodying a principle and servile copyism of a feature, and it was his knowledge of this difference and his constitutional repugnance to the latter which gave his work its unquestionable freshness and individuality.

If he had to build in a southern country, he set himself to infuse into forms which should be analogous to those of the architecture of the country some of the spirit of northern work.

The earliest instance of such a design—though here two closely kindred styles had to be brought into relation with one another—was that for the cathedral at Lille. The conditions of the competition had laid down that the style should be French-Gothic of a particular date, and my father fully carried out the spirit of his instructions; but into the French work he infused in a subtle way so much of the English spirit as not merely to give a charm and freshness to the design of a special kind, but to show—in case of its ever being carried out—that the church was built under English influence, thus permanently and unmistakably stamping its history on its face.

Other examples are the Memorial Church at Constantinople, admirably adapted to the conditions of the climate, and full of most original work, which is as beautiful as it is useful; the English Church at Genoa, where local peculiarities have been happily made to serve as a basis without being slavishly borrowed; and the American Church at Rome, where, by his skilful manipulation of the native style, my father succeeded in rousing the enthusiasm of Romans themselves, teaching them that they have architectural treasures of their own in plenty, of the existence of which they were hardly aware. Of the English church there it is difficult to speak with patience; details misunderstood, leading features omitted, and a style of workmanship which leaves very much to be desired, have done their worst for it.

To turn to smaller examples, there is much suitability in the little churches at Vevay and Lausanne, though they have unhappily suffered from the want of intelligent supervision; while the little stone and timber chapel at Mürren, though still effective and appropriate, would have been much more so had not the enthusiastic landlord of the neighbouring hotel tarred the interior with the same brush as his *salle-à-manger*. It is distressing to see good work marred by the want of really intelligent supervision; but that is what the architect who works abroad has often to reckon with, while the vagaries of the local superintendent are all laid at his door.

My father confined himself to the style of no particular date in his original work, though he certainly preferred that

of the thirteenth and the first half of the fourteenth century; but as a young man he was not so liberal in his
tastes, and showed a decided preference for " first-pointed."
Sir Gilbert Scott, in his *Recollections*, says: " In my own
office Mr. Street and others used to view every one as a
heretic who designed in any but the sacred phase. The
revived style was one, and its unity was middle-pointed." Sir
Gilbert's memory was at fault here, because as a matter of
fact my father used, in his own words, "to swear by first-
pointed; and we called Scott's work ' ogee ' because we
thought it too late in character." Again he says: " My
first church—Biscovey—built in 1848, was of the purest
first-pointed." In 1853, while he was still in practice at
Oxford, he showed his predilections plainly enough in a
pamphlet which he published, the subject of which was
the best type to be adopted in new college or university
buildings. He protested equally against the choice of
classical or fifteenth century models—the only alternatives at
that time; against the first, because he saw how ill-suited it
was to serve the purposes to which it was put; and he
pointed his moral by instancing the Taylorian (a building of
which, viewed merely as an architectural monument, I have
often heard him express his approval), with its great portico,
which neither a modern Socrates nor any one else has ever
been seen to use, and its costly windows only made to be
blocked up, as a good illustration of the way not to do it.
Further, he contended that for mere purposes of contrast
there was already classical work enough with the Bodleian,
the Clarendon, the Taylorian, etc. Against fifteenth-century
Gothic he protested, because he held that what is best in
itself must be under all circumstances the best; while the
theory which seemingly prevailed that Gothic in its perfection
is only fitted for ecclesiastical work, while the same style in
its decadence is everything that could be desired for domestic
work made him eager to prove its futility. He pointed to
St. Mary's and to Merton, and asked whether fourteenth-
century work is not as convincingly the more beautiful as it
is constructively the more scientific. It must be confessed
that Oxford was not fortunate in its first example of an

earlier style, and the museum in the Parks, if it did not actually constitute an unanswerable argument against the adoption of fourteenth-century forms, showed at least that the style, though very good at its best, is not so safe to deal with as that stereotyped in Oxford.

My father's preference for the earlier style was founded no less on admiration of its moral attributes and the rightness of the principles which it sustained than on its actual beauty of form.   He maintained, as Ruskin had done, that the early plate tracery was right in principle, while the elaborate line traceries of middle-pointed were wrong.   In the plate traceries the openings were always simple and beautiful, while the lines, if there were any, were full of dignity and order, besides being easily intelligible.   In later work the piercings were no longer a matter for consideration, and generally assumed the most fantastic and capricious outlines, whilst every effort was directed to making the stonework of the tracery curve about in an irregular and unconstructional way with the idea of getting a pretty effect.   To illustrate the beauty of early openings, my father took one particular form as a specimen.   He pointed out that the trefoil of early work is as different as possible from the form which we are accustomed to now.   The lower curve was almost always stilted, while the upper one was somewhat smaller.   The result was a beauty and vigour as well as a truth in construction which uniformity does not give.   What was true of trefoils was equally true of cusps. Here again we are accustomed to a lifeless equality, but in mediæval work the curve of the lowest cusp was always greater than that of the centre one, so that there was an avoidance of any abruptness in the transition from the upright line of the jamb to the curved line of the cusp. The tendency, as Gothic deteriorated, was always towards lines as opposed to bold rounds or hollows.   The contrast, my father said, may be easily seen at Worcester Cathedral, where the nave is a fourteenth-century copy of a thirteenth-century choir.   The shafts of the early work are replaced by mouldings in the later, while the arch moulds are all on a chamfer plane, instead of being on a succession of

squares,[1] with a consequent loss in light and shade. A natural
result of the discontinuance of the detached shaft was a loss
of boldly designed and effective capitals, and the substitution
of flowing curvilinear foliage for the more decided and
characteristic forms of early work. If the comparison of
thirteenth-century work with later developments in England
seemed to my father to decisively establish the superiority
of the former, a reference to foreign examples seemed to
him to make it all the more obvious. Among French
buildings he ranged on one side Nôtre Dâme, Paris, and the
cathedrals at Chartres, Amiens, Laon, Sens, and Rouen, as
examples of a style which was nervous and strong, lapsing
at Rheims into beauty merely, marvellous indeed, but nothing
beyond beauty, and at Troyes into quaint picturesqueness.
He compared St. Gereon at Cologne with the cathedral, to
the disadvantage of the latter, its magnificence being marred
in his eyes by the vaingloriousness of the effort. Lastly, in
Italy, he saw a great fall from St. Mark's, Venice; San
Miniato, Florence; San Francesco, Assisi; and Sta. Anastasia,
Verona, to the cathedral at Milan and San Petronio,
Bologna, the earlier buildings in every instance clearly
preaching a higher purpose and a loftier morality. Much
of this superiority he attributed to the fact that the influence
and control of the architect-in-chief did much to prevent
the ebullitions of eccentricity which none of the noblest
examples show, while in the fifteenth century it had become
common for deans and chapters to employ different men for
the various kinds of work without having any supreme
control. The result was that the masons, carpenters, and
the men of the other trades were all developing for themselves, and producing an architecture full of quaint conceits,
and remarkable chiefly for manual dexterity.

The works which I have already mentioned would be enough
in themselves to show that Gothic lost none of its plasticity
in my father's hands, while they are a standing evidence of his

---

[1] In England, however, mouldings on the chamfer plane became common at
an early period, owing to the use of circular moulded caps, and they were so
skilfully managed as to give as much light and shade with much greater variety
than could be obtained on the other system.

complete grasp of Gothic in all its varieties and developments; but there are other instances in England itself which
make the case stronger.   Perhaps the most remarkable
among them is the transformation which he effected in the
interior of the classical temple which served for a chapel at
the Wellington Barracks.   Looked at from outside there is
little sign that anything has been done, except for a small
semidomed excrescence at the east end, and a glimpse of
internal tracery to the great plain window openings; but
inside a magician seems to have been at work: the
windows have been gracefully treated, divided into two
lights by a delicate marble shaft, and filled with very good
stained glass: the great bare parallelogram has been
divided into nave and aisles, with a chancel and transeptal
chancel aisles in two stories, with charmingly treated staircases.   The eastern wall of the old work has alone been
broken through, in order to give the chancel sufficient
length.   This addition ends in a circular apse and a semi-
dome.   The nave arcade is of brick, stone, and terra cotta,
and supports a barrel vault in brick with stone bands with
transverse arches.   The aisle walls are all panelled in
various marbles, each panel being filled with a figure in
marble mosaic, while above are a range of small subjects in
terra cotta.   The spandrel over the chancel arch and one of
the east walls of the chancel aisles are already filled with
glass mosaic, as is the drum of the apse; the semidome is
eventually to be treated in the same way.   The appropriate-
ness and beauty of all the ornaments, enrichments, and
carving are not to be surpassed.   The handling shows much
freedom and originality, but all is in perfect harmony.   The
designs for the fittings, such as the septum wall with its
ambons, the font, the stairs in the chancel aisles, and the
whole of the metal and woodwork, have been evidently a
labour of love.   They are charmingly conceived and worthily
carried out.   The reconstruction of St. Luke's, Lower Norwood, was a work of a less sumptuous character; but all I
have said in praise of the Guards' Chapel may, *mutato nomine*,
be understood of it.   Of my father's power of adopting the
design of another, and preserving its main features, while

giving it a special and distinct character, I shall speak at some length when I deal with the rebuilding of the cathedral nave at Bristol. Suffice it to say now that in that case he felt himself morally bound to follow the evident intentions of the architect of the choir so far as the general forms went ; but while adhering rigidly to his predecessor's main scheme, he succeeded in transforming a work which, while possessing a gracefulness of its own, was somewhat weak in character and poor in detail, into a purer, nobler, and more dignified edition of itself.

Of his skill in the utilisation of a site there are many instances. At St. Mary Magdalene, Paddington, for instance, every bit of the oddly-shaped site is turned to advantage, and made to yield picturesque effects. The lopsided arrangement, which the division of men and women must always demand so long as the churchgoers among the latter preponderate so greatly in numbers, is turned to valuable account, and gives occasion for a plan which is artistically good, but hardly justifiable without a strong reason. The planning of the English Church at Rome is again a most ingenious piece of work. The eastern boundary, which runs at an odd angle, is made to fit exactly to the projection of the apse, while the tower carries on the line in a natural way. The use of a four-sided apse with the angle in the centre is an uncommon feature, but not ineffective. Here it has a particular reason, but my father had made use of it once before—at St. Saviour's, Eastbourne,—where it was simply a matter of choice.

People are apt to think and say that the design of the elevation is the more technical part of an architect's work, while a good plan may really be made by any intelligent man, however unskilled in architecture. It may be simple enough to arrange a number of rooms or blocks of rooms in convenient relation to one another, but the intelligent unprofessional man who had got so far would find that, beyond this simple disposition, there are the questions of light and air, of roofing, of getting good masses, which make planning a more complicated thing and more technical than he had been wont to think. To use my father's words :

" There is the highest art in so disposing the plan that the arrangement shall be convenient for the purpose, and yet admit of well-balanced masses in the elevation and well-managed outlines and skylines."

Whatever the effect of iron may ultimately be on our architecture, there is one point at least in which my father thought it ruinous to good work, unless most sparingly used, and that is in planning. The basis of Gothic work is, of course, that construction should be displayed, while iron is directly favourable to a fatal illegitimacy in this respect. The architect is able now, when he finds himself in a dilemma, to put in a girder here or there, and thus the old knack of disposition under difficulties, which should be one of the especial functions and signs of a skilful architect, tends to be lost. In fact, the power of using concealed iron supports naturally leads to those apparent *tours de force* which are likely to be wonderful and admirable in the eyes of the public.

It requires a great deal of courage to cry out against the use of iron, or to ask for some limit, because the detractor of a material which has such powers and opens up such possibilities, naturally lays himself open to the charge of being unpractical and a visionary. My father, as a lover of the truth and beauty in old building, felt bound to protest in strong terms against, not its use, but its abuse. He maintained that iron as it is used at present is the bane of good architecture and the fruitful parent of bad architects.

Great engineering works, where iron does what stone and wood could not do, he cordially admired. There it is the right material in the right place, but used in close conjunction with brick or stone, or copying the lines of stone construction, it seemed to him to abnegate its great powers and to sink into vulgarity. Such works, however, hardly belong to the province of the architect properly speaking. The false construction and false architecture which he had in his mind was that which unhappily we see in its highest development and at its lowest depths in the principal streets of our great towns, where great upper stories seem to stand on nothing more substantial than a sheet of plate glass, and solids are superposed over voids as if nothing could be more satisfying to the eye than such an inversion of the natural order of things.

May we not, he asked, claim of the engineer or the architect in iron that he shall show us how an iron building can be made pleasing for its own sake, rather than be content to let it be the servant of inferior stone and brick architecture? and secondly, he asked whether it is really necessary, for so experience would seem to show it to be, that the more scientific construction in iron becomes, the more artistically unsatisfactory it should become also? In his own work he never used it unless some obvious advantage was to be gained by doing so, but preferred invariably to let timber do what it is capable of.

In the use of a material such as wood, he thought it better where it is seen—as in open roofs—not to be content with what is sufficient, but to increase the scantling to such an extent as to satisfy the eye of its solidity and sufficiency. This is an opinion which, in the matter of masonry, he did not hold. It of course has its dangers, and may soon lead to unscientific work if the line be once overstepped.

I say that in masonry my father did not make his work heavier than was necessary for perfect strength. His works have, indeed, often a simplicity which gives them a look of massiveness greater than they possess. He was always crying out against the ephemeral character of modern work, and his dearest wish and most constant aim was to leave memorials behind him which should resist the inroads of time as successfully as those of our forefathers did.

In his opening address as President of the R.I.B.A., his last public utterance, he laid particular stress on the need of reform—more especially in the vernacular art, the builders' and workman's art of the country—in this very respect :—

"In the last century," he said, "there was a simplicity and restraint in design, an absence of vulgar display, which makes one feel a charm in work, most of which is the art of the bricklayer, mason, smith, carpenter, and plasterer, and certainly never passed through an architect's hands. Go from the house of 1750 to one of those which rise in countless numbers on all sides now, and your verdict as architects and artists must always, I fear, be given in favour of the former; compare the two and you will find that the preference of the eighteenth-century builder was for simple and good work rather than ornamental.   My only suggestion is that we architects should show by example that simple building may be quite as good as extravagant, and that the essence of all good architecture is that it should be solid and lasting before it tries to be ornamental, and that ornament is a feature which grows out of utility and cannot be applied to a building like a loose-fitting garment to cover defects or to distract attention from parts which are not supposed to be seen. It is unworthy of architects to build what is in its very nature ephemeral; and I wish heartily before all questions of style that this vital one of solidity were always present to us when we are making our plans."

Again : "Whole towns rise among us and around us in which not one building in a hundred is well, solidly, or lastingly constructed, and in most of them the construction being concealed as well as flimsy can scarcely be called honest; whereas, formerly, there was no thought of self or of building only for one's own time; now there is a strangely different state of affairs.   The art of building has come to be the art of building not for all time but for a certain time. Houses are built with the distinct idea that they are not to last much longer than the term of the lease, or say, than ninety-nine years.   The idea that building for a certain time is the only wise course of policy for a great country is even formulated by us into a system.   I have myself been told by a high Government official that the best building is not that which will last longest, but rather that which will last a limited time, and may then be rebuilt with all the latest improvements.   He maintained that the difference of cost between a building erected to last and one intended to survive a certain time only would, if invested and reinvested in the funds, produce by the end of the term so large a capital sum as to pay for the whole expense of the reconstruction, and he concluded that the only true policy was to build with this view."

My father's thorough practical acquaintance with every branch of his work earned the respect even of those who might have come better off with a less vigorous and intelligent supervision.   Experience had taught him how best to use his materials as well as their capabilities and their limitations.   It seemed to me as I went over his works with him, as I very frequently did, that his keen eye lighted on every blunder or delinquency with unerring certainty, while his settlement of all the difficulties, great and small, which a

clerk of works is apt to spring on the architect, was made
with the utmost promptitude and decision.

Workmen who came in contact with him felt a pleasure
in working under a man who was as sure to show his appreciation of good work as to condemn bad.

The work of most architects,—of all, probably, who are
connected with church work, is twofold in character. First,
there is purely original work ; and secondly, there is that of
dealing with old buildings, restoration, reconstruction, enlargement, or whatever it may be in the particular case.

Restoration is a difficult and tender subject to deal with,
and there has been within the last decade or so a great outcry against it. There has been, it must be owned, much
exaggeration and high-handedness in the sayings and doings
of many of the champions of anti-restoration, but their influence has been none the less salutary. It is hopeless to
expect that complete accord can ever be established between
the architect pure and simple and the almost fanatical
admirer of anything a hundred years old, be it a mere rude
wooden prop or a tottering blank wall. Architecture and
archæology are different things, but their connection is intimate ; no architect is worthy of the name who does not
reverence old work for itself and for the story it tells as well
as for its absolute beauty, but he ought not to be expected to
worship a piece of comparatively modern work which hides
or mars the effect of something much better worth seeing,
simply because it proves that somebody at such and such a
date had so little sympathy with earlier work as to obliterate
what, on the showing of the anti-restorationists themselves, he
should have been anxious to preserve. The ultimate test for
the architect must after all be the absolute value or worth-
lessness of the work with which he has to deal, unless it have
some peculiar archæological or historical interest.

My father, though an active member of the Society for
the Protection of Ancient Buildings, felt himself unable to go
all lengths with them, and indeed he was himself the subject
of their strictures on at least one occasion. It would have
been odd if a man who had such strong predilections in favour
of one particular style should not, when the opportunity

came, have hastened to free it from the prison which had so often been reared about it during the last two centuries. I think he yielded to none in his respect for the domestic work of the eighteenth century ; the quotation from his opening address shows how he appreciated its good qualities; but that man must be a zealot indeed who would maintain that the incrustations and mutilations of good work, which were so freely indulged in a hundred years ago, have much claim in themselves to be retained. My father may have respected the sentiment, but it was one he could not share, which goes near forbidding us to point up old brickwork for fear the mortar should be taken to be of the same age as the wall, and so make false history. There are walls—such as those at St. Mark's—which have been mellowed and coloured by time into so harmonious and glowing a tone that to lay a rude finger on them is to take away what ages alone can restore. No one fought more energetically for the preservation of this venerable building than my father, and I believe it to have been attributable to his warning and his exertions that the west front was not practically rebuilt. Similarly, he spared no pains to avert the danger when the Corporation made their proposal to broaden London Bridge with a couple of iron gangways. The mere mutilation of a fine work was enough to call him to arms, but the manner of the mutilation and the folly of widening a bridge, when the approaches would inevitably have had to be left as they were, appealed at once to his veneration for old work, his artistic feeling, and his practical common sense. In such cases as these, where the work had a special attraction, my father was the first to cry " Hands off!" but he could not go the length of objecting to the removal bodily of an old work of ordinary type—every stone being, of course, marked and replaced exactly—on the ground that it involved a loss of sentiment. The stones in the old work, so common sense tells us, were set by men who were simply acting under orders, and with no more skill or intelligence than is shown by the workmen of the present day. There is a passage in my father's description of the restoration of Christ Church Cathedral, Dublin, which puts this view of the question very clearly.

"The work to be done at the cathedral was absolutely necessary and brooked no delay, but it was as difficult as it was urgent. There were portions of the fabric, as *e.g.* the north side of the nave, which might have been rebuilt at less expense than was incurred by their repair, but Mr. Roe was entirely in accord with the architect in desiring that not a single ancient stone which could be retained in its old place should be removed, and such a resolution involved a great deal. To have restored in any other spirit would have been opposed to all right principles. The interest of an old building is twofold. There is, first, the interest of a purely artistic character, which we take in the architectural design ; and there is, next, the antiquarian interest which accrues by mere lapse of time to the stones which form the building.

"In my opinion, the latter sort of interest should be regarded as hardly, if at all, inferior to the former. It was necessary too, in this case, to consider above all things the importance of making a building as far as possible suitable for our day and our services. Ireland is not rich in such buildings, and an opportunity was here given, such as it would have been culpable not to have made the most of, to show that it was possible to restore an old cathedral with the most reverent respect for all its old features, and yet in such a way as to make it suitable in the very highest degree for the solemn services of the church, for which it had been originally planned.

"No doubt such good intentions have only too often led to the destruction of work which ought on no account to have been interfered with. In our own days we have seen so much mischievous alteration done that we can hardly feel surprise that, as a natural result, an obstinate objection should exist on the part of many men well entitled to speak, to *all* restoration upon any pretence whatever. Their complaint is, that it is impossible to restore an ancient building, inasmuch as each age puts its own impress on everything that it does, and that to pretend in the nineteenth century that we are doing work exactly as it would have been done in the thirteenth, is wholly inaccurate and untrue. Now this assertion, correct as it might be under certain circumstances, and clear as its results seem to be, is after all only a half truth, and therefore almost wholly misleading. A building is the work not of one man, but of a number of men, working from instructions given to them, probably by one man, certainly by comparatively few. No feature, for example, is more important, or affects the general character of a building more, than the great moulded plinth which, as in the Yorkshire Abbeys, forms the base to an entire fabric ; yet this base must have been designed by one man at once, in the space of, at most, a few minutes,—whether marked on a stone or drawn on a sheet of paper matters not at all,—and then its execution may have occupied a

gang of workmen for weeks or months.   All those workmen had to
work the moulding drawn on certain uniform conditions, of the same
material, and with the same tools.

"To give an instance : The whole of the stonework at Salisbury and York Cathedrals, executed in the thirteenth century, was
finished with a 'claw' tool.   Evidently no workman was allowed to
use any other, and the conclusion is obvious, viz. that the men in
the thirteenth and nineteenth centuries work on the same principle,
which is that of obedience to one controlling authority, so as to
leave no room whatever for the exercise of any of the personal
fancies or tastes of individual workmen.   What is true of the plinth
is true also of almost every other portion of the truly architectural
features of any building.   Yet the combination of these strictly architectural features in one harmonious whole is no less the work of one
mind and one hand than was the first section of the first moulding.
The mere workman of the thirteenth century was in no respect
whatever superior to the mere workman of the nineteenth century.
He confined himself to doing what he was told, implicitly following
the directions of the master.   An illustration of this is afforded by
the construction of the nave columns of Christ Church.   They were
all built in the worst possible way, with small pieces of stone, all
cut without any allowance for bonding them into the work, and the
consequence was that they all gave way to pressure.   It is a fair
assumption that some thirty masons at least were at work on these
columns, and can it be supposed that not one of these men was
aware that the work he was doing was very bad, and could not be
safely done ?   The supposition would be absurd ; and it is clear that
what happened was that the workmen absolved themselves of all
responsibility, worked the stones they were ordered to work, and ate
their meals between times with the same absolute *sang froid* that
marks their successors at the present day.   They had no more
pleasure in their work, no more originality in their way of doing it,
than our workmen have at the present time, all the pretty fables to
the contrary notwithstanding.   It may be confidently asserted then,
that the spirit of the age, as far as it affected the mere workmen,
had nothing whatever to do with the highest excellences of ancient
architecture.   It is not so much the spirit of the age as the marks
of age that have to be respected.

"The truth is, that these old buildings were built like all others,
each at one time, by some one artist ; and the only justification for
the assumption that this was not the case—which is the question
begged by the extreme anti-restorationists—is the fact that in the
Middle Ages, in *certain kinds* of work, the individual workman was
often allowed, under certain rules and guidance, to do pretty much
as he liked.   This happened, no doubt, chiefly in the case of wood

and stone carving. . . . So far from mediæval buildings being remarkable for the evidence of the handiwork of the individual workmen who assisted in their erection, the exact opposite is much
nearer the truth.   Wherever we do come on old work which has
this precious personal impress of the workman, no one can agree
with the anti-restorationists more cordially than I do that we are
bound not to restore, but only to save from further damage, and to
deal gently and lovingly with that which cannot possibly be repeated.
It is precisely the same thing to restore an ancient piece of sculpture
as it is to restore an ancient picture.   The whole interest of the
work lies in the mark of the artist's own hand on every part of it."

This is what my father says about the restoration of the
porches at Chartres :—

"I believe the porches of Chartres are to be restored.   Can
any one who has ever had the privilege of seeing them hear it without dread ?   They are almost, if not quite, the most precious relics
of northern art still left to us, and who is to measure the damage
which may be done to them by rash and wholesale cleaning and
repairing ?   Much better were it to let them go for the rest of time,
as now, propped here and there with a heavy timber shore, than to
let irreverent hands scrape off every weather stain, repair every
damaged feature, and leave the whole as clean and new-looking as
when it was first built.   In such a case there can be no difficulty in
drawing the line between what is lawful and what is unlawful.   It is
only possible to restore sculpture on the principle that it has no art
and no inherent individuality of character."

These are very explicit declarations of principle, and
should satisfy all but those of extreme views.   But, as my
father truly said, the touch of the individual is absolutely
lacking in the actual workmanship of many of the greatest
buildings.   What is there in the architecture of the temple
of Pæstum which could not be exactly repeated to-day ; or
in any one of those glorious Cistercian abbeys, where no
sculpture of foliage was allowed, much less of figures ?   In
these works, whatever variety there was was almost certainly
due to one mind.   And, at any rate, there was no scope for
the individuality of the workman to show itself.

"No one with an atom of judgment," says my father, "would
destroy, except under absolute and immediate necessity, work to
which time had given that charm of colour which is one of the most
precious qualities that age gives to architecture ; nor would any one

be justified in destroying the works of a later period in order to
bring back a whole building to one uniform condition as to style.
This is to obliterate the history which successive generations have
left on the face of a building. Marks of this kind are of supreme
interest. . . . The architect who would destroy such marks ought
to be condemned as a barbarian."

There are cases, of course, where the enlargement of an
old church may be quite unavoidable, but even in such a
work it is possible to proceed on lines much less destructive
than those pursued by the restorers of the Middle Ages.
Their respect for the work of their predecessors was little
more than a minus quantity, and the freedom of their proceedings is almost justified by the superiority of the work
executed under such circumstances to that which resulted
from the attempt to bring it into harmony with something
already existing.

My father, naturally, in the course of his professional
work, came across many works which had been added to and
altered again and again. He cites Bloxham Church, Oxfordshire, as a proof that the mediæval architect as a rule did
better to work with perfect freedom in his own style. That
church was to a great extent rebuilt in the fourteenth century. The new building took the place of a very ornate
Romanesque church, in which there was a great deal of enrichment, chevron and other. In rebuilding the chancel
the architect, with the view of retaining somewhat of the
old work, used the old enriched stonework in making the
inside arches of the windows, with a result which was far
from satisfactory.

At West Walton, Norfolk, the thirteenth-century church
was enlarged by simply widening the aisles; the result of
which was that the glorious south porch was half swallowed
up, and the proportions of the whole church were ruined;
yet so much use was made of the old stonework that, till
my father saw what had happened, the church had been
generally accepted as wholly unaltered and perfect. Here,
then, was an instance of history falsified, and a fine conception obliterated by conservatism of the most clumsy kind.
Ottery St. Mary Church stands almost alone as a fourteenth-

century attempt to copy thirteenth-century style, and one so successful as to have deceived many. Here the attempt was evidently a conscious one, and the architect was doing pretty much what we do nowadays, except that he laboured under an additional disadvantage—that of having to forget the style which was familiar to him. The model was of course the neighbouring cathedral of Exeter, and, though the work is not earlier than the middle of the fourteenth century, the windows are all lancets, and obviously meant to look like first-pointed, but the mouldings in themselves are sufficient to betray the date. The effect of the work on my father was conclusive as against eclecticism even under the most favourable circumstances.

There are instances, though not many, of similar copyism in continental work, and he quotes as an instance the pulpit in the church of San Giovanni Evangelista at Pistoia, erected by Niccola Pisano, as being an almost literal copy of Guido da Como's pulpit, dating from 1250, at San Bartolommeo, in the same town. The idea once taken was then reproduced with variations, as in the famous example in the Baptistery at Pisa, where the plan is hexagonal instead of square; and again in the pulpit in Siena Cathedral.

There is sometimes a sort of grandeur of utility, a splendid disregard of the means, in mediæval additions which compel admiration on their own account. My father mentioned many examples which he thought worthy of being put in this category. Among them, Cuddesdon Church, Oxford, which may be taken as a sample. In this case the original church had consisted of nave, chancel, transepts, and a central steeple, there being no aisles. Early in the fourteenth century, when more accommodation was wanted, aisles were added. This was done in a bold way, by inserting arches in the old walls, without removing the upper part, where, to this day, the early windows and corbel table remain, cut into and half destroyed by the new arcade. But the church with its wider aisles was soon found to be very dark, and the outer walls being very low, a dormer window under a stone gable was added; then, this expedient not having proved satisfactory, the aisle walls were raised, the roofs flattened,

the old dormer was encased in the new wall, and large
windows were inserted.   Subsequently to this the chancel
was rebuilt and made longer.   Any experienced eye might
detect all this, my father says.   And, indeed, the remarkably
decided way in which things were done was likely to leave
much more evidence of what had been than a more gradual
and thorough process.   This is the way in which history was
made; and such history is immensely interesting and instructive.   It is, however, not to be accepted as a precedent
for us to-day.   Our work makes no history, except in so far
as it tells of the Gothic movement, and is thus quite without
one striking merit which all old work had; but there is a
limit to the weight of fetters with which the architect to-day
is to load himself.   The limit, I think, is reached in such a
case as that of the Fratry of Carlisle—the restoration of
which by my father was so bitterly opposed by the anti-
restorationists.   Here was an early building, almost intact,
if it could but be seen, deformed and hidden by late and
squalid additions, which were without architectural value or
significance.   Great stress was laid by the Society for the
Preservation of Ancient Buildings on the necessity of leaving
intact certain square-headed classical windows, which were
said to have been inserted by the archæologist Machell.
These they dignified with the name of " Venerable Historical
Evidences;" but it seems very pertinent to ask, why the
architect of to-day is not to be allowed to have his word as
much as the archæologist of yesterday?   Historical evidence
in these windows there was none, beyond their showing that
the classical style was then floating on the top of the wave,
as Gothic was later.   All my father did was to clear away
what was incongruous from a very charming building, not
to make a conjectural restoration of something which had
actually been destroyed.

Not only did my father in his treatment of old works
display the greatest regard and handle them in the most
tender way, but he possessed a quite remarkable power of
grasping and realising the historical growth or decay of a
building; and his great knowledge and real insight into the
spirit of old work enabled him, as some learned man will

construct an entire prehistoric animal from a fossil footprint, to do much the same in his own field. The most striking instance of this is perhaps Christ Church Cathedral, of which I shall speak somewhat fully hereafter. What I refer particularly to now is the fact that he designed a new western door there without a fragment to guide him. And afterwards one of the original jamb-stones having been discovered in the wall was found to be almost identical in section with that which had just been worked. This was no more than a happy accident, still it seems to throw a light on the immense difference—in kind rather than in degree—between a restoration which is merely careful, and one where deep thought and something like inspiration have given, as it were, the keynote of the whole.

Out of a whole host of parish church restorations none, I suppose, was more remarkable than that of Clun Church, Salop,—a building which was declared in the time of Charles II. to be beyond repair, but in my father's skilful hands was restored from squalor incredible to its original grandeur. And there, as elsewhere, it is the genuine old work which has been made to tell its tale, and there is little new work comparatively.

"Mr. Street's idea of church restoration must certainly be admitted to possess an undeniable sentimental charm. Spare everything that is authentic; cherish everything that is genuine; even the æsthetic incongruities which come of successive alterations during the later Middle Ages do not disturb. The Tudor work itself regard with all respect; despise not even the Stuart work if it be anywise lifelike. Let the history of the fabric, for good or ill, be treated as a sacred record—there it is, there let it be."

These rather stilted phrases sum up the impressions of my father's teaching on the subject of restoration, and give us concisely the principles with which he was actuated and on which he worked.

CHAPTER VII

IT seems almost superfluous to say that an architect ought to be a good draughtsman. Most people would regard it as a truism. Still there have, no doubt, been not a few who have become eminent in the profession without ever having obtained any mastery over the pencil; and the great works of the Middle Ages must have been executed from drawings of a very different kind to those in vogue now,—all the full sizes being no doubt drawn on the spot by the architect, whether on the stone or on paper, the small scale or 'general designs being of a comparatively rough character.

This much is clear, however, that the man who has the advantage of a ready pencil is at once able to register for himself, and in such a way that he will be little likely to forget it, every noteworthy feature he may come across. The value of ancient examples for educational purposes cannot be overestimated. But they must be used and not abused; for individuality is a necessity in a great artist, and copyism is the almost infallible sign of a bad one. This, however, does not make it any the less advisable for the architect to register in his memory or in his sketch-book the beauties which are all around him; for in this way he may insensibly impregnate the imagination with a delicate sense of gradation and proportion, and a right perception of form and outline.

Some have denied that it is good to sketch much; have even gone so far as to decry it altogether; with some idea, perhaps, that it must inevitably lead to copyism, or possibly from believing that a too clever pencil may give a drawing a fictitious charm not due to any merits in the design which it represents. I remember an article in one of the weeklies on

my father's perspective view of his design for the New Law
Courts, as proposed to be built on the Embankment, in
which there is the expression of a fear of this sort.   It was
as follows : " Mr. Street has a gift, the witchery of which
may not have been fully revealed to himself, in the exercise
of which, as he is great, so he ought to be merciful, for he
cannot realise the force of his own hand.   He is not only a
great architect, but a consummate landscape artist.   Of those
who in our time have had his gift, it has never been developed
to so exquisite a degree as in Pugin and Mr. Street."   There
may be a grain of truth in this, but it must be remembered
that the busy architect turns out hundreds of purely architectural drawings for one perspective.   The working drawings
which came from my father's office were of the most simple
character, and did not contain an unnecessary line.   They
were, in fact, severely utilitarian, and as different as possible
from the shaded and beautifully suggestive productions of
French ateliers ; the praises of which some are never tired of
sounding.   My father was wont to say that where so much
time is given up to making pretty small-scale drawings, the
details run a good chance of being left to take care of themselves.[1]

In intimate knowledge of all the best mediæval examples, I believe my father yielded to no man ; and in
speaking of his sketching I am tempted to say, remembering how many sheets of a sketch-book he would cover in a
few hours, and how incessantly he was at work at it whenever he was away from his desk, that he did it to an extent
unsurpassed either before or since.   This is a strong statement ; but I am sure it is no exaggeration to say that there
are none of the principal or most beautiful mediæval
buildings in Europe from which he did not in a manner
extract the goodness ; but I can say with equal assurance
that he never referred to a note-book for a suggestion, and
that he never even so much as reproduced a moulding in

---

[1] The advocates of the French mode of getting up drawings lay much stress
on the fact that everything is shown in them—carving, ornament, and figures ; but
in my father's work all such detail was invariably given, not to a small scale, but
full size.

his life except in so far as the storehouse of the brain may have unconsciously yielded up some remembered outline.

My father believed as little as any one that mere good draughtsmanship is the end, and should be the aim of the architect ; but he records himself how, as a matter of fact, experience had shown him that artistic merit and power of drawing were almost invariably to be found together, and that among young men and architectural students the best executed designs were nearly always the ablest.   I believe there is a feeling at the time I write that good draughtsmanship tells in a way that it ought not to do in competitions, and it was perhaps with the view of making this less probable that, in various competitions recently decided—that for the Edinburgh Municipal Buildings, for example,—it was laid down as one of the conditions that there should be no perspective view. The object is a right one, but the result must be that even for the trained professional assessor the merit of the general arrangement and massing of the various designs must become infinitely more difficult to determine with certainty. Subjectively speaking, it seems perfectly clear that facility in the use of the vehicle by which the thoughts are expressed is of as great value to the architect or artist as a corresponding power over language is to the literary man. On the subject of sketching my father says :—

"I plead guilty to having told men to sketch, but I have never thought it the end of an architect's life.   I do I don't know how many drawings a year without any attempt at picturesqueness to five or six perspectives.   The architect's business is to build and design rather than to draw ; but though a good building may be erected without good drawings, it is still certain that the best architect is likely to be one to whom drawing is so easy as to present no impediment to him when he wishes to put his ideas on paper. Our working drawings are perfectly simple without any of the sponging and shading of French drawings. . . . I think an architect should do his own perspectives ; nor do I hold that those drawings have much to say for themselves when the sky and trees and background are even more judiciously dealt with than the design itself."

This was *à propos* of certain strictures which had been uttered by a brother architect—presumably not a first-rate draughtsman himself—on the too great attractiveness of my

father's pen-and-ink drawings; the ground of complaint
being that skill of hand was made to atone for and disguise
want of imagination or feebleness of design   Mr. Edmund
Sharpe—no mean authority—maintained on the other hand
that it was rather the merit of my father's designs which
made pen-and-ink drawings go down than the converse.
Pen and ink is so familiar to the present generation—no
other medium being indeed so much affected for purposes of
exhibition,—that it is difficult to imagine its not having always
been popular ; yet not very many years back it was practically
unknown, and, indeed, the credit of having founded the great
modern school of pen and ink lies with my father as much as
any one   There are endless varieties of style and method
now, but they have all one common origin ' The rapidity and
effectiveness of my father's own workmanship have not yet
been surpassed, and it was perhaps natural that a man with
so unusual a power should wish to make it a *sine quâ non*
that drawings sent for exhibition should be by the architect's
own hand.   Still every busy man, even if he have the power,
may not be a sufficiently rapid worker to be able to do more
than his purely architectural drawings ; and it seems hard
that he should be excluded from the benefit or the satisfaction
of showing such of the public as ever glance at an architectural drawing what his powers of design may be.

My father then advises the student to sketch, and with
no doubtful voice , and he further gives him this piece of
counsel, which is paid too little heed to among us, viz. that
he shall begin by making a diligent study of the human
form coincidentally with or before applying himself to more
technical subjects.   A truthful and beautiful portrayal of the
highest types of the human form must always be the highest
and noblest thing in art, but as it is naturally the subject to
which the most consummate artists turn, so should it form the
groundwork of the student's education.   It teaches us, so my
father said, a sublime indifference to certain qualities which
are now exerting the worst possible influence on our architecture and our arts of production in general—the qualities
of minute and rigid exactitude, of lifeless repetition, of utter
sameness, the perfect similarity of colour, line, and texture

which are, or, it may perhaps be now said, which were, supposed to be the *summum bonum* of artistic production.

"I venture to say," my father exclaims, "that there are
varieties in the best works, and that, just as God makes
every man and every animal unlike his brother or the rest
of his kind, so the variety which is absolutely incompatible
with exact accuracy of execution is really the highest quality
which any of man's works can have." My father would
have had the hand and eye trained by constant practice to
work in perfect unison,—a state of things which is particularly
to be desired in the case of a young architect, because he
is then under less temptation to save himself trouble or to
make up for the deficiencies of an unskilful hand by the use
of mathematical instruments. "Nothing does so much
harm to design as a too frequent dependence on mathematical instruments." Once let the habit be indulged, and it
will grow and grow till the smallest design or pattern is
arranged so that its curves may be struck. My father
insisted that what is worth doing at all is worth doing well
and thoroughly. Thus, when the architect is drawing a
pattern or an ornament, divided, say, into eight equal parts, it
is not enough—it is wrong rather—to draw only one part as
a sample of what all are to be, or to do, what is so common
a habit, viz. draw one and trace two or three others from it ;
but each one of the eight parts should be drawn, and with
only so much approximation to exactitude as the eye will
give. The result is worth the additional trouble, for,
whereas the perfection of accuracy gives a tameness and insipidity to the best arrangement of forms, the hand will produce, what Nature invariably gives, a charming irregularity in
order. If proof were wanted, my father would have pointed
to mediæval and eastern embroidery, or to old Venetian glass,
or to ancient painted glass, for in this last is seen even more
fully than in the others those beautiful gradations of tints in
its golds and blues and rubies, clouded here and brilliant
there, which give it such a rich and sumptuous beauty.

While I am on the subject of drawing, I may perhaps as
well refer to my father's views on the use of natural forms
in design.

"There are two ways," he says, "of using Nature in art. The one is copying her exactly, the other is giving a conventional representation of her. Direct copyism is obviously right in certain works, but in a picture it is absolutely impossible to represent every leaf, or the complete stratification of a rock, and the painter is forced to betake himself to a certain sort of conventional treatment which enables him to give the general effect. In decoration, as you cannot copy exactly, it is better frankly to accept the conditions and boldly adopt a conventional treatment Take a leaf and you will find its leading features to be its outline, the lines of its fibres, and the way it grows out of the stem; your conventionalised leaf must give you the essence of these three facts in the simplest way and with the least complexity. . . . Nothing is more common nowadays than the practice of making ornaments by the combination or repetition of natural forms, and perhaps it is not going too far to say that nothing is more contemptible.".

My father's own powers as a sketcher were of a very remarkable kind. Very often have I looked over his shoulder while he did a complete sketch, and I cannot say what entire confidence he inspired with his powerful handling. A mistake seemed almost out of the question. The first few touches of the pencil, the putting in of those first lines on the accuracy of which all may depend, showed the master hand. There was never any wavering or faltering, apparently no consideration as to the best way to put the subject on paper, or as to the scale which the size of the note-book would make necessary All seemed to have come in a flash and to be as vividly present to him as though—imperceptible to others—the subject were delicately outlined on the paper before him. He delighted in the most difficult subjects, not in the least because of their difficulty, but simply because a subject which gives the gist of a great building must necessarily be an intricate one. It was his custom, I believe I may say invariably, to make the ground plan of every church of much interest. On the Continent, where chevets are so frequent, no two being quite alike, and almost every one displaying cleverness and ingenuity, he certainly made a point of doing this. It was done in many cases and with sufficient correctness for all practical purposes by stepping The relation of every part was at any rate established in this way with a close approach to accuracy. The ground plan of a cathedral taken in this way was put on paper in an incredibly short time.   He very frequently took the most comprehensive interior and exterior views, looking up the choir from the nave or nave aisle or across it from one of the transepts.   A sketch of this kind involved every difficult feature which the architectural sketcher has to grapple with, and it necessitated a great deal of drawing of groining, the correct delineation of which I have often heard my father say is a pretty conclusive test of a man's capabilities.   All this was sketched with as much ease and rapidity as the most simple and straightforward parts.   But it is futile to try to indicate the subjects which fill my father's note-books. They are of course infinitely varied.   Pages and pages are filled with details, accurately and thoroughly measured. This is a feature which, it is to be noticed, characterises all his sketches, except those which obviously dealt with too large a subject.   These sketches—executed in such a brilliant way—have in themselves the highest artistic value ; and besides that they are a most accurate and thoroughly intelligible record of what they represent.   There is not an arch-mould, or an abacus, or a base, the section of which is not faithfully indicated.   Lastly, my father's sketches prove that he knew exactly how much to do and how much to leave undone.   They are not worked up to concert pitch in every part, but they omit nothing which should be shown, and have a delightful suggestiveness which tells one everything quite as well and in a more attractive form than the most carefully elaborated drawing could do.[1]

Firm and decided as every line is, looking as if it must have been drawn under the most favourable circumstances, such was far from being the case.   I have stood with my father at eight o'clock on a bitter early spring morning, after having just got out of the train in which we had been travelling through the night, and have watched him use his pencil as though it were as warm as midsummer, though my

---

[1] In spite of the artistic merit of his sketches, it is quite certain that it was never his aim to make them look pretty.   What he tried to do was to show as much of some fine piece of work as he could, and in as few lines as possible.   He never sketched for mere sketching's sake.   He was essentially the architect, not the architectural draughtsman.

own hands, cased in warm gloves, felt as though they were frozen stiff.   He drew just as well and firmly whether he supported his book on his knee or merely held it in his hand as he stood   The latter indeed was his habitual method, because he was then free to move, to get a nearer view of some detail, or to take measurements as he worked.   His habit of drawing on square note-books obliged him very frequently to extend his sketch over two pages ; but the lines which travel down into the valley between the two sheets and climb up again are none the less straight or decided for having done so.   In fact, I think he never felt it to be the least discomfort to have to do so.   His advice to young sketchers turned always on the paramount importance of getting perfect self-reliance.   He practically said, " Burn your boats behind you," for the young draughtsman without indiarubber is like the army without retreat.   Indiarubber may of course be useful once in a way to the most practised draughtsman, but it is the fatal power of drawing what is wrong with the knowledge that it is not done beyond hope of recall, the sense of security which its possession gives which is the mischief of it, and my father thought it better to cut the knot by simply refusing to carry it   It was in this way that he trained himself to be accurate.   I never remember his carrying indiarubber.   I think if he ever borrowed mine (for I am afraid I did not follow his advice) it was only once or twice ; and certainly there are but few sketches of his, except among those of his earlier days, where there is anything that needs correction.   He was no doubt possessed of unusual powers ; but it is none the less true that sketching, as he did, in ink or in pencil without resorting to indiarubber is the best way to avoid a slipshod and careless style, and will in the end give a freedom to the hand and an accuracy to the eye which is never gained by a less Spartan system of training.   Of my father's rapidity in making the pen-and-ink perspectives of his designs which always did him so much credit, I am able to speak with exact precision in one case at least.   Two years before his death, in 1879, he exhibited at the Royal Academy a most effective bird's-eye view of the convent of St. Margaret, East Grinstead : the drawing is 34 inches by 22, a very fair size, and full of buildings all running at odd angles to each other, and consequently presenting an unusual quantity of work for the amount of paper to be covered. My father began this one evening at nine o'clock, and before he went to bed at one o'clock had put it all in in pencil, *i.e.* all that needed pencilling. The next night he worked, and again the next, and on the fourth night he finished it completely, having taken, as he himself records in his diary with some pride, just sixteen hours about it. Any one who remembers the drawing will allow this to be remarkably quick. What was true of my father's sketching was equally true of his original work. There was the same certainty and the same perfect co-operation of hand and eye in the one as in the other. For some time he drew all his full-size mouldings in ink—a conclusive testimony, if there were no other, of his self-reliance. He had no first thoughts and second thoughts about a thing, but he decided rapidly and once for all what would be suitable ; and his hand was engaged in registering before the brain had ceased creating, so that in making his details, or even his general designs, there was a complete absence of hesitation or tentativeness. He had, in truth, and of all his qualities it was the highest and rarest, that power of instantaneous and complete mental conception which but few in a generation can lay claim to. It is a power which the reader of Nasmyth's *Autobiography* will recognise to have been present in him. He tells us in a simple and straight-forward way how he received a letter one morning at break-fast, in which his opinion was asked as to the feasibility or the wisdom of having a cast-iron paddle-shaft for the *Great Britain* steamship, which was then being built, no hammer at that date being of sufficient power to make a shaft of the required size. He goes on to say that the principle on which a hammer should work to be capable of doing what was wanted struck him on the instant, and in half an hour from the time he received the letter he had put down in a note-book his design for the great steam-hammer, which is now known all over the world, with every detail complete. " I rapidly sketched out my steam-hammer, having it all clearly before me in my mind's eye." This sketch was not a mere suggestion to be worked out at leisure, but it actually embodied almost everything that is found in the hammer of to-day. "This, my first delineation of the steam-hammer, will be found to comprise all the essential elements of the invention" To take another instance, this time in the sphere of art: All who have studied Turner's life and work in any degree know that it was his habit to jot down his impressions of natural objects and natural phenomena in the most rapid and seemingly undecipherable way. Some of these are reproduced in the pages of *Modern Painters*, they are partly in writing, and partly in the roughest kind of sketching. The impression is in fact recorded with all the speed possible, and with as few words and touches as will serve the purpose. Now some of his water-colour drawings, embodying the experience which he had gained by constant observation and had registered in the way I have mentioned, were, I believe, hardly more than a morning's work What Turner gives us is not an exact and literal transcript from Nature, but it is the record of an impression not merely gained from the actual piece of scenery which is included in the picture, but, as Ruskin says, the impression received depends on the temper into which the mind has been brought, on the scenery which has been seen in the course of the day, so that when Turner sits down to paint a scene on the St. Gothard, what he gives us is not a bare and accurate reminiscence of one spot and its surroundings, but it is a scene which is strongly characteristic of the mountain forms to be found throughout the St Gothard Pass. This is only possible when the brain has the necessary power of receiving indelible impressions, and of conceiving something which unites and blends all their essential qualities "The powerfully imaginative mind seizes and combines at the same instant, not only two, but all the important ideas of its poem or picture; and while it works with any one of them, it is at the same time working with and modifying all in their relations to it, never losing sight of their bearings on each other" (*Modern Painters*, vol ii part iii.) Fuseli laid down that "Second thoughts are admissible in painting and poetry only as dressers of the

first conception ; no great idea was ever formed in fragments ;" and Ruskin too says : " He alone can conceive and
compose who sees the whole at once before him."

Now this power of complete and instantaneous conception
belonged to my father just as much as it did to either
Nasmyth or Turner.   I have said that his original work was
drawn with just as great, or, to be accurate, with even greater
rapidity than his architectural sketches.   It is clear that the
ability to design as rapidly as a skilled hand can work must
denote the existence of a complete conception in the brain
of the designer.   My father's pencil—of remarkable facility—
could not yet move as fast as he wished.   I have mentioned
the rapidity with which he threw off details, but he dealt
with complete designs in just the same way.   A hostile
critic once animadverted on his habit of completing the
designs for a church in a morning, and professed himself
scandalised to find that an architect of position could do his
work in a way which must of necessity be so slipshod ; but
happily one can refer with confidence to the admirable
results of this rapid work.   Putting aside the question whether
my father's designs are beautiful or not, it can easily be
shown that they are not slipshod.   There is not a work of
his which bears the mark of carelessness or want of attention ;
on the contrary, there is about them every evidence of the
most careful consideration of details.   Any one who was
ever in my father's office can bear witness to his rapidity in
designing ; but I think a particularly good instance of his
power of conception is afforded by the American Church in
Paris, lately opened.   My father had been with the rector
to see the site which it was then proposed to buy, and had
found it sufficiently suitable to decide in favour of it.   On
his return to the rector's house, the latter asked him whether
he would be able to let them have a sketch of his design
when he had thought it out, so that intending subscribers
might know to what their money would be devoted.   My
father in return asked for paper, and without further consideration made a detailed sketch to a scale of about a
twelfth of an inch to the foot.   I don't remember how long
he took to do it, but he was described as putting his pencil to

paper with apparently no pause at all for reflection, and as fast
as his hand could work   Now this sketch is, like Nasmyth's,
not a mere suggestion of what might possibly be, but it practically represents the church as it stands there now.   It is true
that one large window has taken the place of two smaller ones
in the west front, and that the tower and spire have been
shifted from the south side to the north, but these are the
only important modifications.   Every proportion is exactly
similar.   The height of the church in relation to its width,
the design and proportions of the tower and spire, the proportion of the whole to the site on which it stands.   The
artistic qualities of the sketch and the beauty of the design
are obvious to the most unskilled eye, but the great
point is the wonderful power of imagination which is implied
in such a *tour de force* as this, and the immense self-reliance
which could enable a man to bind himself, definitely, once
for all, and at a moment's notice, to a design for a church,
which was about the most costly parish church which he had
ever had to build, and was to stand in a great and splendid
foreign capital as a monument of what the boasted English
school of church architects could accomplish.   I lay particular
stress on this example because of the importance of the
church, but in other respects it was not a whit more remarkable than scores of others; and, indeed, I never remember my
father's designs being produced except, as it seemed to me,
by inspiration.   I have already spoken of his laying great
emphasis on an architect's not restricting his own personal
interest in a work to the shell, but on the contrary designing
every fitting or piece of furniture in it   Such was invariably
his own practice, and much of his most imaginative and
beautiful work is to be found among his designs for em-
broideries, for plate, for metal, marble, and woodwork of
every kind.   Of these, I think, it is difficult to speak too
highly   Of the merits of his ironwork no one who lives in
London need be ignorant, while he has the infinitely varied
series of the designs at the Law Courts at his doors   It is
difficult to pick out single pieces as being better than others,
but there are some among the more easily found which are
quite among the best.   What, indeed, can be finer than the

gates on the Strand front, those, for instance, at the entrance
to the office quadrangle, and those again in the archway under
the clock tower? or, on the Carey Street front, what more
charming than the little gates in front of the Judges' entrances?
The variety is infinite, the curves have all the beauty of
natural outlines, the sections are piquant. It is not uncommon
in good and interesting churches to find even nowadays ironwork, hinges more particularly, which seem to have had
little or no attention given them by the architect. Even
where the outline has been sketched, it is obvious that the
section has been forgotten or has been ignored; yet the
section is hardly less important than the form, and a commonplace outline with a varied and well-designed section will be
quite likely to look better than a good outline where there is
no section at all. There is much beautiful ironwork of my
father's at Kingstone Church, Dorset; at All Saints, Clifton;
at Christ Church Cathedral, Dublin; at St. James the Less,
Westminster. Indeed, there is probably not a church with
which he had to do where there is not some ironwork which
is worth study, even if it is nothing more important than
hinges. His ironwork was to a great extent executed by
Leaver of Maidenhead. Of his work Sir Gilbert Scott said:
"I believe Mr. Street has made great progress in metal
work, acting through a smith at Maidenhead. I have only
seen a little of his work, but that was first-rate." It is
impossible to describe embroidery designs, but altar-cloths
and hangings of my father's design exist throughout the
length and breadth of the land. They rarely, if ever, have
any representation of figures—a feature in which it is difficult
to strike the happy mean between realism and conventionalism, and the results of which are not usually very
satisfactory,—but are composed of patterns, devices, and
monograms of great originality and endless variety, inter-
spersed with conventionalised flowers and foliage. My
father often made conventional studies from the flowers
themselves, so that no characteristic should be lost or
reduced to insignificance in the conversion from the natural
to the conventional form. The arrangement of colours was
always at least as satisfactory as the patterns.

There is a last point to be noticed in dealing with his thoroughness, and that is, his ability in designing carving and enrichment. This is not unfrequently, I think, classed with hinges as one of the minor adjuncts of a work about which an architect need not trouble himself, beyond perhaps, glancing at a model or two. To quote Sir Gilbert Scott again :—

"My friend, Mr Street, during this period, has been working up the pure conventional foliage, Mr Earp being his handpiece, and he has done very great things I think that his work and mine together, for the last few years or so, has been a noble development He can lay claim to his more personally than I can to mine, as he gives drawings, while I do my work by influence ; but the results in both cases are of a high order."

Without in any way disparaging Sir Gilbert's method, it is impossible not to feel that the true and thorough way of getting your work done, *exactly as you want it done*, is to design, to sketch, or even to model, it yourself Busy as my father was, he yet found time to go into the modeller's shed, which adjoined his office, every time he went down to the Law Courts—two or three times a week—while the work was going on. In that shed he not only made numerous sketches, not willingly foregoing making the design for even the smallest piece of enrichment, but in very many instances he worked on the clay models The carving throughout the Law Courts is probably of as high a character as any Gothic carving which has been executed in our day, and does every credit to the men who were engaged upon it Its great value, however, lies in its not being only a near approach to what the architect desired, but in its being literally the embodiment of his designs. If there was one thing more than another which my father would never have tolerated, it was the modification of a design by the carver, smith, or whatever he might be, who was employed in carrying it out. ' Skidmore kicked over the traces," says Sir Gilbert Scott of the well-known ironworker who did so much for him. *That* my father would never have allowed. A work once put into his hands, he was determined that all its merits and demerits should be due to him and to no one else His earliest work, both in iron and carving, though as full as it could be of originality and go, erred on the side of crudeness in some measure—a fault which was, however, very soon eradicated

In addition to his imaginative faculty my father had great powers of critical observation and comparison, the results of which are obvious in all his contributions to architectural and archæological literature, whether in his books or in the more fugitive pieces   This power enabled him to illustrate, in the most ample way, any architectural feature which he was discussing, or any dictum which he laid down.   He never treated a building merely from the artistic point of view, but rather subjected it to a searching analysis, looking for analogies or contrasts, traces of foreign influence, or local idiosyncrasies,—paying the most careful attention to the historical aspect generally   His advice to students shows how necessary a part of an architect's duties and training he held such a course to be.   The history of the building which they have to restore, he tells them, must be deciphered with as near an approach to accuracy as possible, before all.   The architect, who would deserve the name, must be an archæo-logist as well as an artist, and a builder as well as both. Diligent exercise of scientific observation, combined with a retentive memory and powers of logical classification, enabled my father to make considerable additions to the store of our historical knowledge as to the connection between various works in different parts of our country and in different parts of Europe   The habit of thoroughly co-ordinating and sys-tematising his experiences enabled him to trace the action of various laws in the development of style, and to point to the production of like effects by like causes in different parts of the world   The following short quotation on the subject of the brick architecture of Europe will explain my mean-ing :—

"The great fields for brick architecture were (1) the north of Italy ; (2) the north-east of Germany ; (3) the west of France ; and (4) various parts of Spain   There were other districts, but these were the most important.   The developments of each were different, but they all agreed in the discovery of certain qualities in bricks   In the first place, they all found that if brickwork is to be strong, it must be built with an enormous quantity of mortar, and so, instead of specify-ing, as some enlightened nineteenth-century architects would do, that

' no mortar joint is to be more than one quarter of an inch thick,' I
think if we could find a mediæval specification we should find it run
in this form, ' No mortar joint to be less than half an inch thick.'
Then next they observed that bricks might be moulded, and that, if the
earth used were well tempered and fine, any delicate pattern might
be reproduced in a hard material which would almost defy weather.
In subsequent times we have seen it become the fashion to ignore
this vulgar view of the question, and to regard brick as a material
which ought to be so soft as to be cut and rubbed easily. Moulded
bricks of course made easy a plentiful use of a mould when once it
had been made, and there was consequently a temptation to use a
pattern over again as often as possible. The result of this was that
in most brick districts we see moulded brick traceries used and
repeated all over a building, not because they were very beautiful, or
because they were required, but because they existed, and therefore
had to be used. Look at the cornices of the Italian churches, with
their endless repetitions of the same form of tracery, and you will
see what I mean, whilst in North Germany the traceries all over
the transepts of St. Katharine at Brandenburg show precisely the
same kind of result. Still more curious is it that in Italy, in France,
and in Germany, the use of brick led to the erection of sham fronts
in front of the roof-gables, the main or only use of which was to
show off the variety of moulded bricks. You will also see a close
affinity in cause and principle between such fronts (to take typical
examples from each country) as those of the Town Hall of Lübeck,
the gables of the churches in and near Toulouse, and the transepts
of Cremona Cathedral; whilst, nevertheless, each is entirely independent of the other in style, and evidently their architects knew
nothing of each other's work. And here I am reminded of the
curious effect of brickwork upon stonework in the same districts, as,
e g. in Venice, where one cannot look at such traceries as those of
the Madonna del Orto, consisting of groups of quatrefoils cut out to
fit an arch, and not growing naturally as our own English traceries
grow, without seeing that the necessary repetitions of brick traceries
had probably suggested them. So again in North Germany we see at
Brunswick, Halberstadt, and in that district generally, a remarkable
type of west front, consisting of a raised gable between the towers,
the sole object of which seems to have been the exhibition of magnificent traceries, both to the east and west, which looks almost as
if it had been suggested by the common exhibition of grand brick
traceries in the churches not far off, as, *e g.* in the transept of St.
Katharine, Brandenburg, though, no doubt, the Romanesque
examples of the same arrangement would rather militate against this
theory. In the south of France, in Toulouse and its neighbourhood, the use of brickwork led to almost exactly the same kind of

development as we may see in the front of St. Taur, Toulouse, or
that of Ville Nouvelle or Villefranche, not far off; but the details
of the works in all these districts are different, and yet in each the
style has been affected by the material, and is quite unlike what it
would have been if stone had been available for use."

The power and habit of critical comparison made my
father's books on *Brick and Marble in North Italy* and *Gothic
Architecture in Spain* most valuable ; the latter perhaps particularly, because the architecture of Spain was influenced
in so great a degree by foreign examples or executed by
foreign architects, and previous accounts had been so meagre
and so unscientific In that book he tells us how the
cathedral of Santiago must almost certainly have been
inspired by the church of St. Sernin, Toulouse Lérida,
Tarragona, Tudela, Benavente, Salamanca, and other northern
examples all show a foreign hand,—and not improbably the
same hand,—but not that of the man who was responsible
for the cathedral of Santiago. Toledo, Léon, and Burgos
all bear on them the marks of French influence, but their
architects must have come from different parts of France ;
while at Toledo alone is the influence of the popular art of
the country visible. Léon has been built without any
thought of the conditions to which it is exposed, and the
Spanish sun blazes fiercely into a church which is greatly
composed of windows—a mistake which my father notes was
also made by the German architect of Milan Cathedral.

On the Continent—in England of course—he is able to
group churches as exhibiting similarities which are due to
the use of some particular material, such as granite, for instance. He draws his examples from far and near, from
every point of the compass, all of them illustrating the
natural working out of the same principle. In like manner
he was able to lay his hand on many a group of buildings in
which the hand of the same architect is discernible either in the
plan or some other fundamental feature, or possibly in some insignificant and almost unnoticeable details. He finds that the
architects of the fourteenth and fifteenth centuries were frequently in the habit of copying the forms of earlier work, though
using their own detail, illustrating this among other examples

by the towers and spires of Normandy and Valencia. He
shows how one style may act on another and be itself reacted
on by it, and instances some of the work in the Ile de France
and in the Rhineland, more particularly the cathedrals of
Laon and Bamberg. He discovers that Gatton Church and
Bristol Cathedral, dissimilar as are their designs, own a
common author, and establishes beyond a doubt that Stone
Church, Kent, was the work of the architect of Westminster
Abbey I might multiply examples indefinitely, but I have
said enough to show how systematically my father worked,
and how thoroughly he cultivated the scientific as well as
the artistic side of his profession.

It may be of interest to take one case and examine it
with greater particularity to show the minuteness of my
father's investigations, and the convincing nature of the
evidence which he required before he was satisfied with having
established his contention

Stone Church is at once interesting in itself, and because
of its almost certain connection with the Abbey; and I think
I could hardly find an example of a more typical kind, or one
which displays better the kind of analysis to which my father
subjected a building.

"Few subjects," he says, "are of more interest to me than this
of the extent to which the work of the same artist may be traced in
different buildings. I have been able, in a considerable number of
cases, to prove pretty clearly what I now wish to prove about Stone
and Westminster, but I need hardly say that the evidence is
always of a kind which it is extremely difficult to give in writing,
though it is hard to resist its force if the two buildings are examined
one after the other, and their special peculiarities noted."

My father in this instance observed (1) that the
arcade round the chancel at Stone was almost identical
with those round the choir at Westminster, the proportion of
the trefoil cusps being very peculiar and almost identical
The spandrels are filled with foliage, carved exactly in the
same spirit; the labels terminate in both cases on small
corbels level with the capitals; and the arch moulds are similar
in character, and both undercut at the back. (2) The
original window tracery at Westminster is the same as that

at Stone. My father discovered a window at Stone of precisely the same character as those in the south triforium of the nave at Westminster. The lights in both are of exceptional width ; again the tracery bars at Stone, richly moulded on the inside, and with a very broad simple chamfer on the outside, find their parallel at Westminster, and the cusping is let into the stonework in the same way at the two churches. (3) The carving in the spandrels of the arcades is treated in just the same way. The foliage of the capitals is generally alike, while the foliage in the chancel arch of Stone —arranged like an enormous dog-tooth—is almost a repetition of the archivolt enrichment in the triforium at Westminster, and the roses round the archivolt of the south door at Stone are of the same kind as those round the inside arches of the north transept doorways of Westminster. There are also some carved crosses in trefoils at Stone which have their counterpart in the Abbey. (4) The materials used in the Abbey and the church are as nearly as possible the same. The wrought stonework is executed in Caen stone and Gatton stone, and a great deal of chalk is used for wall-lining and groining, and all the shafts are of marble. (5) The general system of proportion is observed in the minster and the village church. In both the width from the aisle walls to the centre of the columns is equal to half the width of the nave. At Westminster the height is given by three equilateral triangles, whose base line is the width across the nave from centre to centre of the columns, and two of these triangles give the height to the springing of the groining, and the third the height of the groining to its apex. At Stone, if triangles are set up on the same base line, the first gives the top of the caps of the nave arcade ; the second—within a very little—the height of the top of the wall ; and the third may very well be supposed to have marked the height of the ridge of the timber roof. The width of the bays in the nave of Stone is equal to the diagonal of half the width of the nave ; and the width of the bays in the chancel is equal to the diagonal from the centre of one column to the centre of the nave or aisle opposite the next column ; while the height of the chancel

is given by two triangles similar to those in the nave, whose
base is the width from centre to centre of the groining
shafts

It is further to be noticed, as my father pointed out, that
in carefulness and beauty of workmanship the village church
is undoubtedly superior to the minster   The carving particularly is of the highest kind.   It all seems to be the work
of one man ; and he must have been, if not the best of the
Westminster sculptors, at any rate equal to the best   This
tells very strongly against the supposition that the church
was copied from the Abbey, because detail rarely gains in
such a process ; while the fact that one or two pieces of carving (for spandrels), which had actually never been fixed, were
found by my father, looks as if the architect had been getting
the carving done by one of the carvers at the minster, and
having it sent down to Stone in a finished state.

The thoroughness which is apparent in these investigations pervaded all my father's work.   The high-road to success
—he would have said—lies through hard work, and sustained
hard work must depend on enthusiasm.   Enthusiasm, if it
does not come at once, must be diligently cultivated.   His
own indebtedness to it was great indeed, for from what other
source could he have derived the energy which enabled him
to turn play into work and work into play, to spend his
holidays measuring and sketching and taking notes as he
used to do from morning to night ?   His frequent foreign
tours and his diligent study of Gothic under every condition
and in every part of Europe were the carrying out of his
maxim, that a man should make himself cognisant of even
local peculiarities, firstly, so that he should never be taken by
surprise or find himself obliged to design on lines which
were unfamiliar to him ; and secondly, because the more
broad and liberal the education is, and the more thorough
the knowledge of good examples, the less likely is a man
to desert the great principles which underlie the highest
forms of art in architecture, wherever it may be, for tricks
and mannerisms which may perhaps claim the attention for
the day, but which no one will care to glance at to-morrow.

CHAPTER VIII

THE NEW LAW COURTS

THE concentration of the Courts of Law, which had some-
time previously been mooted in legal circles, was brought
prominently forward in 1832 by Mr. Freshfield, who introduced the subject in the House of Commons on behalf of
the Incorporated Law Society.

In 1842 a proposition was made to utilise part of
Lincoln's Inn Fields as the site for the new buildings ; but
the space was so obviously inadequate for the purpose that
the proposal dropped, as also did the half measure of Lord
Chelmsford—subsequently laid before the House of Commons
—which provided for building the Equity Courts only on
that site. These less ambitious schemes gave place to others
of a more comprehensive and thorough kind ; and in 1865 a
Commission, presided over by Sir John Coleridge, selected
what came to be afterwards known as the Carey Street site,
as eminently fitted for the purpose in view. In the same
year two Acts were passed : the first for buying the Carey
Street site, and the second for providing the necessary funds ;
a Commission of about forty members was also appointed
in June ; the requirements were gone into with great minuteness by three separate Committees, and instructions were
drawn up for the future guidance of the architect.

In February 1866, a limited competition having been
decided on, invitations were issued to six architects, viz.
Messrs. Scott, Street, T. H. Wyatt, Edward Barry, P. C. Hardwick junior, and Alfred Waterhouse. Five judges of designs
were nominated (two being named by the Commission), viz.

The Right Hon. W. Cowper, the then First Commissioner of Works, Right Hon. W. E. Gladstone, the Chancellor of the Exchequer; The Right Hon. Sir A Cockburn, Lord Chief Justice; Sir Roundell Palmer, Attorney-General, and Sir William Stirling Maxwell. Messrs Shaw and Pownall were subsequently added to the number as professional advisers The conditions of the competition laid down among other things that £800 should be paid to each competitor, that no design was of necessity to be selected for execution, and that the successful competitor should not undertake any new work requiring his personal attention for a period of three years, unless with the consent of the Treasury. The second of these stipulations, which robbed the competition of all finality, proved to be a source of so much dissatisfaction that it was withdrawn

Of the six architects who were originally invited to compete, Messrs T. H. Wyatt and P C Hardwick at once declined. Their places were filled by Messrs. Raphael Brandon and Deane The third stipulation proved a stumbling-block to Messrs. G. G. Scott and Edward Barry, and they retired, to be replaced by Messrs. Garling and Gibson.

On 22d March 1866 a resolution was passed in the House of Commons affirming the inexpediency of limiting the competition to so small a number as six, and the Treasury in conjunction with the Royal Commission, in consequence of this resolution, raised the number to twelve. To cut a long story short, designs were finally sent in in January 1867 by Messrs. Abraham, Garling, Raphael Brandon, Edward Barry, Scott, Street, Seddon, Waterhouse, Lockwood, Deane, and Burges.

The award was made in the following July, and was to the effect that the judges felt themselves unable to recommend the adoption of any individual design, but that Mr Barry's seemed to them best in the distribution of the interior, while Mr Street's took the first place in regard to merit as an architectural composition; and they recommended that these two architects should be employed conjointly—Mr. Barry to be chiefly responsible for the internal arrangements, and Mr. Street for the elevations. This recommendation was at once protested against by Mr. G. G. Scott; his contention being that the conditions did not allow of the judges taking the sum of two men's merits and weighing them in the balance with the individual merits of the others.

This view, or something like it, was evidently shared in other quarters, and the judges were asked to reconsider their decision, as being one which their conditions did not allow them to come to. The officers of the Crown further pronounced such a decision to be invalid; but in spite of this, and after a delay of four months, the judges announced that they could do nothing but repeat their recommendation.

This double appointment was accepted by the two principals and by the majority of the competing architects as a sufficiently satisfactory conclusion; but public opinion, as represented by the press, was much divided as to what was the proper course to pursue. It was contended that the first competition should be regarded merely as a means of showing the legal gentlemen more fully what they wanted, and that a second competition should be held, perhaps primarily for ground-plan only. This truly afforded a pleasant prospect for the unfortunate competitors.

The decision of the judges was published in July 1867; and from that time till June 1868 rumour said first one thing and then another, till at the latter date it was authoritatively announced that my father was to be the sole architect of the new Law Courts, while to Mr. Barry was given the building of the new National Gallery. It would be both bewildering and unprofitable to attempt to pursue the subject through those eleven weary months. It was naturally a time of great anxiety to the principals. The decision was accepted in a loyal spirit by Mr. Barry, though he would have been more than human if he had not felt, and said, that he had been dropped a little unceremoniously. Some notice was taken of his case in both Houses; but a proposal for the appointment of a select Committee to inquire into the circumstances, made by Mr. Goldsmid in the House of Commons, was summarily rejected.

There was some carping at the adoption of Gothic for the new building, but it was generally allowed to be in

keeping with the venerable age and traditions of legal institutions ; and any interference with the architect, on the same
lines as Lord Palmerston's, was looked on as impossible, with
the results of that unfortunate and ill-advised proceeding
always in evidence.

For some six months the subject of the Law Courts was
in abeyance ; but from the beginning of 1869 it again came
into prominence, while the vexed question between the respective claims of the Carey Street and Embankment sites
was fought out.

The battle of the sites was started in the columns of the
Times by Sir Charles Trevelyan. He contended that the
Commission of 1858, in selecting the Carey Street site, had
been led to do so simply from the want of a better ; and that
at that time the merits of a site on the Embankment could
not be imagined, while even in 1865 a great deal had to be
taken for granted. He himself made a sweeping and comprehensive proposition which, shortly stated, amounted to
this .—

1 That the building for the new Law Courts should be
erected on a site bounded by the Temple and Somerset
House on the east and west respectively, by the Strand on
the north, and the Embankment on the south.

2 That the occupants of Lincoln's Inn should move
down to Somerset House, so as to be near the Courts.

3 That King's College and its school should move from
Somerset House to Lincoln's Inn

4. That the Carey Street site should be covered with
buildings adapted for use as chambers

5. That Somerset House should be enlarged by the
addition of a story.

6. That the occupants of Gray's Inn should move to
Clement's Inn.

7. That the site of Gray's Inn should be covered with
industrial dwellings, to accommodate those who had been
rendered homeless by the clearance of the Carey Street
site.

8 That the occupants of Somerset House should move
down to Westminster.

Naturally there was much in this impossibly large scheme which gave a great handle to its opponents ; still the fact remained that the Embankment might possibly be made, as Sir Charles Trevelyan averred it would, a great quay of palaces ; and that when such a good opportunity for making a splendid commencement was at hand, it would be folly to reject it without ample discussion

The advantages of this site were set forth not only by its first promoter, but by many others, in a number of letters to the daily papers ; and it may confidently be said that the cause did not suffer for the want of able advocacy.   The advantages claimed for it have subsequently proved to have been founded, to a considerable extent, on misapprehensions and illusions.   It was taken for granted that the Embankment road would be, what it has not yet become, a great thoroughfare from east to west.   Thus Sir Charles Trevelyan argued that the approaches to the new buildings would leave nothing to be desired, with a great thoroughfare on both the north and south fronts.   The really fatal objection to the scheme was the immensity of the outlay which it would have entailed.   It can hardly be denied that if the building had been placed on that site, the removal of the block of buildings up to Holywell Street would have been a matter of necessity, otherwise the already congested Strand could by no stretch of the imagination have been regarded as a good approach.   The cost of buying this block of buildings would therefore have had to be added to the actual cost of the site, which Sir Charles Trevelyan put at a million and a half sterling.   On the other hand, it was at that date assumed that a million would have to be spent in making proper approaches on the north of the Carey Street site, that the Law Institution and King's College Hospital would have to be bought, Clare Market swept away, and that £700,000 would have to be spent in additions to the original site, the cost of which had been £800,000.   But how does the case stand at the present time ?   Not one of these improvements, much though they are needed, has proved to be absolutely necessary ; and consequently this extra two millions has remained in the pockets of the public.   It is not too late to hope now that some opening may be made on the north side ; but it certainly needs not to be on the colossal scale which the opponents of this site took to be necessary.

There were others—Sir William Tite among them—who favoured that subdivision of the building which had long ago been condemned, but they did not succeed in ever catching the public ear.   Their suggestion. was that my father might be entrusted with one building, and Mr Barry with the other.

From a very early stage the conflict became, or was made by the partisans of the Embankment site, a question between the public and the legal profession, and complaints were made that the clients were being sacrificed to the convenience of the lawyers

It is pertinent to ask what the public is ?   Does it not mean in reality the public litigant ? and how could the Embankment site be shown to be the more convenient site for them ?   It was not denied—nay, that was the actual ground of complaint—that the Carey Street site was in the · heart of the legal district, instead of being at its southern extremity.   Now it had been further proved that of those who enter the Courts ninety-two per cent do so from the chambers of barristers or the offices of solicitors, while the residue was, as it always is, composed to a great extent of the idle and out-at-elbows, who hang about the Courts every day of their lives for want of other occupation.   All this was very well put in a letter to the *Times* of that date.   It was further argued on this side, that a building on the Embankment would be visible to the people on board the penny steamboats, and to few besides ; and that the inducements to enter the building from that side would not be very great, as it would entail mounting a perfect Jacob's Ladder to reach the Strand level.

My father was at this time, both on practical and æsthetical grounds, in favour of the Carey Street site.   His reasons were : firstly, that a building there would crown a hill, instead of clinging to a steep declivity ; secondly, it would offer the architect more chances of a picturesque treatment than would be possible in the formal front which the Embankment site would require ; and lastly, that—*cæteris paribus*—a building on that site would be the cheaper of the two

The controversy, after raging for some time in the public press, was taken up in the House of Commons by Mr. Gregory, who presented a petition, to which the signatures of a considerable number of legal men were attached, on behalf of the Embankment site   He said little that had not already been well said by Sir Charles Trevelyan, but he presented two estimates of comparative expenditure, in the compilation of which he appeared to have drawn largely on his imagination.   He made out somehow or other that the Carey Street site would cost in all over three millions, while the other, he maintained, would not be likely to exceed a million and a half ; and he represented further that the land already bought might be very profitably disposed of.   Sir Roundell Palmer followed him in a very able speech, and advocated the Carey Street site on the ground of superior convenience both to suitors and lawyers.   He quoted Mr. Edwin Field's dictum that " every day saved to the suitors saves £25,000 , " and showed that the extra five minutes' walk to the Embankment would make this estimate no mere figure of speech, but a tangible fact.   Further, he pointed out that the Embankment site would in all probability cost two millions and a quarter, while some £400,000 would be lost in the resale of the land already bought.   Again, while the Carey Street site would be the more convenient for 5087 solicitors, the other site would only be the more easily accessible to 1119; and of the houses so placed as not necessarily to prefer the one site to the other, a majority of 1519 were in favour of keeping to the land already bought.   He also drew attention to what I have noticed above, that the nature of the foundations and the steep slope of the ground from the Strand to the river made it quite impossible to put a building erected there at as low a figure as would pay for one on solid and level ground.   An unexpected termination was put to the debate by the speech of the Chancellor of the Exchequer (Right Hon Robert Lowe), which made both sides feel that they had been made cat's paws of.   Mr. Lowe began by saying that when he came into office and was confronted with the proposal of the Commissioners to spend a sum of £660,000 on additions to the Carey Street site, he was struck with such dismay that he at once put a veto on it   He showed that the money, far from coming from the suitors' fund, was in reality to be taken out of the pockets of the ratepayers   Once, he said, exchange the frenzy of concentration for a rational desire to group together all the really necessary offices, and you will find that neither the swollen Carey Street site nor Sir Charles Trevelyan's exaggerated scheme is in the least necessary.   All that is wanted may very well be built within the boundaries of Essex Street, Howard Street, Somerset House, and the Embankment

Audacious as this proposal seemed at the first blush, and scouted as it was by the press with hardly an exception, it was not long before it had quite superseded the larger proposal.   It was felt that there was a good deal of truth in the phrase "frenzy of concentration," and that it would impose on the architect a less impossible task were the building reduced to more reasonable limits ; at the same time it was strongly held that, if any good purpose could be served by a larger expenditure, this was not the occasion for grudging a half million or so.

The first and most obvious criticism on the Howard Street site was that if it were thought possible to build all that was essential on this restricted site, the necessary buildings could be at least as well contained on the ground already bought and cleared, the interest on the purchase-money of which was all this time being wasted

Mr Lowe's action seemed to have been modelled on the judgment of Solomon   He settled the question by destroying the subject-matter.

The Howard Street cause was damaged by the proposal to utilise an old design for a water front by Inigo Jones as a part of the new building, with the view of saving a modicum of the architect's fees.   This treatment of the architect as an importunate and superfluous middleman was conspicuous at the time ; and my father incurred certain strictures in some quarters for having contravened the usages of the profession in accepting a lump sum in lieu of commission, which represented somewhat less than the usual percentage on the cost It was doubtless a pitiful piece of cheeseparing on the part of the authorities to make the demand, and it is probable that such a mode of encouraging a man at the outset of a great undertaking is peculiar to this country ; at the same time, when pressure was applied, the individual had no alternative but to give way.   It is difficult, out of the multitude of estimates presented by either side, to arrive at the exact truth as to the relative cost which the rival sites would entail.

The cost of the Embankment site was put at £600,000 by Mr. (now Sir H. A.) Hunt, and at £662,000 by Mr Pownall , but these estimates did not take into account the inevitable widening of Essex Street at the upper end, which would have meant a further sum of £150,000.   This would have brought the amount up to a figure almost identical with the £765,000 spent on the Carey Street site.   There was another factor to take into account, viz the probable result of a resale of the latter piece of ground ; but on this point Mr Hunt announced that he had been in communication with people of means who proposed building chambers there, and who were prepared to pay seven per cent per annum on the amount of the purchase-money.   Mr. Eiloart asserted that many years of experience had proved to him that chambers could never be made to pay : still Government had an apparently *bonâ fide* offer, with the result that they were free to choose quite unreservedly between two sites which were practically identical in value

Directly my father entered seriously into the consideration of a building on the Embankment, he arrived at the conclusion that it would be mere waste of money and space to build a vast basement similar to that of Somerset House, a course which had hitherto been always taken for granted. He decided to start from the Embankment level, and found that by doing so the slope of the ground, so far from being a stumblingblock, might be made to lend itself to an ingenious and convenient treatment of the different levels. This alteration did much to equalise the probable outlay on the two buildings, or reduced the difference in favour of Carey Street to a minimum

On 4th May Mr. (now Sir H. A.) Layard asked for leave to bring in a Bill to enable the Commissioners of Her Majesty's Public Works to obtain a new site for the concentration of law business. He had previously announced that the Government were preparing to submit to the House a scheme for a building on the Howard Street site at a total cost (inclusive of the site) of £1,600,000 From the point of view of economy the Howard Street site struck him as having at least one very satisfactory feature, viz. that it did not admit of expansion. The announcement of this negative virtue was received with ironical cheers. As regarded style, Mr. Layard suggested that something after the manner of the Ducal Palace at Venice would be very much in keeping. Sir Charles Trevelyan continued as active as ever in promoting a river site ; and, indeed, only two days after Mr. Layard's speech, he wrote a letter to the *Times* claiming for the Howard Street site that very capability for expansion, the absence of which had, in Mr. Layard's eyes, been its chief attraction. He also continued to suggest schemes for the rearrangement of that part of London of about as comprehensive a character as that which Colonel Fougas submitted to Napoleon for the better ordering of Paris It seemed as if the great and crucial question of style was to be settled by everybody except the architect. Sir Charles Trevelyan expressed himself as strongly in favour of some style which would admit of the ground floor being devoted to shops. Let them but be contrived with granite or iron supports and plenty of plate glass, and he thought they would present an appearance of great cheerfulness. Whether his idea was that the form of London's great buildings should symbolically remind us that our empire is founded on trade is not clear, but even that could hardly have been sufficient compensation for such a Lowther-Arcadian style.

A fortnight later my father, who had now thrown himself with great zest into the Embankment scheme, had completed his sketch plans of the new design, and published a report on the respective capabilities of the two smaller sites,

with plans of the buildings as proposed on each. The
Architect of 29th May said :—

"The intention of the Government to move the Law Courts to
the Embankment was first known on 20th April. On 4th May
Mr. Layard was able to announce that Mr. Street was already engaged on the plans ;" and added, "Even those acquainted with the
extraordinary rapidity with which this brilliant architect works may be
astonished to know that finished sketches of the new design are
already complete."

Mr. Layard, on his part, said in the House that it "had
not been their fortune to see a more artistic production than
the sketch of the new design by Mr. G. E. Street."

Other architectural critics thought there was a little want
of simplicity in the design, but attributed it to the fearful
way in which the architect had been hurried, and eulogised
the general grouping of the parts, and more particularly the
way in which the building was brought forward in front of
Somerset House, in échelon, as it were, so as to follow the
sweep of the river.

I have already mentioned that my father's early predilection for Carey Street had been seriously modified. The
Embankment site, though too much in a hole, still offered
superior facilities for the admission of light and air, and the
shape was also more favourable to a convenient arrangement
than the square Carey Street plot. In his report he pointed
out that, whichever of the sites might be decided on, the
original plan would have to be completely reconsidered, as
it involved the widening of Carey Street and the readjust-
ment of Clement's Inn on the west and Bell Yard on the
east.

The surroundings of the buildings on this site (the Carey
Street one) were all amply provided for in the plan approved
by the Commissioners ; but every portion of them—except
on the Strand side—depended on the power to make additional purchases of land. "If these purchases are not made
under compulsory powers, I do not see," he goes on to say,
"how a public building can properly be placed on this
site."

Dealing first with the Howard Street site, my father pronounced it to be extremely well off in the matter of access   the streets running down from the Strand, to use his words, are wide and have no traffic   The railway station and steamboat pier will be in immediate proximity.   Essex Street on the east will be widened, Howard Street will be widened and lengthened, and both these streets will then afford capital means of access.

The terrace of Somerset House is to be utilised as an entrance for the judges on the level, and Essex Street is to be treated in a similar way to the Rows at Chester, so that lawyers may cross the Strand by a bridge and enter the Courts without going up and down.

Light and air are good, though a considerable opening should be made into the heart of the building from the Embankment.   In my father's own words :—

"It is difficult to conceive a public building being erected in London with greater advantages in its surroundings than this site affords. . . . At first sight the rapid slope of the ground presented considerable difficulties, there being a rise of no less than twenty-three feet from the Embankment to the highest point of Howard Street. .   . I have preferred to adopt the more common-sense plan of taking the levels of the ground as they are, and building to suit them , and the advantage of this course is that I am able to make entrances at various levels, and so give to many offices the practical effect of being on the ground floor, which, on a level site, would have to use flights of steps up or down   Thus I have ground-floor entrances on the Embankment, and at higher levels in Essex Street, and still higher in Howard Street, and from the Somerset House Terrace ; and if my suggestion of a bridge across the Strand is ever adopted, there will be the still further advantage of enabling people to go from the Strand to the upper part of the building with an extremely moderate ascent of steps "   On the question of the architectural advantages of this site he added, "Before I thoroughly went into the question of a design for the Embankment site, I had not realised some of the advantages which it affords.   It is true that I allowed in the discussion on the subject, which took place at the Society of Arts Rooms, that the Embankment site was preferable to that on the north side of the Strand , but I protested against the unfair disparagement of the latter site, as it was proposed to be formed by means of additional purchases, and I pointed out how these had enabled me to design a building, which would not only be very convenient and very conveniently placed, but which would also, I hoped, be an ornament to London. At that time I thought of the Embankment building as raised upon a terrace like that in front of Somerset House. I foresaw that my building would then rise far higher than Somerset House, and that the suggestion made by some one to add a story to Sir William Chambers's building was not one which I could ever endorse. I foresaw also considerable difficulty in planting my building on the curved line of the Embankment, without danger of producing an unpleasant result. But in working out the plan to suit the site, I think, as is often the case in architectural designs, that the very difficulties of the case have proved in the end to be its greatest gain "

My father, however sensible he was of the merits of the original Carey Street site, was unable to speak in very high terms of the restricted one   To begin with, the shape of the site seemed to him unsatisfactory. It had less light and air, and promised to be more noisy, than that south of Howard Street. The levels worked out fairly well, but could not be made to yield any noticeable advantages, such as that afforded by the ingenious use of Somerset House Terrace. The height above the river was an excellent point, but this was rather negatived by the loss of the lofty towers which had formed part of the original design.

He pointed out what liberties the Incorporated Law Society had taken in their report on and plan of the rival sites. The inaccuracies were many, and, curiously enough, they all favoured their pet scheme. He goes on as follows ·——

"The object of the map is obtained by altering the eastern boundaries of the ground already bought, and bringing them considerably nearer to Chancery Lane than they really are; and in order to do this, the whole block of houses, from the Law Institution on the north to those which front the Strand on the south, is drawn of much smaller dimensions than it ought to be,—for example, from the east side of Chancery Lane to the west face of the Law Institution the Law Society's plan gives 135 feet; in reality it is 180 feet So again the distance from the south-east angle of Chancery Lane to the south-east angle of the purchased site is shown as 105 feet; whereas, in reality, it measures on the Ordnance map 145 feet. Again the clear dimensions from east to west between the houses in Bell Yard and the houses in Clement's Inn is shown as 630 feet, out of which two 60-feet roads being taken would leave an area 510 feet in length for building on; in reality the exact length on the Ordnance map, between the two points, is only 560 feet, which, if the proposed roads are deducted, leaves a building area of not more than 440 feet. Any one may see that this alteration has really been made on this map by comparing it with my plan of the building on this site, or with the Parliamentary map of 1st August 1845, from which it professes to be, but is not, accurately copied. It will be seen that while the south-east angle of my building only projects about 10 feet to the east of Temple Bar, the yellow (or building) site on the Law Society's map projects 50 feet east of Temple Bar. The result of this examination of the actual dimensions of the ground is that, allowing the same depth from north to south that I have shown on my plan, viz. 470 feet, and allowing for the two roads east and west of the building, the site coloured yellow on the Law Society's plan, and described as containing 6 acres, would, in truth, only contain 4 acres 2 roods and 1175 square yards.

"As I have felt obliged to show the inaccuracy of this plan in regard to this site, it may not be out of place to say here that it is similarly inaccurate as regards the Embankment site; but the inaccuracy in this case makes the distance from the north side of Howard Street to the line of Somerset House Terrace about 40 feet less than it ought to be, and so diminishes the apparent size and value of this site in the same degree that it increases those of the other."

The report concludes thus :—

"On the whole, it appears to me that the Embankment site affords by far the best opportunity for a great work, now that the reduced scale of the building is accepted by the opponents to your scheme (*i.e* the Howard Street). I have found, I am bound to confess, that the more I worked at the plan for the building on the Embankment, the more did it seem to be possible to make the work one with which men of taste might be satisfied, from an architectural point of view, and I have good hopes that, if the building is in the end put on this site, it would be possible, in the way I have indicated, to make it so really convenient to all those whose business would lie in it as to involve no very serious sacrifice, if any, of the present use or associations of the great Inns of Court or other centres of legal business."

In spite of the apparently general agreement of outside opinion in favour of the site which my father in this report so decidedly upholds, the professional party finally gained the day, and in August it was known that the restricted Carey Street site had been definitely decided on. Probably the right choice, in view of the convenience of those attending the Courts, was made, and I remember my father, in later years, expressing to me his real satisfaction that the choice had fallen where it did.   The site is beyond all question too small for the buildings which it has to contain, but that is a misfortune which seems quite inevitable in London, and would have been almost as much felt on the other site.   Many improvements there no doubt are, which, if not imperatively necessary, are yet earnestly to be desired, such as the clearing away of the Holywell Street block, the demolition of the low and squalid houses at the north-west angle of the building, and the widening of Searle Street, and its continuation through the great turnstile into and across Holborn.

The decision was generally accepted as a relief even by those whom it most severely disappointed.   An extremely good article appeared in one of the papers which had consistently supported the Carey Street site throughout.   It was shown, with great truth, that the Thames can never, owing to its breadth, be a great water highway in the sense that the Seine is.   Its volume naturally dwarfs whatever is on its banks, and it is better to accept this frankly, and treat the Thames quay as a servant and not as a master, spacing the buildings out, and allowing wide and ample inlets for fresh air up to the Strand.   Were the wishes of the lovers of the Embankment to be carried out, the writer went on to say, the architectural improvement of the whole of the rest of London would have to be postponed to the one object of accumulating on that Embankment the most numerous and most unbroken series possible of monumental constructions. Somerset House standing on its foundations,—now made painfully public,—and jostled by a neighbour rising from the ground level, would, in the words of the same writer, look rather like a person in a smart Court dress, with his legs encased in rough jack-boots.

The Committee must have been firmly convinced of the superiority of the Carey Street site in the matter of convenience, for it cannot be denied that the claims of the Embankment were presented in a most attractive way in my father's drawings   His perspective view of the river front of the proposed building met with the most flattering criticisms on all hands.

Thus ended the well-fought battle of the sites. A settlement once arrived at, the Law Courts ceased for the time to be one of the burning questions of the day.

My father had at first intended perfecting the scheme shown in the block plan of his report, that being a modification of the plan originally submitted in the competition, but he eventually decided on an entire rearrangement of all the principal blocks, and in his new scheme placed the office wing and the quadrangle which it formed with the main building on the east side instead of on the south, while the central hall was now placed north and south, instead of east and west. There was one conspicuous advantage in the amended scheme, viz that it at once gave the opportunity for a great centre in the Strand front—a feature which it would have been difficult to obtain legitimately with the old arrangement

In August 1870 so much progress had been made that Mr. Ayrton was able to promise to lay upon the table of the House an estimate of preliminary work, so that as much as possible might be done before the meeting of Parliament in the next year.

The foundations were meantime being put in, and the drawings for the superstructure made, and it was hoped that tenders might be sent in in the course of 1871. The preliminary or sketch plans were submitted on 1st January of that year, and were provisionally approved in the following August, but in that word "provisionally" lurked a thousand worries and delays, bickerings and criticisms, parings and cuttings down, so that it was not till 25th March 1873, or a year and three-quarters later, that tenders were actually submitted, and the contract was not signed till 4th February 1874.

During the whole of this period my father was the subject more or less continuously of bitter and personal attacks by the self-elected upholders of the canons of art, while, instead of being supported by the Office of Works, his task was daily made harder and more thankless by their penny-wise economy and persistent red-tapeism.   While irresponsible critics asked for a lofty and sumptuous palace that should bear visibly on its front the imprint of the majesty of the law, the architect had to meet the views of a First Commissioner who professedly regarded and spoke of architecture as a trade of the same dignity as the market-gardener's, and of architects as mere servants who owed a slavish obedience to every utterance from the Office of Works. Unfortunately this quasi-Oriental habit of mind was not accompanied by a correspondingly warm imagination or love of beauty, and in spite of the acknowledged fact that prices were rising in every trade, the hard-and-fast limit of expenditure was rigorously kept to, and the omission of features most vital to the dignity and beauty of the building, no less than to its unity and completeness of arrangement, seemed to give the only possibility of satisfying the official love for false economy.   I allude especially to the central hall, the loss of which would have made the building little better than limbs without a trunk   It was not indeed sacrificed, but it was not for want of suggestions to that effect on the part of the chief official   The design, moreover, does suffer from the want of a tower of grander proportions than that which marks the south-east angle of the present building.

I should be glad to pass over in silence the hostile and unreasonable criticisms which filled the columns of some few of the papers in 1871, albeit emanating chiefly from one or two sources, but they must have been read by thousands, and were no doubt generally accepted without question.   The merits or demerits of the building speak for themselves now, but in those days a few architectural elevations afforded the only food for the critics, and these were often misunderstood, and quite as often not so much as looked at.   It was recognised even at the time that the attack was a good deal personal to the man and not so much against his art, and partly a supreme effort by the anti-Gothic party to prevent the erection of an important building in the style of their abhorrence.

The first, as he was the bitterest opponent, was the late Mr. James Fergusson, who, in letters, in leaders, in the pages of magazines, consistently waged war against the architect, against Gothic, against what he termed mediæval-ism, generally.   To him as to most of the critics the building resolved itself into a Strand façade and a central hall.   For all purposes of criticism the rest of the building did not exist, or was possibly beneath notice.

Mr. Fergusson declared the central hall to be "an imper-forate gloomy vault, which nobody wants but Mr. Street" . . . "It is not a Gothic hall in any true sense of the term either."   . "No Gothic hall of anything like this size and applied to civil uses was vaulted in the Middle Ages."   To call the same erection a gloomy vault, and at the same time a bigger hall than any erected for the same purpose in the Middle Ages seems to show a slight confusion in the mind of the critic.

To an architect or to any one versed in architectural terms, the word "vault" simply means the "vaulted ceiling;" but to the general public it would be calculated to suggest dark and mouldy crypts, wholly or partially underground, and if Mr Fergusson were to be implicitly believed, without a single window.   This is the same gloomy and cavernous cellar in which the opening ceremony took place.   Not a feature of the design which Mr Fergusson stigmatised in such ridiculous terms has been changed   The hall is forty-eight feet wide, eighty feet high, and proportionately long   It has large windows at its north and south ends, and eight very large ones on each side.   It stands clear of buildings all round, and may probably be said to be the lightest hall in Europe, yet all this was shown exactly in the plans from which Mr Fergusson may be supposed to have obtained his information.

Again he complains, Gothic is bad enough, but this is not even Gothic: and why?   Because, he says, no Gothic architect in the Middle Ages would have vaulted it   The criticism is meaningless in itself, but is still more so as coming from a man who, doubtless from strong convictions, spent his life in decrying all mediæval precedent and in prophesying the uprising, or rather the invention, of a nineteenth-century style, eclectic and all-embracing, allowing the fullest use of all the latest inventions, and of every modern appliance and material. It was seemingly a part of his theory of the impossibility of Gothic, remarkable as that style really is for elasticity and power of assimilation, to deny to it the faculty of utilising any improvement posterior to the thirteenth century, even those so obviously unconnected with any particular style as heating and ventilating.

The windows throughout the building were, he declared, to be filled with rich stained glass, the chairs to be high and straight-backed, and, generally, discomfort was to reign supreme.

With regard to the Strand front, Mr. Fergusson expressed himself as follows :—" I have no hesitation in saying 'that it is the meanest design for the principal front of so important and pretentious a building which has been produced in our day." He objected more particularly to the arrangement by which the recessed Central hall was made to form the central feature, and advised that it should be closed up so as to make one face with the rest of the buildings. No long time before he had, I believe, been telling the world that Somerset House would be much improved if the centre were recessed, and the wings brought forward.

From other criticisms couched in more general terms, and smacking rather of the literary than the professional man, I take a few quotations at random, which are a fair sample of the whole —

"The design lacks pure and noble form." . . "Mr. Street has given us a chaos of ill-distributed masses of weak and confused outline." . . "It looks more like a street in a collegiate town—some goodly houses, a church, and a town hall." . . "The general effect of the front is too ecclesiastical" . "Mr Street has written ably on secular Gothic, but he has clearly not mastered it." etc etc

Now what does all this amount to when it is divested of its fine phraseology ? To this, I think : that the writer or writers had just looked at the drawings—had seen that the building did not present one level parapet throughout—that all-desiderated unbroken skyline—that the central hall was not in the exact centre of the site, and that, consequently,

M

"there was not a perfect balance of parts," that a certain
number of pointed window heads were used (arched stone
heads over square openings invariably in the rooms however),
that in some cases window openings did not come exactly
under the centre of the gables, and a few other points of a
similar character.   It was on such merely superficial points
as these, without inquiry into the conditions of internal
structure, which might explain and justify the external
irregularity, that the attack was based.   For all such criticism I can find no other epithet but "ignorant."   What is
the objection which is put in the forefront?   That the building
is too ecclesiastical in style, and that Mr. Street, however
well he may write of secular Gothic, is evidently unable to
rightly use it.   Now let the writer be credited with all that he
deserves ; he has indisputably the merit of having discovered
this distinction without a difference—this secular Gothic as
opposed to, or at least strongly differentiated from, the ecclesiastical form of that style.

But in what, to the mind of the writer, did the difference lie?   Difference of plan, difference in degree of ornamentation, there naturally must be.   The purposes of a
house make it impossible that it should bear any resemblance
in form to a church, the same is in a lesser degree true of a
hall ; but where does the difference in style make its appearance?   Is Westminster Hall or is the hall at Eltham
Gothic?   If not, wherein is the Central hall of the Law
Courts Gothic? for it bears precisely the same relation to the
church work of its date as the other two halls do to that of
their date,—that is to say, the art is identical, but the circumstances are different.   Enough, however, about this great
discovery, for the distinction, if never professedly given up,
was at any rate put very much into the background.

The Strand front was compared by one gentleman to a
group of almshouses.   The most charitable supposition is that,
not being habituated to the use of a scale, he had got confused.   The same also may be said of Sir George Bowyer, who
regretted that the front was so squat.   Does it seem squat
in reality? and what would the occupants of the upper floors
have said to the endless flights of steps which Sir George

Bowyer's impossibly tall ideal would have entailed on them ?
Some one else complained that the main entrance to the building was by one little church-like door.   Seventeen feet wide,
answered my father   No, no more seventeen than seventy,
retorted the critic , it is only twelve feet wide, and is divided
by a central pier into two openings of five feet apiece. This
explanation made it obvious that the intelligent critic had been
looking at the doors into the central hall, a long way back,
while the real entrance had been seemingly too large for his
visual capacities, or had at any rate quite escaped his notice

Let me touch on another point in which "ignorance" is
strikingly manifested   I mean the implied necessity of
regularity of elevation without any regard to plan.   Now the
new Law Courts were meant to accommodate people and
fulfil needs of the most varying descriptions.   There were
primarily the Courts, the judges' rooms in connection with
them, consulting rooms, offices in immediate connection with
Courts, offices not necessarily so near, and so forth.   All
this does not signify.   If the building has an office wing, it
must be carefully assimilated to the other part ; no part of
the exterior is to show what is inside.   It is merely an outer
shell.   Windows must be in the centre of gables even if it
involves a partition wall coming into the middle of one ;
regularity is everything, and all in all ; the beauty of truth
and usefulness nothing.   The examples held up for imitation
were sufficiently ludicrous.   The town hall at Brussels, a
very picturesque but fussy building, and obviously deficient
in dignity ; the town halls at Louvain and Ghent, beautiful buildings in themselves, though much over-decorated,
but quite small and by no means admitting of being multiplied indefinitely ; all, moreover, town halls, the very name
one would have thought predicating a use, and therefore an
outward appearance, as different as possible from that of
Courts of Law.   One large room was an essential, so that
the regularity, instead of being a sham, was a piece of truthful designing.   Still more unintelligible was the suggestion
of the Cloth Hall at Ypres as a model ; one of the most perfectly beautiful buildings in Europe without a doubt, but a
cloth hall and not a house of justice, and presenting on its

upper floor one great unbroken chamber throughout. These were, however, not the only suggestions. Mr. Sidney Smirke gravely cautioned the architect to keep the Flavian amphitheatre before his mind's eye as a model. To this Mr. E. W. Pugin retorted that he surely must have meant the pyramids ; but Mr. Pugin himself had a suggestion to make, viz. that the architect would do well to take the Granville Hotel at Ramsgate as his guide. He laid down the law in the most decided way, so much so that the general public must have felt that it was very stupid of them not to have realised before that he was the head of his profession, and should rightly have had the work. When my father was first appointed, Mr. Pugin was so good as to approve. " I have little doubt," he was pleased to say, " that Mr. Street is perfectly competent to improve and perfect his ground-plan ; but I have far less doubt about Mr. Barry's incapacity for mending his elevation." This is rather hard on Mr. Barry, but my father's new and vastly superior design for the Strand front drew from him criticisms which, always humorously written, were equally funny in being so much *de haut en bas.* I am afraid the Strand front never did approximate to the high ideal which he had formed, and his original advocacy, or rather approval, of the selection of my father must have stuck very much in his throat. All the critics united in condemning the profusion of detail and ornament which were scattered over the face of the building, even those who held up as an example the simple grace of the Belgian town halls. Where, it may be asked, is all this detail ? I think it may be confidently said that there is no great public building, new or old, with so little. Compare it with Louvain or Brussels, or with the Houses of Parliament at Westminster ; where, indeed, is it possible to find window mouldings more simple and restrained, a more sparing use of carving or enrichment ?

I return to Mr. Fergusson, who, determined that the nineteenth century should not have to admit its inability to invent a style, had, after much rumination, had the good fortune to light on what he termed a growing, living style, one which would be perfectly suitable here, and which would be handled well by a hundred architects whom he could name.

" It is sometimes called Italian," he said   So then his wonderful discovery meant neither more nor less than deliberately transplanting an exotic and laying it in here by the heels in a cold and uncongenial soil.   One thinks how wise M. Taine was ; he shuddered to see Somerset House shivering on the banks of the foggy Thames, and when he came to Westminster Abbey exclaimed, " Here is the true style of the country, serious and earnest, capable of battling with fogs and storms ' " Mr. Fergusson gave the new heaven-sent style the best credentials · " It can use either pillars or pinnacles as may be required ; it admits of towers and spires or domes ; it can either indulge in plain walls or pierce them with innumerable windows ; it knows no guide but common sense : it owns no master but true taste "   Now every single word of this might at least as well have been said of Gothic.   Mr Fergusson then condemned Gothic because it *was* Gothic, and my father's design because it was in that hated style, without any particular reference to the individual design.   Lord Grimthorpe (then Mr. E B. Denison) condemned it because, as he said, it was Streetian (a very sufficient reason to him), because it showed the outcome of foreign study, and of the outcry for a new style, because it was not slavishly mediæval.   One critic, who objected to the design because it lacked unity, regularity, majesty, had two years before expressed his objection to all the drawings submitted in the competition because they aimed at making one great building of what should have been, and in the Middle Ages would have been, a group of several.

One wonders what is the way to set about inventing a new style   The forms and methods of construction have been tested and proved.   If we are to invent new ones we must be content with something inferior.   To be radically new, they must be radically bad.   An arch is the most convenient form of bridging an opening , a pointed arch is the most convenient and adaptable form ; an arch of an entirely new shape could not but be hideous both in its shape and from its comparative uselessness.   Mr. Fergusson said : " Let the architect leave this to the engineer."   It is for him (the architect) " to construct ornamentally, and to ornament his construction;" but how does that dictum concern style?

Gothic, so far from being indigenous of the soil, seemed in his eyes so ill adapted for our needs or our conditions, and so inadaptable, that one would almost imagine it to have been imported from some other planet. But are our climate and our conditions so different from what they used to be? We have learnt to need more, doubtless, and we have also learnt concurrently how to gratify those needs; but Gothic lends itself in the fullest and most liberal way to the most complete satisfaction of our latest requirements, though Mr. Fergusson would not have it so. This is what he said: "The Houses of Parliament are two centuries nearer our time than Mr. Street's building, and thus incorporate all the improvements that were introduced during those two hundred years." It is hardly to be believed that this can have been written seriously. Why did he not go a step further and say, as some one suggested, that none of the improvements in legal procedure could be admitted into such a monastic edifice? "We shall be reminded of manorial and baronial privileges, of gallows and villeinage, and all the *bric-à-brac* of the Middle Ages."

The building, of course, was not without its warm adherents in public, while private expressions of sympathy and admiration were without number. The former—gentlemen of acknowledged taste and knowledge like Mr. Ruskin, Mr. Edmund Sharpe, Mr. E. W. Godwin, Mr. Paley—showed that Gothic had a dignity and a majesty eminently fitted to express that of the law, that it was a revival, but founded on the needs of our climate, and not necessarily to be taken up in exactly the same state in which it had been left. Its animation had simply been suspended; it could grow to meet the manifold wants of modern times, and would show itself possessed of a flexibility unknown to many of the later growths.

What my father's object had been in designing the Strand front, and, indeed, the whole building, as he had, was justly and clearly explained. He had tried, or it had been natural to him, to make his exterior not merely contain the interior,

but explain it and express its uses.   First and most important was of course the plan ; this once completed so as
to meet what was required, then was the time for turning to
the elevation.

The building, as it has come from his hands, explains
itself.   To the east you have what is obviously a wing of
offices, distinct from the rest, but connected with it.   Westward is a symmetrical block, the nucleus of which is the
central hall, with its dependencies grouped round it   The
building is thus roughly divisible into two parts, but these
two parts are ingeniously and beautifully welded into one
group by the entrance to the office quadrangle.   There is
then to the west the central hall with its wings, next the
entrance to the office quadrangle, also with wings, but with
that to the east the more important, and terminating in a
tower, and lastly, the office block, forming a whole by itself.
There are then in a sense two centres, though that to the
east is quite subservient to the main centre ; the result is
that in the narrow Strand thoroughfare, when the passer-by
looks up, he is confronted not by a slice of a monotonous
front, but a piece of building which in itself makes a satisfying whole.   The front towards Clement's Inn, as being more
open, has been more regularly treated   On the subject of
his design for the Strand front, I quote a few pregnant
words from a published letter of Professor Roger Smith :—

"His observation also points out that Mr Street has well understood this canon of street architecture, viz that a large building in a
street will be seen as a whole when seen from up or down the street,
but will be extremely foreshortened, and must be designed so as to
look well when so foreshortened.   The observation of 'Point of
Sight' (the writer of a letter on the subject) points out a second
canon of street architecture, which may be stated thus   a large
building in a street will be seen only piecemeal when seen from the
opposite side of the street, and must be designed so as to look well
when seen in detail.   Both these principles are sound, and both of
them have been conformed to by Mr. Street in designing his Strand
front."

Here are well-measured, thoughtful, practical words,
giving tersely and clearly the rationale of this design, and

worth a whole world of flimsy sentiments about dignities, unities, lines which carry on the eye, and the like.

I have already said that my father was engaged from the middle of 1871 till early in 1873 in finally settling his arrangements so as to meet every requirement, and in endeavouring to cut his building down to the hard-and-fast limit. However, as it happened, prices continued to rise throughout these two years, and consequently when the tenders were sent in, the lowest, that of Messrs Bull, was found to be somewhat over the amount which Mr Ayrton considered requisite. In spite of remonstrances both inside and outside the House, the First Commissioner made the continued reduction of this unhappy building a personal matter. He allowed himself to speak in insulting terms of the architect, explaining, for the edification of the House, that they ought to force their servant strictly to obey orders at any price. A more false and unreal piece of economy than that on which Mr. Ayrton was insisting can hardly be conceived, when it is remembered that all this time the interest on the £800,000 paid for the site was simply being lost, while rates and taxes were being paid to the amount of £9500 per annum. Nineteen tenders were sent in on 25th March, and Messrs. Bull, who submitted the lowest, undertook to erect the building in Portland stone for £744,000, with a further sum of £804 for the fittings of each of the eighteen courts. This sum, added to the £31,500 spent on the foundations, made a total of £790,000, whereas the limit for the fabric had been put at three-quarters of a million.

Deaf to all arguments, the First Commissioner again returned the drawings to my father for still further reconsideration, meaning reduction. This resulted finally in the contract being signed on 4th February 1874 for £680,000 Messrs. Bull therein undertook to hand over the eastern or office block to the authorities in August 1877, and to complete the entire contract in six years and a half. My father had, for his part, been forced to undertake his share of this more than usually onerous work for a sum considerably under the recognised fee of an architect,—a piece of economy which, let us hope, commended itself to Mr. Ayrton's constituents, as it certainly can have affected no one else except the victim.

In the design, as it went first into the hands of the contractors for the purposes of tendering, there was very little carving or enrichment; but the building, as it was finally contracted for, had less by £15,000 worth—an amount which, spread over such a mass of work, was little enough in itself, but of which every pound's worth would have told, and the omission cannot but have meant a direct loss of effect.

Hitherto the history of the new Law Courts has been on one side the record of skill in surmounting difficulties, thoroughness in details, and unequalled forbearance under the greatest provocation; on the other, of misrepresentations and attacks, where even personal hostility was not wanting, and of a cold, unsympathetic, petty treatment by a Government who were content to lose the substance in grasping at the delusive shadow of economy

It has ever been the prerogative of the British public to bully its architects. Wren, at St. Paul's, could have said something to this. Witness, too, the building of Regent Street, or, later, of the Palace of Westminster, but I doubt if the architect in any of these cases had to bear as much as my father had, or would have borne so much in silence as he did

It is possible that my father had to some extent to suffer for the sins of his predecessors. There is no doubt that, owing probably to the number of small, ill-defined contracts, the Houses of Parliament did very greatly exceed the amount which had been settled on, and nothing could persuade people that the same would not happen with the new Law Courts, whereas, now, there was one definite contract in the place of many, and a mass of details thoroughly completed at an early stage instead of their being deferred till over-late, as had been the case at Westminster. That the public were wrong in anticipating a great excess, or indeed any excess, over the contract amount, the sequel will show.

Before concluding, I ought to mention that the first stone, or, to be quite accurate, the first brick, was laid by the contractor and his wife, in a perfectly private and informal way, in May 1874   It is usual with a building which has the least claim to importance, that the laying of the first stone should be attended with some little attempt at ceremonial, but probably fresh scruples of economy interfered to prevent such a totally unremunerative outlay.

Public opinion, which had been so much exercised on this subject, was, after a brief space, again directed to it by the discovery or the suggestion that Temple Bar was in a dangerous state, owing, as it was alleged, to the proceedings of the contractor for the Law Courts   Perhaps it is hardly necessary to say that, if danger there was, the contractor was perfectly innocent in the matter.   The substitution of solid concrete for rubbish immediately against the foundations of the Bar was not likely to make it unsafe, and, as a matter of fact, all that was done was much more calculated to prolong the existence of that venerable structure than to shorten it.   I have heard my father say many a time that the whole scare was in a great measure groundless, and that the crack which created so much dismay was an old one, the filling in of which had been either accidentally or purposely displaced. The Bar, however, cut adrift on its north side and dwarfed into insignificance by the lofty pile which was rising out of the forest of scaffolding almost immediately over it, looked sadly out of place, and its reputation would no doubt have suffered more by its retention than it has by being taken away ; for, whereas its memory is now cherished with a certain regret as one among many of the relics of the past which the utilitarianism or indifference of to-day has sacrificed, it would, in the contrary case, have had to bear some measure of the odium which the present obstruction so justly incurs.

In any case, it is quite untrue to say that my father was anxious for its removal.   From his point of view it would have been a most useful foil, and would have served to give scale to his own building, and he could consequently have had no possible objection to its being retained.

The history of the Law Courts for some years is a chronicle of bricks and mortar, of workmen to be counted by their hundreds, of machinery in unequalled profusion,

of scaffolding of unprecedented ingenuity, of order reigning
in apparent confusion, and of a thousand springs and checks
working with the regulaity of clockwork. Such is the
record of the next three years and a half till July 1877.
Then came a sudden interruption which threatened to throw
the whole of the complicated machine out of gear. This
was occasioned by the claim made by the masons for a reduction in the working hours, and the strike consequent on
the refusal of the contractors to entertain their demands.
Messrs. Bull, with praiseworthy pluck and promptitude, finding the strikers resolute, made immediate arrangements for
the importation of stone-masons from Germany, Italy, Canada,
and the United States.

The strike was not without its stirring and dramatic
elements. The imported workmen were at first starting lodged
in the vicinity of the site, but not actually on it. This
arrangement soon proved to be impracticable, as the men
were subjected to frequent attacks on their way to and from
the works at the hands of the Trades Unionists or their
rough hangers-on The lower stories of the main block were
accordingly made to supply a rough species of accommodation, and the foreign workmen were permanently lodged there,
and were from that time in no way obliged, unless so disposed,
to quit the security of the site.

Great complaints were made by the strikers of unfair-
ness, of hitting below the belt, and the like ; and it must
doubtless have been a great disappointment to them to see
their well-concerted scheme so easily and so successfully
foiled The strike itself formally terminated on 18th March
1878, after having lasted seven months and a half ; but men
had been dropping in by twos and threes for a long time,
and there were at the date of the termination of the strike
quite a number of Englishmen engaged. Some hundred
and fifty German masons were retained on the works till
the stonework was complete. They were employed in a
separate shed, and continued to work on terms of friendly
rivalry with their old antagonists. The contract had provided
that the eastern or Chancery Lane block, which was to be
occupied mainly by masters, registrars, chief clerks, etc,

should be handed over complete to the Government in August 1877, but it was not actually done till April 1878, various unavoidable causes having contributed to the delay. Owing to an unfortunate difference of opinion between Government and the contractors, the accounts for the main building at the moment of writing still await settlement; but the accounts for the eastern block were settled shortly after the completion of the building, and the strictness and exactitude with which the amount provided for in the contract was adhered to—a matter, as all who are experienced in such things know well, of immense difficulty and very rare attainment in so large an undertaking—bore a mute but striking testimony not less to my father's business capacities than to the earnestness and thoroughness with which he had considered every detail of the work.

The strike once settled, the contractors had no adverse influences, except those of weather, to contend against till the completion of the works.

It has often been said before that the individual attention bestowed by the architect, not only on the larger questions but on details, on every detail, I might almost say, in this vast work, was something which would be incredible, were it not that there are many witnesses to testify to it, the writer among others. I think I may say without exaggeration that there is not a single feature in the building which he did not accurately draw, not a piece of carving which he did not sketch or touch in the clay, not a single moulding of which he did not give the full size, perhaps hardly a chamfer or splay the angle and depth of which he did not decide.

Some writers have almost hinted that there was something morbid in my father's love for variation and variety, that he loved them for themselves as ends, not means; but I think that any one who looks at this building thoughtfully will see that it is not so. Immense variety there is, but not in juxtaposition. To take an instance: Every court differs from every other; each roof is a single design in itself, and borrowed from no other. In the principal rooms again every mantelpiece of any richness is a distinct design; but surely variety of this kind implies no more than the proper use of materials, such as wood and stone. They are not run in moulds like terra cotta ; if the fancy is there, let it run riot where it has the scope But I have said that this variety does not occur in features which are in juxtaposition. You cannot see two courts at once, you cannot see two mantelpieces at once, the eye is consequently not worried by a want of restfulness in the design, because each *coup d'œil* comprises an organic and harmonious whole , but it is spared that aching sense of weariness which the constant reiteration of one ornament or of one feature is sure to give.

Now let us take a larger instance . Take the Strand front, take the western front, or indeed any of them. Are there not here masses which balance masses, not with exact regularity or with absolute similarity of detail, but with great and sufficient resemblance of general outline and arrangement ? Can it be denied ?

The most regularly arranged front is of course the western, for the reason that it is the only one which can be seen in its entirety. Its little differences in, detail give it life and vitality ; its general symmetry of massing gives it repose and dignity. Quite as well balanced, but not so much as a whole, because it can by no possibility be seen as a whole, is the principal front, that to the Strand. This may perhaps be said to be composed of two parts ; not of two parts which are distinct from one another, but of two parts which overlap each other, and have some portion in common ; of two parts which, seen in abrupt perspective— the only possible view—do form a whole, which is a masterpiece of inspiration and reasoning Many have been the criticisms on this front, various the suggestions, mostly or all by amateurs, or by gentlemen who were prepared to find fault with any style not that which they themselves particularly affected. It has been said that the tower at the Fleet Street end should have had its exact counterpart opposite St. Clement Danes. A truly delightful suggestion, and one which, if carried out, would have the effect of shortening the front one-quarter in appearance ! What an opportunity was lost when the clock tower at Westminster was made so

dissimilar to the Victoria Tower! and yet, in spite of this
astounding freak, the Houses of Parliament are generally
condemned as being over-symmetrical.

One word about the illustrations of the building which
have from time to time appeared. These have in many
cases—nay, it may almost be said, invariably—been taken
from utterly impossible points of view, denoting in the artist
a power of seeing not merely through deal planks, but even
through blocks of houses. There are strong objections to
such a proceeding which must be patent to every one who
considers the matter, but there is a convenience in so doing
which is quite sufficient to outweigh the objections so long
—and this is the important point,—so long as the mistake
is not made of criticising the design as it appears under
conditions which were rightly never considered and will
never in reality exist. The mistake, unfortunately, is only
too often made, and even the artist himself again and again
stands convicted of ignorance of the first principles of design
by deliberately basing his criticisms, whether favourable or
unfavourable matters not, on an assumption which deprives
them of all application, and scatters to the wind every
element of value they might otherwise have possessed.

It is true that the building itself is now in evidence ·
impossible points of view are things of the past ; but prejudices notoriously die hard, and such is our nature that
most of us, having been told that the front lacks oneness,
assume that it does, and when we have occasion to pass the
building, do not trouble ourselves to see whether personal
observation verifies the criticism or the reverse. Suggestions
as to the puniness of the great entrance, the squatness and
unimpressiveness of the whole pile, are bits of highly imaginative description, which seem to be sufficiently refuted by
the reality.

The amount of actual physical and mental work which
my father underwent in the execution of his task must have
been a severe strain even to so robust a constitution, but he
would have been more than equal to it had not his work
been embittered by constant worry, the result, I feel bound
to say, of an ill-advised economy on the part of Govern-

ment in letting the work to a firm which had no inexhaustible funds to fall back upon, and for an amount which really was inadequate for the profitable carrying out of the work. My father was consequently harassed day and night by his efforts to get the work through without a stoppage.

He was successful, but it cost him his life. He may indeed be said to have died in the service of his country just as really as the soldier who falls with his face to the enemy. For years he worked without recognition from the Bar or from Government, and it remained for death to bring about a public expression of the value of his services.

CHAPTER IX

JUST about the time that the competitions for the Law Courts and National Gallery were announced, a move was being made in Bristol towards getting funds for the rebuilding of the cathedral nave, and some time in 1866 my father was called in to advise the Committee thereon. He made a careful examination of the site, and his report was laid before a public meeting in June of the following year. The unusual character of the nave, which was afterwards erected from his designs, makes it interesting to see what his reasons were for the course he took. To make a brief *résumé* of the report.

It appears that when he came to examine the ground, he found some remains of the original church, dating from 1142, still in place. These showed the chapter-house, the outer angles of the north transept, the south wall of the south transept, and the south-west angle of the south aisle. These fixed points were, from the importance of their positions, sufficient to give the complete dimensions of all that part of the original scheme. The probability is, that this church was still in its entirety when, early in the fourteenth century, Abbot Knowle began his work of complete demolition and partial rebuilding, to which it was now contemplated putting the finishing touch.

Abbot Knowle began, after the manner of these days, by simply pulling down the old choir, and then building up another entirely independent of it. This new choir is the one still existing,—a work of great originality of conception, and full of the evidences of the genuine constructive skill of its architect. Its unusual features are the uniform height

of the choir proper and its aisles, and the omission of triforium and clerestory, which is a natural consequence of such
an arrangement. Whatever may have been the motive for so
complete a departure from the stereotyped form of a cathedral church, the result certainly justifies it ; for we have here
an interior which looks both dignified and spacious in spite of
there being a good deal to reprobate in the detail. One possible explanation of the design is that it was thought desirable
to retain the central tower—an unusual piece of conservatism,
— and that the church was consequently strictly limited in
height, or it may have been that the whole design was
simply an ingenious way of getting a church of large area
at much less than the usual cost.

The choir completed, a similar course was evidently to
have been followed with the nave, but the work never got
beyond the earlier stages. My father discovered the foundations of the new north wall that was to have been, with an
arrangement of buttresses precisely similar to that of the
choir, and he also found a portion of the south-west angle
of the south aisle. The fragments of the Norman south
wall, never removed, bore mute but convincing testimony to
the sudden stoppage of the works at this stage. Subsequently to the building of the new choir, the old central
tower was taken down and rebuilt.

The fourteenth-century foundations showed so incontest-
ably what the outlines of the nave were intended to be, and
the similarity of the size and arrangement of the buttresses
to those of the choir pointed so distinctly to a general
scheme similar to that of the completed work, that my father
felt that there was really no course open to him but to
build on the old foundations and on the same lines as the
choir, and to make the distinction between the old and new
work in the detail, such as a greater elaboration of the
mouldings, a variety in the window-traceries and in the
character of the sculpture, and a different treatment of the
groining. He also made fresh designs for all the monumental recesses which, following the old model, he introduced under the aisle windows. The only additions to the
old scheme were the north porch—placed in the same posi-

N

tion as the old Norman one—and the western towers. The
treatment of the west end was necessarily hypothetical.
Still, my father's opinion that the probabilities were certainly against there having been western towers in the
original scheme, did not deter him from including them in
his own, because he thought they would be specially valuable
in a building which was both unlike the ordinary cathedral
type, and on an unusually small scale, as expressing the
fact of its being a cathedral. The unique and effective
vaulting in the choir aisles was reproduced in those of the
nave, but with considerable improvements. I am tempted
to quote from a letter which appeared in one of the Bristol
papers, wherein a comparison was drawn between the character of the nave and that of the choir, because, though
rather ludicrously fanciful, it does not give altogether a bad
idea of the difference between the old and new work. It
runs as follows :—

"The construction of the nave may be regarded as the providing
of a husband to the widowed, or perhaps virgin, choir. A comparison of the details of the choir with that of the new work of the
nave will show this. The choir is essentially female in its character
and expression. Dean Eliot is wont to say to his friends : 'I have
always regarded the arcading of this choir with its graceful lancet
arches, rising in unbroken sweep from floor to apex, as the most
perfect realisation of female grace and virgin purity yet achieved in
architecture ;' and the Dean is right, and Street is right too. He
was restricted to the style of architecture of the choir ; he has complied with the restriction, and has saved his reputation as a poet by
simply changing his sex. Out of the rib he took from the female he
has made a male ; every member of the one is to be found in the
other, and yet no member is precisely alike in both ; every nerve
and muscle, every vein and artery, every bone and every articulation
is in each, and yet not alike ; the one are those of the female, the
other of the male structure."

The work was commenced in 1867, and for some years
progressed surely and peaceably, till in 1876 the placing
of the statues of the four doctors—SS. Jerome, Gregory,
Augustine, and Ambrose—in the niches which had been
prepared for them in the north porch, the exclusive gift of
Mr. W. K. Wait, raised an outcry among a section of the

townspeople A meeting was held at Colston Hall, at which incredibly strong language was used, though strong protests were made by Dr. Perceval and others against the outrageous character of the proceedings A memorial was thereupon drawn up and presented to the Dean and Chapter, in which the removal of the four figures was asked for, and special exception was taken to the figures of the Virgin and Child over the door. In the words of this temperate memorial, our Lord was said to be " seated on the goddess, predominant above all the saints, the object of special worship and adoration."

There was no satisfying the Protestants when once they had drawn blood. To doctrinal objections were added purely architectural ones, and the whole was now condemned, where a short time before only a part had been called in question. One gentleman asserted that the architect had gone out of his way to make the "gateway as uninviting as possible, and has certainly given us a signally debased specimen of architecture." The good taste in thus characterising the special gift of a most munificent donor is no less notable than the conjunction of such adjectives with the particular piece of work. Others who may reasonably be supposed to know better hold this porch to be amongst the most completely successful and beautiful pieces of work that the architects of the Gothic revival have given us The Dean and Chapter determined (*diss* Norris and Wade, to the former of whom the inception of the whole scheme was chiefly due, and to whose exertions and offerings the Building Committee were largely indebted for their success hitherto) that the offending statues should be removed, and informed Mr. Wait of their resolution, the Building Committee having already refused to move them unless ·legally compelled to do so. Without more ado a gang of men made their appearance one morning and proceeded to the defacing of Mr. Wait's sumptuous and beautiful gift. " The figures," the Dean courteously said, " will be retained for the disposition of the Committee." If, however, the evidence of an anonymous correspondent of the *Pall Mall Gazette* is to be credited, at least one figure, that of the

Virgin—and presumably the Child—would have reached the Committee in small pieces. The figures of the four doctors now adorn the tower of one of the many churches which my father built for Sir Tatton Sykes in the Wolds.

A short time after this event the Dean wrote to my father to say that " the substitution of Scripture characters for those which had been removed must be taken as a *sine quâ non.*" My father's own position and views are well defined by two letters which I quote below ; one to the Dean, and the other to the *Guardian* paper.   To the Dean he wrote :—

" When it came to be a question as to what figures should be introduced, there was a discussion in the usual way with the executive, and it was finally decided to erect the statues and subject to which you have so great an objection.   The names of the saints to be represented were never given or suggested by me in any report, nor did you, as Dean, at any time between 1867 and this day ask me a single question about them, or my intentions as to them ; yet, when you first saw the drawings of the nave in 1867, the six figures of the saints were very distinctly shown on the plans, and when I exhibited a large drawing at the Royal Academy, these statues were equally conspicuous.   This drawing was photographed, and circulated extensively, in Bristol, and I myself frequently saw copies of it in shop windows near the cathedral.   I cannot doubt that you, too, saw it. But you will excuse my saying that, seeing with what singular care you avoided discussing anything connected with the new works with me, I should have thought it a grave impertinence to ask your opinion of any of the details.   I gathered from your manner that you did not much like the work being undertaken, nor cared to make yourself in any way responsible for the character of any portion of it.   You left all the responsibility, both for the cost and execution of my designs, to the Committee.   When the subjects for the figures were settled, I never thought even of consulting you, and I should have felt certain, if I had thought about it at all, that after you had sanctioned six indefinite figures of saints, you would never have objected if we put four figures of such universally acknowledged worthies as SS. Gregory, Augustine, Ambrose, and Jerome, and a subject from the life of our blessed Lord Himself, instead of that from the life of St. Augustine.   I am bound to say that I think Mr. Redfern, the sculptor, was injudicious in making so much of some of the insignia of the four doctors.   They were finished and fixed during my absence from England.   Had I seen them before they were sent down, I should have been inclined to ask him to omit the cardinal's hat and papal tiara, and these alterations could be made even now if the statues have not been damaged (as I am informed they have been) by the careless and hasty way in which your removal of them was effected."

In the *Guardian* my father wrote :—

"The statues of the four doctors were not selected by me, nor ordered until I had received authority to order them   The designs of the figures were not mine, but those of the sculptor, Mr. Redfern, who executed them."

He then supports the choice of subjects and their treatment by a reference to symbolism in general :—

"It is," he goes on, 'a more generally interesting question, I think, whether or no the usual dresses and symbols of saints are properly to be criticised as being 'both doctrinally and historically objectionable.' . . . I do not gather anywhere what the doctrinal objection to the symbols ordinarily used in figures of the four doctors may be, but certainly, if there is any such objection, I should be very sorry to use them.   I have seen them only to-day on statues introduced within a few years in four niches in the south porch of Gloucester Cathedral, where the Dean cannot be charged with any desire to favour Popery, and where the bishop is the same as at Bristol, and the architect Sir G Gilbert Scott.   They have been used for hundreds of years over a great part of Europe, and certainly during the last seventy years have been introduced without any such intention in scores of instances, either in stained glass or sculpture, and (so far as I know) without serious objection on the part of any one.   The historical objection appears to me to be equally untenable, unless for the future we are all to be bound to a purely realistic treatment of all figures and subjects introduced into any kind of church decoration.   For myself, I do not think that reverence for our blessed Lord's person would be at all aided, if each artist represented Him as he thinks it possible that in reality He appeared. .   . The conventional representation of Him, clothed in the accepted attributes of sovereignty, is, I venture to think, even if historically inaccurate (as it certainly is), far more reverent

"So with the saints.   No one supposes when St. Michael or St. George, or scores of other saints, are represented in dresses and armour which they never wore, that a real historical blunder has been committed.   A cope or vestment decorated with patterns never thought of before the fifteenth century cannot certainly have been used by a bishop or priest who lived in the seventh, but the object of the representation of such vestments is not, and was never supposed to be, to give an exact picture of the man as he lived, but to show—as it does clearly—what the office was which he filled.   So in the case of the four doctors, it is said to be 'historically' inaccurate to give St. Gregory a tiara, seeing that he never wore one ; the only object being to show that he was Pope, as to which fact there is no dispute, and of which office there is no other symbol so conveniently represented or so universally understood. In the case of St. Jerome, it is true, there may be disputes as to whether the office he occupied was certainly that now held by cardinals or not. I suppose the College of Cardinals would affirm that it was, and it was hardly for Mr. Redfern to decide that question against their view and against the consenting custom of the painters and sculptors of the last five centuries. Many of your readers will agree with me, I hope, in believing that the study of Christian iconography is not only very interesting, but may also be made very useful in a religious way. Take the extreme case of an allegory like that of St. Christopher, and is it not very narrow and blind to see no virtue and no beauty in its most matter-of-fact representation on the walls of old churches ? and, undoubtedly, the symbols of saints have often a real value, either of a historical or a figurative kind. St. Ambrose's scourge has the former, and, to my mind, St. Augustine's burning heart the latter. Those who wish to get rid of all sculpture of figures in our buildings are right in objecting to all unhistorical representations or symbolical attributes. These once swept away, they would have reduced all single figures to a dead level of similarity ; and when we could not tell who was meant to be represented, we should hardly care to have the representation. I am not ashamed to say that, whether in a new or in an old work, the details of the religious iconography are not those which interest me the least, and I view with real dread any serious attempt to deprive us of all but so-called historical and realistic representations. The religious conventions of many ages of often very devout artists are worth more than the latest conceit of the nineteenth century, and I trust you will allow me space for this protest against any attempt to make us give up the former in favour of the latter.

"In the case of the Bristol sculptures, the Dean has stated that I had regretted what had been done. This is true ; but it was because a degree of prominence appeared to me to have been given by the sculptor to all the insignia which was unnecessary, and, to some extent, apparently aggressive. I thought and said at once that this effect might be modified to a large extent ; and Mr. Redfern very kindly acquiesced in my suggestion. But then it appeared that the Dean of Bristol's objection was not really to the symbols and apparel carved on the persons of the four doctors, but to any representation of their persons at all ; and, that being so, it was obviously impossible to satisfy the objections even by the largest modification of details."

As a natural result of the arbitrary conduct of the majority in the Chapter, the Building Committee, who had worked together so long and so successfully, issued a statement explaining the impossibility, under the circumstances, of continuing to act, inasmuch as there was no guarantee that other parts of the fabric might not be arbitrarily mutilated in the same way. For month after month everything seemed to be at a deadlock; but it was clear to every one that the almost complete church could not be allowed to stand there permanently in its unfinished state as a monument of party bitterness. Funds were eventually collected sufficient for the purpose of so far completing the fabric as to admit of the nave being used for public worship

In October 1877, a year and a half after the resignation of the Committee, things were far enough advanced for the opening ceremony to take place. A more unfortunate ending to what had prospered so greatly at every stage but the last there never was. Those who had been most instrumental in getting the work started were, as was only natural, absent from the ceremony which, as it were, crowned the edifice which they had built; and my father, who did attend, did so with very mixed feelings, in spite of the sincere satisfaction he felt in the success of the work as a piece of architecture, for he missed the familiar faces of those—his whilom fellow-workers—with whom his sympathy had never been deeper than at that moment.

It was something like a year before the Bristol Committee first consulted him that he made the acquaintance of Sir Tatton Sykes, for whom, in the next few years, he was to do as large a number of works probably as any architect has ever had to do for a single client. His first visit to Sledmere was in 1865, and on his way there he visited Beverley again.

"Here I had an hour to spare, which I spent in the minster—a glorious poem in stone—now turned into the saddest prose by a Simeon Trustee Vicar. I never saw anything more disheartening. One dreams of noble churches nobly served, and when one comes across such a church, one finds it being used by a man who probably loathes every moulding in it as a silent protest against the vulgar idleness of his mode of using it."

If my father was disheartened at Beverley, he had the satisfaction of finding in the Master of Sledmere a client who was as anxious as he could have been himself, not only to give every village a building where the people could meet for public worship, but such a building as should be an incentive to worship, and should, by the purity and beauty of its architecture and the completeness of its arrangements, insensibly affect for good those who were gathered together within its walls.   This is what our old-time architects did, and what, I think, my father also succeeded in doing.

I am reminded of what the late headmaster of Uppingham told me about his own chapel which had been opened not long before this time   He was showing it to the present Bishop of St. Alban's (Dr. Claughton), and the words " consecrated building " somehow came up in the course of conversation.   Mr. Thring explained that the chapel was not consecrated, whereupon Dr Claughton turned to him and, putting his hand on his shoulder, said, " Never mind, Mr. Thring, never mind   It's a holy building."   The chapel is indeed a work of unusual grace and dignity   Its windows are rather richly traceried, and are set equally all along the wall between buttresses which, as a combination of strength and delicacy, are the perfection of their kind   Two or three days before the opening, when my father was paying his last visit to the works, he was standing with Mr. Thring looking at the chapel; and the latter, speaking of the language of architecture, told him that he must say, though it were to his face, that the building which he had given them spoke the language of truth if ever building did.   " Yes," answered my father ; " you let me build a good wall."   These words impressed Mr. Thring greatly ; and, indeed, they are an epitome of the differences between a good and beautiful and truthful style and one which is the reverse of all these.

My father's skill as a restorer, his intuitive perception of the right method in each case, had resulted in many successful works of the kind.   It was in Ireland, where he had already done a considerable amount of work for Lord Bessborough and others, that his great opportunity was to come This was the restoration of the older of the two cathedrals of

Dublin, Christ Church or, as it was formerly called, Holy Trinity.   The state of this church had long been a standing disgrace to the town, and its squalid meanness became all the more noticeable when private liberality had restored to the sister church—St. Patrick's—a semblance of its former beauty.   My father had been originally called in in 1868 to advise the Dean and Chapter as to the restoration of all that part of the church which was west of the transepts, but with the passing of the Irish Church Act all hope of getting subscriptions sufficient for so large an undertaking seemed at an end, and for some time no further steps were taken   The Duke of Leinster then took the matter up, and my father was instructed by him to make plans showing how the choir might best be restored to its original state ; the rehabilitation of the nave my father had estimated to cost £16,500, and the work on the choir he now put at £14,500   These amounts are very small indeed compared with what was ultimately spent ; but it must be remembered that they represented simply what was necessary for making the church at all fit for use, while, on the other hand, the works when carried out were, by the desire of the donor, treated in the most expensive way in order to make absolutely certain of preserving all the old work intact and without removal   A scheme for a synod house, which it was at that time intended to place on the site of the old Conventual buildings on the south side of the cathedral, made a further addition of £15,000 to the proposed outlay.

It was at this juncture, in March 1871, when things looked none too hopeful, that the Archbishop of Dublin, who was also by virtue of that office Dean of Christ Church, received a letter from Mr. Henry Roe jun., a wealthy and public-spirited citizen of Dublin, offering to take on his own shoulders the whole burden of restoring the cathedral in a thorough way and building the synod house, and proposing to entrust the entire work to the exclusive control of my father.

This offer having naturally been accepted, the work was commenced almost immediately, and was carried on with so much vigour that the opening services were held almost exactly seven years afterwards

In the inspection of the western part of the church, which my father made in 1868, so far from confining himself to that part with which he was then chiefly concerned, he had made careful investigations of the eastern arm of the church, with the result of discovering that the original choir had been built on lines of a very unusual character and at the same time most suitable for the requirements of the services of the church as they are conducted to-day. The plan of the choir was in effect discovered through the medium of the crypt. This showed—very roughly—a chevet planned with an apse of three sides with an aisle round it, there being only one bay of choir between the apse and the central tower. Perhaps it would be more correct to say that the choir was composed simply of a five-sided apse ; east of the apse were three square-ended chapels, the centre one having a greater projection than the other two. This plan was as far removed from that of the fabric which then stood upon it as the poles are asunder.

The church, as my father found it, was a cruciform one, with a nave and north aisle of six bays, north and south transepts and a long choir, in the form of a simple parallelo-gram, with choir aisles extending to not much more than half its length. The site of the old south aisle of the nave was occupied by a library, a chapter-room, a robing-room for the choir, and a lobby leading to the sexton's house, which was attached to the south-west wall of the nave. On the south side of the choir was a modern entrance with a vestry-room or waiting-room attached to it. The tower, which belonged to the seventeenth century, was mean in appearance both inside and out. It was supported on rude whitewashed limestone piers and arches. The transepts had only one old feature left to them externally, viz. a doorway in the south transept. Inside they were defaced with whitewash and ceiled with wretched lath and plaster vaulting. The north wall of the nave was in a highly dangerous state : cracked all over, and bulging in every direction ; the triforium and clerestory were as a natural consequence much out of the perpendicular, and my father was of opinion that the wall had given way before the nave vaulting fell in in 1562. The south wall of the nave had been dragged down in the ruin of the vault. The vaulting of the north aisle had fallen—presumably at the same time,—and the whole aisle wall had been propped up externally with an immense mass of masonry which entirely covered, while fortunately preserving, the old windows. The south wall of the nave itself had been replaced by a curious sixteenth-century attempt to reproduce thirteenth-century forms The west front had been completely modernised, and every trace of old work obliterated. The choir was divided from the church by a solid screen, on which stood the organ The walls were covered with plaster panelling, cornices, and pinnacles of a contemptible character and redolent of Batty Langley. The floor was closely packed with pews, and the choir aisles had been converted into galleries Throughout, not merely the choir, but the whole church, there was absolutely not one single old window remaining open. Externally there hardly remained one old wrought stone. A certain importance the church still had, which it owed to its considerable size and to the roofs and gables which retained their old forms, but a feature of beauty would have been looked for in vain.

In spite of the incredibly degraded and deformed condition into which the church had been allowed to drift, or into which something worse than indifference had hurried it, there were still found some wrong-headed enough to protest against the removal of these squalid accretions of comparatively modern date. More especially did they clamour for the preservation of the interesting sixteenth-century nave wall, rendered all the more historically valuable as it was by the pithy and genuinely Irish inscription, " This wal fel in 1562 ; this wal was built in 1562." The removal of such a relic may have revealed the cloven hoof of vandalism to the eye which always seeks for such appendages in the architect of a restoration, but moderate men were agreed that if ever a restoration was legitimate it was here. The building seemed to cry aloud to be released from its bonds It cannot, of course, be said of this restoration that every feature had its warrant in what existed before ; much of the old work had been so completely destroyed as to make that impossible.

There are features which may never have existed at all, such as the flying buttresses which are so conspicuous outside, but they have the merit of extreme usefulness, if indeed not of necessity. Innovations were unavoidable, but a survey of what was done, and a consideration of the principles on which my father acted, will, I venture to think, make it clear that any real history, which the variety in the styles of the different parts of the church might convey, was rather rendered more conspicuous than obliterated by the course which was pursued.

Interesting as the entire restoration was as a work of revelation, the plan of the choir, as verified by my father, could boast an originality which made it perhaps the most engrossing part of the whole work. I have already said that he found a long narrow choir, remarkable chiefly for its utter poverty of design and detail. Its east end was square, as were the ends of its aisles. This plan my father was at once able to pronounce to be of much later date than the foundations, and the process of verification and analysis by which his old plan—first suggested by the rough outlines of the crypt—was made a matter of certainty, is full of interest even for the unprofessional man, and to the architect is eloquent of my father's skill and learning. Mr Thomas Drew, R.H.A., a Dublin architect of eminence, and since appointed as hononary architect to the cathedral, writes: " To Mr George E. Street's marvellous instinct for the comparative anatomy, as I may term it, of an ancient building, and profound architectural erudition, we owe the recreation of the perfect and unique twelfth and thirteenth century church from the merest shreds of evidence." My father has himself described his work of restoration, and I don't think I can do better than adopt his words for the time ·—

" By the time the modern fittings and decoration of the choir had been removed, it was evident that more could be restored than at first sight seemed probable Right and left of the choir, close to the tower, there remained two arches, opening to the aisles, of very rich transitional work of the end of the twelfth century. These had been much repaired and disguised with plaster mouldings and other ornaments, but were evidently in their old position and of old construction. Next to them came two wide stone piers, and beyond these were two stone arches generally similar to those already described; but on close inspection it became clear that of these the northern one only was ancient, the other being a copy made in plaster, probably at the last refitting of the interior in 1831. Here, then, we had three old arches to deal with, and one of them—that to the east on the north side—clearly not in its old place, as its supports came over voids and not over piers in the crypt below. I then proceeded to cut into the south pier, east of the old choir arch, and soon discovered the wrought stonework of the commencement of the canted side of an apse; some of these stones were quite perfect, and gave all that was required for the plan of the apse, for, in addition to the angle-stones, which gave the slope of the side of the apse, there remained also the springing-stone of the second arch from the west, which started at a lower level than, and at a different radius from, the others. It occurred to me at once that the arch which had been rebuilt on the north wall was really the eastern archway of the apse, and that the two intermediate archways which formed the canted sides of the apse, springing as they did at a lower level, were no doubt also narrower than the others. Worked out in this way, the whole of the stones came together perfectly over the old foundations in the crypt, and there can be no doubt whatever that in this most singular, if not unique, portion of the plan and design, the choir, as now rebuilt, up to the level of the string-course above the main arches, is an exact reproduction of the original work, being indeed to a large extent reconstructed, with the old carved and moulded stones brought back once more to their old places.

"As to the exact date of the earliest portion of the church above the crypt, it is a little difficult to speak with certainty, but the mixed character of what at first sight looks like Norman detail proves that it is really nowhere earlier than the transition from Norman to first-pointed, whilst, if we regard the circumstances under which the church was built, we may fairly assume, I think, that it would be rather later in date than the corresponding class of work in England . . .

"In making the designs for the completion of the new choir, of which the lower portion had been so fortunately and with so much certainty recovered, it was decided to introduce freely the same kind of enriched mouldings throughout as those of the five arches of the lower stage. To have adopted a more advanced style would have been to establish a violent discord between the several stages of the choir, as also between this and its aisles and chapels, and though it is true that the church gains by the great difference between the choir, the transepts, and the nave, it is equally true that the completeness of each portion in itself is one of the charms of the building."

The triforium and clerestory of the choir having wholly disappeared, my father adopted a scheme of window openings similar in arrangement to the beautiful ones in the nave, while he so arranged his design as to be able to put a single-light window over the two narrow bays, and double lights over the three wider ones. In the transepts, which are of about the same date as the choir, my father found none but round-headed arches used internally, so he reproduced that form in the outer wall too.

In the south transept he placed the organ on a groined gallery, which takes up hardly any room on the floor of the church and hides no architectural beauties. It is also directly at the back of the choir, which is placed at the crossing.

The transepts my father looked upon as the productions of a man who was copying English works with only imperfect understanding of them. The mouldings seemed to him to be of a mixed character and not quite in keeping with the round-headed arches. The design altogether lacked the decision of that of the nave, which he did not doubt to be that of another man, though one educated in the same school, the English school namely, which had its headquarters at Glastonbury and Wells and spread thence to Llandaff, St Davids, and Cwm Hir Abbey, the arcade from which now adorns the parish church at Llanidloes.

The interior of the nave as now completed presents few, if any, features for which there was no authority The vaulting, of course, had fallen in, but the wall ribs remained, and the curve of the vault and the section of the ribs were accordingly a matter of certainty. The whole south wall was rebuilt, and it would have been more economical to have treated the old north wall in the same way, but so deeply was Mr. Roe imbued with reverence for the old work that he permitted my father at great expense to treat it as it stood. The wall had to be carefully shored up while the columns were removed and replaced. These columns, though as much as six feet in diameter, were so miserably constructed in the thirteenth century that they had proved quite unequal to the task of carrying the vault, the weight of which they

should rightly have been able to bear many times over
Beautiful indeed as they are with their clustered shafts,
they really subtract something from the merit of the design
from the utter want of science which they display, the
diameter being actually equal to half the space between each
pair.

The exterior of the nave having been almost wholly
destroyed, my father boldly put a series of picturesque flying
buttresses to resist the thrust of the vault.   It is needless to
say that the columns of the nave, now that they have been
properly reconstructed, are very much too strong for the
purpose, but no other course was open.

While the work was in progress, the remains of a chamber groined in three bays were found on the north side of
the nave near the west end.   This my father has rebuilt
from rather fragmentary evidence, and the chamber, which
he has made a very beautiful one, now serves as a baptistery.

The west front, I have already said, seemed to be hopelessly modern, but the jambs of a west window of five
lancet lights were discovered in the wall, and after my father
had designed a new west door with a double entrance and
central pier, and even after some part of it was fixed in its
place, one of the old jamb-stones was found, and by an extraordinary chance proved to be of almost the identical
section of the new stonework, insomuch that, I believe, it was
incorporated with it   My father was rather proud of this
testimony to the harmonious nature of his own work   From
the south wall of the nave aisle, in the westernmost bay, a
picturesque staircase starts, this crosses the street by a bridge
formed of one bold segmental arch, and connects the
cathedral with the new synod buildings.   The synod hall
with its accessory offices was built on the site of the
modernised St Michael's Church, the tower of which—its
only old feature—was incorporated in the new work.   As
for the tower of the cathedral itself, it was, as I have said,
wholly without interest, but a bold and withal most simple
treatment of it has made it a very effective crown to the
whole pile.

Internally it rested on low rough arches and plain whitewashed limestone piers. Those piers were slowly elaborated *in situ* till they became rich enough to harmonise with the plentiful detail of everything about them, and the arches were replaced by others some ten feet higher. This work was done in the way the mediæval workmen would have done it, —that is to say, the stones were cut out and replaced by new ones separately and without any system of shoring. The whole was successfully finished without a sign of a settlement.

There is one feature in the restoration which has been freely subjected to criticism, and that is the exterior of the nave clerestory. Undeniably it is ugly, and my father felt it to be so ; but at the same time he had assured himself to his own satisfaction that it was undoubtedly old, and he felt bound to reproduce it without modification.

The church was of course elaborately fitted with furniture. The pavement in particular is remarkable for its extraordinary richness. No less than sixty-three different patterns of old tiles were found, and were all reproduced from accurate sketches in colour.

On this subject and on the ironwork I may quote the criticism of an architect :—

" Unmeasured praise is bestowed on the ironwork. The grilles which surround the choir are simply the culmination of Mr. Street's ablest designs in a branch in which he excels. When a future school of architects historicise the architecture of the middle of the nineteenth century, and point to the best examples of what the Gothic architects of the Revival did at their best, they will probably point to this work as exemplitive of what they could achieve original in treatment, perfect in technical manipulation, and characteristic of nineteenth-century feeling fired with admiration and appreciation for the honesty of mediæval art. Then, as for the pavement of the entire church, it is simply a gorgeous sight. So brave in originality and so striking in aspect, it is not to be wondered at if, on the opening day, it somewhat appalled the timid souls of men used to the simplicity and breadth of effect to which the hideous black and Carlow blue flagging have accustomed too dismally the eye of the Dubliner."

Every window throughout the church was filled with stained glass. Under the western tower arch was placed a delicate open screen in marble and alabaster—a feature for

which there was plenty of evidence in the old work. Everything had been done with a thoroughness which was almost
lavish, and, to quote an unprejudiced opinion, "with a
studious desire to avoid symbolism or accessories which
would touch the sensitive feelings of a not very liberal or
well-informed section of the Irish people." All the chief
authorities—Dr. Stephens, Dr. Studdert, and Dr. Battersby,
the Archbishop's chancellor—agreed in stating that the whole
work without any exception was both within the letter and
the spirit of the law.   In spite of this a letter appeared on
1st May 1878, written on the very day of the opening, in
which these sentences occurred —

"'The large, unmeaning stone cross over the arched screen
should be removed   The picture of the crucifix in the east window
should be exchanged, and if the Agnus Dei and the stone structure
(meaning the simple retable) behind the communion table offend
those for whom the building is intended, I feel certain that Mr Roe
has too much good sense not to take them away also.   If not, the
cathedral must be closed, or the Protestants of Ireland will themselves pull down the obnoxious emblems."

Surely bigotry and bad taste could no further go ; and
yet this is only a sample of many letters all in the same
tenor, emanating from the small and illiberal community of
ultra-Protestants, gentlemen who, after the work was complete, said that Mr. Roe ought to have left it to be done
by the Protestants of Ireland, but at an earlier stage of the
proceedings had been discreetly silent.

Dr. Battersby, who had been specially enjoined to take
note of the "obnoxious emblems," wrote to the Archbishop :—

"There is nothing in the church, as I saw it, that would justify
your grace, either as dean or archbishop, in refusing to take possession whenever the work shall be finished.   The cross and Agnus
Dei were so little striking that, although I went expressly to see
them, I did not observe them until they were pointed out to me "

I should not have touched upon this unsavoury subject
but for its having drawn a reply from my father, which is
interesting as showing his views :—

"I have read the address to Mr. Roe on the subject of one of the screens in Christ Church Cathedral with much interest. I had seen various statements as to its artistic effect on the building, and its moral effect on the worshippers, which appeared to me to be so extremely one-sided and unreasonable, that I was anxious to know what might be urged by those whose objections to what I have done might be assumed to be well considered and marked by sobriety of statement. The objections to the screen, stated in the Memorial, are twofold. That which is stated to be the greater is, that many people object to it on religious grounds. The answer to this, though it is not an architectural one, is obvious, viz. that many people on the same grounds object to its removal, and that their opinion is as much entitled to respect as the opposite one, if the screen is a legal article of furniture or ornament, as to which, I suppose, there is no question. The other objections are :—

"(*a*) That it is of no practical use. (*b*) That it spoils the beauty of the church. (*c*) That it lessens its apparent dimensions, and (*d*) greatly obstructs the majority of the congregation from hearing, seeing, and intelligently taking part in divine service. I will, with your permission, say a few words on each of these heads, premising only that they are all matters of taste and opinion, and not matters of fact; and that, therefore, my judgment on all of them must be allowed by candid men to be of more weight than that of gentlemen who have not had any artistic or professional training.

"(*a*) The choir screens or enclosures of our cathedrals are of so much practical use as to be almost universal in the English communion. The office-books and music-books remain in the choir when no service is going on, and it is always found inconvenient to leave them unprotected. When screens surround the choir, it is possible to leave the whole of the rest of the church open all day. This is the custom in all or nearly all English cathedrals, and I hope that ere long it will be equally the custom at Christ Church.

"(*b*) In my opinion the screen adds greatly to the beauty of the interior. The old architects thought so, no doubt, for we found remains of their screen during the progress of the works. Of the design of the particular screen it does not become me to speak; but I am obliged to say in self-defence that it is as good and as successful as anything I have ever done, and certainly equal in merit to the rest of my work at Christ Church.

"(*c*) Those who have studied the question know that the effect of a partial obstruction or subdivision is to increase, not to decrease, the apparent size of a building. An unbroken area, like that of St. Peter's or the Pantheon at Rome, always makes buildings look smaller than they really are. The subdivisions of Gothic buildings were evidently meant by their designers to increase to the utmost their apparent size. The subdivision of parts (such as 'mouldings') was carried to the utmost point with the same object The cathedral of Christ Church is really one of small dimensions, and, thanks to its subdivisions and, above all things, to the screen between the choir and the nave, it now looks much larger than it really is, and its scale would suffer immensely if the screen were removed. Of this I am as certain as I can be of anything

"(*d*) The memorialists are bold in their assertion that they could hear better without the screen My confident belief is that in its absence there would be almost a certainty of a considerable echo At present I have found myself able to hear perfectly well in all parts both service and sermon If the screen is removed, I do not believe that I should any longer be able to say this. The other objection, as to seeing and joining intelligently in the service, can hardly be quite serious. This does not apply at all to that part of the congregation which sits in the aisles out of sight of the screen, and for those who sit in the transepts, the removal of the transept screens is equally required; while for those who sit in the nave, in full view of the screen, I assert that there is no difficulty whatever in an equally intelligent joining in the service, whether there is a screen or no screen, and that for some reasons in all cathedral churches it is more productive of devotional feeling to be able to join in the service without seeing every attitude and every expression of the face of those who are engaged in the musical portion of it.

"Allow me to say, in conclusion, that it is a matter of extreme pain to me that there should be any controversy about any portion of this great and important work I have done my best to make Christ Church all that it should be, and I declare, on my honour, that if the particular alteration now asked for is conceded, my work will be immensely damaged, and much of its architectural and artistic effect destroyed. Surely the artist, though he may not be infallible as you say, is at least the person whose opinion is of the most weight as to what will or will not damage or improve his work. If in such a building he does what is illegal, of course there can be no question whatever that his work must be altered; but if, as in this case, he has not done so, and has devoted the whole of his powers and knowledge and taste to make the work as good, as harmonious, and as perfect a whole as he could, he has a fair claim to ask that it may be left in its entirety as it came from his hands. Every one would concede this in the case of a painter or sculptor, and I see no reason why the work of the architect should be less respected than that of the artist '

Within the last two or three years Mr. Drew, the honorary

architect to the cathedral, in excavating for a drain at the south side of the cathedral, discovered the ancient level of the cloister garth.   This is nine feet below the church floor, and the level explains the nature of what seemed to be an old cellar door adjoining the cathedral at its south-west angle. It was no doubt the Abbey gateway.   Further investigation has shown that what was formerly the Exchange must have been the old chapter-house ; while Mr. Drew has also discovered the blocked-up entrance from the south-west angle of the south transept up into the dormitory.   At the time of the restoration this piece of land, at one time destined to hold the synod hall, was occupied by masons' sheds, and all the paraphernalia which so large an undertaking makes necessary, and consequently no thorough investigation was ever made into its possible hidden treasures.

In 1868 my father was made Diocesan Architect of Ripon, a post which he already held in the dioceses of York and Oxford, to which Winchester was subsequently added ; besides this he was appointed, almost at the same time, Architect to York Minster, and, later on, to Salisbury and Carlisle Cathedrals.

The high estimation in which his work was held on the Continent was shown by his election to the Corresponding Membership of the Viennese Academy of Fine Arts in 1869, while in England he attained the highest distinction open to an artist by his election as a Royal Academician in 1871.   A year before this he had, in the absence through ill-health of Sir G. G. Scott, who then held the Professorship of Architecture in the Academy, given a couple of lectures, which were an earnest of the admirable series which he was to deliver when he himself occupied the chair a few years afterwards.   These lectures, which attracted much attention, are appended to the present volume.

Directly after his election to the full membership, it became my father's duty to serve on the Council in common with the other newly-elected academicians.   As a member of Council, his energy of character and good business qualities made him very valuable.   He entered thoroughly into his duties, and devoted himself with special zest to the attempt to place the teaching in the architectural schools on a par with that which the student of painting received. I am indebted to Mr. R Phené Spiers, F.S A, the Master in the Royal Academy Architectural School, for the following note on his work in that particular :—

"My first recollections of the late Mr. G. E. Street, in connection with the schools of the Royal Academy, date from the year 1871, when, having become a full member, he took his place on the Council. A Committee was appointed to revise and reorganise the schools, and Mr. Street was placed on the Committee to advise respecting the architectural school. The time, however, was not ripe for the changes which were proposed, and the Committee was dissolved without any definite action having been taken.

"Subsequently the work of this Committee was brought forward, with the result that many changes were introduced into the working of the schools Among other propositions was that of Mr. Street, that the architect members should in future take their turn as visitors in the architectural school, in the same way as had always been done in the painting schools by the painter members of the Academy

"At first I did not think the proposal was likely to succeed, for it seemed improbable that architects in busy practice, whose works necessitated their frequent absence from town, would be able to attend regularly at the schools to give the students the advantage of their experience and criticism. In this, however, I was mistaken The architectural visitors made their weekly visit an appointment always to be kept, and, foremost among them, Mr. Street (who was the first to undertake the task) not only never missed an evening, but arrived punctually at six o'clock, and remained till the closing of the school at eight o'clock " (My father made his first visit in January 1878)

"The immense value of his teaching was apparent from the first. He threw all his energy into the task, and commenced on his first visit by sketching altogether a fresh design for each student. Subsequently, finding that the students preferred to wait for his designs, instead of thinking for themselves, he changed his plan, and confined his attention to the correction of their work when placed before him; and it was interesting to note how a poor commonplace cardboard design gradually became developed, under his advice, into one showing vigour and boldness in its treatment, with simple but effective mouldings, and with its construction well insisted on. Mr. Street invariably required a portion of the design to be set out at an early stage to a half-inch scale, on one half of this he would draw in all the sections of his mouldings, and alter the design of the tracery and other features, requiring the student to copy them on the other half. These he would correct again, if necessary, on a subsequent visit, and revise from time to time on the final drawings

"Mr Street from the first ingratiated himself with the students by the kindness of his manner; he always seemed to try and work with them to ascertain their ideas, and point out how they best could realise them, instead of putting forward ideas of his own,—the result being that the students took a much greater interest in their work than they would have, had they been simply carrying out some one else's design.

"Mr. Street continued his work in the schools till within a short time of his death, and it was only on the occasion of his last visit, I think, that for the first time I heard him complain of feeling tired, though he had frequently passed the night before his weekly visit in the railway train, and had then been hard at work all day.

"His untimely death was a great and serious loss to the profession at large, and to no section of it more than to the Academy students, who profited so much by his sound advice."

My father-in-law, Mr. Wells, the Royal Academician, writes to me :—

"Although your father and I were elected into the Royal Academy on the same day, it was, of course, not until we had passed through our probation as Associates, and had become full members of the Institution, with the right of taking our parts in its business and management, that I had the opportunity of seeing how valuable his services were likely to be

"As a newly-elected academician he took his seat upon the Council at a time when it so happened he was able to be of especial use to the Academy, for the new galleries had been recently opened, and the members were awaiting the completion of Burlington House itself for the removal of the entire establishment from Trafalgar Square to its new home.

"It was a time of change and expansion. The schools had commenced working on an increased scale; there was a launching-out in every department; and, besides the rising yearly expenditure, very large dealings with the builders were going on. Under these circumstances, and when there was danger lest the ideas and habits of business, which were the traditions of the comparatively small establishment at Trafalgar Square, should be too strictly adhered to, your father fortunately came among us with his clear perception and knowledge of affairs. It was my fortune to sit at Council with him during his first year of office, when his mastery in dealing with all the various kinds of business which came before us soon made itself apparent. I also served with him on the Audits and on the Finance Committee, where his vigilant supervision of our new expenditure came into full play and led to reforms in many important matters.

"But the work for which he will be most generally remembered at the Academy, as I am sure he would himself have wished, was his putting of the architectural schools on their present footing Strangely enough, until he intervened, the students of architecture, unlike those of painting and sculpture, had never received their teaching from members of the Academy, and had thus been excepted from the advantages of the system of visitorship which puts the student in contact with the most eminent artists of the country Without doubt there were obstacles to making the different schools alike (I may instance that architectural students are generally employed in offices during the daytime, and are prevented from giving the hours of attendance of the other students, and from following the general routine of the schools). Your father, however, took up all the conditions of the problem in his practical way, and when in 1877 he introduced to the General Assembly his measure for the creation of visitorships to the architectural schools, he presented it in such a form that it obtained the ready acceptance of the academicians and, if I remember rightly, by an unanimous vote.

"The measure at once gave life to these schools Very naturally your father was closely associated with their success, and was seen to be ever watchful for their further development His opportunities came in the years 1880 and 1881, when the General Assembly, with the help of a special committee, on which he served, devoted much time to the whole subject of teaching, and revised the laws and regulations with a view to increasing and improving the schools.

"In this remodelling, the architectural division came in for quite its full share of additions, and the new regulations for it, which took their shape chiefly under your father's advice and by his advocacy, are those in force at the present time.

"The interest your father took in everything connected with the Royal Academy was shown by his unremitting attendance at the schools, and at the various meetings of Council committees and General Assembly, at a time when his great professional practice was calling him away to all parts of the kingdom, and even to the Continent On one of his professional visits to Italy my own services, I remember, were enlisted to keep him informed of the course of Academy business, for it so happened an important General Assembly was impending, and he was so anxious not to be absent from it that he intended to hurry back to England if the then unannounced

date of the meeting made it necessary for him to do so   Indeed,
he seemed to make his own personal engagements, as far as
possible, dependent upon the course of business at Burlington
House.

"That his devotion was a consequence of his belief in the Royal
Academy as an instrument for benefiting the Arts he made clear on
a notable occasion shortly before his death, when he gave his address
as the newly-elected President of the Institute of Architects.   On
that occasion, after expressing his conviction that the two institutions
had work to do in common, and were not in the least antagonistic,
he said that were it otherwise he would not then be addressing his
audience   Knowing, as I did, how much he had been gratified
by the honour of election to that chair, I was struck by this burst
of manly candour, which threw a meaning into all the services I had
been a witness of through several years of comradeship

"His death fell as a great blow upon his colleagues.   He had
become our Treasurer, and was looked at as a pillar of strength to
be counted upon for many years to come   He was apparently in
the fullest vigour of health ; and as he sat in front of us at the last
meeting he attended, no thought but of life could be associated with
him.

"When at the meeting that followed his death the formal
announcement of it had to be made by the President, Sir Frederick
Leighton could not refrain, although the custom of the Academy was
against him, from putting into words what was uppermost in all our
hearts, and when he ended by saying that our late colleague would
always have to be remembered by us as a 'great academician,' I, for
one, felt he had most correctly defined our loss.   In my own time
I have known of no one to whom that title so well applies."

There are many entries in my father's diary during this
time which show how much interest he took in the experiment, and how thoroughly satisfactory he could conscientiously take the result to be

To his hard work was now added the worry of having to
sit still under the strictures which were launched almost daily
from a certain quarter against his design for the new Law
Courts   He was able to write lightheartedly enough about
it though :—

"The only bother about the Law Courts is the abuse of my
plans in ——   *They have never seen them,* so the criticisms are all
the more free and unprejudiced, of course ! but I don't suppose it
has any weight with any one capable of really arriving at any reason-

able conclusion on such questions, and every one else has written most favourably about me and about my work. This work, of course, engrosses me very much ; but I am obliged to find time for plenty of other business, among other things for a great work— the restoration of the south transept of York Minster. I am also just making plans for the restoration of the ruined cathedral of Kildare, and of course I have told you of the grand work I have in hand at Christ Church, Dublin, which is almost tantamount to the building of a cathedral "

Besides these, and a whole host of less important works, the chapel and house for Lord Crawford at Dunecht were now in progress. Here he had to add his own work on to a bald piece of building with which it would almost have seemed hopeless to find any common ground , yet my father managed with such skill that the noble chapel and dignified pile of building for which he is responsible, at least produce no discord, as they stand side by side with the original commonplace modern house. The whole work looks grave, simple, and large, as my father would have wished. The chapel is something more than that.

The work at York Minster gave him peculiar pleasure. Its two great transepts had always stood out to him as representing in perfection first-rate English work. It was no common satisfaction then that a piece of work which he regarded in such a light should owe its restoration to its original and beautiful state to his own care.

It was in 1871 that he was first applied to by the chapter, the state of the south transept having become obviously so dangerous as to call for some immediate and decided action. My father found, upon examination, that the weight of the roof had thrust the clerestory walls very much out of the perpendicular, with the natural consequence that the groining had spread, while the south face of the transept was in a terrible state of decay, and much spoilt and concealed by modern additions. Two great longitudinal stages were erected on the floor of the transept, and support was thus given to the entire roof, while the clerestory walls were rebuilt The slates on the roof were replaced by lead, and the plaster filling-in of the groining by oak, while the groining itself was lifted up into its proper position Besides this, the east and west walls were underpinned. The south front and the eastern aisle were the first to be entered upon, and the work on them was finished for the most part in three years, but it was as long again before the octagonal turrets which flank the front were completed. These were designed to take the place of the modernised remnants of the old ones, and were to some extent conjectural. Indeed, it is probable that the old turrets had never actually been finished ; at least my father was inclined to that view.

This, however, was the solitary innovation, and it certainly seems a most warrantable one, for the simple restoration to the *statu quo* would have been worse than quixotic. The rebuilding of the clerestory was of course fallen foul of by those who would let our old buildings become small by degrees till there was nothing left of them, but my father made haste to give extremely good reasons for having laid his rash hand on the work :—

"If I had not rebuilt the clerestory of the south transept it would have fallen. Much of the external stonework was so effectually tooled and redressed many years ago that in parts hardly any of the untouched face of the original stonework remained. By care and great pains we can find the original mouldings almost everywhere, and these I am substituting for the bad copies of an ignorant period. To those who do not value our matchless English mouldings, such a work may be repugnant. To me, I confess, it is one of the very greatest interest. We have no finer or more classical work in England than the transepts of York Minster, and I am not a little proud to have a hand in exposing them to view again in their old state, and minus whitewash and modern alterations."

In 1874, when the work was complete, my father wrote from York to my mother :—

"The transept of the Minster looks so magnificent now; I think more interesting and striking than anything we have seen in France, and on such a grand scale ! The Dean is charmed with it, etc."

The restoration of the cathedral of St. Brigid, Kildare, was another of those cases where the disagreement of opinion between those who would leave a ruin to moulder away till its place knew it no more, and those who prefer to preserve a design and save a church, showed itself markedly.

St Brigid, when my father was asked to report as to the feasibility of again making it fit for service, had the side walls of the nave still standing as well as the south transept and the south wall of the central tower. The west wall of the nave and the north transept had entirely disappeared, and an ugly modern tower had been built close to the ruins of the old one. The choir was chiefly modern, and what was old had been altered so much as to be almost unrecognisable as such. My father reported favourably as to the possibility of restoration. The wall that remained he regarded as striking in design, and well worth preservation, and such parts of the church as were destroyed could, in his opinion, be at least built up so as to harmonise with the rest without difficulty :—

"The south transept and nave," he said, "have lost their roofs, but almost all the other architectural features still remain, either intact or in such a state as to make their restoration a matter of no difficulty. The south elevation of the south transept is one of great simplicity, and of good character and proportion, its window is a well-designed triplet, simple externally, but with shafts and mouldings internally. The side walls of the nave present a very remarkable design. The windows are simple lancets, separated from each other by buttresses; between these buttresses bold arches are formed nearly on a face with the front of the buttresses, and with a narrow space between them and the face of the wall. The effect of this arrangement is to throw a very bold shadow over the windows, and the effect produced is most picturesque . . . The central tower is a mere wreck; one side only—the south—is fairly perfect, the whole of the rest of it has been destroyed. It is a work of fine design and proportion, not very lofty, but, in its complete state, so large as to give a good deal of the dignity of a cathedral to what might otherwise have looked somewhat too much like a parish church."

I have already said that the thoroughgoing anti-restorationists exclaimed against anything being done, and argued that there were other national improvements on which, at any rate, the money might more profitably be spent, but the feeling among Dublin architects and archæologists, as expressed by one of their most representative men, was distinctly in favour of the contemplated work of preservation, and of its being entrusted to an architect—a foreigner though he might be called by some—who had shown himself in so many cases capable of masterly and conservative work   There is a beauty in usefulness, and, to those who thought of it, the objections of the *laisser-aller* party seemed whimsical and absurd   My father, after paying one of his periodical visits to the church, wrote: "The work at the cathedral getting on bravely; what a pleasure it is to see the nave walls all restored, and the north transept rising from the ground on its old lines!   It is really a grand work to restore a ruined church exactly to its old state"

During the same period important churches were in progress at Torquay, Clifton, Kingstone, Kennington, Liverpool, Eastbourne, Bournemouth, and Paddington.   All of them have their special features of beauty and interest, though it is impossible to give them in words.   Toddington and Kingstone, built respectively for Lords Sudeley and Eldon, and both built without a contractor, are examples of churches where money was not spared.   The first of these is remarkable for the beauty of its window-traceries, the delicacy of its detail, and its charming tower and spire—a feature in which my father may be said to have always succeeded.   Take a group of his larger designs for towers and spires, beginning with Lille Cathedral, then St. Philip and St. James, Oxford; Boyne Hill; St. Saviour's, Eastbourne; St. Peter's, Bournemouth; St. Mary Magdalene, Paddington; Edinburgh Cathedral competition design, and, among those only partially built or not begun, Whiston, Kennington, Chapel Allerton, and the American Church, Paris, and, diverse as they are, they all have a marked beauty of outline, and exhibit great skill in the treatment of the junction of the tower and spire, whether there are pinnacles and parapets, or one of the many forms of broaches, and in the treatment, placing, and projection of the spire lights, so that there is no sense of any abruptness in the change from the perpendicular line of the tower to the slope of the spire, but the whole mass seems to spring to the sky from the ground itself in one great sweep. Many of my father's earliest designs—executed and not executed—included towers and spires, and I think it must have needed but a glance at one of these to see that their youthful author was something out of the common run

Kingstone Church, near Wareham, is probably one of the most complete things my father ever did   It is a regular cross church, with an upstanding central tower, and an apsidal east end   The chancel, crossing, and nave aisles are groined   In the west wall is a great rose window, under which is a narthex of the width of the nave   The mouldings throughout the church are elaborate and beautiful, and the nave arcade, with its richly-clustered shafts, has probably hardly a rival among purely country churches. Lord Eldon being the owner of great quarries of Purbeck marble, that material is used in profusion throughout ; all the windows in the church, with the exception of the roses in the west end and clerestory, are lancets, richly moulded internally, and having shafts in the jambs—this gives the opportunity for the use of Purbeck from end to end.   Two notes from my father's diary, one during the progress of the work, one after its completion, are here given.   The first is as follows :—

"The church is looking well   I hope the interior may be beautiful   It ought to be, for they have already spent a large sum of money on it.   It will be difficult to find, even among old buildings, anything more thoroughly elaborated, I believe.   It is a real pleasure to work for such a man as Lord Eldon."

And afterwards he wrote :—

"To Kingstone, where Lord Eldon met me   I could not help saying that the church looked well.   It is a pleasure to be allowed to make work so much after one's own heart, as this will be ; I think it is the jolliest church I have built"

On this point, however, he was really no better able to make up his mind exactly than other people are, and always objected to people saying, "This or that is your best work" Another design of this period is worth mention, because it showed the power which was afterwards still further exemplified at the Guards Chapel, viz. that for the alteration of St Luke's, Lower Norwood   There my father had to deal with a hopeless kind of temple, which he succeeded in turning into a fine Byzantine-looking church at no great cost.

Of St Mary Magdalene, Paddington, I have already spoken in reference to the way it is planned ; for London church-goers there is no need to describe its architectural features. The only serious mishap which ever occurred, so far as I remember, in any work of my father's, was the partial destruction of this church by fire a few weeks before it should have been opened. A workman with a candle somehow set a light to the felt on the nave roof, and the results were rather disastrous. The roofs of the chancel and nave were entirely burnt, and that of the transept was seriously damaged. Strange to say, the stonework and brickwork and the stained glass, which was fixed, was not materially damaged ; the chancel being saved by its groining. This accident made my father for a time very shy of using felt ; but before long he had to acknowledge to himself that its advantages more than balanced the risk of using it

From 1867 on, the year in which I got into college at Eton, and was able to reap the benefit of the extra week, which was always a feature of summer holidays there in those days, I went with my father and mother on all their autumn tours ; Italy was none too cool at that time of the year, but my father, nevertheless, managed to revisit most of his old favourites in the summers of 1867-69, besides seeing Ravenna. In 1868 we made our way from Venice into Titian's country, and up to Cortina, where the beauty of the country and the primitive simplicity of the people were equally charming. In the course of those years we visited the Engadine, the Oberland, the Val d'Aosta, and a great part of Southern Germany.

So much of what he saw was already in my father's notebooks that he turned to watercolours, and did a great deal of architectural and landscape work in that medium. I remember, on my first visit to Venice in 1867, that he used to appear every morning at breakfast with a large sepia study of one of the capitals of the Ducal Palace—work which he never tired of. As might have been expected, his landscape sketches are chiefly remarkable for the success with which mountain form and structure is rendered, and besides this, they were truthful to the smallest detail, not being intended so much as subject-sketches, but rather as a vivid form of diary. It is easy to illustrate the accuracy of his work. The first time we visited Pontresina, he made a sketch of the valley which runs up to the Roseg Glacier, and is closed at the head by various peaks of the Bernina range, and among them by the " Capuchin " Those who know Pontresina will hardly believe that, during the whole of our stay there, we never discovered the capuchin's face, which, once seen, is a constant torment. Such, however, was the case, and my father consequently made his sketch without having the least idea that he was putting a grotesque head on his paper On a second visit we saw the face at once, and immediately began to wonder how it would appear on the old sketch Directly we got home we had the sketch-book out, and there, sure enough, was the face to a very small scale, but about as true as a photograph. It must be remembered, too, that all these sketches were done very rapidly, which makes the extreme accuracy the more surprising.

In 1870 the war drove us to Scotland, and we saw Hexham, Kelso, Jedburgh, Dryburgh, Melrose, Dunfermline, St. Andrews, Arbroath, Elgin, Pluscardine, Dunkeld, besides getting a glimpse at Fountains, York, and Lincoln on our way home.

The next year, while we were in Switzerland, my father met with an accident which might have had the most serious consequences for him. We were run away with in the dark on the Weissenstein, a mountain above Solothurn, the horses dashed up a bank, and we were thrown out amid the débris of the carriage Luckily we were only some few hundred yards from the hotel, and within sight of its lights. My father suffered so much pain in his left—happily his left— arm, that it was clear it was either dislocated or broken, and apparently the former. As the Weissenstein hotel is three or four hours above Solothurn, there was nothing to be done that night, and he had to grin and bear it. The doctor did not put in an appearance next day till late in the afternoon— about eighteen hours after the event He found the arm to be dislocated, and so firmly fixed had it become that the services of several waiters had to be enlisted to pull it in again. The innkeeper from whom we had hired the carriage demanded compensation , but our landlord with great kindness took the whole thing into his own hands, and we heard no more of the claim. The effects of the accident were lasting; whenever my father used his hand he felt a sensation of cramp, which would have been enough to stop his drawing almost entirely if it had been in the other hand.

Curiously enough, when, some years afterwards, he was making the experiment of crossing the St. Gothard in the winter, his sledge was suddenly upset in a snowdrift, and in trying to save himself he put the arm out again. He got up ruefully, and motioned to the driver to help him into his seat; the boy with rustic awkwardness seized him promptly by the bad arm and gave a lusty hoist. My father was preparing to make as strong a remonstrance as his German would allow of, when he felt that his arm had been pushed into its place, and the more acute pain quickly began to subside. I believe that if you dislocate your arm in the hunting-field, the remedy is to put it over a gate and give a sharp pull from below with the other hand. The principle is the same, but that it should have been applied simply through excess of clumsiness was the most fortunate chance.

In 1872 we struck into some new country

"We went by Luxembourg," wrote my father, "and Trèves, and down the Moselle for the first time to Coblenz. Thence to Munich, and by carriage past the Bavarian lakes, the Tegern and Achen See to Innsbruck. After that we struck south-eastwards into a delicious country full of beautiful mountains, and with no tourists but ourselves. This was in the valleys of the Drave and the Gail. We went also to Heiligenblut, which lies just under the Gros Glockner, a great snow mountain Then we made our way across the Prédil Pass to the Adriatic, and had a few days at Gorizia, Udine, Aquileia, Venice, Verona, Brescia, and Bergamo, and hence again by the Engadine, finishing up at Augsburg, and then down the Rhine. Altogether we agree that we never made a more delightful tour. I worked hard and brought back a well-filled sketch-book, mainly watercolour drawings of mountain scenery."

The first edition of *Brick and Marble* had long been exhausted, and a year or two after this journey a second edition was brought out with a good deal of new matter in it, to which this 1872 tour contributed a good deal.

In 1871 Dr. Nevin, the American chaplain in Rome

had asked my father to build them a church there. The
commission was an attractive one in every way. Dr. Nevin
was a man of such energy and resource that funds were sure
to be forthcoming sufficient to provide a church which should
hold its own even in this centre of the Roman Catholic
world, and, moreover, it gave my father the necessary impulse
—the wish had never been wanting—to make a push for
South Italy. Accordingly, in the spring of 1872, he made
it possible to get away. The first stop was made at Orvieto,
then at Viterbo and Toscanella, and the rail for Rome was
taken at Corneto. Six days was all that could be given to
Rome. We are told that to know Rome at all, month after
month must be devoted to it. The inside of a week was
lamentably short even for a trained traveller who did not
know what fatigue was, who knew what he cared to look at
and what not, and who never forgot what he saw. These
six days at least served this purpose for my father : they
made clear to him the necessity for another and more
lengthened visit. Goth, as he delighted to call himself,
ancient Rome held him spellbound ; the indefinable attractiveness of the city, born partly of its associations, and partly
of what it offers to the eye, of humanity as well as of brick
and stone, made itself felt hardly less strongly in him than
in the student whose heart is wrapped up in the Rome of the
past.

After leaving the Eternal City, my father and mother
made their headquarters at Portici, where her father had a
villa planted on the lower slopes of Vesuvius, flanked by a
hanging orange garden, and looking over the bay to Castel-
lamare and Sorrento · a perfect site, were not the lava too
close to be pleasant. During their stay they visited Naples,
Pompeii, Salerno, and Pæstum, reserving Capri and the exquisite coast scenery between Salerno and Amalfi for another
visit. It was, I think, about a year later that Naples was
thrown into commotion by a great eruption of Vesuvius, the
lava at night-time seeming to the frightened people to be
bearing down directly upon the city. If the Neapolitans
were frightened, the people of Portici were naturally much
more so. My grandfather, who had an Englishman's objec-

P

tion to being disturbed by thoughtless ebullitions, whether on the part of Nature or his fellowmen, and who was also somewhat of an invalid, stood his ground, but he was temporarily deserted by his whole household.

Shortly after his return from Italy, my father started on another competition work, that for the Episcopal Cathedral at Edinburgh, for which, though unsuccessful, he made a design of great excellence.

EDINBURGH CATHEDRAL COMPETITION.

This was held in accordance with the provisions of the will of Miss Walker of Drumsheugh, who left a sum of £45,000 for this purpose. The arrangements were left in the hands of six or eight trustees, citizens of Edinburgh, most of whom were so *ex officio*, as, for instance, the Bishop, the Dean, the Provost, etc.

It was stipulated that there should be six architects, half of them English and half Scotch: the latter being Mr. Alex. Ross, Mr. Lessels, and Messrs. Peddie and Kinnear; and the former, Sir G. Gilbert Scott, Mr. Burges, and my father. I am tempted to describe the circumstances of the competition and the characteristics of my father's design at some length, because, in spite of his want of success, this latter seems to me to have been conspicuous for its suitability and completeness of arrangement. The drawings were to be sent in in August, and before the end of the year it was known that Sir Gilbert Scott had been selected as architect, while Mr. Ross had, next to him, found most favour with the trustees.

The decision was not generally accepted as a good one, certainly not in professional circles; and as more facts came out, it was found to be really indefensible unless the terms of the competition were to be regarded as not binding. Supposing those terms to remain in force, the choice could only have been between my father and Mr. Burges, as they were the only two who had kept themselves within the prescribed limits of expense and fulfilled the requirements.

According to the Edinburgh correspondent of the *Church Times*, only two of the trustees, viz. the Bishop and the

Dean, were Churchmen   The others were Presbyterians, and, as such, unable to appreciate the planning of an Episcopal church.   Further than this, they were men taken quite at haphazard, simply from the fact of their holding certain offices at the particular time, and, in the matter of taste, were generally remarkable for the want of it.   From the same source we learn that the Bishop supported Sir Gilbert Scott through thick and thin, while the Provost did the same for Mr. Lessels, for whom no one else could say a good word. Naturally dissatisfied with the way in which the stipulations of the competition had been set aside, my father appealed to the Press for a hearing.   From his letters it appeared that he had visited Edinburgh in the early part of 1872, and had had an interview with the Bishop, from which he came away fully satisfied that the trustees would not undertake the selection of the architect themselves, but would either appoint a professional adviser or a small committee of skilled persons.   " If I had supposed," he writes, " that the trustees of Miss Walker's will were to be the judges, as I am not a madman I should not have thought twice before refusing to compete "

Many of the trustees being, as I have said, non-Episcopalians, would necessarily have seen special objections in a really good arrangement, such as my father undoubtedly gave

It was originally stipulated that £45,000 was to be the limit of the expenditure, and that the cost of the various designs was to be tested by a qualified surveyor, and an independent estimate made by him.

Two or three months later, when my father had already made his design and done a good deal of work on it, it was announced that the limit was to be extended to £65,000, so that he had to begin his work afresh.

The first thing heard of after the sending in of the drawings was that one of the competitors had broken the stipulations by sending in two designs, and that one of them, in consequence, had had to be returned to him,—a process by which the trustees must necessarily have become cognisant of his name.   Late in the month of August, the drawings having been sent in on the first, my father, who was on a

tour in Carinthia, heard from one of his clerks that rumours
were afloat to the effect that the trustees were, after all,
going to take the onus of deciding the competition upon
their own shoulders. A protest, however, was sent in by
Sir Gilbert Scott, with Mr. Burges's assent, against such a
course, and eventually, to the satisfaction of the competitors,
Mr Ewan Christian was appointed as adviser.

After the authoritative announcement of Sir Gilbert
Scott's appointment, my father applied to the trustees for a
copy of Mr. Christian's report, but they had marked it
"private and confidential," and refused to let him see it,
thus making him pretty certain of what he had surmised
before, that they had not abided by its suggestions. He
was the more certain of this, because it was pretty generally
said that my father's and Mr. Burges's plans were the only
two which could be carried out for the sum allowed

My father, in insisting on the printing of the report of
the architectural assessor, wrote : " If this work was to be
given to Sir G. G. Scott, Mr. Burges and I have a right to
complain that our time and skill have been wasted" On
Mr. Christian's also writing strongly in favour of the publication of his recommendations, the trustees at last conceded
the point, professing at the same time that they had till
then been ignorant of the existence of any such wish on the
part either of the competitors or of Mr. Christian.

Briefly, the report eliminated Mr. Lessels and Messrs.
Peddie and Kinnear at once ; and of the other four, had
their merits in other respects been equal, two should have
been at once put out of count by their failure to keep the
expense within the limit. Roughly put, the estimated cost
of carrying out these four designs was, beginning at the
highest—Mr. Ross, £113,500 ; Sir G. G. Scott, £75,000 ;
Mr. Burges, £63,500 , Mr. Street, 60,500 ; so that Mr
Ross exceeded by more than £48,000 and Sir G G. Scott
by £10,000, the stipulated amount.

Mr. Christian spoke favourably of Mr. Ross's design,
which was, however, obviously on too large a scale when
there was not unlimited money to be spent, with its central
and two western towers and apsidal east end. In view of

the selection of Sir G. G. Scott's design by the trustees, in spite of its cost, it is interesting to notice what Mr. Christian said of it. Briefly, he spoke of the central tower as being designed with considerable power, while other portions of the exterior, and notably the west front, seemed to him much less happy and forcible. Of the interior he said that, in the main, if it showed little originality, it had at any rate a thoroughly church-like and dignified character.

With regard to Mr Burges's design, the report pointed out several shortcomings : firstly, that the accommodation in the transepts and nave and aisles was only sufficient for thirteen instead of fifteen hundred, which was the number to be provided for ; again, that no provision had been made for daily services, and that the chapter-house and approaches were on too mean a scale.

Like Mr. Ross, Mr. Burges had included two western towers and a circular apse, but had substituted a *flèche* for the central tower. Of the design the report said : "It is very beautiful, and is founded on a French type. The interior would be bold and simple, yet rich in effect." The aisle roofs, however, were said not to be well treated, ugly outside, and calculated to hold a great deal of snow. Generally, however, the design was warmly praised in spite of a few defects.

Of my father's plan Mr. Christian said :—

"I may remark on this point that the plan of the church has been very carefully considered, and the result is most excellent. The nave and aisles are admirably adapted for a large congregation, and the arrangement of the choir is such that it would be thoroughly available for congregational purposes Nothing, indeed, can be better than the manner in which the whole building is, as it were, brought together for the purposes of worship, and there can be no doubt that a church so designed would, internally, be both thoroughly useful and exceedingly beautiful. The large area westward of the preacher allows of the central tower being made an open lantern, the effect of which, internally, must needs be good." Of the exterior he says : "The design is throughout very simple in its general character, though bold and vigorous in detail ; but the author has evidently felt himself considerably straitened by the limit of expenditure." And again : "The design is one of great excellence in detail, and, although perhaps severe, is wrought out in a bold and vigorous style, combined with much elegance, and would undoubtedly, if executed, produce externally a dignified and noble result, whilst the interior would be remarkably light and elegant."

The excellence of plan, and conscientious fulfilment of every requirement within the moderate limit of expense, with a reliance on purity and dignity of mass and outline rather than on costly detail, was, unfortunately, very unlikely to win the suffrages of men who had not had experience or knowledge of architecture, and most of whom probably now saw architectural drawings, or troubled themselves to understand architectural plans and elevations, for the first time in their lives

The Edinburgh correspondent of the *Church Times* said of my father's design —

"It is not likely to attract the multitude, but it has a meaning and an interest unattained by the others . . . It is the noblest design for a church that any of our modern architects have produced "

The same sentiments were expressed by many others in the columns of the same paper.

The *Church Herald* said :—

"No architect, Roman Catholic or Anglican, Continental or English, knows so thoroughly and exactly as Mr Street does what is required in a cathedral, and his design for Edinburgh was masterly. Unfortunately some of those who had to give judgment knew no more of architecture then a codfish knows of computation."

The *Building News* spoke of the design as being thoroughly characteristic, and founded on the native style :—

"It is in general conception the most original, and in point of plan and arrangement the most suitable. Had the prize fallen to this design the result would, in our opinion, have been more consistent with the views of the profession."

The same paper's Edinburgh correspondent said :—

"Mr. Street's drawings were unquestionably first in execution and in perfection of detail. The plan too was more full of interesting matter for study than any of the others, having evidently been designed to meet all the possible contingencies of cathedral service. If Mr. Street, by adhering to conditions as to cost, conscientiously refrained from giving the element of popularity to his design, he is not to blame; and we can only regret the more that, while Sir G. G. Scott has been allowed £10,000 for mere ornament, Mr. Street has not been suffered to leave his mark on our architecture "

After the publication of Mr. Christian's report, a long and exhaustive letter appeared in the *Scottish Guardian*, traversing the decision of the trustees. The writer pointed out how distinct and well-defined were the conditions as to cost, the trustees even binding themselves to appoint an independent surveyor to satisfy them " that the design can be carried out for the above sum " Mr Street and Mr. Burges are evidently selected by Mr. Christian; the trustees, however, throw them over for Sir G. G. Scott and Mr. Ross.

It is instructive to note the difference between the views of Sir G. G. Scott and my father as to the cost test.

The former says : " I have made a calculation as to the cost, which gives a result as favourable as I could anticipate , but as such works as this are rarely executed in our day, I will not pledge myself to meet your views with minute accuracy, but content myself with carefully aiming at the prescribed sum; and I believe that with care and reasonable economy, and possibly with the aid of some safety-valves, it may be realised, though it would not be wise, in a matter proverbially so much of a lottery as the cost of a large building, to pledge oneself too minutely. My object has been to give the best and noblest church which your conditions appear to admit I have made this my anxious aim, but beyond this I will not bind myself, further than to say that I believe I have realised my aim with very considerable accuracy. *Some of the more decorative fittings, such as the reredos, may be looked for as special gifts, and the painted decorations would not be included.*"

Contrast with this cloud of words the directness with which my father goes to the point, and the loyalty with which he accepts the limit imposed :—

" I have been most careful not to exceed the limit set ; I have made a careful calculation of the cost, founded upon my knowledge of the cost of corresponding buildings, and am satisfied that the work, *as drawn by me*, will be completed for the sum you have named "

The writer I have quoted goes on to point out that in various respects Mr. Burges had broken the conditions, as the consulting architect's report showed, and that in this respect my father was the only one of the competitors who was quite faultless —

"I think it almost impossible to escape from the conviction that Mr. Street ought to have been the successful man. In conclusion, I can only again express regret at the unfortunate selection the trustees have made."

It only remains to give my father's own explanation of the intention of his design, condensing the language of his report.

1. As to style, he expressly stated that he held it to be a mistake to copy any distinctly foreign feature, such as an apsidal termination, or to aim at importing any novelty of style, but rather to use the style of the country as seen at Dunblane, St. Andrews, and Elgin Cathedrals, and the abbeys of Sweetheart, Pluscardine, Melrose, Jedburgh, Dryburgh, and Holyrood—a style remarkable for its purity and simplicity Further, he pointed out that to provide a large and stately church for the money made it a *sine quâ non* that rich, curious, and elaborate details should be dispensed with

2. As to the plan. This was explained to be on the usual cathedral scheme of a cross church :—

"The choir is of moderate length so as to afford proper accommodation for the clergy and choristers only. The nave and transepts of ample dimensions to accommodate the number required. The choir furnished with aisles for the convenience of passing all round it, and of seeing and hearing well in all parts, and the exterior marked as a cathedral by its central lantern (open from the floor inside), and for the adornment of the city by its lofty western tower. I have made my nave unusually spacious. All its occupants will be within view of the altar, pulpit, and choir, and its length is such as to allow of the preacher and the choir being heard to the fullest extent."

A morning chapel was provided on the east side of the south transept for services with small congregations ·—

"The organist is so placed between this chapel and the choir that he can attend equally to services held in either place, and the organ—opening as it does both to the choir and to the south transept—will be heard equally well all over the church. The organ chamber is vaulted for purposes of sound. There is room in the choir stalls for forty clergy and choirmen. The stalls for the clergy are brought forward under the lantern, so that their occupants may be well seen and heard. The altar is brought forward from the east wall, and placed under a canopy. The space or passage behind the altar will add much to the perspective, and is consistent with all the traditions of British cathedrals. The arrangement of the aisle round the choir will give easy means of communication from the vestries to the altar in the choir, or to the altar in the chapel opening out of the transept. . . .

"The synod house in my plan occupies the place ordinarily taken by the chapter-house on the east of the cloister. . . . I have provided a distinct baptistery for the font opposite the south door-way. This is a picturesque as well as a convenient arrangement. . . I have provided a vaulted gallery in the western tower this might be used congregationally or for a great organ."

3. As to structural arrangements :—

"I propose to build the church with walls faced inside and out with wrought stone . to cover the whole eastern part of the church, *i e* the transepts and the choir with its aisles and side chapel, with stone-vaulted roofs. The tower and the north and south aisles of nave will also be vaulted in stone. The nave I propose to cover with a wooden vault this was a common mediæval arrangement. I may instance the transept roofs of York Minster."

The report concludes with a reference to the acoustic advantages of stone vaults and the estimate of expense which I have already quoted. Here I leave the subject. To my father it was a naturally distasteful one, and he never spoke of it at all ; but I take pleasure in putting down, once for all, in black and white, the rights and wrongs of the matter ; for my father's want of success, due as it was, firstly, to a refusal to pander to love of ornament, and secondly, to a conscientious adherence to the smallest item in the conditions, reflected as much credit on him as did the remarkable beauty and fitness of the design.

CHAPTER X

IN January we had moved from Russell Square, after having lived there several years, to a house at the corner of Cavendish Place and Cavendish Square—a most desirable change in every way, pleasant to my father personally and acceptable to those who had to do business with him. My father used to think that the position could not be bettered. When the succursale of the Langham was built at the back of our house, it made one's mouth water to see the gravel which came out of the foundations, and, to any one with a weakness for a gravel soil, must have inspired the most implicit confidence. We always looked upon it—proper pride demanded as much—as the healthiest spot in London, and were accordingly rather amused to find this view borne out by an old Frenchman with whom we struck up an acquaintance somewhere in France He spoke excellent English, and began to enlarge on the subject of health in towns and the comparative healthiness of the great cities. He was all for London, and out of all London he pronounced the western district to be the healthiest, selecting Cavendish Square as the best part of it ; and, he said, "the best part of Cavendish Square is the north-east corner of it" This was rather startling, and suggested that we might have been playing Box to his Cox in the house It appeared afterwards that he lived habitually at the Langham, which at one point actually touched our house.

My mother had long been urging on my father that he might well treat himself to a *pied à terre* in the country somewhere within easy reach of London, so as to be able to get a little fresh air on Sundays, but the project had taken no definite shape, and might very likely not have got beyond the region of possibilities had not the chance suddenly offered itself of getting a piece of ground in so charming a country as to make consideration little more than a pretence.   It was in September 1872 that my father and mother went down to spend the Sunday with his fellow-academician, Mr. H T. Wells, at his house at Holmbury, in the beautiful Dorking district   The station at which they arrived lies in a valley from which you gradually ascend, till at a certain point the view over the Sussex Weald suddenly bursts on you   As my father and mother came upon it, the distance was seen framed between two great beeches, where there was a rough opening to a piece of ground which had seemingly been lately bought, and was then being stocked with young trees and shrubs.   The view was so beautiful and so unlooked-for that my mother cried out, " It is heaven's gate."   The end of their journey was only five minutes farther on, and I imagine when they got there they were still full of it.   Mr. Wells was able to give them the intelligence that, owing to the death of the gentleman who had bought it, it was actually in the market at the time.   The piece of ground was only some fourteen or fifteen acres in extent—too little in a country which is all up and down, particularly as it would have been liable to have the view quite ruined by a building on the nearest brow ; but when my father found that he could secure so much more as to effectually prevent his ever being over-looked, he hesitated no longer

This new possession was the source of intense happiness to him, and when he was weighed down by sorrow upon sorrow in the years that followed, it may almost be said to have given him a new lease of life.   The actual ground itself, when it passed into his hands, was in the roughest possible state—genuine raw material on which to exercise his skill, but the lie of the land was all that could have been wished for.   Below the hill, on which he proposed to place the house, whenever he should see his way to begin building, the ground swept down in an amphitheatre, open at one end to give a glimpse of the blue distance seen over a bit of parklike foreground, whilst above it rose one spur behind

another of the near hill clothed with junipers and grand
bushes of holly, and over them again the farther edge of the
hill crowned with masses of dark firs

All that was needed was just that touch of man's handiwork which, by contrast, serves to make Nature all the more
lovely ; and that touch my father hastened to give.

He had the wisdom to depart from the orthodox rules of
proceeding, which ordain that, first of all, the brand-new
house, complete in every accessory, is to be planted down in
a rough field, or, may be, on a stony brow—looking as much
out of place as a gentleman in court dress on a snow
mountain,—while the really more important half of the work,
and far the more lengthy, what is to be looked at, instead of
what is to be looked out of, is postponed *sine die*. It requires
a good deal of self-restraint, when you have bought your
ground, resolutely to face a delay of years before actually
settling down on it, but that is what my father did. He
preferred to put off for a time the enjoyment of living on a
piece of ground of his own, in order that it might be without
drawback when the time did come.

The ground which he had to deal with no doubt lent
itself very happily to a quasi-formal treatment ; still he
could not do more than score a success, and that he certainly
achieved, giving every proof of being no indifferent landscape
gardener. The house he decided to place on a brow, with a
terrace running all along its front, overlooking the amphitheatre ; the whole, or nearly the whole, of the garden being
disposed in the hollow below. Here he set a regular gang
of men at work, cutting in and filling up till a certain formal
effect had been obtained by sunk rectangular lawns and
banks, which just gave the required contrast to all the
running lines and wild growth of the surroundings ; a carriage
drive right through the grounds to a lower road, and a
gradual obliteration of hedgerows, bound the whole together,
and opened out the views of the distant country :—

" I have been doing a great deal of gardening and planting this
winter," he writes a year after the purchase, " and am now looking
forward to the spring for a revelation of all the benefits that I have
conferred on my land. I have made a charming arrangement of

terraced garden and lawn in a deep dip between two steep hills, on the top of one of which my château is some day to rise, and then beyond this I have made a long carriage drive, which looks very well, and as I have been planting quantities of rhododendrons, I hope in due course of time we shall be very gay and beautiful I cannot say what a pleasure this hobby is to me, and what a relief I find it from my rather too ceaseless hard work."

Though my father had no intention of building his house till the garden had grown up somewhat, that did not prevent his doing the plans.   As the views to the south and south-east were almost equally good, he planned the house in two wings, forming an obtuse angle one with the other, one facing south-east and the other full south over the sunk garden.   A view of the house from the north-west, showing the entrance, was exhibited in the Academy.   The design was of a simple and unaffected character, with no odd excrescences or extravagant bits of picturesqueness   One-half of this was eventually carried out, but the whole was not completed during my father's lifetime.   In the early summer of 1873, having decided to make some use of his newly-acquired land, and at the same time superintend the earthworks which were in progress, he took rooms at Ockley, a village some three miles to the south, and from there we used to drive up every day to Holmdale—such was the name with which we found the place labelled, — spend the whole day watching the garden grow into shape, and return in the evening laden with peas and potatoes from our own kitchen garden.   Never did vegetables taste so delicious as those—the first-fruits of our own soil.

Just before our visit to Ockley the Bishop of Winchester had met with his death at Evershead's Rough, not more than three miles from our ground.   He was then riding to Mr. Leveson Gower's at Holmbury with Lord Granville, and had intended looking at the proposed site of our house while he was there   My father was much shocked at the sudden death of one who had been his true friend and patron from his earliest days, and the manner and place of the accident made it all the more grievous to him, and seemed like a bad omen at this our first coming.   He attended the funeral, which took place at Graffham near Lavington, where he afterwards practically rebuilt the church for Mr. Reginald Wilberforce, in memory of the Bishop. A few years later he designed the large memorial church of St. Mary's, Southampton, for Canon Wilberforce. St. Mary's is simplicity itself, in no way cheap-looking, but a large church for its cost Internally it is most impressive, very spacious and dignified, and relieved from the possibility of severity by a well-placed richness in various of the fittings There is no chancel arch at all, the division between the nave and chancel being shown by nothing more than a cusped wooden roof principal. The result is that the eye is carried in from the nave arcade across the transept to the chancel arcade, and a great appearance of length is in that way obtained. The vestries are in an unusual position, east of the chancel, and of course at a somewhat lower level than the chancel floor. The chancel is approached from them by two staircases of a few steps through the east wall, one on each side of the altar, the altar itself being protected on either side by a stone wing screen. ' The arrangement is convenient and effective, but would be obviously out of place in any but a very wide chancel, which this one is.

Among the, more important works which my father was doing at this time were the hall, Wigan, for the Hon. and Rev. G T. O Bridgman, for whom he had done work at Blymhill many years before ; the restorations of Thirsk, Oswestry, Dunster, and Clun churches—all of them fine buildings and most successful restorations, more particularly the last, perhaps because of the terrible state of decay into which it had fallen, and the grand look of the church after restoration Besides this he was engaged on various works at Marlborough College, a chapel at Luton Hoo for Mrs. Gerard Leigh, new churches at Blickling and Putney, and what was practically one at Huish for Lord Clinton

The latter part of the summer, which had been begun at Ockley, was spent in the lake country. My father can hardly have been there since he went up to stop at Langrigg in quest of his first commission some thirty years before. He managed to get some architectural sketching at Furness

Abbey, Cartmel, and Calder, and Egglestone Abbeys, and, going back through Yorkshire, revisited Richmond and Easby Abbey, which he had first seen thirty years previously.

During my Christmas holidays a second tour was made to South Italy This time we took an unusual and round-about route to Naples in order to see some fresh places. Stopping first at Ancona, we went next to Foggia—a wild-looking place, unvisited of tourists, and inhabited by something very like banditti; in the neighbourhood—at Lucera —was a most interesting church. From Foggia we made our way by Benevento to Naples. After a stay at Portici my grandfather joined us in our excursion to Salerno, and along the exquisite coast road to Amalfi and Ravello. Ten days were spent in Rome, a good deal of which my father had to give up to business, an English church having been put into his hands as well as the American one, and there being a good deal of difficulty about a site On our way back we stopped at Terni to see the grand fall, Spoleto and Foligno, driving from the latter place to Spello and Assisi, with which my father was enraptured, then to Perugia, Asti in polar weather, and so home.

In the summer of 1874 we saw Troyes, Sens, Dijon, Beaune, Auxerre, Tonnèrre, Pontigny, Avallon, Vézelay, Chartres, and Rouen, besides spending two or three weeks in Switzerland This tour has a melancholy interest, because it was the last my mother was ever to take ; by a strange irony of fate we went on this, her last tour, to several of the places which she and my father had seen on their honeymoon By the light of her illness, which came on gradually during the tour, we could see that for a year or two her health had been gradually failing Physically, but not constitutionally, strong, the many hardworking journeys she had taken part in had possibly helped to sap her strength, though the interest she felt never allowed her to show fatigue, and very likely prevented her feeling it in full at the moment. None of us, she, I feel sure, as little as any, had the least idea that her illness was likely to be serious, and after our return from abroad we went down to a little inn within a mile or two of Holmdale, with the idea that a little perfect rest would put her in the way of recovery. One afternoon she walked on from Holmdale to see Mr. Wells and his family, and I know they were much struck by the change in her; but the doctors gave us no alarming hint; and to us, seeing her as we did every day, a change would be less perceptible. As October wore on she took to her bed, and as late as the 13th we had no suspicion of danger. That day, being my birthday, we had contemplated spending at Holmdale, and my mother insisted on our going, though she felt too unwell to go with us. The next day she became unconscious, intermittently at first, and continued so till the 16th, when she died.

The loss to my father was a terrible one. The companion of a quarter of a century, whose love had seemed to grow with the years, who had shared his joys and sorrows and made them her own, rejoicing in his success more intensely than he did himself, was suddenly snatched from his side.

My mother had not been satisfied to enter only into half my father's life, content to let business be her successful rival in his thoughts during the greater part of each day, but —his office had always been at home, and that made it easier —she had identified herself from the first with the workaday side of his life; she knew all that he was doing, how his works were progressing, his doubts and his hopes, as this promised less well than he had anticipated and something else better; she had soon learnt to take an intelligent interest, not only in his designs, but in architecture generally, and moreover, had her strong likes and dislikes, being a devoted adherent of first-pointed work, and almost intolerant of anything later.

Her admiration for my father was as boundless as her devotion to him. To me she was the best of mothers, always ready to sacrifice herself, if by doing so she could do me pleasure. Almost the last time she spoke to me, it was to blame herself for having spoilt the enjoyment of my birthday by being ill, entirely forgetful of herself. She was the warmest, the most enthusiastic, the most faithful of friends; indeed, I think the number of close and affectionate friendships she formed was one of the most remarkable things about her. One of the earliest of them was almost like a case of love at first sight. She was so much touched by the acting and the looks of a lady who was then almost the first among our actresses, that she could not rest till she had got to know her. The acquaintance once made soon ripened into the warmest friendship on both sides, and only ended with her death.

A nature which was so prodigal of its best naturally craved for much in return, but did so with no tinge of jealousy, and in claiming a rich tribute of affection as its due, would have been pained if it had meant the exclusion of others. She was buried at Boyne Hill, in the shadow of one of my father's churches, built during the earliest years of their marriage, and near, too, to her old home at Geys.

The day after the funeral I went up to Oxford to keep my first term, and my father was left alone in the desolate house. Hard work was his great resource, varied with rapid dashes down to Surrey. His work at Holmdale became every day more and more of a pleasure to him, and in his projects for the future there he found some relief from his thoughts. A month after my mother's death he wrote to me :—

"Before Bishop Wilberforce died, I had offered him to build a chancel if he could get a church built near Holmdale, where we might reckon on decent services. Since your mother's death I have been thinking a good deal about it, and I have now offered the bishop to build a church if he can get a district made for it, to take in Holmdale and the other houses on the hill. I think the present bishop will be inclined to help me, though not so vigorously as the last would have done perhaps. . . . I have had such a happy prosperous life that it is time for me to say, 'Quid retribuam Domino ?' . . . I had a very cold journey back from Dublin again on Saturday night; we were nearly five hours crossing, so that we did not get to Euston Square till half-past seven on Sunday morning; but as I had come up for the express purpose of going to the early service at All Saints, I got home, gave myself a very mild polish, and got into church by 8 A.M. I think, after such a feat as that, I may be expected, ere long, to be figuring on the cinders against some of your athletes; don't you think so? . . . I am going to breakfast very early to-morrow, in order to go to Warfield, near Windsor, and I shall get back to luncheon. After dinner I am going down by the 11.50 P.M. Pullman car train to Leeds, in order to go to a couple of places in Yorkshire, and I hope to get home again on Thursday night. . . . Your uncle and his family are coming on Saturday I am very glad to have some one here, for the solitary confinement does not suit me at all."

This gives some idea of the sort of life my father was leading. Incessant occupation gave the only hope of escaping from his natural depression of spirits. My uncle and his wife and family came at the end of November and stopped some months, so that my father was spared the loneliness which he had felt so much during the first sad weeks.

In 1874 the gold medal annually presented by the Institute of Architects was bestowed on my father. It was, and is, the custom not to confine this honour to Englishmen, nor yet to practising architects, but to confer it at regular intervals on literary, in contradistinction to practical, exponents of architecture, and this particular year it had been decided, in the words of the Resolution, "to confer the distinction on an Englishman distinguished for his literary productions in connection with architecture."

The choice had fallen on Professor Ruskin, and the thing was taken as settled, but, unfortunately for the dignity of the Institute, there were two parties to be consulted in the matter, and Professor Ruskin took the unprecedented step of entirely declining to receive the medal, at the same time rapping the members of the Institute on the knuckles for the numerous delinquencies which were accountable for his refusal of the proffered honour.

The Council then decided to rescind their previous resolution, and to substitute an architect as the recipient in place of a literary man. My father, whose claims to be elected as a writer were considerable, was unanimously chosen as the most eminent practical exponent of the art. The medal with its gilt rubbed off was loyally accepted by him. The presentation took place so immediately after my mother's death that my father was unable to be present, and Mr. Pearson acted as his representative. Sir G. G. Scott, in handing him the medal, after eulogising my father's work and the morality of his artistic character, took occasion to point out that his claims rested by no means wholly on his actual works :—

"Mr. Street is an author," he said, "of no mean eminence, and his book on the *Brick and Marble Architecture of North Italy*, and his *Gothic Architecture in Spain* will always stand forth as practical evidences of this fact, not to mention the more fugitive productions of his pen. These works are not only of the utmost value from the talent of their author, but are so more especially as proceeding from one who has probably extended his studies and his wonderful powers of sketching to the mediæval buildings of a greater number of countries and places than any other living man."

On my return from Oxford we started for Rome and spent some five weeks away. From Mentone we drove along the Riviera. After a day in Genoa we left by a very early train with the intention of going right through to Rome and getting there to sleep. A mistake at Pisa, where, by the misdirection of a porter, we changed into a train which was going back to Genoa instead of that for Florence, upset our arrangements, and gave us an opportunity of seeing the great pinewood of Pisa. The first station we stopped at was Viareggio, ten miles out—a desolate-looking place, but boasting a horse which, harnessed to a strange springless cart, carried us through the pinewood to Pisa in the hour. The rest of the day was spent there, and, starting in the evening, we reached Rome early the next morning, well satisfied with the result of our contretemps. This year from Naples we explored the coast north of it, and on our way home spent a few days at Florence with Lord Crawford at the Villa Palmieri, a house beautifully situated on the road to Fiesole, and the scene of the Decameron.

While he was in Rome my father wrote an interesting letter on the probable meaning of the network of walls which was then being laid bare under the arena of the Colosseum. A letter had appeared in the *Times* a short time before in which some explanation was offered, but it seemed to him so unsatisfactory as to induce him to write.

"I venture," he wrote, "to give what seems a more correct explanation of the results. Your correspondent treats the whole of the substructure of the arena as a comparatively modern addition to the original building, erected on the old paved floor, which remains some twenty feet below what hitherto appeared to be the ground line. If he had compared this substructure with that of the still almost perfect amphitheatre at Pozzuoli, he would have been less likely to have ventured on such a suggestion. The use of the building would involve the necessity of buildings, rooms and passages under the floor of the arena, and when we see them all perfectly preserved, with all the necessary provisions for lighting, for ingress, and for drainage as at Pozzuoli, we might be sure that some similar arrangements must once have existed under the arena of the Colosseum, even if all traces of them had been destroyed.

"Fortunately the excavations already made show that the two buildings were arranged very much in the same way. Looking at the uncovered basement walls of the Colosseum from above, we find that the whole central portion of the arena was occupied with constructions that did not follow the oval lines of the amphitheatre, but were rectangular in plan. They present the appearance of three parallel canals or passages, surrounded by double walls, strengthened at short intervals by cross walls. Though these walls are too close together for use as passages, they are all plastered, and it seems probable, therefore, that this cellular construction of walls, plastered on the face, was devised for the purpose of supporting the weight, and also preventing the escape, of water in the canals above them, whenever the arena was required for nautical combats. In the central passage or canal the masonry is built on a slope from the basement up to the floor of the arena, and at the bottom lies the wooden framework referred to by your correspondent. This is not constructed as a floor would be, but is evidently a sliding way, up which vessels might have been pulled from below into the arena Just in advance of the front seats in the arena, a double row of recesses is constructed all round the basement. Mr. S. H. Parker is of opinion that these recesses were used as cages for wild beasts, and this is the ordinary account of the corresponding recesses at Pozzuoli. The objection to the theory is that there seem to be no remains or marks in either case of any enclosures in front of these dens, and that it would be difficult, to say the least, to put wild beasts into places so difficult of access. The passages in front of them were probably lighted in the same way as at Pozzuoli, where a large number of square openings are left in the floor of the arena. These were fitted with frames let into stone-rebated margins, and probably contained iron gratings which, when required, could be covered with boards. I am myself more inclined to think that two large chambers, which exist right and left of the principal entrance to the basement, were the commonly used dens The metal sockets in the floor described by your correspondent would allow of the main supports for the front of the dens being firmly fixed, leaving a passage-way in front, and allowing of the confined beasts being let loose into the arena without risk to the attendants. The arrangement is somewhat similar to that for the entrance of the bull into the Spanish arena, and the ascending-way would have served for the beasts to reach the arena. In front of the double arcade of recesses or dens are visible pairs of large corbels of travertine at regular intervals.

"These formed the base of square chases made in the walls for the admission, when required, of timber-posts of great strength. These would have formed the supports for a palisading a few feet from the front seats of the arena, leaving an unoccupied alley or passage-way between the arena and the spectators. How necessary such a contrivance is, I need not point out to any one who has ever seen a bull-fight.

"At Pozzuoli, precisely the same provision is made by square holes through the vault of the substructure, which left a space of six feet clear of the front seats. Here the arrangement is more obvious to an ordinary visitor, but once pointed out, every one may see plainly that it existed also at the Colosseum. In both these theatres there are numbers of chases cut in the walls, which are so cut that pieces of cross timber might be inserted, wedged tightly in, and removed at pleasure. In the Colosseum many of these look at first sight as though they had been additions made for the sake of gaining additional support for the walls. But seeing that precisely the same kind of groove is made at regular intervals in the canal at Pozzuoli, I come to the conclusion that they show that the provision for water displays was not of a permanent kind, and that the cisterns, tanks, or canals, were constructed mainly of wood, while, no doubt, when not in use, they were covered over with wooden floors. It would have been quite impossible to flood the whole arena without flooding at the same time all the rooms and passages below its level all round the building, and at the same time stopping all means of access to the arena for combatants. And it is quite clear that a building used at different times for various kinds of displays would be likely to show, as the substructure of the Colosseum does, many marks of removable constructions, such as those on which I have remarked. I will only add that if the suggestion which has been made as to the original level of the arena having been some twenty feet lower than has hitherto been supposed were correct, either the arena must have been reduced to the smallest possible dimensions, or it would have been such a deeply-sunk pit that none of the spectators, except those in the front row, would have seen anything of the performances that went on in it. The suggestion therefore carries its own refutation on its face."

In his journey over the Brenner, my father met with a very interesting fellow-traveller, who, upon an interchange of cards, turned out to be Count George Seckendorf, then on his way to Pegli. My father met him subsequently in London, and was introduced by him to the German Crown Prince and Princess, who spoke warmly of their admiration for my father's work generally, and his little church in Genoa in particular

In the summer of 1875 my father became engaged to Jessie, second daughter of Mr. William Holland of Harley Street, a lady who had been of all my mother's friends the most highly prized, and had been so intimate with us as to have been her companion on many of our autumn tours. This year closed with every promise of a peaceful and happy future ; my father was on the eve of a marriage, of the wisdom of which there could be no doubt. Work poured in as fast as ever, and found him no less able than heretofore to cope with it, while the house at Holmdale was now fast rising out of the ground, with every sign of being ready for living in during the coming summer.

My father was married on 11th January 1876. The wedding tour took them over a great deal of ground which he knew well, and some which was new to him—Capri, for instance. On their way back they stopped a few fatal days in Rome, and then came rapidly home. I was still at Oxford when letters came from my father saying that his wife was not well, then that she had been feverish, but that the doctors were not anxious, and the fever was abating ; and then, again, that all was over. The last flicker had raised hopes which were to be only too quickly dispelled, and Rome was answerable for one more victim. I had never seen my father's wife during the short eight weeks of her married life She was buried at Cranleigh, in which parish part of my father's land lay, under the shadow of the church to which in those days we used to go every Sunday to service

When our church was built at Holmbury her remains were moved there

The effect of this blow following so quickly upon the first was numbing in its effects. I think my father dreaded the prospect of living on. The happiness of the past six months had shown him how much more complete a happiness he might reasonably look for in the future. Hardly had he begun to realise how entirely his hopes were being fulfilled when the cup was, with startling suddenness, dashed from his lips. London became abhorrent to him, and whenever he could spare a day he betook himself to Holmdale, on which his affections and interests became more and more fixed, though he could not but associate it with the memories of those who had not been permitted to go down into the promised land. To dwell on the serene face of Nature was his delight. The spring told him of birth and growth, and the summer of exuberance of life and health, with a reality which his frequent watching in the chamber of death made all the more vivid. Even in autumn he found in Nature the needed contrast: "The autumn tints on the foliage," he wrote, "are exquisite, beyond anything I have seen before, I think ; *calm decay* everywhere."

In the summer of 1876 our house was completed, and the next eight weeks were spent there with only short breaks. I think this time was not an unhappy one. My father had pleasant neighbours and sympathetic friends about him, and the possession of one or two spare rooms, which were rarely empty, enabled him to renew his friendship with many whom, in the long period of isolation caused by his double loss, he had almost lost sight of. From this time forward, winter or summer, there was hardly a Saturday to Monday that he did not spend there, and through all the spring and summer months he, generally speaking, had friends with him. These days in the country were as prolific of work as they were enjoyable ; so rapidly was he able to do his drawing, when quite uninterrupted, that he could, with the best possible conscience, spend much time in the garden which, in London, would have been spent, and very likely half-wasted, in his study. As an instance of what he was able to do in a few quiet hours, I notice in his diary the result of one day's work entered there : "Twelve sheets of full-size drawings for hinges for Christ Church Cathedral, etc. Specification for Melksham Church." I need not say that all the ironwork for Christ Church, Dublin, is of the most elaborate character.

The certainty that he would never be able to give his town house a mistress, and a feeling that there were many more rooms in it than he could ever really use, made him seriously think of moving to some smaller house in the neighbourhood. We had actually settled on one in Park Square, and were trying to pretend to each other that the new house would be all that we wanted when, at the last moment, there was a hitch in the negotiations, and one that proved fatal

The relief was intense. My father wrote to me at Oxford:—

"I saw ——, he told me he never saw so charming a room as this drawing-room, and he was rejoicing that I could not leave it just now. Nearly every one seems to be of the same mind, and I must own that when I heard that —— would not take me for a tenant, I felt as if I had been reprieved after a sentence of death. All my happiest associations are with these rooms, and I begin to think I should be less happy anywhere else."

Naturally my father never had any further thought of leaving a house which he found to be so bound up with his affections With the certainty of keeping his house came the desire to make a better use of it, and of gathering now and again at his table the friends whom his busy life did not allow him to see at other times. There being no lady of the house, it was natural that he should generally have confined himself to men Most of the members of the Academy were his guests at one time or another, and professional brethren, with a smattering of outsiders made up the number I think a sly stroke of business was done in the judicious mixture of members of the Academy and architects. My father never tired of doing all he could to forward the interests of his profession, and get recognition for the talented among its members, and in this way he delicately hinted to his fellow-academicians that there were many architects, still outside the pale, worthy of being admitted within the magic circle.

CHAPTER XI

IN spite of the multitude of his engagements my father was able to devote time and energy to the support of these movements, which have become common of late years, directed now to the preservation of some ancient monument, at home or abroad, from wanton alteration, at another time to the rescue of some work of our own day from the clutches of the reckless improver.

Some of the subjects with which I deal in this chapter do not, as will readily be seen, come, accurately speaking, under either of these heads, but they are at the same time somewhat analogous to those which do come strictly within this category, and have this feature in common, that they show my father, not as the architect in charge, but as the critic, dealing, in some few cases indeed, with the proposals of a brother architect, not, however, unless constrained by the paramount importance of the question in dispute and the general interest taken in it.

The first important subject of this character in point of date was probably that of the decoration of St. Paul's, so long debated,—so barren, even now, of visible result. The fitting treatment of Wren's masterpiece had always been very near my father's heart He, indeed, felt not only a very genuine and often expressed admiration for the building itself, but he had that sort of selfish interest, "οὐδέν τό τούτου 'μᾶλλον ἢ τοὐμὸν σκοπῶν," which every architect should have in keeping intact and unhurt the conception of a great predecessor My father's contribution to the controversy, if it may be so called, was interesting both objectively and subjectively. It displayed so emphatically that feeling which always governed him in dealing with churches old or new, a respect for the building—if it deserved it,—and still more a respect for its sacred use, and a desire to make its purpose more entirely attainable , and again his suggestions had the merit of being unlike anything which had been previously mooted, and were as practical as they were original. First, he premised, a great artist's work ought not to be restored or completed if that process is to involve any departure from what he would conceivably or probably have done himself. Now, in my father's words, it is impossible that much applied decoration (such as was then contemplated) can be done without wholly altering the architectural character of an interior. When a man's real intentions are as much a matter of guesswork as Wren's are in this case, it is cruel to remodel his work. My father insisted strongly that the translation of stone into marble was inadmissible   A design, when made, is arranged for execution either with surfaces of stone or with a marble face, but the treatment in the two cases will naturally be very different. It did, however, seem to him very necessary to alter the existing surface by restoring the stone to sight throughout, leaving the walls otherwise intact. This, he thought, would add sensibly to the dignity and beauty of the interior

Broadly stated, his real proposal amounted to this, that the new work should be done not on the walls or in the dome but on the floor of the church   He gives his reasons for the changes and additions which he proposes.

The service of the church, rightly looked at, needs two things :—

1. An altar, so placed as to be a central object, visible to the whole congregation, and

2. A choir and organ, so disposed as to direct the largest possible number in the most effective way. The modern use of a cathedral in a big town is, as has been said before, not unlike that of a great religious house in the Middle Ages. It has to convert the multitudes which, on special occasions, throng the building ; and at another time to satisfy the two or three who gather day after day at the choir services.

These latter services, continuing the analogy, answer to those of the religious, and the popular nave services to those for which the religious orders provided their great naves and people's altars.

My father was so strongly impressed by the twofold character of the need, that he proposed making permanent provision for two kinds of congregations.

Firstly, the choir was to be retained, practically without alteration ; and secondly, another altar and choir was to be made for the large congregations collected on Sundays, festivals, and exceptional occasions. He pointed out, very justly, that for all purposes of worship, supposing that word to have any meaning, the services conducted in the choir were practically useless for a congregation assembled under the dome. No one but a most devout churchman could under such circumstances dream of kneeling, still less of joining in the chanting :—

"Architecturally," he says, "I can conceive nothing more magnificent than the result which my alternative plan would achieve. I should put a noble altar under the dome, raised on steps, and under a sumptuous baldachin. The arrangement of the choir might be similar to that of the cathedral at Florence. The baldachin might be largely made of metal or of sculptured marble, and the retable behind the altar might rival that of Pistoia in its wealth of enamel and silver ; mosaics might be used for the roof and groining of the canopy. The baldachin and altar alone would more than redeem the church from its present poverty."

The casket would have been glorified by the jewel as Or San Michele is by Orcagna's shrine and baldachin.

Further, the pavements were all to be converted into opus Alexandrinum, and the organ was to be placed over the screen between the choir and the dome—a position acquiesced in by Wren, and one which would have made the instrument equally available for either service. Plenty of room would have been left on either side of it so as to avoid blocking the vista up the choir.

This alteration my father regarded as a *sine quâ non*. One more change would have been necessitated by his plan, viz. the removal of the present pulpit. The new one would have been placed against the marble septum wall of the choir in the form of a grand ambon, following the arrangement so well exemplified at San Clemente in Rome.

For the decoration of the windows—for he contemplated the substitution of colour for the simple white glass as in no way calculated to interfere with the architectural effect—he suggested as a model the exquisite French glass of the sixteenth and seventeenth centuries, the most marked features of which are its delicacy of drawing and the predominance of white background.

This was the complete scheme ; one which, as my father truly averred, had at least this merit, that it destroyed nothing and altered no existing effect except where the alteration was a reversion to the original scheme   It however lacked that tentativeness[1] which seems a necessary ingredient in any plan for dealing with St. Paul's, and the very fact that it was capable of fulfilling so completely the two great essentials as laid down by my father at starting, was likely to frighten all but the stronger spirits   Let us hope that the mosaic designs which are some day to decorate the dome will not have the effect anticipated by my father of destroying the impressive largeness of scale, which is due so much to a sense of atmosphere and indistinctness of colour and detail.

I find from a letter of my father's that the pamphlet— one of some length—in which he expressed the views which I have given here very shortly, was written one night at a client's house after he had gone up at twelve o'clock, presumably to bed.

LONDON BRIDGE.

In 1875 the question of the best means of relieving the congestion of traffic on London Bridge came before the Court of Common Council for consideration, and one morning the announcement was made in the papers, to the general dismay, that a resolution had been passed in favour of widening the bridge by the application of iron structures to its sides—such an arrangement being in accordance with

[1] Written before the new reredos was put up

certain recommendations which had been made by the
Bridge House Estate Committee. My father lost no time
in writing to the papers to protest most strongly from both
the purely artistic and the practical point of view against the
proposals contained in the resolution :—.

"I suppose no one," he wrote, "would consent to doubling the
width of Westminster Abbey by the addition of brick aisles outside
the existing walls ; yet it seems to me that such a proposition would
be no more monstrous than the scheme which seems to have been
approved by the Common Council for widening and entirely concealing the design of Rennie's very magnificent work, London
Bridge . . . In the place of the bridge as it now exists we should
have a network of iron which, as it would have to conform to some
extent to the old masonry outlines, would have none of the merits
of a real and genuine iron construction. . . . The one merit of the
proposal is its economy. the alteration can, it seems, be made for
£65,000 . . . The wisdom of any proposal for mixing up iron and
granite in any structure is in itself open to serious question The
two materials will not decay at the same pace; and the project is,
therefore, on this ground open to objection, on the ground of its
temporary nature, as opposed to the monumental character of the
existing bridge."

From the practical point of view my father argued, in
common with others, that a wider bridge could be of no manner of use unless the approaches were made wider too. His
opposition to this scheme, for which the city authorities did
not cease to battle, met with recognition from various quarters.
Truth especially paid him the compliment of devoting an
entire paragraph to him of the most veracious kind :

"I trust that London Bridge will not be rendered hideous by
Mr. Street's plan to widen it by facing the present granite arches with
iron arches It is a monstrous scheme."

For some time the project was little heard of, but in
1879 there was a decided recrudescence, till fortunately the
Bill was shelved on a third reading in the House of Lords,
and no more was heard of it.

A few extracts from my father's diary will be of interest
as showing the part he took :—

"*June* 23 —Attended meeting of the Committee for the conservation of London Bridge. Afterwards went to London Bridge

to look at the traffic, etc., then at 4 P.M. to a meeting of the Council of the R.I.B.A , where my resolution was again carried unanimously, and ordered to be sent as a petition to the House of Lords This is capital ! '

Again . " Dined at Lord Eldon's He met me with the news that Lord Carnarvon's motion had been quite successful about London Bridge. The question was referred to a committee finally. If there had been a division our side would have had a large majority. I am well pleased at this so far satisfactory result of my protest.

" Went to Lord Carnarvon's to consult about London Bridge Committee. Thence to call on Sir Frederick Leighton, G. F. Watts, Millais, and Poynter; got all of them to agree to give evidence against the alteration of London Bridge. They are all very hot about it.

"*July* 10 —Examined at Lords Committee, and gave evidence against the alteration.

"*July* 11.—As I came out of the Athenæum this evening met Gregory, the engineer, who said : ' Well, you have thrown out our Bill for widening London Bridge.' I was of course delighted to hear that I had done so."

The next day Lord Carnarvon wrote to my father ·—

" I am really rejoiced to have been able to save London Bridge ; but I should have known nothing of the danger, nor could I have averted it, but for your warning and help."

SOUTHWELL MINSTER.

In 1876 my father made a report on this interesting church at the instance of the Ecclesiastical Commissioners, whose architect—Mr. Ewan Christian—had already made a scheme for its restoration. He met Mr. Christian at the church, where they examined it together, and subsequently wrote his report.

The question on which he was asked his advice was that constantly recurring one, viz. the best way to make an old building suitable for our services without pulling it about My father's opinion, as expressed in the report, is another exemplification of the spirit which always animated him in such cases, and shows yet once again the relative importance which he attached to an old building merely as such, and as a thing possessing certain possibilities and having certain functions to fulfil.

He first proceeds to show how admirably adapted the thirteenth-century plan, in its untouched state, would have been for our purposes The choir was a short one, only fifty-five feet in length, and, even when prolonged westward across the transept, only about eighty feet long.   This would not have been too large for the clergy and choir of a cathedral at the present day.   The nave and transepts would have served for the congregation, the noble eastern chapel for early celebrations, week-day morning services, or indeed any services which do not draw a large congregation

The old arrangement my father took to have been as follows :—

The three eastern bays of the choir formed the lady chapel. (These were, at the time the report was written, included in the choir, and Mr Christian did not propose to make any alteration.)   The next bay westward was in all probability left open, so as to form a passage behind the altar and give access to the lady chapel and the chapels at the east end of the north and south aisles   It seemed likely that these chapels were screened off at the ends and sides, and they were almost certainly not used as passage ways, to which purpose, Mr. Christian wished to put them

Had the church been left untouched, it would have presented no difficulty at all, but the fourteenth-century additions offered a problem not easy to solve.   At that time a great stone rood screen and loft was put up.   This was something like fifteen feet in depth from east to west, groined in three divisions, with two staircases leading up to the loft.   Upon it was a large organ, so that the church was actually cut in two.

My father, before approaching the solution of the problem, cleared the ground by stating what he thought should be the aim of an architect in trying to adapt an old church.   The right course, he said, is, first of all, to replace the altar in its original position, to restore all the old arrangements as far as they can be discerned, and when that is done, to see how far the plan can be made to serve the needs of to-day.

If the complete utility of the original scheme is found to be interfered with by subsequent erections of the nature of the rood screen in this instance, then the only true course, if the obstruction is a really serious one, is to have the courage to remove it, preserving it carefully and re-erecting it in some other part of the building.

At Southwell, however, the smallness of the population seemed to make a compromise more than ordinarily feasible.

In calculating the amount of accommodation to be provided, my father would always have wished it to be kept in mind that choir aisles were built as passages and used as such, and consequently should not, under any circumstances, be obstructed by seats and chairs. Having laid this down, he advised that the next step should be the screening off of the lady chapel, leaving the first bay west of it clear, in order to give it a proper access ; there would then be four bays of choir east of the tower and rood screen, with a total length of sixty feet. Bernasconi's plaster screens and stalls should be removed, and their place taken by others of the original design (which my father was able to make out completely from fragments which he had discovered in the middle of lumber). These new stalls should occupy the two western bays two rows deep, and with one row of chairs in front of them would give all the accommodation necessary for week-day congregations.

The difficult question, however, of providing for the largely attended services still remained

My father assumed that the rood screen would be left undisturbed—such a course being in accordance with his own views ; but its retention was obviously a source of difficulty. He explained that unfortunately it did not lend itself to any system of piercing Accepting it, then, as an obstruction, he asked himself what the purpose of its builders had been, and to what use such an ample loft had been designed Far from having been intended as a barrier, it had doubtless been put up by the fourteenth-century men in order to make the service more audible to the congregation in the nave. The organs of those days were very unlike what we are accustomed to now, and took up comparatively little space, so that this screen might well have served as a singing gallery. Why not, he asked, put it to its old use ? There would be ample room for the choir with a pair of small organs, the great organ being put in some other part, as at Canterbury. In this way the people would be enabled to join intelligently in the service, the lessons might then be read from an eagle under the central tower, and the pulpit placed against one of its piers.

My father was convinced that this was .the right way to overcome the difficulty—to face it boldly. For all that he could not disguise from himself that the novelty of the arrangement in our day would be quite enough to frighten "safe" men. With this possibility before him, he alluded in his report to two other schemes, which he gave in the order of their merit.

The first alternative was that of removing the rood screen bodily, and erecting it somewhere else, as, for instance, across the transept. On this point he wrote that he would not mind being responsible for its removal "were I not distinctly of opinion that the screen may be utilised in the way I have suggested." It would, to his mind, have been straining at a gnat and swallowing a camel to alter the *whole* of the old arrangement for the sake of preserving *one* feature, but in this particular case he was glad to feel that the necessity for this strong measure did not arise.

The second and less commendable plan was the same as the original one up to a certain point It involved the restoration of the choir to its old state, but the organ was to be retained on the screen, and a second altar provided in the nave for the services there This arrangement my father did not feel able to say much in favour of, still he preferred it to the scheme which was fathered by Mr. Christian, viz. to throw the whole choir open, to put the altar where that of the lady chapel had originally stood, increasing the number of stalls, and seating the congregation in rows of chairs or seats—facing north and south—between the stalls and the altar ; in one word, upsetting the whole of the old arrangement of the church to preserve one later piece of furniture.

Mr. Christian wrote a reply to my father's report, the gist of which was that my father had no proof of the old arrangement having been what he had suggested. "The only difference between us," he summed up, "is, that Mr. Street wishes to restore the choir to what he believes to have been its original state, while I wish to utilise it as it comes to me with its fourteenth-century additions and alterations." A difference of a very fundamental kind however!

My father was the subject of a bitter attack for his supposed vandalism in having suggested that the removal of the screen was within the bounds of possibility. It was useless for him to repeat that he had merely mentioned it as one of several obvious courses while strongly advocating another. His fault, in the eyes of his critics, lay in his having professed himself courageous enough to counsel the removal of a piece of old work in any instance where it proved an insuperable bar to a proper use of a church, and where no less heroic treatment was possible.

His conclusion is the one to which he had willingly and gladly bound himself in speaking and writing from his earliest years, and it is a perfectly logical one to any one who regards a church primarily as a building which owes its existence to the needs of public worship, and should therefore be made to subserve them properly, rather than to play the part of a museum of architectural antiquities. Indeed, the difference between the man who clings to the dry bones of the building rather than to the spirit which vivifies them and the man who just reverses the order lies very deep, and can hardly be the subject of argument.

ST. ALBANS ABBEY.

Sir Gilbert Scott, at the time of his death, was employed among other things on a restoration of the Abbey Church of St. Albans, but as this was being done piecemeal, it was left a good deal to the imagination of his successors to divine what would have been his action in certain particulars which had never received his full attention.

Foremost among these was the treatment of the nave roof—a subject which was brought very fully before the public in 1878-79, and into the merits of which I do not propose to go except in so far as my father's strong views on the point make it necessary. A good deal of dismay was created in architectural and antiquarian circles when it was found that it was proposed to replace the existing flat roof and panelled ceiling by a roof of steep pitch with parapets.

It appeared that Sir Gilbert Scott had never actually expressed his intentions, but Mr. J. O. Scott, who had taken his father's place, stated that, as far as he could ascertain his father's views, and judging by his action in analogous cases, as, for instance, at Selby, he concluded that a new high-pitched roof would have been substituted for the existing one, which was in very bad condition. His own opinion was that a high pitch was most valuable architecturally, and he was unhesitatingly in favour of sacrificing the rotten old one On 10th August 1878 the St. Albans Restoration Committee passed a resolution that

"The roof of the nave having become ruinous, it is desirable to restore it to the original pitch indicated by the weathering on the tower, keeping so much of the painted and panelled ceiling as is in a sound condition, and restoring the rest in a similar style."

A meeting of the Society of Antiquaries was held a month later, for the purpose of protesting against this resolution. The president, Lord Carnarvon, who was unable to be present, forwarded a letter which he had written to Lord Verulam, the chairman of the St. Albans Committee, in which he quoted from a letter written by Mr. J O. Scott in the June previous, to the effect that Sir Gilbert had taken exact and accurate notes of the roof, and Mr. Scott went on : " I need not say that my father's object was twofold—to preserve the old roof and to render it sound , and," he added, " no doubt a sound roof could be obtained."

It appeared that Sir Gilbert Scott had decided as to the treatment of every separate principal in the roof, and it was clear that he must have contemplated preserving it Lord Carnarvon admitted that a high-pitched roof would not be an absolute novelty, but he argued that it would detract greatly from the importance of the central tower—the best feature of the exterior.

Papers followed from Mr. Neale, F.S.A , who testified to the possibility of making a good restoration of the existing

roof, and from my father.   He (my father) premised that the
roofs were no doubt originally uniform and of a high pitch, and
exhibited a drawing which he had prepared, giving the roof
as nearly as possible as it originally was.   This he had been
enabled to do by the discovery of a great deal of the original
timber which had been reused in the flat roof.   The common
rafters were all marked by the same mortices and corresponding holes for pins through similar tenons.   This gave him
the exact position on the rafters of the collars, braces, etc.
This evidence my father regarded as conclusive.   He further
pointed out that there were two blocked-up doorways in the
west wall of the tower which opened towards the nave from
the galleries of the tower.   The lower doorway fixed the
level of the tie-beams of the Norman roof, on to which it
must have led, for it would have been useless for any other
purpose, and in like manner the upper doorway fixed the
level of the upper side of the collar beams of the old roof.
The existence of the lower doorway suggested to my father
the probability of there having always been a ceiling.

It was impossible that the original roof, as made out in
this way, could have had parapets.   The walls of the choir
were raised at an early period and a flat roof put over it.
If, then, the nave and transept roofs were now to be raised
to their old level, the church would have much the appearance that it had then.   My father parenthetically mentioned
that a raising of the nave roof would necessarily involve a
similar treatment of those of the transepts.

At some date subsequent to the raising of the walls of
the choir those of the nave were raised about three feet.

The date of the flat roof of the nave my father stated to
be between 1494 and 1526.   It was all of oak, and, as Mr.
Scott said, quite admitted of satisfactory restoration.   One
great advantage in leaving it would be that the grand mass
of the central tower would be unimpaired.

The proposal of the Committee to build a steep roof
with parapets seemed the more regrettable because the two
could never have coexisted, so that it would be a complete
novelty, besides which no steep roof which admitted of a
parapet could agree with the old marks on the tower.   The

Committee erred again, inasmuch as they were going to
replace a good oak roof with a light fir one An exact
restoration of the old oak roof would, my father said, be
splendid internally, particularly if the ten western bays were
left unceiled, so that at the end of the long vista of trusses
the eye could rest on the three bays of panelled ceiling at
the eastern end restored by Sir Gilbert Scott. Anything
short of this would be fatal. My father pointed out further
that the good old lead could be recast for the flat roof,
whereas the steep roof would probably be covered with slates.

Messrs. Christian and Blomfield, who had, by request,
accompanied my father to St. Albans on a tour of inspection,
agreed with him in every one of these conclusions. Mr.
Chapple, who was then in charge of the building, had met
them there and given them every facility for arriving at the
truth. At the end of the discussion the Society of Antiquaries passed a resolution condemnatory of the proposal to
destroy the old roof.

My father subsequently wrote to the papers against
what was apparently a new departure of Mr. Scott's, which
was nothing less than a proposal to retain the old roof and
to build the new one over it. This had, Mr. Scott said,
always been his own wish, and had only been given up
when he found that he had no supporters on the Committee.
He further alleged that there were the marks of two
separate roofs on the western face of the tower, the higher
of which he took to be the original

To this my father made the natural objection that
the original roof line would not have been likely to have
cut through string-courses and across windows of the same
date, as this line did, and added that he was strongly of
opinion that all the roofs were of the same height, and that
the transept gables really showed what it was.

A further objection to the Committee's scheme was the
practical one of expense, the probable cost of the new fir
roof being double that of the repair of the old one.

The Building Committee seems now to have come round
to Mr. Scott's view, and he was able to announce publicly
that it was their intention to restore and retain the old roof

under the new one if their funds admitted of it. Thus was a piece of spurious renovation as opposed to genuine conservation decided on. The flat roof, though admittedly not the original one, was none the less genuine. It was the typical roof four centuries ago, and consequently much superior, even apart from historical associations, to any modern copy of a supposed original.

Lord Grimthorpe, the Lord Paramount of St. Albans, strongly favoured the high-pitched roof, particularly on æsthetical grounds, and when my father hopefully asked whether judgment could not be suspended as the timber for the new roof had not yet been ordered, crushed out the last spark of hope by saying that, on the contrary, a great deal was actually on the spot, and that my father must have been very shortsighted not to have observed it when he "sneaked down" to St. Albans. My father was not wont to go about with his eyes shut, so one is not surprised to find that Lord Grimthorpe's roof timbers were in reality scaffold poles. Lord Grimthorpe's version of my father's views was that he wished to rebuild an ugly and debased roof, while he and his meant to rebuild the handsome one of the best period. If this had been a fair statement of the case there would have been nothing more to be said.

Still undaunted, my father returned once again to Mr. Scott's theory of the two high roofs, and showed that this theory had at any rate never commended itself to Sir Gilbert, even if it had seemed to him within the range of possibility, for in cleaning down the tower he had done his best to make the lines, which he must have thought the original ones—on three sides of the tower—as conspicuous as possible, while obscuring the line on which Mr. Scott laid so much stress.

If a simple explanation of the double roof line were wanted, it would be that the higher roof belonged to the same date as the raising of the walls. With regard to the existing parapets, my father said that he saw no evidence of their being old, the section of the coping appearing to him to be of very uncertain date, while the moulding below might well have belonged to a corbel table under the eaves.

The general correctness of my father's views was soon proved in a remarkable way through the untiring exertions of Mr Neale.

That gentleman had, under the most adverse conditions, succeeded in drawing full size all the important parts of the west wall of the tower, and the result of his work was shown in a diagram which was published in the building papers. This absolutely accurate reproduction of the stone-work of the tower proved, in Mr. Neale's words, that "the only high-pitched roof which has been conclusively proved (by the actual grooves) to have existed could not have stood between the Tower parapets" The outlines of the grooves as fixed by Mr. Neale's measurements and tests showed that my father's original drawing, founded, as I have said, on the evidence of the old·rafters, had only varied from the actual line by some few inches

Mr Christian now wrote urging strongly that some consideration should be given to their view now that its correctness had been so triumphantly vindicated.

Mr. Scott had himself made a drawing, the object of which was to establish the fact of there having been two roofs. Mr Neale showed that its accuracy might be simply and effectively tested. "Hammer in," he said, "a nail at the apex of the proposed roof, and hold a cord from it to the required point, and you will find that the line actually passes over original and untouched tilework."

With evidence thus piled on evidence it might have been hoped that the Committee would have seen the reasonableness of abandoning their high-pitched roof, the right course, as Mr. Scott himself admitted, providing my father's drawing could be proved correct.

It could not be seriously urged in favour of their proposal that they were carrying out Sir Gilbert's scheme, because my father was able to show that he had written very strongly in a contrary sense on a very parallel case.

If justification is wanted for the strong line my father took, it must be looked for in the interesting character of the building itself, and in the unfortunate result of the decision of the Building Committee—now fully revealed.

St. Mark's, Venice.

The year 1879 saw the beginning of the movement which had for its object the preservation, not of one of our great national monuments, but of a building which may almost be said to belong to the whole world of art—St. Mark's.

In this agitation my father was one of the prime movers and most unwearying workers. The safety of the whole west front was at stake ; for the restoration, had it not been happily checked in time, would have involved rebuilding it absolutely from the ground, and on lines by no means identical with the old.

The feeling in this country that the Italian Government, ever ready to spend money in the preservation of the monuments of antiquity, which do so much to make Italy what it is, was in this case, with the best possible intentions, spending large sums of money in destroying the interest of a unique building, had become so strong as to overcome the natural scruples which so delicate a step as interference with a foreign government would be likely to give rise to.

In furtherance of the view that representations should be made on the subject to the Italian Government, a meeting was held at Oxford in the Sheldonian, in the latter part of November, at which resolutions were carried to the effect that the works contemplated by the architect in the employ of the Government were unnecessary, and destructive of much of the interest and beauty of the building, and that the Government should be memorialised on the subject.

My father, who moved the first resolution, argued that, from the nature of the construction of the building, any attempt at restoration was necessarily attended with considerable risk. "Once begin to tamper," he said, "with the thin incrustation of marble which overlies the brick core, and it will be almost impossible to stop short of absolute renovation." The glory of St. Mark's lies, as he said, in the warmth of colouring given by its marble and mosaic incrustations. These it would be suicidal to touch ; and he instanced as an example of what might be confidently looked for in such a contingency, that part of the façade which had already been restored with its cold and dirty-coloured marbles and its staring new mosaic.   Among other things he noticed the commonplace effect produced by a pavement which was laid dead-level instead of being undulated like the old.

Other resolutions were moved and seconded by Messrs. E. Burne Jones and William Morris, Professors W. B Richmond and Holland, and others, and were carried by acclamation

A few days later my father stated the subject of complaint more explicitly in the columns of the *Times*, and showed by instances how one piece of new work led, almost inevitably, to another ; the new wine having the usual effect on the old bottles.

The baptistery roof and a part of its walls were covered with ancient mosaics.   The works in progress on the outside of this part of the church caused a settlement in one of the vaults.   In 1877 my father saw that it was shored up.   Two years later there was not a particle of the old mosaic on either the walls or vault ; all was brand-new.   He returns again to the subject of the pavement, on- which he felt very strongly. The whole north aisle has been repaired, he goes on ; the old designs have not been adhered to ; and the surface has been made absolutely level, instead of being raised and sunk in undulations as the old one was.   This arrangement he held to be nearly, if not quite, unique   If not the first to conceive the idea, he, at any rate, seems to have first given expression to the opinion that this undulation of the floor was due to design and not to accident   It is, perhaps, a startling theory at the first blush, and one which in our matter-of-fact days is difficult to credit without some very strong evidence in its favour.

Objections were not wanting from Mr. Fowler and others, the first-named gentleman stating that the subsidence of the ground, owing to the sinking of the water underneath, was quite enough to account for the phenomenon, and he further maintained that he had carefully noted the undulations on his numerous visits, and had found them to vary considerably.   The accurate verification of these supposed changes can have been no easy task, and my father, at any rate, felt that he had such strong grounds for his contention, that he refused to be convinced of the accuracy of Mr. Fowler's observations.

In the first place, he urged that if the pavement had been giving way owing to imperfect foundations, inasmuch as it is composed of countless small pieces of marble arranged in combination with a few large pieces, every particle would naturally have been broken up, and some parts would have sunk abruptly and broken away, while others, getting a permanent support on the foundations of piers or walls, would have kept their original position. At St. Mark's there was nothing at all like this.

To epitomise his arguments. The pavement against the chancel screen is distinctly undulating. The screen itself dates from the eleventh century, the upper part, however, being fourteenth-century work. It is perfectly upright, and shows not the least sign of giving. Clearly, then, there is no settlement here, at the screen itself, and yet the pavement is noticeably out of the level. Had a settlement taken place westward of the footings of the screen, then the pavement would naturally have been drawn away from it, or there would have been a distinct lateral crack running parallel to the screen, and at a little distance from it, just beyond the support of the footings.

There is nothing of the sort.

Again : The choir is built over a crypt ; the crypt itself is perfectly firm, and shows no trace of a settlement ; the floor above, however, is quite uneven. The entrances to the crypt are by staircases and passages under the choir aisles ; the pavement above these is also uneven. The great slabs of gray marble which form a sea before the choir—many of them unbroken—are waved on the surface.

"I remember," my father continues, "how we are told that the pavement of St. Sofia was made in the form of a central sea, from which the four rivers of Paradise flowed to its four doors, and I ask myself why, if this symbolism might be avowed in the mother church at Constantinople, it might not also be indulged in the daughter church at Venice? I look, too, at the architecture of St. Mark's, and I see that there is nowhere in it a hard line.   The angles are all rounded off, the ceilings are all domes, the very front is planned on a curve, and the dimensions of apparently corresponding parts are almost invariably dissimilar ; and I ask again, why, if there was this love of irregularity and of curves everywhere else, the pavement alone should have been of that exact and hard level which not unnaturally commends itself to Mr. Fowler's professional instincts ? "

I have admitted that my father's theory seems at first rather startling, but I think it not unfair to set it at least on a par with that of men whose work, though it may be in some ways highly imaginative, still rather tends to the glorification of the matter of fact as embodied in straight lines, right angles, and dead levels ; my father's view, at any rate, was supported no less by hard facts than by senti- ment, and I have never to this day seen any explanation offered for some of the chief features on which he rested his case.

It is to be noticed that another opus Alexandrinum pavement at Venice—that at Murano—is also undulating like that of St. Mark's.   This might be an argument for either side, except that a special reason given for the in- equality of the St Mark's pavement—which I shall allude to presently—is certainly not applicable at Murano.

In the spring of 1880, on our way to Rome, we made a detour to Venice, as my father was most anxious to see how Signor Meduma—the architect then employed by Govern- ment—was doing his work.   He found that a start had been made at what was apparently to be an entire rebuilding of the west front.   The work had been commenced at the south-west angle, and the few feet of new work which had been built agreed neither in elevation nor on plan with the old.   The waved line of the west front seemed to have been just as distressing to the eye of the architect as the waved line of the pavement, and he had set himself resolutely to redress it.   The consequence of this proceeding was that, where the new work joined the old, there was a distinct hiatus, the marble step or slab round the base of the church being, where the new work stopped, as much as twelve centimetres higher than the old work, and fifteen centimetres in advance of it westward. My father felt himself, in consequence, able to justify fully the statement made at the meeting at Oxford, that it was proposed to do neither more nor less than rebuild the west front.

The justification for the action of those who started the agitation against this act of constructive vandalism is found, if any is needed, in the constitution of the Comité de San Marc de Venise, and in the temperate character of the remonstrance which was presented by them. Therein it was stated with great justice that, looking to the utter destruction of all the interest of the Fondaco dei Turchi and St. Maria di Murano by over-restoration, the members of the Comité were naturally unable to trust blindly in the self-restraint of the Italian authorities.

The memorial was signed by men of eminence, representing not art alone, from England, America, France, Germany, Austria, Belgium, the Netherlands, Bavaria, Poland, Switzerland, and last, but not least, Italy itself. St. Mark's, with its glorious and irreplaceable harmony of colouring, is indeed something quite by itself, the heirloom of all cultivated peoples, a monument in admiration of which painters and architects, experts, and the world at large, can more fully and sympathetically share than in the case of any other raised by man's hands. To counsel its thorough restoration was, my father said, as though a man should propose to clean down the Sistine Chapel and replace the masterpieces of mediæval giants by the daubs of a scene painter.

At the end of last year (1886) the question of the pavement again cropped up in the newspapers, the Secretary of the Society for the Protection of Ancient Buildings writing to protest against its restoration, though he pronounced the undulations to be certainly due to subsidence, and added, as with a touch of scorn, that some enthusiastic admirers have actually gone the length of asserting that the undulations were purposely introduced when the pavement was laid, to mark the connection of the building with the Queen of the Adriatic—one of the last things which a mediæval builder would have done. This last assertion is rather

startling ; the direct contrary may really be asserted without hesitation. Ancient Christian Art is so instinct with
symbolical meaning that the probability of there being a
symbolism in the waves of the pavement naturally suggests
itself to the student of mediævalism ; but that the architect
should have intended to typify the queenship of the Adriatic
implies a remarkable power of prophetic instinct on his
part. That, however, was not the symbolism which suggested itself to my father ; as he read it, the pavement and
the fabric above were to be taken together : the pavement as
the sea, the building itself as the ark of the Church, resting
upon the waters. Such a symbolism is not unknown. We
are told of the church of St John Baptist at Ravenna (a
votive building erected by Galla Placidia, after escape from
shipwreck in 424) ·

"Jubet Augusta ubique naufragii sui præsentari formam
ut quodammodo tota operis facies Reginæ-pericula loqueretur.
Pavimentum undosum undique mare, quód, quasi ventis agi-
tatum, procellosæ tempestatis gerit imaginem "

It is argued on the other side that this merely means that
the marble was laid in wavy patterns ; but surely the mouth-
filling alliteration *undosum undique* could hardly have been
applied to so feeble a portraiture of the tempest as these
interminable little niggling patterns all over the pavement
would imply   Dr. Saccardo, the present architect, explains
the unevenness of the pavement of the nave by reminding
us that there was once a vault under it, as there still is
under the choir   This, he tells us, was demolished, and the
space filled up with rubbish, without the precaution being
taken to remove the piers and columns, the result being that
they offer a firm support to the pavement above, while the
loose earth around them gives way   This accounts for the
so-called waves of the sea.

So much for the nave : the removal of the vault sufficiently accounting for the state of its pavement.

Now for the choir. in this case we are told by another
writer that the sinking of the pavement is beyond all question attributable to its being laid on a vault, as it would be
very likely to sink into the pockets unless the filling in was

firmly rammed down.   Accepting this explanation, let us now turn to Murano and ask what is the explanation of the similar feature there.   What but the subsidence of the water, and the consequent sinking of the ground?   Here, then, are three different causes all producing an identical effect in the same place, all very plausible, taken singly, but rather confusing when taken together, and none of them explaining how it is that the inclines of the pavement are all so rounded and flowing when we should naturally have looked for abrupt sinkings and gaping cracks in places where they certainly do not exist.[1]   It is the fashion to laugh at symbolism ; much has doubtless been clothed with a meaning which would surprise no one more than the mediæval builders who are made responsible for it, but those who deny are at the least as wrong as those who exaggerate ; and I think that with examples before us of pavements which are known on credible evidence to have been meant, in one way or another, to represent the sea, my father's theory requires a more logical and connected attempt at refutation than it has yet had, before it can be pronounced confidently to be baseless or chimerical.

[1] It is argued with some reason that the waste of marble consequent on the working of the uneven surfaces in large pieces makes it unlikely that such a course should have been taken, but how are they to be explained then ?

CHAPTER XII

THE years 1877-78 were not very eventful ones, though they brought in much new and important work. In the latter year, as I have already said, the east wing of the Courts of Justice was opened in a perfectly quiet way

My father was at this time appointed Architect to Salisbury Cathedral—a post which he was very glad to hold, and he was also called in to advise at Gloucester and Winchester Cathedrals.

In May he went abroad for a short time, revisiting many of the places which he had seen under such far happier circumstances seventeen months before. The tour was an experiment, and not a successful one; he himself soon began to doubt the wisdom of dwelling too exclusively on old associations He travelled about alone for the most part, but met Ruskin at Venice, and joined him in a chorus of lamentation over the evidences of the all-pervading spirit of the age, which, now that the city is in the way to be prosperous, is changing its whole character. The following Christmas we passed at Brussels, making excursions to all the old towns which lie so conveniently in a nutshell for the traveller's benefit.

The nave of Bristol Cathedral was sufficiently complete in October 1877 for the opening ceremony to take place. My father speaks of it thus in his diary :—

"Bristol Cathedral nave opened; not a very imposing service for such an occasion. The whole of the arrangements of the choir are so thoroughly bad that the sooner they are altered the better I think every one sees how unsatisfactory they are. Went to Canon Girdlestone's for lunch, but as every one was marshalled in before me, I took the opportunity to slip away instead of going into the dining-room. It suited me, as I was in rather a hurry for time, and really it does seem rather absurd that all the young parsons and elderly aldermen should be thought of first, and the architect left to himself on such an occasion."

The summers of both those years were spent for the most part at Holmdale ; in the latter year my father induced the Royal Academy Club to make their annual outing to Dorking ; many of the members came to Holmdale for lunch, and then drove over Leith Hill to Dorking for dinner. In May he wrote :—

"Last week seems to have been given up to bishops and other swells. Lord Beauchamp gave two breakfasts, to both of which he invited me, and we had eight or ten bishops at each, and as many distinguished laymen. They were both pleasant gatherings"

These breakfasts, at which there was much discussion of Church prospects, were great meetings of the most important ecclesiastical and lay representatives of the High Church party, and for some years my father was frequently present at them

In October he paid a brief visit to Paris to see the exhibition, and soon afterwards writes :—

"I saw in this morning's *Times* that I am to be made a Knight of the Legion of Honour, as a reward for sending some drawings to the exhibition. I cannot say I am much elated."

Meantime the chief object of my father's life had been steadily marching to a successful issue. An ecclesiastical district had been formed from outlying parts of the six parishes of Shere, Abinger, Ewhurst, Cranleigh, Ockley, and Ockham, under the name of Holmbury St Mary. So much of the tithes of Ewhurst and Cranleigh as were drawn from the district were contributed by their respective rectors. The parsonage house and school at Felday, the latter of which had up to that time served also as a chapel-of-ease for Shere, was transferred at the same time to the living. They had been erected chiefly at the expense of Mr. Reginald Bray, the Lord of the Manor, and Mr. Laurence Adams, the Rector of Shere. A site for the church of unusual beauty was also given by Mr. Bray, and the church itself was begun in the course of 1878 The next thing was to find a suitable man for the first vicar. My father had arranged that the presentation to the living should be in the hands of the bishop of the diocese for the time being, with the sole reservation that the first appointment should be one with which he could heartily concur. The offer of the living was made to Mr. John Shearme, who was then acting as curate to Canon Sapte at Cranleigh, and in November he signified his acceptance of it—a fact fraught with the happiest augury for the future of the parish

My father's gift of the fabric of the church was met by a most generous response on the part of the parishioners generally to an appeal for funds for an endowment. The site of the church had been given, and the laying out and enclosing of the churchyard with its high gate were also due to private munificence.

The church which my father built, whether it is to be numbered among his happiest efforts or not, is something quite out of the common run of village churches, from the picturesqueness of the site, the beauty and congruity of the building itself, and the completeness of its furniture and fittings. It stands under the lee of a wood of Scotch firs on a hillside which slopes rapidly to the east and north, advantage has been taken of the considerable difference in the levels to place the sexton's room, etc., under the chancel, while over the vestries is a raised north chancel aisle, which is in itself an unusual and picturesque feature. Here the school-children are placed—apart from the rest of the congregation, and so visible as to make good behaviour a necessity The common Surrey feature of a great roof embracing both nave and aisles is reproduced, and the chancel is only divided from the nave internally by a cusped wooden roof principal, and a graceful open wooden screen. At the west end is a simple open screen which serves to support the bellcote above, and forms a sort of internal narthex The outer door of the church is left open, and that of the screen kept closed, so that the building is always open for private prayer, and at the same time there is no opportunity for horse-play in the body of the church itself.

The stained glass, the altar-plate and coverings, are very complete and of beautiful design. The altar-cloths were worked by the East Grinstead sisters as a gift to one who had been largely the benefactor.

The 6th of November 1879 saw the consecration which my father had so set his heart upon The energy and *bon-hommie* of the vicar had already made the church a power in the village such as it had never been before, and the enthusiastic and overflowing congregations on the day of consecration and after testified in an unmistakable way to the appreciation of the people Since that day there has been constant progress. What the actual building has done for the outward beauty of the place has been equalled by the moral influence which has been exerted by the services It is happily still our boast that we can show what my father earnestly desired we should show—a church which belongs to the poor just as much as to the rich, where the villager does not fear to take a good seat or hesitate to sit side by side with his master.

Not long after the opening, Gladstone told my father that he thought our congregation more rapt than any he had ever seen in a village church.

"He told me," my father wrote, "he was so glad to see me in the midst of my own work. He came to service again in the evening, and walked back with me as far as this house (Holmdale) afterwards. He discoursed much about hymns, defending the emotional character of modern hymns, but regretting their too great number He was very warm in favour of free and open churches, and told me they had lately made theirs at Hawarden so. . . . Shearme tells me that Gladstone went to see the church last week, and spoke very warmly about it."

The night after, my father was his next neighbour at dinner, and jotted down in his diary afterwards some of the topics of conversation.

"Gladstone talked about London improvements and the increasing height of houses. He saw no reason why, in fifty years or so, London should not have ten millions of people living in it, and England seventy millions. He expressed himself strongly about the treatment of the lower orders in such a matter as not being allowed to drive across the parks He denounced our divorce laws, to which his objection is evidently no slighter than it was when the Act was passed Talking about a gate which had been found locked across a public thoroughfare, I said that if I saw any one breaking the lock I should certainly not interfere 'No,' said he, 'nor should I ; and after all, in defence of what we consider our rights, we should all do what the Irish are attacked for doing.'

"In various ways I thought I saw evidence that the dominant idea in Gladstone's mind at present is that of treating all men on equal terms, and doing away as far as possible with all favours to particular classes. He inveighed against the custom of sending venison from royal parks to men in his position "

In the summer of 1879 we made a short tour through Normandy and on by le Mans to the Loire, returning by Orleans and Bourges. My father seemed in better fettle for sketching than ever, and though we saw little that was new to him, except Mont St. Michel and some of the chateaux on the Loire, he naturally found subjects without number.

In the spring of 1880 another visit to Rome was necessary, and we made some most interesting excursions into the country round about. Starting from Tivoli, we went through a wild-looking country to Subiaco (above which lies Sta Scolastica, the mother of religious houses) ; Olevano, much frequented by the German painter fraternity ; and Palestrina , and afterwards to Albano and Frascati.

In the following autumn we made a tour through the series of magnificent houses in Wilts and Somerset I remember on this occasion that my father, who felt that church-building could not go on much longer in such volume, strongly impressed on me the advisability of turning my attention more particularly to house-work. The seven years that have passed since then have, however, seen little of the diminution which he anticipated

The death of Mr Edward Barry made a vacancy in the Professorship of Architecture at the Royal Academy My father had tried unsuccessfully for the post two years before.

"I offered myself for the Professorship of Architecture, and had eight votes against fourteen (I think) for Barry. This is certainly as uncomplimentary a snub as I ever received, but, on the other hand, it is a great relief not to have to lecture, and they cannot say that I shirked it."

My father only lived to deliver one course of lectures in the spring of 1881, but they were so able and so suggestive as to attract a great deal of attention both inside and outside the institution on behalf of which he gave them.

The writing of these lectures was a serious inconvenience to so busy a man, and my father must have offered himself for the post with rather mixed feelings; still he valued so highly any opportunity for advancing the study of architecture that, in his heart of hearts, he was no doubt glad to avail himself of this, though it entailed considerable personal sacrifice.

The greater part of the writing was done in the evenings at Holmdale. The sound of the pen used to be almost continuous. The hard facts and the deductions to be made from them came to hand with equal quickness and reliability

In November of the same year he was elected, practically unanimously, to the Treasurership of the Academy, the post next in honour to the presidentship, and, till his death, generally, if not invariably, filled by an architect

Mr. Barry's death had been preceded by that of my father's old master and consistent friend, Sir Gilbert Scott. Death was indeed busy among those with whom he had worked long and happily. The Dean of York, Dr. Duncombe, in whom my father had had a constant friend and supporter throughout his work on the transept, had just died; as had also Mr. Bennett of Bournemouth, who had been his client for seven and twenty years. During the whole of this period that truly untiring man had gradually been elaborating St. Peter's Church, and it was not till after his death that the last touch was put by the completion of the spire

It would be tiresome to give a long list of all that my father was doing at this time, but his work at Carlisle should be mentioned because it made a certain stir in some circles.

My father had done a good deal of work at Carlisle Cathedral at one time or another, including the Paley memorial pulpit—a very elaborate and beautiful work—and a fine canopied bishop's throne, but the most important undertaking in connection with the cathedral was the rehabilitation of the interesting old Fratry. This was a building dating from the fifteenth century, but cut about and defaced and maltreated at various times and in different ways till little enough of the old work was visible to any one but an expert, and much of that which could be seen was evidently out of its place.

Windows had been wholly or partially blocked up, square-headed openings had been inserted which had themselves come to depend for existence on rough brick piers and wooden props of eccentric and hideous form, niches had been torn down from one place and put up incontinently in another, string-courses had been broken away, floors and ceilings had been inserted at fancy levels, and a wall with a fireplace in it erected so as to cut the original chamber into two rooms—a larger one to the west and a smaller to the east. The additions belonged for the most part to the ends of the seventeenth and eighteenth centuries, the square-headed windows being attributed to Machell the antiquary. My father's proposal to root out all the rank growth, which had wellnigh stifled the life out of the original work, met with much reprobation at the hands of certain archæologists ; particular stress was laid on the iniquity of moving any of Machell's work ; but, as it was pointed out at the time, the fact that the windows were the work of an archæologist really made them valueless as historical evidence, and all they showed was that the style in which they were built was the one which Machell, who was an ardent promoter of the classic revival, chiefly affected. Others cried out that if the programme of the architect were adhered to nothing would be left of that old Fratry where, as some say, Edward I. held his Parliament ; of all the pleas in favour of retaining the ramshackle accretions which did so much to damage a fine building, this was probably the oddest. Even had my father proposed to sacrifice the old work to the new, the exact

converse of which was, of course, the case, he would even
then have been counselling the destruction of a building
which was not begun till nearly two centuries after Edward's
death. My father's reply to those who objected to the
removal of the "venerable evidences of history during two
centuries," and the "genuine remnants of a past living architecture" (which is just the last thing which could be rightly
said of Machell's work), was of the nature of a *reductio ad
absurdum*. He contented himself with sending to a building
paper a literal and truthful representation of the Fratry as
it was at the time (early in 1880), when some part of the
clearing away had been done, and much of the old work
exposed.

He subjected to the searching light of publicity the
venerable eighteenth-century roof—one of the meanest conceivable,—the much-belauded windows—mere square openings, without the strength to stand a day if deprived of the
motley group of pillars and posts on which their sagging
lintels rested. The true nature of the historical evidences
by which so much store was set became immediately apparent, as did also the real and solid character of the evidence on which the proposed restoration was based.

Luckily the destruction of the old work had not been
thoroughly carried out ; much had been merely hidden or
removed instead of being actually destroyed, and it did not
need a professional eye to see that what was wanted was
rather the rehabilitation of work still existing, after due lop-
ping off of fungus growths, than actual new work

Time after time did my father, where he found additions
or alterations with an intrinsic value of their own, or when
the nature of the work supplanted was in any degree problematical, time after time did he accept the later form, and
do his utmost to preserve it , but he felt that the architect
who knows his work should exercise his judgment on each
particular case as it arises, and should refuse to be bound
by sentimental phrases, which only cramp and disable the
exercise of that wisdom which is the natural outcome of a ·
properly utilised experience

Only a year or so before the time when the controversy

over his projects at Carlisle was raging, he had been examining Brewood Church, Staffordshire, with a view to its restoration   After his visit he wrote in his diary :—

"Completed the plans of Brewood—a very curious church
The most remarkable features were altered or almost destroyed in
the fifteenth century.   This is the real puzzle of a restoration—how
to restore the interesting portions of two periods, one of which was
destructive of the other."

Here, then, is an unsolicited concession to the claims
of history, though to ask for it would argue great ignorance
of my father's works ; but when the evidence of history is
confined to a few flimsy obstructions which, without any
artistic claims or anything to show their date, serve but
to make the building which they adorn useless, it is mere
Quixotism to insist on their retention, and common sense
refuses to be shackled by such feeble bonds.

About this time I find a note in my father's diary, brief
enough, but telling a tale to those who can understand it, of
admirable management and remarkable forethought :—

"Went to the Office of Works with the accounts for the east
wing of the Law Courts.   These show a saving of between two and
three thousand pounds on the amount I was authorised to spend   a
result which Sir Henry Hunt calls 'wonderful,' certainly very rare
in any case.   Here the cost was about £190,000, and there were
no provisions to meet any extras."

In 1879 it became my father's turn to serve on the
Council of the Royal Academy, and in consequence of the
amount of time which his duties there were sure to take up,
he sent in his resignation of the vice-presidentship, and his
seat on the Council of the Institute of British Architects
In his letter he said :—

"This year (and next year will be the same) so much of my
time is taken up by being on the Council of the R.A., that I have
really no time to spare for other similar duties ; and as, under the
present system at the Institute of Architects, any chance of getting
new blood into the Council ought to be seized, I feel that I ought
to resign my post as Vice-President and Member of Council   Will
you be so good, therefore, as to see that my name is struck out of
the House list ? etc "

The notification of his resignation appeared shortly afterwards in the following terms :—

"The Council have received, with great regret, a letter intimating that, owing to large demands on his time at the Council of the Royal Academy during the next two years, and to the feeling that he ought not to hold a position, the business of which he cannot in consequence discharge to his own satisfaction, Mr. Street resigns · his seat on the Council"

It is clear from the misinterpretation of my father's note, and the entire omission of the real gist of it, that some sting lay in the sentence expunged ; and, indeed, his resignation was generally taken, as it was meant, to be an emphatic protest against the Council as reorganised during the presidentship of Mr Charles Barry, and the scheme of succession to the chair with which it was associated. The reconstituted Council was to consist of the leaders of the profession in perpetual succession. This order had been, in the first instance, decided by an incidence of votes, which was in some measure fortuitous. Each member of it in turn was to be nominated by the Council, as a body, for the presidentship. The attainment of the chair was thus to be along the highroad of patience. My father's view was that the arrangement was unfair to the younger men, who at once had the thing settled for them, and were themselves kept at a distance by that settlement, and that it was as injurious as it was unjust to substitute for the old mode of selection, by which the man was chosen who at the time of the election was best qualified to fill the post, a new cut-and-dried inelastic system in which a healthy competition had no place.

My father speaks thus of his resignation :—

"I have resigned my vice-presidentship because it would lead by routine to my being president, and I don't think that is the way in which the presidentship should be conferred, if it is to be an honour"

This feeling was shared by a considerable section of the members of the Institute, but it is quite likely that it would not have found emphatic expression had it not been for the ıetirement of Professor Hayter Lewıs early in 1881 from the succession to the presidentıal chair—shortly to be vacated by Mr. Whichcord—which it would have been hıs turn to fill

This gave an unexpected opening for the election of my father, who had refused to take advantage of the new by-laws, and without in any way postponing the expectations of others. The next ın order to Professor Lewıs was the late Sir Horace Jones (then Mr Jones), but the opposıtıon to him was simply the affirmatıon of a principle, and had nothing the least personal in it. This is sufficiently shown by a letter of Mr. E. C Robins, in which he said :—

"Mr. Street's personal fitness is not now in questıon. That ıs admıtted   Hıs claım to electıon ıs on the ground of thc prıncıple of freedom of election"

The opponents of this principle based their action on a technıcal dısapproval of my father's act of resıgnation. They contended that his candidature was a breach of ordcr and a stultification of their body, inasmuch as it directly broke a by-law which had only been enacted a short time before

It was on the reading of this by-law that the whole question turned, and ıt was argued by the opponents of the Council's nominee, Mr. H. Jones, with great apparent justice, that the nomination of the next in successıon on the lıst of the Council by the Council was a formal and unavoıdable act, and not a personal expressıon of opinion by the members severally, and that, far from its of necessity carryıng the vote and sympathy of the general body, it did not even plcdge the member of Councıl as an individual to ratify by his vote the recommendation which his official posıtıon had oblıged him to make.

It followed, then, that the nominee of the Council being merely "recommended" to the general body of the Instı-tute, it was quite opcn to any indıviduals to start a rıval candidate.

My father's own view may be put shortly ın his own words —

"I am thc person," he said, "who, when the order of presıdents was settled four years ago, was placed next in succession to Mr Whichcord, and above Mr. Horace Jones   But feeling that I could not possibly take the presidentship on the strength of such an election, in justice either to the Fellows or to myself, I retired   Since that time I have been absolutely passive on the subject, but I have always felt that it would be an honour to be elected to the office, and when I was asked by a member of the Council whether I would serve if elected, I had no hesitation in agreeing to do so on this occasion."

Again he said : " I resigned my vice-presidentship because I did not choose to succeed to such a post as a mere matter of rotation   I think the system an extremely bad one, and if I am ever president it will be in spite of this rule "

My father's consent to serve having been obtained, he was duly proposed by certain members of the Council. Much as the sticklers for order deprecated the idea of a contested election, the more liberal section of the Institute felt that, even at the cost of displaying to the public the internal dissensions of their body, they could not logically refuse the battle

On 9th May my father was elected after a hard fight, but he only lived to hold the post for a few months.

It is interesting to notice what his attitude was towards the movement in favour of closing the profession, and how far he was satisfied with the position of the modern architect. There was in his lifetime—there is still more now—a tendency by means of qualifying examinations, and by the granting of diplomas, to make the practice of architecture as impossible for any one outside the close corporation as is the practice of the law for those not duly qualified.   The architect is from this point of view primarily the professional man, the man of business, and secondarily the artist   He will be the first to approve of the system on which architects are at present paid—the percentage on the outlay—because it appeals to business instincts , and, indeed, the system has able supporters, for has not Lord Grimthorpe himself raised his voice in favour of it, and has instanced in a way as flattering as it is convincing the terms on which a broker is paid ? yet happily there are some who hold strongly to the opposite view, and even go so far as to refuse to be stigma-

tised as professional men. My father did not go so far as
this, but he was profoundly dissatisfied with the low stand-
point which many of his brethren were prepared to take,
and of the system of payment he said : " In old days men
were paid for their work and for the exercise of their talents,
and not on our ludicrous and unsatisfactory percentage
system "

His opposition to the illiberal spirit which prompts the
closing of the door against all who will not submit themselves to the tender mercies of the examiner, dated from his
earliest days, and continued without abatement to the end of
his life. Here is a letter written to the *Times* five and
twenty years ago, which makes his position plain :—

" Mr. Cole's very natural and affectionate reference to Captain
Fowke might well, I think, have been allowed to pass without
question , and remembering how very rare the instances are in competitions where the second prizeman does not think himself unfairly
treated by the judges, one may be permitted to think also that a
competitor, fairly defeated by Captain Fowke, was the last person
who should have allowed himself to utter the protest which has been
addressed to you to-day.· As, however, your correspondent has
raised the question of Captain Fowke's claim to be called an architect
at all, I pray you to allow me, as one who entirely believes that he
has just as much right to do so as most of us, to say a few words on
this subject. Mr. ——'s ' specially educated architect ' earns his
right to call himself one solely by the process of paying a premium
to some practising architect, and spending from three to four years
in his office ; after which, if he can persuade any one to give him
work to do, nobody will object to his calling himself an architect and
undertaking the work.   Captain Fowke, on the other hand, adopted
a profession which at least involved a great deal of scientific education, and trained him in many ways most admirably for the practice
of a constructive art.   Then, after many years' successful pursuit of
his profession, accident or his own choice induced him to devote
some eight or ten years of his life almost entirely to the preparation
of designs for buildings of various kinds and various degrees of
importance, from the simplest volunteer shed to the museum buildings at Edinburgh, South Kensington, and the like

" In common fairness one must admit that he was at least as
likely to do his work well as any man ' specially educated ' in the
usual way would be. The real test of his claim to be an architect
in the best sense of the word is the examination of the works which

he carried into execution.   Had Mr. ——'s theories as to architects
been invented long enough ago, many of our greatest men would
have been utterly unknown.   I will take two examples only from
among many of all ages, and ask whether or no Giotto was an
architect when he built his campanile at Florence, or whether Sir
Christopher Wren—who probably began to practise as an architect
at about the same age as Captain Fowke—ever acquired any right
to the title, seeing that he had never been 'specially educated' for
the purpose?

"The simple truth is that he is the best architect who can erect
the best building, and whatever doubts many of us may have as to
Captain Fowke's exact rank in the profession, there are but few, I
hope, who would pretend to charge him with being a mere amateur;
while I hope that all those who regard architecture as an art, instead
of a mere trade or profession, join me in a decided opinion that,
as all arts owe very much to the enthusiasm of amateurs, so he is
no real artist who wishes to shut us up within the narrow bounds
of routine and conventionalism, which it is the tendency of special
education to establish for its pupils

"To many of us it was rather a pleasure than the reverse to find
so accomplished, so able, and so earnest a man as Captain Fowke
willing to throw in his lot with us, and to most of us, I am sure, it
is a pain rather than a pleasure to find that the grave has no sooner
closed over his body than the first opportunity is seized with avidity
to proclaim that after all he was only an amateur"

This manly protest against professional cliqueism excited
many warm expressions of agreement from other " specially
educated " architects, and brought my father proof that he
was not alone in the view he took.   The position then assumed
was resolutely maintained, and naturally so, for is it not one
which all must take who do not wish to see their art degraded
into something not worthy the name, and who prefer the clear
ray of Art strong and unfettered to the fitful gleam of the
rushlight of professional routine?

A society which is recognised as having on its roll the
names of many of the most illustrious in their calling, and,
if numbers are a test, representative of the general views of
those who practise in the metropolis, should, as a consequence,
have an influence, if not an authority, of a more real kind
than the Institute can be said to have.   My father felt this
strongly.   He was of opinion that the Government or the
governing bodies of large cities should be encouraged and

urged to consult the Council of the Institute as to the preliminaries of any great operations, as to the best routes for
streets, the best sites for great public buildings, the best
openings for architectural improvements.   Had this been an
established custom we might, as he said, have been spared
the vast and barnlike sheds at Cannon Street and Charing
Cross, which are a disfigurement to the riverside, or indeed
the recent half-hearted improvements at Piccadilly Circus
and Hyde Park Corner.   He would have also welcomed
most gladly the extension of the influence of the Institute
in saving works by deceased architects   Such a surveillance
would have made it impossible to put up a series of
erections on the top of the General Post Office, or to
leave the Colonial Office without the towers at the angles of
the Whitehall front ; it might well be even extended to all
our architectural treasures.   The instances where the exercise
of such an influence might have saved us from Vandalism are
legion.   There is the colonnade of Burlington House heaped
up somewhere on the other side of the river ; Temple Bar
laid up in some similar limbo ; the Buckingham Water Gate
half covered by earth, and used as a sort of rockery by the
gardener of those parts.   All these cases seemed to my
father to cry out to be dealt with at once.   They are still
waiting for some one with influence enough to give the
necessary impetus.   Then, again, there are city churches
whose towers and spires, though far and away the most
picturesque features in a general view of our great city, are
yet given over to the destroyer one after another.

Here my father felt there was a boundless field for the
exercise of a salutary and intelligent influence.

The natural solution seemed to him to be the formation
of a ministry of fine arts, to which such a body as the
Institute would naturally stand in the relation of a consulting
architect.   Not very long before his election as president, a
request had been made to the Institute to exercise a control
over or advise upon the general designs of certain buildings
in Northumberland Avenue   My father felt that the position
of the Institute on that occasion was a difficult one, and not
likely to be of service to architecture.   Though the individual

members of the Council might, as he said, be excellent judges, yet as a body they were unwilling to criticise too much the work of one of their brethren, or to recommend conjointly any alterations.

In this particular instance only elevations were submitted, so that only simple modifications could be suggested. What advice was given did not appear to receive any attention, and the sole consequence was that buildings over which the Institute had really exercised no control were erected with the cachet of that body. "For myself," my father said, "I have no hesitation in saying that if we are to have no more power than at present, we should have less."

The election of my father as president "seemed to augur," as I have seen it said, "a prosperous epoch for architecture in England He was no sooner installed in office than he took by storm both friends and opponents by the broad, impartial, and far-sighted view which he took of the responsibilities of his office, and the dignity of a profession in which he used his authority as a peacemaker and a reformer."

The moral influence which my father wished to see evidences of in our vernacular art does indeed seem to have become somewhat more apparent since he uttered his much-applauded presidential address. The solidity for which he argued so forcibly is not so transparently lacking as it was even in actual shop-fronts, and if much of the less inferior work in our main streets is nothing more than copyism, sometimes rather ignorant, yet this is better than bad work pure and simple, and the good houses which are sprinkled about may be confidently said to have done something to leaven the mass in the last decade.

In the early part of 1881 an event took place which caused my father more real happiness than anything affecting him alone could have given, viz my engagement to the elder daughter of his friend and colleague, Mr. Wells. My father had a peculiar affection for my wife, and had looked forward to the possibility of our engagement with an interest which did much to make him forget his own grief A couple of months later—in June—not feeling in the best of health, he proposed that we should go abroad together, perhaps for the last time as he said, only too truly.   His first idea was to show me something of Spain, but finally he decided on Germany as being more accessible.   From Cologne we went to Ems, Limburg-on-the-Lahn, Dietkirchen, Wetzlar—name familiar to lovers of Goethe—Marburg, Gelnhausen, Eisenach, Erfurt, Arnstadt, Naumburg, Schulpforta, Halle, Merseburg, Leipzig, Dresden, Meissen, Jüterbog, Berlin.   During the early part of the tour my father seemed well ; he entered into the sight-seeing with his accustomed zest and made no complaint, but as we went on symptoms of suppressed gout began to show themselves, and his ailment, though seemingly trivial, spoilt his pleasure so much, that he decided to try whether Surrey air would not have a better effect.   We had intended going from Berlin into the brick country of the north, particularly to Stralsund and Stettin, which my father had never seen, but we now made straight for Aix-la-Chapelle, where he spent a few days unprofitably in drinking the waters, and so home.

Once in England he went about his work in the ordinary way, and with not less than his usual vigour.   His great work at East Grinstead was now drawing to a close, and on St. Margaret's day we attended the annual gathering there, to see how things looked.   " There," as my father characteristically said, " we found a great mob of people, among whom the shy architect seemed the least important."   If the architect did occupy a subordinate position that day, he had himself to thank for it   He had a natural horror of being made much of in his own person, which it was difficult to reconcile with the importance which he rightly attached to his official position as architect of the building, the completion of which was being celebrated   On this occasion the health of the architect was certainly proposed, probably in flattering terms, but the architect himself was unconscious of the fact, as we had effected our retreat from the tent just before the speeches began.

I think after this time my father never felt thoroughly well. He began to suffer from headache, intermittent at first, afterwards chronic, of a worrying rather than a painful nature

On 6th August he writes in his diary : " Went to see the doctor, being troubled a little with headache ; he puts it down to overwork, and wants me to go to the Baths of St. Gervais." Nothing could have been much less acceptable than such a suggestion ; he was never so happy as when he was in harness, and looked forward dismally to the prospect of vegetating for weeks at a place of which he did not then know the attractiveness, without companionship, and with the knowledge that there was lots of work at home which wanted doing. Luckily Mr. Pearson, R.A., was meditating taking his holiday at the same time, and arranged to go with him They started in the latter end of August and went straight to their destination, where, for a fortnight, they conscientiously submitted themselves to the daily baths and walks ; a day or two before my father left they were joined by Mr. Ewan Christian From St. Gervais my father went to Chamounix, and, after looking at the churches at Vevay and Lausanne, joined his colleagues again at Aix-les-Bains He was away about four weeks altogether, and was troubled more or less by headache the whole time ; but his general health did not seem bad, and he did a good deal of walking and sketching in spite of very bad weather

After returning to England he seemed to get gradually better, and by October had even got rid of his headache. In the course of the month he went down to Combe Bank to spend a Sunday with Mr. Spottiswoode, a strange coincidence, for these two—host and guest—were the very next two to whom a resting-place in the Abbey was to be given.

Early in November I went down to Southwold and Blythburgh with my father, and we sketched and measured the churches together ; and on the 7th of the month the winter session at the Institute began, and he gave his wise and thoughtful opening address ; on that evening I was present as a visitor, and the cheers which greeted my name, when it was read out among the list of candidates for election to the Associateship, testified to the popularity of the new president.

On the 18th of November I went with my father to

Salisbury, and we spent the whole afternoon sketching and measuring an old house, which it was intended to convert to some other use   I never saw my father more alert ; he did his work quickly and thoroughly.   That evening he saw the dean on some cathedral business, and the next morning we left early for Holmdale.   I noticed that he was unusually drowsy while we were in the train, and while we were walking up from the station to the house it became evident to me that something had happened , I feared that he had had a paralytic stroke, though I could not tell at what moment. He began speaking of my mother as though she were still living.   I noticed too that there was a hesitation in his walk which was unusual

Two days later we came up to town, and my father seemed to mend, though very slowly   He made no attempt to do work of any kind.   Friends came to see him, and his progress towards convalescence was such that we made all our preparations for a lengthened tour in Egypt.   It had been arranged that I should accompany him during the earlier part of the journey, and my place was then to have been taken by Mr. Frank Walton, the painter, who, for friendship's sake, was prepared to take upon himself this anxious and responsible position

Three or four days only before the date fixed for our start my father was again struck by paralysis.   He was sitting at the dinner-table talking to Mr. Wells, who had been dining with him, when the seizure took place   He must have realised then that his end was near ; it is more than probable that he had done so before, though he always made light of his illness, and affected to see no reason for behaving as an invalid.   Once in bed he soon sank into sleep, and the next morning was seemingly almost unconscious, just able to say to me, " I am glad to hear your voice," and never speaking again   On 18th December he gradually passed from unconsciousness into death

CHAPTER XIII

MY father is said, by some at least of those who knew him, to have been of rather a serious disposition as a child, with a propensity to seek the society of his elders. This preference was due in some measure to the circumstance of his having been thrown so much into the company of a brother several years older than himself, whose tastes and occupations he had learnt to share at an age when most boys would have found them irksome ; and it is a very natural one in a child with an active brain, who innocently looks upon his elders as walking encyclopædias for supplying information and solving difficulties.

I gather, however, from various little signs, that my father was boyish enough among boys, and as full of life and fun as a healthy high-spirited child naturally is In manhood, though he gave evidence of a grave and earnest disposition— "a mixture of gentleness and strength," as I have heard it called,—yet he was the best and most cheery of companions, knowing when to be serious, but the last person in the world to stalk through the lighter scenes of life as though it were all high tragedy

His merits and demerits were those of the typical Englishman. He told me once that at her last breath my stepmother murmured, "*The* English face" The face was a faithful index to the character He may have had some of that insular exclusiveness which makes an Englishman hesitate before he gives his friendship, or the semblance of it, to every one he meets ; possibly to those who did not know him he may have seemed hard of approach, but such an idea was soon dispelled on a better acquaintance, and

where he once gave his friendship he did not lightly with-
draw it ; nor was it of that selfish type which would take all
for itself and give nothing in return. There are many who
could testify to services rendered again and again by him, to
a thoughtfulness always on the watch, to a willing sacrifice of
time and trouble at friendship's call

Effusive he was not , but he was straightforward, sincere,
and charitable , not one of those who utter unpalatable truths,
but a man who, where he could, gave praise, and, where he
could not, was silent

Few can honestly say that they have cast no stones at
their neighbours My father had to put up with unusual
provocation, but he spoke no uncharitable word when it
might well have been forgiven His weapon, when he had
to draw it, was the good broadsword of honest outspokenness
and not the rapier of innuendo.

His charity was large, and so given that he himself could
not know its extent, others certainly not. After his death I
had ample opportunity for gauging, what I had till then
been only able to guess at, the extent to which he had been
in the habit of helping those who, from bad health or want
of ability, had fallen out of the teeming ranks of his profession to swell the vast multitude of the respectable unem-
ployed ; nor was this help by any means restricted to that
form which is easiest for the giver and the least useful to
the recipient—money,—but it represented an expenditure
of time and thought on his part in the attempt to secure a
relief which should be of a more permanent kind, and less
wounding to the susceptibilities.

What he did on behalf of the church in whose welfare
he took so deep an interest is too well known to need
recapitulation In many instances, where his sympathy was
strongly in a work, he freely gave his services as architect,
with the proviso, however, that his having done so should not
be known In the case of the very first work which came
into his hands, when as yet he was quite uncertain whether
a second was ever to follow, he expressed his intention, as
a true son of the Church, of giving his earliest work to her
as a free offering.

But, though generous when a cause commended itself to him, he had on occasion to assert his rights in no doubtful tone, when, as sometimes happened, he found that it had been taken for granted that he was prepared to devote his time and talents on some one else's behalf, for the mere love of the thing. More than once, after having been asked to make designs by some one of whom he had had no previous knowledge at all, he was met, when he asked for payment, by an outburst of righteous indignation at the request, and nothing more substantial. To be generous to the gentleman who is engaged in rifling one's pockets is not in human nature, and he rebelled in an unmistakable way.

Without any trace of self-conceit, he must early have become conscious of the possession of considerable powers That he admitted to himself satisfaction in much of his own work his diary and his most intimate letters bear witness, but he confesses with equal frankness the presence of a blemish where he perceives one He criticises the products of his own imagination, but that he should have felt proud of much that he did was no more than the logical consequence of his never allowing a design to leave his office unless he was thoroughly satisfied at the time that he could not better it

There must be hours and days in the life of every man when the imagination cannot answer fully to the calls made upon it. It may be that the frame is jaded with overwork or weakened by illness, or there is some thought which dominates and engrosses the mind with paralysing completeness. The products of the imagination working under such disadvantages as these must almost necessarily be below the usual standard of excellence My father's robust health, and the strength of will which enabled him to give an undivided attention to his work directly he applied himself to it, made such occasions rare with him, but I can remember instances of designs done under such conditions which were afterwards discarded wholly and ruthlessly when he came to look at them again

In his dealings with his clients he never placed himself on the pedestal of infallibility His relation to them was

that of friend and adviser, not that of an autocrat to his
subject. He held his business to be to carry out their
wishes with exactness, when expressed, and so to manipulate
their ideas as to make them susceptible of translation into
brick and stone, not to begin by showing them that what
they wanted was wrong or impossible, and then insisting on
their acceptance of something quite different. But with
all this there was a limit which self-respect would not allow
him to overstep   The free criticism which seems to come
most readily from those who know the subject least, the
sweeping suggestions which are made so glibly as if it were
an architect's business to be constantly doing the same
plans over and over again, generally found him inflexible.
What, indeed, would be left to the architect, or to what
purpose his training, if, himself an expert, he were to be
always bound to defer to the views of those who were
not so ?

It is true that those who put themselves in his hands
were generally content to do so with little restriction.   His
obvious self-reliance and strength of character begat a
corresponding feeling of security in those for whom he
worked which often became enthusiasm.   It is rare, indeed,
for me to meet a client of his who does not cherish his
memory as a man and as an artist.   Much more commonly
does it happen that they will speak of him with unaffected
emotion and respect, and welcome the son for the sake of
the father.   I fear to exaggerate, but I think it true that
wherever he bestowed his friendship he exerted by his steadfastness and right-mindedness a real and appreciable moral
influence ; certainly none who were thrown much against
him could help feeling sensible of his power.

I am indebted to General Philip Smith, for whom my
father restored Wendover Church in 1867, for the following
notes on their relations as architect and client :—

"In 1877 the reconstruction of the interior of the Royal Military
Chapel, Wellington Barracks, having been entrusted to your father,
I was, as Treasurer to the Committee which had charge of the work,
brought into intimate relations with him.

"There was a great mass of detail to be prepared besides the general arrangement of the decoration, which had to be considered, not only with reference to its artistic effect, but also with regard to the religious feeling to be produced by it

" Whether in making the sketch for a capital, or criticising and modifying the designs for a stained glass window, a mosaic, or a relief, Mr. Street was equally remarkable for the ease and correctness with which he decided on what was requisite and desirable, while he never failed to maintain the religious character of the building, and to appreciate the sacred object for which the ornamentation was intended.

" He invariably received suggestions with perfect patience and forbearance, and discussed carefully points which were brought before him, accepting what was good, and declining what, for valid reasons, he knew to be unsuitable   The result speaks for itself

" As regards myself, I was often amazed at the readiness with which he grasped a suggestion, the facility with which he put on paper the sketch of what was proposed, and his decision in pronouncing on its merit or the reverse.   I always felt the greatest confidence that he would not allow a mistake to be made   I look back upon my work with him with the greatest pleasure, and with gratitude for the manner in which he often discussed ideas which no doubt had at once appeared to him to be crude and inappropriate

" I had the greatest possible admiration for him, and, whether as regards his feelings or his powers, I always found him equally superior.

" I consider myself most happy to have been so well acquainted with him "

I have said something of the energy with which my father worked for his own profession generally and its individual members   He had its good very much at heart, and did not spare time or pains to better it.   This is well illustrated by his action in starting the visitorships in the Royal Academy Architectural School, in his willingness to read papers, to give lectures to advance the study of the art generally, in his constant attendance at the Royal Institute, and the prominent part he took in the business when any vital question arose, in the diligence with which he sought out the younger men whose ability he had marked, and gave them what prominence he was able.   He had a hearty admiration for the work of many of his brother architects, and his relations with them were kindly and cordial.   If he had any feeling of jealousy or rivalry he did not show it, and it certainly did not influence his words or actions.   I have often heard him congratulate himself on belonging to a piofession in which jealousy had so small a part, and where men were glad and eager to praise each other's work frankly and cordially.

My father's dealings with those in a lower station showed consistent kindness and consideration.   To the thousands of workmen with whom he had to do at one time and another he was an object of sincere respect, because they saw that he knew his work in no superficial way, and because, so knowing it, he was never unjustly severe or foolishly lenient   At his death the men employed at the Law Courts tendered an unsought testimony to his merits as an architect and a master.   The same feeling showed itself among all with whom he had business relations   His thoroughness commanded respect, and his strict and equal justice was welcomed with much more real satisfaction than a weaker and less consistent course would have been.

As a master he was sincerely esteemed by those in his service, while in the little village where he had made his home, one and all recognised what an epoch his coming among them had created, and how great the benefits he had secured for them.

Our vicar tells me that his devout example, his reverence and devotion in the house of God, have borne fruit in the heartiness and orderliness of the churchgoers to-day, and that many of the people have told him as much   As to the esteem in which his memory is held by them, he says : " It is a significant fact that in many of their cottages there is hanging on the wall the best printed likeness that their means could procure "

Of his intimate life day by day, of his relations to my mother and me, I have said little or nothing, though it is the home side of him that I knew best and remember most, because I feel it to be hopeless to try and put my recollections into words   Our fireside circle was so small in itself that I fancy there was more than the usual intimacy, sympathy, and affection between us ; and the very length of my father's work-a-day hours, while keeping him somewhat apart, made the mutual enjoyment of his rare leisure all the greater.   As

far back as I can remember it was his practice to be down by
half-past seven or earlier, winter and summer, to set to work
upon his correspondence, which was voluminous   During
my mother's lifetime our breakfast hour was nine, and not
unfrequently a little later, mine the fault, I am ashamed to
say ; for I well remember now how often it happened that
while I was guiltily snatching a few minutes' extra sleep, I
would hear my father's step as he came running up like a
big brother, to tumble me out of bed and joke me out of my
laziness.   By that time he had done a good hour and a half's
work, which sufficed as a rule to clear off the arrears of un-
answered letters of the evening before, and to make a good
start at those of the morning   The majority of the letters he
received were answered personally, on the others he wrote in
pencil a brief outline of what he wished written in reply.   It
was his custom to go with my mother every Saints' Day to
early celebration at All Saints, Margaret Street.   This rule
was never departed from, and involved some slight alteration
in the arrangement of the day's work.   Breakfast, however,
was always at the same time, and did not take more than
half an hour, so that by a quarter to ten my father was in
his study again ready to deal with the series of questions
arising out of the office business ; and then, when they were
disposed of, buckling down to his work for the day.   During
the next three hours he did as much designing as he could,
but a great deal of time was necessarily—and sometimes
unnecessarily—devoted to long interviews with clients and
others

After lunch, which he took soon after one o'clock, he saw
no one except his clerks, so that he was comparatively free
from interruption   What exercise he was able to get he took
in the afternoon, generally between three and five ; he would
then inspect any work he might have going on in town.
Very frequently he would have to attend a meeting or fulfil
some engagement ; once in a way he would look in at an exhibition of pictures.   During the progress of the Law Courts
a considerable proportion of his afternoons was spent at work
in the office there or on the building—two, three, or even
more in a week   These visits generally lasted two or three

hours, and one such visit, provided there was no interruption, would give more than enough work for the whole
of the staff there. We used to hear the rattle of his
T-square through the door as it dashed up and down' the
board, and then my father would come out of his room
with a sheaf of papers, put them down, and go out. No
sooner was his back turned than we would all run to see
what he had done for us, making a selection, so far as I
remember, according to our likings and our various degrees
of proficiency.

My father sometimes looked in at his club after leaving
the Law Courts, but he was, generally speaking, home again
between five and six, and would then set to work at letter-
writing again at once Afternoon tea was a thing quite unknown to him ; I doubt if he ever took it, in his life except
on Sundays and when he had visitors It came at a time
which was too valuable to be wasted—just before the post.
Letter-writing kept him employed till nearly dinner-time,
but he was usually able to make a start at his evening's task
before being called away. From seven till half-past nine he
put business wholly aside. After dinner in his early days
he very often sang. Music of all kinds had a great charm
for him, but he became a listener rather than a performer
while I was still quite a boy. If there was no music, he
either read or we had a few games of cards. Unfortunately,
victory almost always inclined to the same side, whether my
mother or I opposed him, for he had, as far as I could judge, the
makings of a card-player of excellence—memory, judgment,
power of combination, dash. In the summer we often enough
sat out in the square or on the balcony while my father
smoked the cigar, at first rare and afterwards habitual. Then,
as the cloud of smoke rose slowly up, we seemed all of us to
see visions of fair towns and pleasant countries still unvisited.
Those were the hours when we talked over—with what enthusiasm !—our summer holiday My father's keenness for
travel was never dulled so long as he lived The change
from the weary routine of professional life, the intensity of
his enjoyment of the beautiful in art and nature, the robust-
ness of a constitution which never failed to respond to the

benefits of change of scene and fresh air combined to make those few weeks precious to him hardly less by anticipation than actually.   The cigar finished, my father had tea, and then went to his study for three good hours of work, rarely going up to bed till half-past twelve.   This was the time when he felt most at his ease in designing, and worked most rapidly, because he knew that he should not hear the step on the office stair which foreboded interruption.

The day thus systematically divided allowed but little time for reading   My father generally managed to exhaust the paper during the short intervals before going to work after breakfast and lunch   In politics he took a decided though not an active interest , his convictions were strong and his opinions well known.   He was able to read very quickly, and yet to retain what he read with considerable accuracy.   Novels he rarely touched in my recollection, but he was familiar with all the best.   When he did read them he was often much moved.   I remember how, after my stepmother's untimely death, he took up the *Heir of Redclyffe ;* he found, as he expected, a sort of companionship in Amy's loss which soothed him even though it made him dwell on his own bereavement.

With the literature of architecture, art, and religion he was widely conversant.   He had read and studied these subjects diligently as a young man, and had thought them over so seriously that the views he then formed underwent comparatively little change.

It resulted from the immense amount of railway travelling which his practice entailed, that he read a great deal of that literature in the form of journals and reviews which can be finished at a sitting   He was never idle when he was in the train ; if he was not reading he was writing, or if the country through which he was passing was an interesting one, he would constantly make rough sketches of what struck him as worth seeing   In this way he was able to note down places to be included in a future tour, with the amount or kind of interest attaching to each.

I remember on the day when he was first struck with paralysis, how surprised and even disturbed I was to see

him constantly dozing off in the train between Guildford
and Gomshall. Soon after our arrival at the latter station
the seizure took place ; we were walking at the time, but so
indomitable was his energy even then that he walked two or
three miles farther to our home, though it was evidently ex-
hausting to him. His servant told me afterwards that for
two or three mornings previous to the attack he had had a
little difficulty in waking him in the morning. The circumstance had struck him particularly, because, as a general rule,
my father was wide awake on the instant.

Of his earlier work-a-day life Mr. R. Norman Shaw, R.A.,
writes to me as follows :—

"My first introduction to Mr Street was in the early part of
1859, when I went to arrange with him about going into his office,
as successor to Mr. Philip Webb, who was about to leave. We
soon completed our arrangements, and he was uniformly kind and
courteous from that day till the last time I saw him, which happened
to be at the Academy in the autumn of 1881 My feeling is that
he was a man of an even temper, for whilst in his office I had ample
opportunities of seeing him tried in many ways ; of course business
matters did not always go smoothly—he had often to alter or modify
his work to suit the tastes or caprices of clients,—and he had disagreeable letters just as other people have, but they rarely seemed
to ruffle him, and never made him in any way unreasonable with us
in the office.

"We worked hard—or thought we did,—we had to be at
the office at nine o'clock, and our hour of leaving was six o'clock—
long hours,—but he never encroached on our own time, and
as a matter of fact I am sure I never stayed a minute past six
o'clock

"There were some interesting men in the office, and we were
thoroughly happy I am sure we were loyal, and believed in our
master entirely, so that our work was really a pleasure , he was our
master—and let us know it,—not by nagging or in an aggressive
spirit, but by daily showing that he knew more than any of us, and
could in a given time do about twice as much

"When a new work appeared, his custom was to draw it out in
pencil in his own room—plans, elevations, and sections,—even putting in the margin lines and places where he wished the title to go ;
nothing was sketched in , it was *drawn*, and exactly as he wished it to
be, so that really there was little to do, except to ink in his drawings,
and tint and complete them

"The rapidity and precision with which he drew were marvellous.

I have never seen any one, not merely to equal, but to approach him, and he was as accurate as he was rapid.

"We used to prepare for him a dozen or fifteen sheets of details —all slightly set out to a large scale with full-size mouldings, etc., and these we placed in his room of an evening When we came in the morning we flew to our boards to find the whole carefully corrected and any amount added, both of drawing and of notes Often, in fact generally, the sheets were covered on both sides; every piece of tracery had been ' amended, every moulding drawn with a fine clear line, and perhaps half a dozen sheets of ironwork (in designing which he was very fertile and original) drawn full size with all the sections indicated. No wonder that we were enthusiastic with such performances going on under our eyes daily

"I well remember a little *tour de force* that fairly took our breath away. He told us one morning that he was just off to measure an old church—I think in Buckinghamshire,—and he left by the ten o'clock train About half-past four he came back and into the office for some drawing paper; he then retired into his own room, reappearing in about an hour's time with the whole church carefully drawn to scale, with his proposed additions to it, margin lines and title as usual, all ready to ink in and finish. Surely this was a sufficiently good day's work ! two journeys, a whole church measured, plotted to scale, and new parts designed in about seven hours and a half

"He was the beau-ideal of a perfect enthusiast He believed in his own work, and in what he was doing at the time, absolutely, and the charm of his work is that when looking at it you may be certain that it is entirely his own, and this applies to the smallest detail as to the general conception

"I am certain that during the whole time I was with him I never designed one single moulding."

I spent a great deal of my time in the study while I was a child, leaning as far as I could over the high table at which my father used to work—generally standing—and watching his pencil perform feats which fascinated me, none the less because the results were not intelligible to me My father liked to have me there, but I often wonder now at the forbearance he showed, for whenever his T-square moved up or down the board the chances were that it encountered my elbow at just the critical moment. That is my most vivid recollection I knew the iniquity of my proceeding, but my memory was as short as his patience was long No

doubt he was glad that I should take an interest, however unintelligent, in what he hoped I should make the
business of my life He never in any way forced my in-
clinations, but I could see that it would be a disappointment to him if I did not follow in his steps so far as I
was able

From very early days he encouraged me to look over
his shoulder while he sketched , and he was unaffectedly glad
when, of my own will, I set myself to try and put something
on paper.   Generally speaking, he left me free to choose my
own subjects , at other times he would make a choice for
me, putting in some of the leading lines when they presented a
difficulty which would be likely to discourage me, and correcting my finished attempt.   If by chance I achieved anything
above my usual average he was so obviously glad and proud
as to make me anxious to do much more   His own sketches
he was never in the habit of showing people unless specially
asked to do so, but he delighted in showing mine to his
friends if the opportunity came, talking them over with a
pleasure which might have made me think them better than
they were had I not known what a more than lenient critic
he was in all that concerned me.

Our foreign journeys, in which so much time was devoted
to architectural sightseeing and sketching, might easily have
become distasteful to a schoolboy, but my father contrived to
make them so entirely holiday trips, giving me information
in so interesting and apparently unmethodical a way, leaving
me free to do exactly what I liked, and apparently always
satisfied so long as I was happy and contented, that these
tours, in which I hope I learnt something, were the source of
infinite enjoyment to me

Even during my mother's lifetime many of my days
abroad were spent in the sole companionship of my father
Miss Holland, who was subsequently to be my father's
second wife, was often with us, so that we were able to leave
her with my mother while we made walking expeditions.
My father's pleasure in walking was hardly less than it had
been when he was a young man ; but it was a much more
severe exertion, and a good deal of pluck was wanted to keep

abreast of a boy who had no weight to carry   Mountain scenery had a great charm for him, in fact he had a strong sensibility to the beauties of Nature, though he must have been a little wanting in eye for colour, as his landscape work hardly ever avoided a certain coldness, which he was quite conscious of himself.   My own watercolour sketching was contemptible enough, but I was not afraid to put a little of all the warm colours in the box on my paper, so that my father often expressed a sort of amused admiration at the generous richness of the effect.

His drawing of form and structure and of the lie of a country was as good as it could be ; it was in the pure use of colour that he failed.   This criticism hardly applies to his watercolour sketches of architectural subjects, which were of great merit, though he rarely devoted the time to making anything like a finished drawing.

The fact of my being an only child naturally threw me much into his company, and during the seven years that followed my mother's death we were almost constantly together , but he never let me feel the want of a brother or sister.   He was boyish when I was a boy, and entered into all my amusements and interests with a life and spirit which was not assumed.   His companionship was better to me than any one else's, and he must have known it ; but in the un-selfish desire to do what he thought would be pleasant to me, whatever the loss to himself, he expressly furnished a room for me, so that I might be able to see my friends *tête-à-tête*   The evidences of his kindness and thoughtfulness might be multiplied indefinitely

He trusted me implicitly and unreservedly, rarely giving me advice, but doing better by setting an example which I could not fail to accept as a good one.   In money matters he took the same line.   He was most generous to me, giving me in fact what I wanted, and only begging me never to get into the habit of leaving bills unpaid.   When I was quite young a couple of hundred pounds were left me   The money burnt in my pocket , vague possibilities haunted me My father waited some time hoping that I should make a proposal on my own account ; and then, though I could see he did not like doing it, he told me jokingly that "the worst bank in the world was my breeches pocket," and that I had better let him invest the money. The suggestion was really a relief to me. The money was invested accordingly in some mysterious stock which yielded me from that time a marvellously high rate of interest

I remember his distress at accidentally opening a lawyer's letter sent to me from Oxford in respect of some small and long-forgotten bill He was always so prompt in payment himself that he had rather a horror of lawyer's letters ; but he was distressed most by the idea that I might have left this bill unpaid because I did not like to ask him for the money. Such was not the case, for he always made such requests so easy that I never felt at all concerned when I had to make them.

He never spoke a harsh word that I remember, and I felt that anger which it took so much to rouse would be a terrible thing. Perhaps his temperament may have been an equable one, but he certainly always impressed me as exercising a great command over the expression of his feelings. In the display of his affection, on the other hand, he had no care for concealment ; his love for those who were dear to him was evident in his whole demeanour.

I have said that his face was a typical English one eloquent of strength and rectitude. His forehead was broad and high, of a noticeable capacity ; his hair brown, inclining to light, and soft in character——that on his face being decidedly darker His eyes were a peculiarly light blue, penetrating and critical, but full of kindness, often twinkling with fun, but too clearsighted to make deception advisable. His lips were well formed and slightly compressed, in a way that was suggestive of firmness and self-control , when opened they displayed a row of white and even teeth, which never gave their possessor a moment's pain his whole life through. His chin, hidden for the last twenty years of his life by a beard, was square and strong. His complexion was fair but a little weatherbeaten and with a good deal of colour.

In height he was a little over five feet ten, thickly and muscularly built, and framed to bear any amount of fatigue ,

his shoulders were broad and rather sloping, his chest deep
His hands were well shaped and rather small, with tapering
fingers. He suffered a good deal at times from delicacy of
their skin, which made them liable to become cracked and
painful ; this affection gave them latterly a rather unnatural
thickness, but did not destroy their characteristics. The
hand was not that of a listless or indolent man, but in repose
was habitually slightly clenched. When he sat reading in
his easy chair he was hardly ever quite still ; either he was
tapping with the paper-knife, or moving his leg gently up
and down These motions did not in the least resemble
those which come from a fretful or worrying nature, but
hand and leg both were clearly parts of an organism which
rejoiced in an intense vitality.

Such a frame has all the elements of strength and endurance in it, and my father was strong and healthy much
beyond the generality Till the brief and fatal illness for
which a long business life spent at too high a pressure, and
with insufficient relaxation was mainly responsible, he had
hardly known what it was to be sick or sorry for a day
Headache and toothache were alike unknown to him Busy
days and short nights seemed to leave no mark At fifty
he seemed to be as happy in the consciousness of perfect
health, or as happily unconscious of sickness, as he had been
thirty years before

He did not know what it was to have a personal interest
in a country life till he was verging on fifty, but the zest
with which he entered into it, and the rapidity with which
he became conversant with all the arts of making a country
place, were remarkable. I have said elsewhere how skilfully
he disposed his grounds—a skill, by the way, which not so
long ago was justly regarded as part of an architect's necessary equipment,—but he was not content to be responsible
merely for the general scheme. As in his own sphere of
work his motto seems from the very beginning to have been,
" If you want a thing done, do it yourself," so it was with his
gardening. Every detail of our garden at Holmdale was
his and no one else's He speedily made himself acquainted
with all the trees and shrubs which are of the essence of the

garden of to-day, their capabilities, their uses, and their limitations, and superintended every bit of planting, laying-out, or disposing, as though to the manner born. It was not merely that he preferred doing his own work, but he took the greatest possible pleasure and interest in it

Associated as it was in his mind with a succession of sorrows, Holmdale speedily became an unequalled source of consolation and happiness to him. His love for the rhodo-dendrons and azaleas, of which he had made a great feature, had something almost personal about it. The calm beauty of the great masses of flower, with their glowing tokens of life and vigour, appealed strongly to a heart which had been lately wrung by death. Whenever he could escape from town he did so, and he was able to get through an amount of work there which in town would have þeen an impossi-bility. More than this, the rapidity which perfect quiet assured for his work allowed of his devoting a comparatively short time to it

In his earlier years he had been very fond of riding , for many years he had contrived to get a ride with me nearly every day when I was at home, but I think he felt that he had arrived at the time of life when it is not wise to risk an accident   Not long before coming to Holmdale he was riding a horse which was in the habit of pulling up short when it was frightened. My father was cantering along a lane at a good pace when the horse suddenly stopped dead. He was on the look-out, and kept his seat, but his weight threw the horse down. The horse was badly cut, and my father's confidence in it was destroyed, so that he got rid of it at once. Almost at the very same time his old friend, Bishop Wilberforce, met his death in a way so nearly identical as to bring home forcibly to his mind the serious possibilities to which he laid himself open by riding , at any rate he gave it up from that time and took to driving instead. The whole country round Holmdale was practically new to him, though he had been in the near neighbourhood on some of his walks with his brother in his boyhood, and he took a keen pleasure in finding out all its beauties and showing them to his friends   Even when he had visitors in

U

the house, which was almost more often than not, he usually devoted his morning to work, except for a stroll in the garden after breakfast. In the afternoon he would give himself a holiday, either driving, or roaming over the hill, or playing lawn-tennis, which he enjoyed heartily and un-affectedly, and without any of the usual gravity of the middle-aged man who regards it as a serious pleasure, and is proportionately sensitive to defeat

When he was alone with me, he devoted more time to work and less to leisure, otherwise the routine was the same He rarely did any work in the evening except writing.

To feel dull in the country never occurred to him; nothing pleased him more than his own garden, where he would sedulously pick off the dead rhododendron blossoms or weed the lawn, encouraged by the approving glances of his collies, Gyp, and old Rory his inseparable com-panion. He liked, however, to have his friends round him As a host he was full of humour and gaiety, and his obvious enjoyment of their company put his guests on the best terms with themselves. His disposition was an eminently sociable one After my mother's death he was terribly depressed by loneliness, London gives no companionship to the lonely, but in the country he found something sympathetic in all his surroundings. With many of his neighbours he was on a footing of warm intimacy; with all he was on good terms. He did not love cliques, nor did he refuse an acquaintance that was proffered to him

Even in town my father never seemed to bring the atmosphere of the office into the drawing-room, but in the country the professional man was sunk altogether "Shop," pure and simple, was abominable to him One friend he had, I remember, not in the profession, who seemed deter-mined to meet him on his own ground, and went on describing church after church, till my father was fairly wearied out. I can hear now the unconscious sigh of relief he gave when the unfortunate gentleman, who no doubt was congratulating himself on his admirable selec-tion of subjects for conversation, took his bedroom candle

His interests were those of the country-side, not merely by choice, but from his very nature. No need for him to assume tastes and ways not naturally belonging to him ; rather, it may be said, the simple, affectionate disposition of the man which had come unscathed through the fiery ordeal of a long professional career found in the country life surroundings which were thoroughly congenial

Throughout the winter he spent his Sundays in the country Sunday was his holiday, and he did not think it wrong, after having been to church in the morning, to put on his skates in the afternoon. I confess I always saw him do so with fear and trembling. He had a perfect confidence in his own ability to do difficult figures which was really not justified. Twenty years before he had been able to do them, but he had lost most of his youthful ability through want of practice, and the result of his rash attempts was not unfrequently a heavy fall, in which the back of his head suffered most severely. In the days I am speaking of we used to drive in nearly all weathers some six miles to church at Cranleigh every Sunday morning ; after our own church was built my father as churchwarden gave up the habit of skating or playing lawn-tennis on Sunday afternoons, for fear of its being misunderstood by the villagers, besides which he never failed to attend evening service Not only did he give the church to the village, but he showed in his own person how it should be used ; of his demeanour there and its effect our vicar has spoken. Amid all the satisfactions of the place the church, the memorial of his griefs, was the greatest, and he rarely failed to take advantage of the week-day service when he was there. The establishment of week-day services was one of the aims of his life, and he was happy in having been able to carry out his wish so near his own doors

---

The death of an architect must almost necessarily cause some break of continuity in the works In an undertaking of such magnitude as the Law Courts, such a break might easily have been fatal to the unity of the whole Happily, however, the design had been brought so near absolute completion in all essentials as to make such a misfortune impossible.   In reality, little more remained than to see that my father's intentions were strictly carried out.   This duty the Government entrusted to me in conjunction with Mr Arthur W. Blomfield, A R A, a friend of my father's— in sympathy with his work,—one whose name he had mentioned during the course of his illness as being well fitted for the task,—a man, too, in whom the public were sure to put implicit trust

Though, structurally, so little remained to be done, all those little odds and ends which, even in a small building, are so fruitful a source of delay, made another year's work necessary, and it was not till 4th December 1882 that the opening ceremony actually took place

If the laying of the first stone had been performed in almost too unpretending a way, the same complaint certainly cannot be made of the proceedings which attended the opening   It is not for me to enter here on the absolutely unique character of the ceremony of the day, the meeting of the sovereign with the whole body of her judges, and the formal completion and fulfilment of the long-cherished idea of concentrating all the branches of the judicature under one roof It is enough to say that everything combined to make the pageant worthy of the occasion   The rare sunshine came opportunely to make the scene a gorgeous one

The ceremony itself was brief and impressive.   Having proceeded up the great hall, which was filled with a brilliant throng, the Queen, standing on a dais at the northern end, received the key—the outward symbol of possession—from the hands of the First Commissioner of Works, and gave it to the Lord Chancellor, at the same time declaring the building to be open for ever.

After a speech from the Lord Chancellor, in which sympathetic reference was made to the absence of the architect, the Queen passed out through the north cross corridor, and the proceedings were so far complete   Later on in the day the various Inns of Court celebrated the occasion in a sumptuous way.

Immediately after my father's death the Council of the

Institute took the initiative in asking the Dean of Westminster to allow of his being publicly interred in the Abbey.
This request was backed up by representatives of the Royal
Academy and many distinguished men, and was at once
acceded to.   It was the first time since Dr Bradley entered
on his office that he had been called upon to exercise his
prerogative

The, funeral, which took place on 29th December, was
remarkable for the extraordinarily large attendance of the
members of architectural and artistic bodies.   The pall-
bearers were : Right Hon A J. B Beresford Hope, M P (President of the Architectural Museum) , Sir Frederick Leighton,
Bart., P.R A , Right Hon. G J Shaw Lefevre, M P (the First
Commissioner of Works) ; Mr. W. H. Gladstone, M.P. (representing the Prime Minister) , Mr Edwin Freshfield (representing the Society of Antiquaries) ; Professor T. Hayter Lewis
(acting President of the R I B A.) , the Bishop of Winchester
(Dr Harold Browne) ; and Mr Justice Kay (representing the
Lord Chancellor)   Delegations from all the chief societies
with which my father had been connected attended, and the
Prince of Wales sent a fully-equipped carriage.

The place of interment was immediately at the foot (*i e.*
eastward) of that where Sir Gilbert Scott had been laid
three years and a half before, the grave of Sir Charles
Barry being again at the head of the latter—a most happy
and appropriate selection.   The coffin bore the simple inscription :—

"GEORGE EDMUND STREET, R.A.
" Born June 20, 1824.   Died December 18, 1881 "

The grave is now marked by a beautiful brass from the
design of Messrs. Bodley and Garner.

On the Sunday following a funeral sermon was preached
by the Right Rev. Dr. Barry (now Bishop of Melbourne)

It was felt generally that some memorial of a permanent kind should be raised, and a committee was formed
forthwith, with Mr. Beresford Hope as Chairman, and Messrs
Alfred Waterhouse, R.A., and A W. Blomfield, A.R.A., as
Hon. Treasurer and Hon Secretary respectively   A meeting

was held in the central hall of the Courts of Justice on 4th April 1882, at which it was resolved -—

First, upon the motion of H.R.H the Prince of Wales, seconded by Sir Frederick Leighton, P.R.A :—

"That the intended memorial shall be a mural monument, including a full-length figure of the late Mr. Street, and that it shall be placed on the east side of the central hall of the Royal Courts of Justice, in the second bay from the south end "

And secondly, on the motion of the Right Hon G J Shaw Lefevre, the First Commissioner, seconded by Mr Henry Hucks Gibbs :—

"That Mr Armstead, R A , be appointed as the sculptor to carry out the work, etc."

The memorial thus auspiciously started was unveiled on 24th March 1886

The Lord Chancellor (Lord Herschell), in unveiling the figure, spoke as follows :—

"I have been requested, as representing for the time being those who are engaged in the administration of justice, to attend here to-day to unveil the memorial of Mr. Street. We must all feel that it is most fit that it should rest here, for this Palace of Justice was the crowning work of his life, and he was engaged upon it at the time of his death He was a man whose success in life was eminently due to his own merits, genius, and energy. While this is the crowning work of his life, there is scarcely a county in England—I believe there is no part of the United Kingdom—which does not owe to him some monument or work of beauty He was a man who not only by his own genius was enabled to realise beautiful creations and to give them visible form, but he found time amid the labours of a most laborious life to devote himself to some works of literature, to assist and benefit those pursuing the profession of which he was so great an ornament, and to write some instructive books on Church Architecture.

"His merits were recognised by those best able to judge of them. The Royal Academy made him one of their body, and elected him Professor of Architecture.

"No doubt, however, he devoted to this Palace of Justice more patience and loving effort than to any other of the works to which I have alluded

"It is impossible for any one to examine this vast building without being struck with astonishment at the enormous amount of labour that was expended upon it. He was not satisfied, having many courts to construct, to design one as a pattern for all Every court was separately designed with all its details of ornament by himself No doubt the building has been criticised,—I believe it would have been equally the case whatever human architect had been engaged Human tastes differ, and human ideas of human wants and requirements and views differ as to the best way of meeting them. It must also be borne in mind that the architect was not left an entirely free hand. He had to work under certain conditions, and some of the greatest faults laid to his charge, if faults they be, were due to the conditions

"I am quite sure of this, that the more this building is studied, and the longer the profession live in it, the more reason they will see to be grateful to the architect who designed it, and to be satisfied with the result of his labours I remember on the day when the courts were opened, a gentleman, whom I see present now, said he was quite sure that every day we lived in them we should discover some fresh beauty in them. As far as I am concerned, that observation has been completely verified. It is not in a day or a year that the minute care and pains bestowed on this building can be thoroughly appreciated or known It was not unnatural that those who admired the work of this great architect, not only in this building but in other parts of the country, and those who enjoyed his friendship, should unite to rear this monument to his memory, and that they should desire that it should rest in this his last and greatest work He has exhibited qualities of the true artist; he has created things of beauty, and I am quite sure that as long as there exists in this country a taste for the beautiful, so long —and I hope it may indeed be long—will the work of Mr. Street in various parts of the country be regarded with admiration and delight "

The memorial, which is composed of a seated figure, with paper and dividers in hand, raised on a pedestal which stands on marble shafts, and is covered with reliefs illustrating the various arts of design, fills the space of two bays of the wall arcading which runs round the hall, and is enclosed under a single large arch. The sculpture is Mr Armstead's, and the architectural design Mr. Blomfield's. The idea of making the memorial an integral part of my father's greatest work was a singularly happy one, and has certainly lost nothing in the carrying out.

There were two other memorials : one in the form of a bust, also executed by Mr. Armstead, which was subscribed for by members of the R.I.B.A., and is now placed in their rooms in Conduit Street ; the other, a churchyard cross, put up by some of his intimate friends and relations in the churchyard at Holmbury as a more personal tribute to a loving and beloved friend.

ORIGINAL WORKS BY G. E. STREET

NOTE —This list does not pretend to complete accuracy nor to exhaustiveness, nor is it intended to include any designs made but not executed. Those works which are mentioned in the Memoir are marked with the number of the page on which they occur.

ABERGELE Schools.
Adderley, Salop, cottages, etc
Amington Church, Staffordshire
    Schools, Staffordshire.
Ardamine Church, Ireland
Arthingworth House
Ashbury Schools, Bucks
Ashley-Green Church, Bucks
Aston Church, Salop
Aston (Little) Church, Warwick.

BANBURY (South) Schools
Barford (Great) Parsonage, Oxon.
Barton Schools, Warwickshire.
Bere Heath Schools, Dorset
Bettisfield Church, Flintshire
Biscovey Church, Cornwall, 11, 106
Bishopstoke, Hants, Longmead House.
    Mission Church
Blaston Church, Notts
Bloxham, House for Rev J. A Gould, Oxon
    Grammar School, Oxon.
    Parsonage, Oxon.
Blymhill Parsonage, Staffordshire
    Church, Staffordshire.
Bolton - le - Moors Church, Lancashire
Boston Spa Church, Yorks.
Bournemouth, St. Peter's Church, 21, 204, 260.

Bournemouth, Schools.
Boyne Hill, Church, 13, 204, 225
    Almshouses.
    Schools.
    House for Miss Hulme
Bracknell Church, 11.
Branstone, School Chapel
Bright-Walton Schools
Brimpton, Agricultural College
Bristol Cathedral, new nave 50, 110, 140, 176
Buckingham, School Chapel.
    Curate's House.
Buckland Schools, Berks.
Burford Schools, Oxon.
Burton-on-Trent, House for Mr. A. Bass.
    Schools.
Butcroft Church, Staffordshire.

CALDYMANOR Schools
Carlton Church, Yorks
    Vicarage, Yorks
Chadstone Schools, Northants.
Challow Schools, Berks.
    Parsonage, Berks
Chalvey Schools, Bucks
Chapel Allerton Parsonage
Chapmanslade Schools
Charleywood Church, Herts.
Chatham Schools
Chesham Schools, Bucks.
Chinnor School, Oxford

Chipping Norton, Schools.
    Workhouse Chapel.
Churchill School.
Clapham, Christ Church Vicarage.
Claremont Estate, Lancashire.
Cleobury Mortimer Schools, Salop.
Clifton, All Saints' Church, 50,
    100, 135, 204.
Coatham, Hospital Chapel.
Collingbourne-Ducis Schools.
    Vicarage.
Colmere Church, Staffordshire.
Colnbrook Vicarage.
Constantinople, Memorial Church,
    30, 50, 105.
Cotebrook Church, Cheshire.
Cuddesdon Theological College,
    Oxford, 20.
    Vicarage, Oxford.

DAFON Church.
Denchworth Schools, Berks.
Denstone Parsonage.
Diss School, Norfolk.
Ditton (Long), Surrey.
Down, St. Mary's School.
Dublin, Christ Church Synod Hall.
Dundee, House of Mercy.
Dunecht, House and Chapel, 50, 201

EASTBOURNE, St. Saviour's Church,
    100, 110, 204.
Eastbury School.
East Grinstead, St. Margaret's
    Convent, 20, 50, 258, 271.
Eastleigh Church, Hants.
East Parley Chapel School.
Eccleshall School, Staffordshire.
Ellon Church, Aberdeen.
Eltham Church, Kent.
    Schools, Kent.
Erlestoke Parsonage, Wilts.
    Church, Wilts.
Eton Schools, Bucks.

FARLINGTON Church, Hants.
Ffynnon Grouw Church, N. Wales.
Filkins Church, Oxford.
Fimber Church, Yorks.
Fylingdales Church, Yorks.

GADSDEN (Little) Schools.
Garston (East) Church.
Genoa, English Church, 105, 230.
Goosey Schools.
Graffham Church, Sussex.
Granborough Schools.
Gravesend Mission Church.

HADDO House Chapel.
Hadington Church, Oxon.
Hadleigh Vicarage.
Hatford, Cottages.
Hedsor, Parsonage.
Helperthorpe Church, Yorks.
    Parsonage, Yorks.
Heslerton (East) Church, Yorks.
    Parsonage, Yorks.
Holmbury, St. Mary Church, Surrey,
    69, 90, 101, 257.
    Holmdale, Surrey, 221, 223,
    225, 231, 255.
Horsham, House for Miss Paget.
Howsham Church, Yorks.
Hull, All Saints' Church.
    Parsonage.

IDE Hill School.
India Monuments.

KETTERING Church.
Kingstone Church, Dorset, 135,
    204, 205.
    Parsonage, Dorset.
Kirkburn, Yorks, Cottages.

LAMBOURNE Schools, Berks.
Lausanne, English Church, 105,
    272.
Laverstoke School, Hants.
Leeds, St. Andrew's Parsonage.
Leicester, St. Peter's Church.
Leigh Schools, Staffordshire.
Lichfield, Monument to Archdeacon
    Hodson.
Liverpool, St. Margaret's Church,
    204.
Llanasa Church, N. Wales.
Llandulas Church.
Llanelly Church, S. Wales.
    Parsonage, S. Wales.

Llanelly, House for E. Phillips, Esq, S Wales.
Llanon, Parsonage, S Wales
Llysfaen Schools, Denbighshire
Lockinge Schools, Berks
London—
 All Saints' Church, Putney.
 No 4 Cadogan Square, S W.
 Norwood Cemetery, Monument to P Ralli, Esq.
 Royal Courts of Justice, 50, 134, Chap. VIII, 200, 278
 St. Cyprian's Home, Marylebone
 St. James's, Paddington.
 St James the Less, Westminster, 37, 103, 135.
  Schools, Westminster
 St John the Divine, Kennington, 100, 204
 St. Mary Magdalene, Paddington, 50, 76, 204
Lostwithiel, Cornwall, House of Mercy.
Luton Hoo, Private Chapel.
Lutton (West) Church, Yorks
Lydford, Parsonage
 Schools

MARLBOROUGH School, Bradley Memorial Buildings
 Mr. Gilmore's House
 Mr. Thompson's House
Marlow (Great) Parsonage
Melksham Schools, Wilts
 Parsonage, Wilts
Mersea (East) Schools
 Parsonage
Middlesborough, All Saints' Church
Milnrow Church, Rochdale, Yorks.
Milton Schools, Gravesend
Milton Schools, Shipton
Minehead Church, Somerset.
Monkland, Cottages
Monmouth, St. Mary's Church.
Moordown Schools, Bournemouth.
 Church, Bournemouth.
Murren Church, Switzerland, 105.

Muskham Parsonage, Notts

NASH Schools, Bucks
Noke Parsonage
North Moreton Parsonage, Berks
North Muskham Parsonage, Notts

OXFORD—
 St Ebbe's Schools
 St Ebbe's Parsonage
 St Paul's School
 St Philip's and St James's Church, 19, 204
 St. Sepulchre's Cemetery Lodge.

PARIS, American Church, 133, 204
Peasemore Rectory, 11
Pewsey Schools, Wilts.
Pitsligo Church, Aberdeen.
Pitstone Parsonage, Bucks
Plymouth, St Peter's Schools.
Pokesdown Schools, Hants.
Polesworth, Dordon Chapel
Probus Grammar School.
Purbrook Parsonage, Hants.

RAUND'S Schools, Northants
Rollright (Great) Schools.
Rome, American Church, 93, 105, 208.
 American Clergy House.
 English Church, 105, 110

SANDHURST, Lodge.
Sheffield Schools.
Shipton Schools, Oxon
Sledmere Schools, Yorks
Southampton, St Mary's Church, 222.
Speenhamland Church.
 Vicarage
Stanford, Cottages
Stanford le Vale Schools
Stantonbury Church.
 Parsonage.
 Schools
Steventon School, Berks.
Stone Parsonage, Kent.
Stoney Stratford Vicarage.

Stourbridge Church.
Summertown Church, Oxon, 19.
Swindon Church.
    Parsonage.
    Schools.
Swinton Church, Lancashire.

TEDDINGTON Church.
Thixendale Church, Yorks.
    Parsonage, Yorks.
Tinsley Church, Rotherham.
Toddington Church, 50, 204.
    Schools.
Torquay, St. John's Church, 204.
Towyn Church, N. Wales.
    Parsonage, N. Wales.
    Schools, N. Wales.
Treverbyn, St. Peter's Church, 11.
    Parsonage
    Schools.
Trinidad, Magistrates' Courts.

UFFINGTON, Schools.
Uppingham, School Chapel, 50, 84.
    Libraries and Schoolrooms.
Upton Magna, Parsonage, Salop.
Upton, Vicarage, Bucks.

VEVAY, English Church, 105, 272.

WANSFORD Church, Yorks.
    Parsonage, Yorks.
    Schools, Yorks.
Wantage, Vicarage, 11, 13, 15.
    House of Mercy.
Warminster Schools, Wilts.
Wellington, St. George's Church.
Wendover Schools.
Wescott Church, Bucks.
    Schools, Bucks.
Wheatley Schools.
Whelford Chapel, Wilts.
Whiston Church, Lancashire.
Whitwell Parsonage, Yorks.
Wigan, Schools.
    St. Michael's Church.
    The Hall.
Winchester, Master's House.
Windsor, Holy Trinity Vicarage.
    St. John's Schools.
    St. Mark's School.
Winkfield Schools.
Wolverton, Mechanics' Institute.
Woodstock, Workhouse Chapel.
Wycombe, Chapel School.

RESTORATIONS AND ADDITIONS

ABBOTS Bromley Church
Aberdeen, St Andrew.
    St. John
    St. Machar
Abingdon, St. Helen
Acton Trussell Church.
Addington Church, Bucks
Adel Church, Yorks
Alnwick Church
Arley Hall, Cheshire.
Armitage Church, Staffordshire.
Ascott Church, Oxon
Ashburton Church, Devon
Ashbury Church, Berks
Ashchurch Church.
Aston Abbots Church, Bucks
Aston Clinton Church.
Astwood Church, Bucks

BACKWELL Church, Somerset.
Balscott Church, Oxon.
Banbury Church.
Banstead Church, Surrey
Barford (Little) Church
Barnstone Church, Cheshire.
Barrow Church, Salop
Barton-in-Fabis Church, Notts.
Bathwick Church
Baydon Church, Wilts
Beachampton Church
Benfleet (North) Church
Bensington Church, Oxon
Bere Regis Church, Dorset.
Bicester Church, Oxon.
Bicknoller Church, Somerset.
Bignor Church, Sussex
Bilton Church, Warwickshire

Bishops Wilton Church
Blakedown Church, Worcester-
    shire
Bletchingley Church.
Blickling Church, Norfolk.
Blithfield Church, Staffordshire
Bloxham Church, Oxon.
Blymhill Church
Blythburgh Church, Suffolk
Bolton Abbey, Yorks
Boningate Church, Salop
Bow Church, Essex.
Bow Common, St Paul's Church
Brackley School.
Bradenham Church, Bucks
Bray, St. Michael's Church.
Brayfield Church.
Brewood Church, Staffordshire
Brickhill (Great) Church, Bucks
Brickhill (Little) Church.
Bright Walton Church.
Britford Church
Brize Norton Church, Oxon
Brodsworth Church, Yorks.
Broughton Church.
Buckden Church, Hants
Burford Church, Oxon.
Burnham Church, Bucks
Burton Church, Staffordshire.
Butcombe Church, Somersetshire.

CALDYMANOR, Cheshire
Canford Church, Dorset.
Cardiff, St. Fagan's.
Carlisle Cathedral, 196, 261
    Fratry, 121, 261
Castle Ashby Church

Castle Rising Church, Norfolk.
Catton Church, Yorks.
Chadderton, Manchester.
Chaddesden Church, Derbyshire.
Chaddesley Church, Worcester-
    shire.
Chaddleworth Church.
Chadlington Church.
Chalfont, St. Giles's, Bucks.
    St. Peter's, Bucks.
Challow Church, Berks.
Chalvey Church, Bucks.
Chapmanslade Church, Wilts.
Charlbury, St. Mary, Oxon.
Charlton Church, Oxon.
Chartham Church, Kent.
Chatham Schools.
Cheadle Church, Cheshire.
Cheddington Church, Bucks.
Chiddingstone Church, Kent.
Chilton, All Saints' Church, Wilts.
Chilton Church, Berks.
Chipping Sodbury, Gloucester
    shire.
Chislehurst, St. Mary's Church.
Claybrooke Church, Leicester.
Claycross Church, Derbyshire.
Clifton Campville Church.
Clifton Hampden Church.
Clun Church, Salop, 122.
Cobham Church, Surrey.
Colebrooke Church, 43.
Coleshill Church, Bucks.
Collingbourne-Ducis Church, Wilts.
Colton Church, Stafford.
Colyton Church, Devon.
Corfe Castle Chapel.
Corsham Church, Wilts.
Cotterstock Church, 43.
Coventry, St. Michael's Church.
Cowley Church, Oxon.
Crawley Church, Hants.
Croxall Church, Stafford.
Croxton Church, Norfolk.
Cubert Church, Cornwall, 11.
Cuddesdon Church, Oxon, 120.
    Palace, Oxon.
Cuddington Church, Bucks.

DEDDINGTON Church, Oxon.
Denchworth School, Berks.
Denham Church, Bucks.
Denstone Church, Derbyshire.
Derby, St. Peter's Church.
Diddington Church.
Dinton Church, Bucks.
Dover Priory.
Downham Church, Essex.
Down, St. Mary Church, Devon.
Drayton Church, Banbury.
Drayton Church, Wallingford.
Driffield, All Saints' Church.
Dublin, Christ Church Cathedral,
        80, 101, 115, 122, 135, 184.
    Archbishop's Palace.
Dunmow Church, Essex.
Dunnington Church, Yorks.
Dunster Church, Somerset, 43.

EALINGTON Park, Warwick.
Eastbury Church.
Eccleshall Church, Stafford.
Edgmond Church, Salop.
Edwinstowe Church, Notts.
Elford Church, Stafford.
Ellesmere Church.
Elmley, St. James's Church,
    Kent.
Elsfield Church.
Enfield Church, 11.
Enstone Church, Oxon.
Ercall (High) Church, Salop.
Eton College Chapel.
Eyam Church, Derbyshire.

FAGAN'S, St., S. Wales.
Fairhamstead Church.
Farlington Church, Hants.
Fawley Church, Berks.
Fenny-Stratford Church, Oxon.
Fiddown Church, Ireland.
Filkins Church, Oxon.
Fingest Church, Bucks.
Finmere Church, Oxon.
Finstock Church, Oxon.
Firsby Church, Lincolnshire.
Foresthill School, Walthamstow.

Freckenham Church, Cambridge-shire.
Frenchay Church, Gloucestershire.
Fringford Church, Oxon.
Fritwell Church.
Frosterley Church, Durham.
Fulmer Church, Bucks.
Fyfield Church, Berks.

GARBOLDISHAM Church, Norfolk.
Garton Church, Yorks.
Glympton Church, Oxon.
Graffham Church, Sussex, 222.
Great Bedwyn Church, Wilts.
Great Marlow Church.
Great Smeaton Church, Yorks.
Greenhithe Church.
Gresford Church, Denbighshire.
Gressage Church, Somerset.
Grwych Castle, Abergele.
Guilsfield Church, Montgomery.

HADLEIGH Church, 11.
Hadley, St. Mary's Church.
Hadzor Church, Worcester.
Hagley Church, Worcester.
Hallow Church, Worcester.
Halton Church, Lincoln.
Hampnett Church, Gloucester.
Hampton Poyle Church, Oxon.
Hanbury Church.
Hanley Church, Worcester.
Hanney Church, Berks.
Hanslope Church, Bucks.
Hardwick Church, Bucks.
Hartley Wespall Church, Hants.
Hartwell Church.
Harwell Church, Berks.
Hatfield Church, Herts.
Hatfield Peverell Church, Essex.
Hawes Church, 11.
Hayling Church, Hants.
Headbower Worthy Church, Hants.
Headley Church, Surrey.
Heallom Church, N. Wales.
Hedon Church, Yorks.
Hedsor Church, Bucks.
Henbury Church, Gloucester.

Henley in Arden, Stafford.
Herne Hill Church.
Heston Church, 11.
Hethe Church, Oxon.
Highgate, St. Michael's Church.
High Halden Church, Kent.
High Wycombe Church.
Hilgay Church.
Hillingdon Church, Middlesex.
Hilmarton Church, Wilts.
Hinton Admiral Church.
Hognaston Church.
Holkham Church, Norfolk.
Hollington Church, Stafford.
Hope Mansell Church, Hereford.
Huish Church, Devon.
Hulcott Church, Bucks.
Hunsdon Church, Herts.
Hutton Church, Essex.
Hythe Church, Kent.

IDE Hill, Sevenoaks.
Ightfield Church, Salop.
Ilmer Church, Bucks.
Ilsley (West) Church, Berks.
Isleham Church, Cambridge.
Iver Church, Bucks.
Ivinghoe Church, Bucks.

KEMPSFORD Church, Gloucester.
Kerry Church, Montgomery.
Kew Stoke Church, Somerset.
Kidlestone Church, Derbyshire.
Kidlington Church, Oxon.
  Parsonage, Oxon.
Kildare Cathedral, 201, 203.
Kildwick Church, Leeds.
Kilkenny Cathedral.
Kiltennell Church, Ireland.
Kilverston Church, Norfolk.
Kingston Lisle Church, Bucks.
Kingstone Church, Stafford.
Kirby Grindalyth Church, Yorks.
Kirby Underdale Church, Yorks.
Kirby Wiske Church, Yorks.
Kirkburn Church, Yorks.
Kirkby Overblow Church, Yorks.
Kirk Hallam Church, Derby.

LADOCK Church, Cornwall.
Lambourne, St. Michael's Church.
Lanreath Church, 11.
Lapworth Church, Warwick.
Lavington Church, Sussex.
Leckhampton Church, Bucks.
Lee Church.
Leeds, Parish Church.
    St. Saviour's Church.
Leek Church, Stafford.
Leicester, St. Margaret's Church.
    St. Martin's.
Lewknor Church, Oxon.
Lichfield, St. Mary's Church.
Lilleshall Church, Salop.
Lillingstone Dayrell Church, Bucks.
Limerick Cathedral.
Linton Church, Hereford.
Little Petherick Church, Cornwall,
    11.
Llanasa Church, N. Wales.
Llandinam Church, Montgomery.
Llandysilio Church, Montgomery.
Llanidloes Church, Montgomery.
Llanilterne Church, Glamorgan.
Llanithern Church.
Llansantfraid Church.
Llysfaen Church, Denbigh.
Lockinge Church, Berks.
London——
    All Saints' Church, Lothbury.
    All Saints' Home Chapel,
      Margaret Street.
    Christ Church, Clapham.
    St. Andrew's, Wells Street.
    St. George's, Bloomsbury.
    St. George's Hospital Chapel.
    St. Luke's, Lower Norwood,
      109.
    St. Matthew's, City Road.
    Wellington Barracks Chapel,
      94, 96, 109.
Long Eaton Church, Derbyshire.
Longfleet Church, Hants.
Looe (East and West) Churches,
    Cornwall.
Lostwithiel Church, Cornwall.
Luffenham (North) Church.

Luffenham (South) Church.
Luton Church, Bedfordshire.
Lydford Church, Devon.
Lydiard Millicent Church, Wilts.
Lyndhurst Church, Hants.

MADRESFIELD Church.
Malvern (West) Church.
Marlborough, St. Mary's Church.
Melksham Church, Wilts.
Middleton Cheney Church, North-
    ants.
Middleton Stony Church, Northants.
Milbourne St. Andrew, Dorset.
Milcomb (Great) Church, Oxon.
Milland Church, Sussex.
Milton Church, Gravesend.
Milton Church, Oxon.
Milton Church, St. Blaize, Berks.
Milton Church, Wilts.
Milton Keynes Church, Bucks.
Mimms (South) Church, Middlesex.
Mixbury Church, Bucks.
Mollington Church, Oxon.
Monkland Church.
Monks Kirby Church, Warwick.
Monks Risborough Church, Bucks.
Moulsford Church, Oxon.

NASH Church, Bucks.
Newport Pagnell Church, Bucks.
Newtown Church.
Normanton Church, Leicester.
North Benfleet Church.
North Leigh Church, Oxon.
North Moreton Church, Berks.
Norton Church, Derbyshire.
Norwich, St. Peter Mancroft Church
Nutshalling Church, Hants.

OLDLAND Church, Gloucester.
Oswestry Church, Salop.
Otford Church, Kent.
Oving Church, Bucks.
Oxford——
    Holy Cross Church.
    Jesus College Chapel, 19.
    St. Aldate's Church.

Oxford—
    St. Ebbe's Church.
    St. John's Church.
    St. Michael's Church.
    St. Thomas's Church.

PEASEMORE Church, Berks.
Penkivel, St. Michael Church, Cornwall.
Pewsey Church, Wilts.
    Parsonage, Wilts.
Pickhill Church, Yorks.
Pitcombe Church, Somerset.
Plymouth, St. Peter's Church.
Pokesdown Church, Hants.
Polesworth Church.
Pontesbury Church, Salop.
Portsmouth, Garrison Chapel.
Prees Church, Salop.
Prestbury Church, Gloucester.
Probus, SS. Probus and Grace, Cornwall.
Purley Church, Berks.

RODNEY Stoke Church, Somerset.
Rollright (Great) Church.
Roydon Church, Norfolk.
Rye Church, Sussex.

SABY Church, Yorks.
Salford Church, Oxon.
Salisbury Cathedral, 117, 196, 255.
Salisbury, St. Thomas.
Saltley Church, Warwick.
Sandford Church, Oxon.
Sandhurst Church.
Scotton Church, Lincoln.
Seckington Church, Warwick.
Shepton Beauchamp Church, Somerset.
Sherrington Church, Bucks.
Sheviocke Church, Cornwall.
Shiplake Church, Oxon.
Shipmeadow Church, Stafford.
Shipton-on-StourChurch,Worcester
Shipton-under-Wichwood Church.
Shottisbroke Church.

Shrawley Church, Worcester.
Shrivenham Church, Berks.
Skirbeck Church, Lincoln.
Smeaton (Great) Church.
Solihull Church, Warwick.
Soulbury Church.
Sparsholt Church.
Speen Church, Berks.
Spratton Church, Northants.
Standon Church, Stafford.
Stanford-le-Vale, St. Denis.
Staple Church, Kent.
Steventon Church, Berks.
Stewkley Church, Berks, 98.
Sticker Church, Cornwall.
Stogumber Church, Somerset.
Stone Church, Kent, 36, 140.
Stoney Stratford Church, Bucks.
Stoughton (Great), Hunts.
Stratton Audley Church.
St. Austell Church, Cornwall.
St. Mewan Church, Cornwall.
St. Neot's Church, Cornwall.
Sundridge Church, Kent.
Sunningdale Church.
Swanbourne Church, Bucks.
Swavesey Church, Huntingdon.

TACKLEY Church, Oxon.
Talk Church, Stafford.
Tanworth Church, Warwick.
Taunton Church.
Temple Balsall Church, Warwick.
Tettenhall Church, Stafford.
Tew (Great) Church, Oxon.
Tew (Little) Church, Oxon.
Thirsk Church, Yorks.
Thornhill Church, Yorks.
Thorpe Arch Church, Yorks.
Thrumpton Church, Derby.
Thurgoland Church, Yorks.
Tilehurst, St. Michael's, Berks.
Tong Church, Salop.
Trumpington Church.
Tuddenham Church, Norfolk.
Turweston Church.
Tutbury Church, Stafford.
Twyning Church, Gloucester.

UFFINGTON Church.
Upham Church, Hants.
Upton Magna Church, Salop.
Upton Scudamore Church, Wilts.

WALSGRAVE Church.
Walsingham Church, Norfolk.
Walton Church, Stafford.
Wantage Church.
Warfield Church, Berks.
Warminster Church, Wilts.
Warnborough (South) Church, Hants.
Watchfield Church, Berks.
Waterstock Church.
Waters Upton Church, Salop.
Weaverthorp Church, Yorks.
Welshpool Church.
Wendlebury Church.
Wendover Church, Bucks.
Westbury Church, Bucks.
Westcott Barton Church.
West Keal Church, Lincoln
Weston (South) Church, Oxon.
Weston - under - Penyard Church, Hereford.
West Walton Church, 8, 119.
Wexham Church.
Whatley Church, Somerset.
Wheatley Church, Oxon

Whitchurch Church, Bucks.
Whitchurch, St. Nicholas, Somerset.
White Waltham Church.
Whitwell Church.
Whixhall Church, Salop.
Wiggenhall, St. Mary's Church, Norfolk.
Winchester, Hospital Chapel
Winkfield Church, Berks.
Winterbourne Church.
Winterbourne, Kingston Church.
Witcombe Church.
Withington Church, Salop.
Witney Church, Oxon.
Wolverton Church.
Wombourne Church, Worcester.
Woolborough Church, Devon.
Woollavington Church, Sussex.
Wootton Basset Church, Wilts
Wootton Rivers Church
Wootton Underwood Church, Bucks.
Wretham Church, Norfolk.
Wymering Church, Hants.
Wymeswold Church, Leicester.

YATTON Church, Somerset.
Yatton Keynell Church, Wilts
York Minster, 117, 196, 201, 217.

INDEX

ABBEY, Arbroath, 207
  Dryburgh, 207, 216.
  Easby, 223
  Fountains, 207
  Furness, 222
  Hexham, 207
  Jedburgh, 207, 216
  Lanercost, 7
  Melrose, 207, 216
  Westminster, 65, 79, 81, 140, 165, 279
Academy, Royal, 50, 196, 260, 263
Aix-les-Bains, 272
All Saints, Clifton, 50, 100, 135, 204
  Margaret Street, 48, 67, 68, 76, 91, 94
Altar, 66, 70, 73, 101, 234, 239
American Church, Paris, 133, 204
  Rome, 93, 105, 208
Amiens, Cathedral, 108
Ancona, 223
Angelico, Fra, 40.
Aquileia, 208
Arbroath Abbey, 207.
Architectural principles 58, 59, 62, 111, 113
Architecture, Greek, 78, street, 111, 113, the practice of, closed, 266
Armstead, H H, R A, 294, 295
Art and Religion, 8, 56, 57
Assisi, San Francisco, 91, 108
Athenæum Club, 50
Ayrton, Right Hon A S, 158, 159, 168.

BALDACHIN, 66, 71
Bamberg, Cathedral, 140
Barry, Sir Charles, 280.
  Edward M, 51, 55, 143, 145, 164, 259
Battersby, Dr, 193
Beauchamp, Lord, 256

Bennett, Rev. A M, 21, 260
Beverley Minster, 183
Biscovey, Church, 11, 106
Blencowe, Rev. Mr, 8
  Miss, 9
Blomfield, A W., A.R A, 245, 292, 293, 295
Bodley, G. F, A R A, 11, 20, 31, 293
Bournemouth, St Peter's, 21, 204, 260
Boyce, G P, 38
Boyne Hill Church, 13, 204, 225
Bradley, Dean, 293.
Bray, Reginald, 256, 257
Brick and Marble, 21, 49, 139, 208, 227
Brick architecture, 84, 137
Bristol Cathedral, 50, 110, 140, 176
Brussels, town hall, 164
Bull, Messrs, 169.
Burges, William, 25, 30, 31, 144, 210
Burne Jones, E, A R A, 38, 93, 249
Butler, Dean (of Lincoln), 11, 13, 15

CAREY Street site, 146, 157
Carlisle Cathedral, 196, 261.
  Fratry, 121, 261.
Carnarvon, Lord, 238, 243
Carter, Owen, 4, 5.
Cathedral, Amiens, 108
  Bamberg, 140
  Bristol, 50, 110, 140, 176, 255
  Carlisle, 196, 261.
  Châlons-sur-Marne, 25
  Chartres, 108, 118, 223
  Cologne, 17, 88, 108
  Cremona, 138.
  Dublin (Christ Church), 80, 101, 115, 122, 135, 184
  Dunblane, 207, 216
  Edinburgh, 210

Cathedral, Elgin, 207, 216.
    Exeter, 3, 120.
    Genoa, 82.
    Gloucester, 181, 255
    Kildare, 201, 203.
    Laon, 98, 108, 140.
    Léon, 139
    Lille, 24, 105, 204
    London (St. Paul's), 71, 100, 233
    Milan, 108, 139
    Paris (Nôtre Dâme), 108
    Rheims, 108.
    Rouen, 108, 223
    Salisbury, 117, 196, 255.
    Santiago, 139.
    Southwell Minster, 97, 238
    St. Alban's, 242.
    St Andrew's, 207, 216.
    Toledo, 139.
    Winchester, 5, 196, 255
    Worcester, 107.
    York Minster, 117, 196, 201, 217.
Cathedral Services, 3, 63, 183
Cavendish Place, 218
Châlons-sur-Marne Cathedral, 25
Chapel, Merton College, 106,
    Wellington Barracks, 94, 96, 109
Chartres Cathedral, 108, 118
Christ Church Cathedral, Dublin, 80,
    101, 115, 122, 135, 184.
Christian, Ewan, 212, 238, 241, 245
Church planning, 97, 99, 110
Clifton, All Saints, 50, 135
Clun, Church, 122
Cockerell, Sir C., 50
Cologne Cathedral, 17, 88, 108
    St. Gereon, 108
Colosseum, The, 227.
Constantinople, Crimean Memorial
    Church, 30, 50, 105
    St Sofia, 251.
Conventionalism, 89, 128
Crabb Robinson, H , 40.
Cranleigh, 230, 256
Crawford, Lord, 201, 227.
Cremona Cathedral, 138
Cuddesdon Church, 120.
    College, 20

Decoration, 79, 87, 91.
Drew, Thomas, 188, 196
Dryburgh Abbey, 207, 216.
Dublin, Christ Church Cathedral, 80,
    101, 115, 122, 135, 184
Dunecht House, 50, 201.

Easby Abbey, 223
Eastbourne, St Saviour's, 100, 110, 204
East Grinstead, St Margaret's, 20, 50,
    258, 271.
Ecclesiological Society, 12, 17, 22
Edinburgh Cathedral, 210
Eldon, Lord, 204, 238
Elevation and plan, 163
Elgin Cathedral, 207, 216.
Eliot, Dean, 178, 180
Embankment site for Law Courts, 146,
    157.
English Church
    Genoa, 105, 230
    Lausanne, 105, 272.
    Murren, 105
    Rome, 105, 110.
    Vevay, 105, 272
Exeter, 3
    Cathedral, 3, 120

Fergusson, J , 159
Field, Edwin, 149
Foggia, 223.
Fountains Abbey, 207
Fowke, Captain, 267
Fowler, J , 250
Fra Angelico, 40
Fratry, Carlisle, 121, 261
Free seats, 67, 69
Furness Abbey, 222.

Galleries in churches, 96, 99.
Gallery, National, 50.
Gatton Church, 140
Genoa Cathedral, 82.
    English Church, 105, 230.
Gervais, St , Baths of, 272.
Geys House, 12, 14, 225
Ghent, town hall, 164
Gladstone, Right Hon W E, 41,
    144, 258.
    Mr W H., 293
Gloucester Cathedral, 181.
Gothic architecture in Spain, 47, 139,
    227.
Gothic, capabilities of, 34, 61, 99,
    constructional merits, 80, 166,
    ecclesiastical and secular, 162; for
    the new Law Courts, 145, 159, for
    the National Gallery, 52 ; not a
    dead style, 77 , position of, 33, 49,
    unity, 34, 78 ; variety, 83.
Government offices, 33, 103
Graffham Church, 222

Greek architecture, 78.
Grimthorpe, Lord, 165, 246, 266.
Guildford, 1.

HADLEIGH Church, 11.
Haseler, Mr., 3, 4.
Herschell, Lord, 294.
Hexham Abbey, 207.
Holland, Mr. William, 230.
    Miss (Mrs. G. E. Street), 230, 274.
Holmbury, 219.
Holmbury St. Mary, 256.
    Church of St. Mary the Virgin, 69, 90, 101, 257.
Holmdale, 221, 223, 225, 231, 255.
Hope, Right Hon. A. J. Beresford, 293.
Houses of Parliament, 34, 170, 174.
Howard Street site for new Law Courts, 150.
Hunt, Sir H. A., 151, 263.

INSTITUTE, Royal, of British Architects, 49, 50, 112, 226, 238, 263, 282.
Iron construction, 111.
Ironwork, 37, 134, 135, 192.

JEDBURGH Abbey, 207, 216.
Jones, E. Burne, A.R.A., 38, 93, 249.
    Sir Horace, 265.

KENNINGTON, St. John the Divine, 100, 204.
Kildare Cathedral, 201, 203.
Kingstone Church, 135, 204, 205.

LANERCOST Abbey, 7.
Laon Cathedral, 98, 108, 140.
Lausanne, English Church, 105, 272.
Law Courts, the new, 50, 134, chap. viii., 200, 278.
Layard, Sir H. A., 151.
Leighton, Sir F., Bart., P.R.A., 200, 238, 293, 294.
Léon Cathedral, 139.
Lewis, Professor T. Hayter, 265, 280.
Lille Cathedral, 24, 105, 204.
Liverpool, St. Margaret's, 204.
London Bridge, 115, 236.
Louvain, town hall, 164.
Lowe, Right Hon. R. (Lord Sherbrooke), 149.

MACHELL, 261.
Mark's, St., Venice, 72, 91, 94, 108, 115, 248.
Melrose Abbey, 207, 216.
Merton College, 88, 106.
Milan Cathedral, 108.
Millais, Sir John E., Bart., R.A., 38, 238.
Monastic system, 8.
Morris, William, 25, 38, 249.
Murano, 251.
Mürren, English Church, 105.

NASMYTH, J., 131.
National Gallery, 50.
Neale, J., 243, 247.
Nevin, Dr., 208.
New Law Courts, 50, 134, chap. viii., 200, 278.
Norris, Canon, 179.
Nôtre Dâme, Paris, 108.
Nuremberg, 17, 96.

OCKLEY, 221.
Offices, Government, 33, 103.
Ornament, workmen's, 80.
Ottery St. Mary, 119.
Oxford, 19, 106, 248.
    St. Mary's, 76, 106.
    St. Philip and St. James, 19, 204.

PADDINGTON, St. Mary Magdalene, 50, 76, 204.
Painted glass, 88.
Palmer, Sir H. (Lord Selborne), 144, 149, 279.
Paris, American Church, 133, 204.
    Nôtre Dâme, 108.
Parker, Mr. J. H., 19.
Parliament, houses of, 30, 170, 174.
Pearson, Mr. J. L., R.A., 226, 272.
Pisa, 227.
Plan and elevation, 163.
Plans, church, 97, 99, 110, 214.
Pluscardine Abbey, 207, 216.
Pontresina, 206.
Portici, 209.
Poynter, Mr. E. J., R.A., 238.
Pozzuoli, 228.
Pre-Raphaelites, 38, 104.
Proctor, Mr. George, 12.
    Mr. Robert, 12, 209, 223.

RATISBON, 17, 88.
Ravenna, 206, 253.
Redfern, Mr., 180.

Religion and Art, 8, 56, 57.
Restoration, 98, 99, 114, 116, 184, 202, chap. xi., 262.
Rheims, Cathedral, 108.
Ripon, 196.
Robinson, Mr. H. Crabb, 40.
Roe, Mr. Henry, jun., 116, 185, 190.
Rome, 209, 223, 230, 259.
    American Church, 93, 105, 208.
    English Church, 105, 110, 223.
    San Clemente, 100, 236.
    The Colosseum, 227.
Rouen Cathedral, 108.
Royal Academy, 50, 196, 260, 263.
Royal Institute of British Architects, 49, 50, 112, 226, 238, 263, 282.
Ruskin, Professor, 132, 167, 226, 255.
Russell Square, 218.

SALISBURY, 273.
    Cathedral, 117, 196, 255.
San Clemente, Rome, 100, 236.
San Francesco, Assisi, 91, 108.
Santiago Cathedral, 139.
Scott, Sir G. G., 6, 9, 50, 60, 61, 106, 135, 136, 143, 181, 196, 210, 226, 242, 247, 260.
    Mr. J. O., 243.
Screens, church, 65, 101, 193.
Seats, free, 67, 69.
Sedding, Mr. E., 20.
Services, cathedral, 3, 63, 183.
Sharpe, Mr. E., 125, 167.
Shaw, Lefevre, Right Hon. G. J., 293, 294.
    R. Norman, R.A., 283.
Shearme, Rev. J., 257, 258, 278.
Sketching, 125.
Smith, General Philip, C.B., 277.
    Professor Roger, 168.
Society, Ecclesiological, 12, 17, 22.
Southampton, St. Mary's, 222.
Southwell Minster, 97, 238.
Spiers, Mr. R. Phené, 197.
Spottiswoode, Mr. W., 272.
St. Alban's Cathedral, 242.
St. Andrew's Cathedral, 207, 216.
St. Barnabas, 71.
St. Gereon, Cologne, 108.
St. James the Less, Westminster, 37, 103, 135.
St. John's, Torquay, 204.
St. John the Divine, Kennington, 100, 204.
St. Luke, Lower Norwood, 109.

St. Margaret's, East Grinstead, 20, 50, 258, 271.
St. Margaret's, Liverpool, 204.
St. Mark's, Venice, 72, 91, 94, 108, 115, 248.
St. Martin's-in-the-Fields, 52.
St. Mary's, Southampton, 222.
St. Mary Magdalene, Paddington, 50, 76, 110, 204.
St. Mary the Virgin, Holmbury, 69, 90, 101, 257.
St. Paul's Cathedral, 71, 100, 233.
St. Peter's, Bournemouth, 21, 204, 260.
St. Philip and St. James, Oxford, 19, 103.
St. Saviour's, Eastbourne, 100, 110, 204.
St. Sofia, Constantinople, 251.
Stewkley, Church, 98.
Stone, Church, 36, 140.
Street, A. E., 22.
    Mrs. A. E., 270.
    George Edmund, in a solicitor's office, 3; goes to Scott's, 6; his first commission, 11; engaged to Miss Proctor, 12; settles at Wantage, 14; made Diocesan Architect of Oxford, 14; his first foreign tour, 16; marries and goes to Oxford, 19; first Italian tour, 21; moves to London, 22; second prize in Lille competition, 29; made A.R.A., 50; elected to Athenæum, 50; appointed to Law Courts with E. M. Barry, 145; sole appointment to Law Courts, 145; the contract signed, 169; the eastern block opened, 172; made an R.A., 196; dislocates his arm, 207; buys Holmdale, 219; my mother's death, 224; presented with R.I.B.A. gold medal, 226; his engagement to Miss Holland, 230; his second marriage, 230; made Professor of Architecture in the R.A., 260; treasurer, R.A., 260; elected President of R.I.B.A., 266; goes abroad for health, 272; his death, 273; burial at the Abbey, 279; memorial in the Law Courts, 280; artistic character, 17, 57, 60, 61, 87; churchmanship, 15, 26, 40, 47,

67, 73, love of painting, 38 ; love of music, 15, 42, 53; power of work, 43, 231 ; business qualities, 172, 196, rapidity in design, 153 ; skill as a draughts-man, 124, 227, accuracy in sketching, 207, power of conception, 131 ; power of critical observation, 8, 83, 120, 122, 137, thoroughness, 134, 172, 276, knowledge of his work, 113, 188, 192, individuality, 103, 104 ; preference for English Gothic, 21, 81, 202, preference for the earlier forms, 19, 106, 107, 108, views on training of an architect, 125, 137, 142 ; views as to the close connection of painting, sculpture, and architecture, 13, 92.

Street, Mrs. G E, 12, 22, 223, 224
    Charles, 1, 4
    Mr. (the father), 1, 3.
    Mrs (the mother), 1, 14, 18
    Miss M. A, 1, 9, 10, 18, 71
    Thomas Henry, 1, 3, 5, 9, 12, 226, 274
Street architecture, 111, 113
Style, Victorian, 86, 160, 165.
Sundridge, 11, 13.
Sykes, Sir Tatton, Bart, 50, 180, 183
Symbolism, 58, 101, 181.
System, monastic, 8.

TAINE, M, 165
Temple Bar, 170
Thring, Rev. E, 184.
Toddington Church, 50, 204
Toledo Cathedral, 139
Torquay, St John's, 204
Town hall, Brussels, 164.
    Ghent, 164

Town hall, Louvain, 164.
Trevelyan, Sir C, 146, 152
Triangles, designing on system of, 141
Turner, J M W, 132

UPPINGHAM, 50, 184.

VENICE, 206, 208
    St. Mark's, 72, 91, 94, 108, 115, 248.
Verona, 208.
Vevay, English Church, 105, 272
Vezelay, 223.
Victorian style, 86, 160, 165

WAIT, Mr. W. K, 178.
Walker, F, 39
Walton, Frank, R I, 273.
Wantage, 11, 13, 15.
Waterhouse, Alfred, R A, 143, 293.
Watts, F, R A, 238
Webb, Rev. B / 13, 22
    Mr Philip, 20.
Weissenstein, 207.
Wellington Barracks Chapel, 94, 96, 109
Wells, H T, R.A, 198, 219, 224, 270, 273
Westminster Abbey, 65, 79, 81, 140, 165.
    St James the Less, 37, 103, 135.
West Walton Church, 8, 119.
White, Mr. William, 11
Wilberforce, Bishop, 14, 221, 225.
Winchester, 5
    Cathedral, 5.
Worcester, 1
    Cathedral, 107.
Workmen's ornament, 80
Wren, Sir C., 76, 170, 233, 268

YORK Minster, 117, 196, 201, 217.
Ypres, Cloth Hall, 54, 164

APPENDIX

A COURSE OF LECTURES DELIVERED BEFORE THE STUDENTS
OF THE ROYAL ACADEMY IN THE SPRING OF 1881,
BY G., E. STREET, R.A.,
AS PROFESSOR OF ARCHITECTURE.

LECTURE I

THE STUDY AND PRACTICE OF THE ART OF ARCHITECTURE[1]

IT is impossible for a professor who enters on his duties under such circumstances as have involved my appointment to this office, not to say at least a few words of a somewhat personal character. Three of my brethren who, in succession, occupied this chair within my time, have all been taken away from us within a brief period. One of them was the master under whom I had studied, and to whose varied information, skill, and enthusiasm for his art I shall always feel myself a great debtor. But the last was one to whom many of you students who are here to-night are similarly indebted. Mr. Barry had, as many of you are aware, held the post of professor in this Academy for some six or seven years His lectures were marked by the variety of the subjects which they embraced, and by the judicial impartiality which it was his aim to show in his appreciation of what was, in his eyes, good in all styles. The sad event which closed his career so suddenly interrupted last year's lectures when their delivery was but half completed. But they are shortly to be published, and will, I doubt not, be well worthy of your study and attention, as containing the advice, criticisms, and views upon our art of one who held a most distinguished place among his brethren. This is not the place or the time to say more on such a subject. But less than this I cannot say on an occasion when all of us would have been so glad that it should still have been his voice to which you listened, and his counsel that you had to accept There is one difficulty which all professors must feel in the work which is to be done here. It is, as I think, our first duty to think of our students and their good. And in successive years it might be necessary, or, to say the least, advantageous, if the simple truths and precepts which are the foundation of all that is best in art were repeated time after time to the succeeding audiences of fresh

[1] Lecture on Architecture to Students of the Royal Academy Delivered Monday, 14th February 1881

students. And so, perhaps, it may matter little if sometimes I repeat what has been far better said before, in hopes that to some at least there may be freshness, instruction, and novelty in what I say. The real difficulty is that a professor who wishes to teach well must, of necessity, inculcate only what he himself believes to be true , and that in dealing with art, as soon as he leaves the domain of simple first principles he comes upon ground where every view is contested, and each man's heart is, to a great extent, independent of his neighbours And my hope is that in listening to me you will none of you forget that, after all, what I tell you is intended to be suggestive before anything. If I tell you of first principles which all acknowledge, and then give you advice which seems to sin against them, you may be sure I have not made myself understood, and in any case it is the first principle which must be held fast by. To-night, however, I shall have to confine myself very much to questions which much concern those of you more especially who are students in our architectural school, but which may, I fear, be comparatively uninteresting to the rest of my audience In subsequent lectures I hope I may find it possible to deal with questions of a different and pleasanter kind—less elementary, and such as all of us who wish to be artists are bound to interest ourselves in It is a good rule of the Academy that compels you all—painters and sculptors, as well as architects—to listen to architectural teaching But no teaching can be worth anything which tries to accommodate itself to the indifference of an audience , and it would be a mistake to assume for an instant that any of you wish to know only a little about any one of the arts, and care only to attend here because the Academy insists upon your doing so. The first test of an artist is that he should feel a real and absolute, if not an almost equal, interest in all the arts, and the painter who does not care to know something about architecture is sure, at least, never to be so good a painter as he might have been , whilst to you students of sculpture, I would say that my art and yours are so intimately allied, neither in their highest developments being ever perfect without the aid of the other, that it is incumbent upon you, if you would excel, to know much more than merely a little about architecture. The three arts are indeed all dependent on each other The most perfect building is that in which not only the architectural lines, proportions, and features are all good and beautiful in themselves, but the one in which provision is thoughtfully and wisely made by the architect for the best display in harmony of the arts of painting and sculpture The architect deals with outlines and masses, with light and shade ; but for that deeper interest which touches one most after these general effects have been produced, he depends, except in the vastest buildings, upon the other arts, and he must know and feel enough about them to make him competent to provide for their worthy and dignified treatment.   And surely it is not less needful that the painter and the sculptor should be so well trained in architectural detail as to make it impossible for them to do or admire work in which ignorance of that art is exhibited—such ignorance being fatal in its effect wherever it exists or is conspicuous Nor should it ever be forgotten that the study of the most permanent of all the arts has a real value if it leads all artists to consider in their work not only what is good for. to-day and for the fashion of the time, but for ages to come, so that it may be looked at with love and respect by their descendants for many generations.   So much only do I think it necessary to say by way of introduction to my subject for to-night, which I have selected as being one on which we ought first of all to understand each other, and on which one who is growing old may well speak decided words of counsel to you who are only on the threshold of your career.   With what conception of art are you bound, then, to begin, your work ?   The work of the architect is evidently complicated by conditions peculiar to itself   It must be useful first of all, beautiful afterwards.   Unless it is useful, it is not really artistic.   Usefulness may be exhibited in trifles as much as in the greatest affairs   You must realise that it is not only necessary to learn how to plan a building so as to make it most thoroughly fit for its purpose, but you must learn also how to design every detail so that it shall be the fittest for the place, and for the work it has to do.   You must therefore begin by studying how to plan well, and how to build well   Good construction is the basis of good art ; though even here a word of caution is required, for new modes of construction may be popular, but not good · and the only test that I know of good construction is the certainty of its being permanent   Unfortunately, you will find that this is the greatest temptation which will assail you from the first in your architectural career   You will be tempted to sacrifice solidity to some fancied necessity for ornament , but it is nevertheless the fact that many very noble buildings of all. ages are almost absolutely devoid of mere ornament, and that no work which is not solid and well constructed and proportioned, however richly it may be adorned, is ever in the end lastingly ornamental   Consider for an instant in what way this rule affects you when in practice   The Egyptian and Greek remains—quite apart from any intrinsic beauty which they possess—affect every one by the evidence of their admirably solid mode of construction.   The somewhat unsightly masses of brickwork which are all that are at first seen of some great Roman works, such as, *e g* the baths of Caracalla, affect. the senses in the same way   In mediæval times, it is when you are traversing some passage formed in the thickness of a wall that the same feeling is

excited, and in all these cases it is the respect for his work which
the builder shows that reacts upon us.   Nothing is ever entirely
unworthy of notice that is done with this feeling, and as it would
be wholly impossible to obtain, as it would also be absurd to
demand, the same goodness of design in a mere temporary erection
as in a permanent one, so the merit of an architectural work will
almost always have some distinct relation to the solidity of its construction.   The reason for putting this fact before all others which
bear on the study and practice of an art is that, if you have but a
firm grip of it, all your studies will bear more fruit, because it will
give you in one vital point an infallible critical test for the examination of all architectural work.   And if I do not attempt to teach
you in my lecture much about the merely practical side of your
work, you must never forget that this is in no degree whatever
because I wish you to ignore what is absolutely essential, but only
because it seems to me that this Academy of the Fine Arts requires
of its professors and of its students that their main devotion shall
be to the artistic side of our art, with but such incidental references
to its practical side as grow naturally out of or tend to illustrate and
explain the other.   Such references, even if only incidental, cannot
be infrequent.

At every turn we are met with the question whether what we
have designed is the best thing possible under the circumstances,
not whether it is the most beautiful—the best thing in architecture
being always that which combines the most sagacious use of the
materials available, the soundest construction, and the most convenient adaptation to the requirements, with thoroughly good artistic
character and proportion in the mass and in all the details, and some
evidence of imagination in the design.   The architect has to work
under limitations wholly unknown to the painter, sculptor, or
musician, and yet his art requires for its perfection no less invention
and imagination and loftiness of character.   If we look carefully at
painters' work, we are struck with the extraordinary extent to which
the artist reveals himself in his work.   On the canvas of a great
painter you see not only the man who sat for his portrait, but almost
equally the man who painted it.   In a more subtle way the architect
is revealed in his work.   His refinement or his coarseness, his love
of truth or indifference to it, are always evident.   In the highest art
it is the man rather than the society or the system that is seen ; and
as in ages when insecurity of life, tyranny of rulers, ruthlessness, or
religious intolerance, were rife, the very existence of these things
involved the existence of men of the strongest and most heroic
character, so in the same times the greatest buildings were erected.
The individual man lived often a higher life, and had a higher conception of his work than is usual in more easy and perhaps more

polished and virtuous times   At the same time, though, the highest art is a reflex of the spirit of the man.   The man is dominated to a great extent by the age , so that the spirit of the age is seen more or less in the architectural works of all times.   Our own history will be read in ours possibly long after all other records of its work are lost, and it lies with us to secure that the record shall be that of the best features, not of the worst of our times   The lesson for you is obvious   you must cultivate in yourselves a high sense of the requirements of your art, and a persistent self-reliance and individuality.   Without these you cannot be great architects. And it is more necessary to insist on this with you than with your brethren of the brush and the chisel, because your daily life may be, and too often I know is, spent in working under influences wholly hostile to this higher view.

It is well to speak thus to you who are still young, and who, being so, are also generous, and I hope enthusiastic   You will soon cease to be young ; but unless you maintain to the end the other qualities you will not be great artists.   There may, of course, be enthusiasm of a certain sort for bad things   Many of us, I fear, fancy whilst we are doing commonplace, if not vulgar things, that our work is worthy to excite such a feeling, never realising any of the necessary conditions.   And it is worth while to ask, therefore, what is it which really does create our enthusiasm in ancient examples ? Enthusiasm is not merely the highest kind of interest   This may be kindled by historical associations , but a bare field on which a battle has been fought has this   Extreme age gives interest, but it is not necessarily lovely   Singularity of situation, of material, of adaptation to exceptional purposes, may all give interest   But none of them create real enthusiasm   And the only architectural work which does excite it is that in which you find evidence throughout that the artist thought nothing of his own part in it, but only of the perfection of his work, of its solidity first, and then of its refinement.   Try by this test such buildings as the Parthenon, the Temple of Neptune at Pæstum, the Campanile at Florence, Amiens Cathedral, or the choir of West-minster Abbey, and you will find that all possess these qualities, and all of them kindle undying enthusiasm.   Once learn to see that such qualities exist and produce their effect, and you have made one step at least towards possessing them yourselves.   Nor is it necessary that you should have any hope of exhibiting your qualities on build-ings of such importance as those just mentioned   Recollect that in Athens, in Italy, in France, and in England small works have been at least as interesting and perfect as large ones, and that no artist depends upon the largeness of the work which he has to deal with for the opportunity of showing his real worth.   I recollect when I sat in your place hearing one of the greatest of my predecessors—the illustrious Cockerell—declare that the most perfect thing he had ever designed was a scraper; and, strange as the illustration is, he was serious, and justified in being serious in such a view   It may be argued that in ancient times there was an intuitive rather than a conscious recognition of the need for refinement which I assume to be necessary; but this I am inclined to doubt   What, for instance, is the story of the long and slow development of Doric architecture, but one of an attempt to secure more refinement by the gradual perfection of every detail?   The enthusiasm for what had gone before being the stimulus to greater perfection, and the refinement being the consequence of the enthusiasm   Or, again, in the whole history of art, is there a more interesting chapter than that of the gradual development, by repeated changes and modifications, of the circular Roman and Byzantine buildings, through the Romanesque apse into the intricate and beautiful Gothic chevet of the French churches in its complete form?—a development which was gradual only in the sense that we can trace all the steps by which it proceeded, but which, as compared with the slow and patient development of Egyptian and Greek art, astonishes us by the rapidity of its proceedings, the fertility of imagination shown by those who conducted it, and the vast and complete change in all architectural forms which in a few years was achieved.   Some among you may have no enthusiasm for your art, and may have no interest in such evidence of what the architects of old must have felt.   You may have been told to be architects, not because you refused to be anything else, but because the profession seems to offer a fair mode of getting a living   This is to reduce your art to the level of the basest trade, to deprive yourselves of all chance of real success, and to condemn yourselves to a career of mediocrity which will benefit neither you nor your neighbours.   If there are any such students here let me beseech them to take a new view of their duty, and to cultivate, by every means in their power, the frame of mind I have been describing.   It does not lie in the power of every one to become a great artist   But it is in the power of even the least gifted among you, by cultivating his reverence for the ways and work of great artists, to make it impossible that he should ever be guilty of anything wholly bad and contemptible.   Consider what a glorious inheritance you have!   In every part of the civilised world, the architect whose eyes are open finds, on all sides, works which speak to him more forcibly, the more he examines them, of the great and eternal lessons of his art.   He, above all men, has a delight in the past, because he can read better than others the most permanent and intelligible of its visible records.   If he is wise he never ceases to learn, for the examples he has to study are of inexhaustible number and variety   Even if circumstances compel him to limit his studies to his own country, there is no cause for regret, for I suppose the man has not yet lived who has seen all that is worth seeing, even of English architecture; and as much may often be learnt by the patient study of small works as by more ambitious attempts to study, to group, and to analyse the origin, principles, and developments of the art all over the civilised world   When you have resolved to look at your work in this spirit, you must be reminded that there are some minor conditions of success which I do not think beneath notice here.   Your first business is to become an accomplished draughtsman   As you will hear presently, good architects have existed, and may always exist, who do not draw well; but no one can safely say to himself that he will elect to be numbered among them   Architectural draughtsmanship is a good training for every one, because its first essentials are clearness and accuracy, and the man who has to depend very much on these qualities for his knowledge of the effect his work will produce must learn so to represent it on paper as to ensure that his drawing is a fair representation of its effect.   The habit of tinting and shading architectural elevations is a bad one, and not to be encouraged.   It is a simple waste of time.   In outlining geometrical drawings, as well as in sketching, never use a very hard pencil, and make up your mind in the latter to dispense almost, if not altogether, with india-rubber The essence of good architectural drawing is not only that it should be clear and accurate, but that it should be done positively and once for all   Nothing is more fatal than a slovenly and tentative habit in architectural draughtsmanship, and if you indulge in it you will find it stand much in your way when you attempt to make original designs.   When you draw these, the first thing you must endeavour to accomplish is to acquire the habit of seeing in your mind what you want to draw before you draw it.   To see some men draw, one might almost suppose that the pencil was gifted with the miraculous power of making a design, so little does it seem to be certainly guided by the hand that holds it   The habit of picturing your design to yourself before you draw it would save a great deal of this confused sort of work   Knowing what your intention is, you have then only to put it on paper, but if you have not taken this preliminary trouble, you will never work with half the accuracy or speed which would otherwise be possible   Good draughtsmanship is a necessity in these days for a really accomplished architect

It is impossible in this respect to put ourselves exactly in the position of men who had not our facilities and our system of education.   It is true we are not better artists than they were; but in one sense we can draw better, and are, therefore, bound to do so   I am not aware that any one knows how a Greek architect set out his design   And as to the mediæval draughtsman, we know, by such books as that of Willars de Honecort, a thirteenth-century French architect, that an architect's drawings then were something like children's drawings now   And even at a later date the still extant original drawings for such works as the front of the church at Louvain, the steeple of Ulm, and the cathedral at Koln were strangely unlike the exact geometrical drawings which we are able to make. These drawings—published in Moller's *Denkmaler*—and Hollar's drawing of the steeple at Mechlin, engraved, no doubt, from an original drawing, afford interesting illustrations of this kind of elevation   You will find that though they are in elevation, they are frequently so far put into projection as to exhibit at all points the plan or horizontal section of the work.   Both the drawing of elevation and plan are, however, so slight, that it must have been impossible for any architect to have satisfied himself without further details, and these, there is some evidence to show, were set out by the architect himself at large on a floor specially provided for the purpose   Such a floor exists in the workroom over the passage to the chapter-house at York, and at Limoges the original setting-out of the groining was found by M Verneille in a similar position   Possibly, also, models were more used than they are now.   At Louvain is still preserved a most exquisite model, cut in stone, of the complete design for the west front of a church, which itself has never been completed   When compared with the design, which is also preserved, it is seen that the model represents mouldings and traceries with an exact accuracy which is not attempted in the drawing   But the making of a model by an old architect, in place of a careful geometrical drawing, is no excuse to any one for making careless drawings in the first place now.   They are sure to lead to careless details afterwards   Too many of you come here wholly ignorant of all works on your art.   Many of them, to which it is always easy to gain access, will give you more evidence of the best kind of architectural drawing than any verbal hints can   But you will find that in these there are united clearness, accuracy, feeling for detail, delicacy, and conformity of line, and you will find no back-lining to mark the supposed shaded side of projections, and none of those provoking splotches of black which are unhappily so much in favour with some young draughtsmen.   A power of drawing in perspective is of the first importance on two grounds   first, that without this knowledge your enjoyment and success in sketching will be very small ; and, secondly, because it will render it more easy to you to realise the effects of your building in perspective, without having the trouble of making a careful drawing or a model, to convince yourself of its real appearance.   Without this power you will hardly be able to realise the real light and shade of a design , and without this ability it were better never to attempt to make a design at all   The delicacy of draughtsmanship on which I have insisted will lead to refinement in other ways.   An essentially vulgar drawing may be made of a refined building, it should be your aim to let the drawing itself have that air of refinement also   You are, all of you, armed with mathematical instruments, the like of which no age before our own has ever seen.   Remember that these are useful servants, and no more, and that, whenever you can do so, you had far better use your hand in place of your instrument.   You cannot practise this too much or too steadily.   Draw accurately, firmly, and, as far as may be, with a single stroke, the outline of a Greek or Etruscan vase, the volute of a good Ionic capital, the sections of Greek mouldings, and equally of our own English mouldings of the thirteenth and fourteenth centuries   The hand trained in this way is, believe me, a much better servant than the bow-pencil.   The curves which can be drawn by a trained hand, under the guidance of a trained eye, are far more beautiful, because more subtle in their variations and prolongations than those of any instrument, and I insist on this point because, unhappily, the bow-pencil and not the hand is at the root of almost all the so-called ornament of the nineteenth century.   Another habit which it is desirable to encourage is that of representing with a few lines the effect of several.   In drawings to a very small scale the attempt to represent every line of moulding and detail is sure to be a failure as well as a waste of time, and the selection of those lines which are essential is always evidence of good draughtsmanship.   This cannot be done without a real knowledge of the character of the details.   And as no one can draw a building accurately without this knowledge, I need hardly say that it is very far from a waste of time for a painter to give some attention to architectural detail.   Some of Turner's pencil-drawings are capital examples of his power of indicating so accurately the details of a building, that no one need be in doubt as to the style in which it is built.   He could not have done this unless he had educated himself by the study of architectural detail, and his example ought to be followed by every painter-student who wishes to be able to introduce any architectural features into his pictures—as who does not?

One word of caution is necessary here   The power of making good and attractive drawings is of immense value, and may make a vast difference in your prosperity and success in life.   But it is a means only, and not the end.   It has its dangerous side.   It is possible to make a design look well on paper which will never pass muster in execution.   Nothing is more suicidal than this, but, unfortunately, there is nothing against which it is more necessary to warn you.   If you do devote yourselves to making attractive architectural drawings, do them always, I beg you, with a conscientious determination to represent your work absolutely as it will appear—

the real object of working out architectural designs in perspective being the discovery of weak points in the design, so that they may be corrected in execution When once you are able to draw fairly well, you are prepared for what is the best and widest field of study —the buildings which are the best illustrations of our art And in these it is well, I need hardly say, to devote yourselves as far as possible only to the best examples In sketching it is best at first to err on the side of formality, to draw, above all, clearly and accurately, the ground plan of every building you visit ; for without this no other sketches are complete, and with it sketches of the elevations or details, however slight, are nevertheless intelligible At the beginning you can hardly take too many dimensions, your work must be sketched and measured on the spot with equal accuracy. At a later period you will be able to generalise more, and to dispense with this elaborate detail in your studies. In sketching, never make the mistake of using the commonest paper. Treat yourselves, from the first, to luxury in this one respect Make your measured sketches in a book, and take care to make your dimensions ample enough to ensure the accuracy of the drawing you make from those sketches ; but in the case of mouldings, of sculpture, of the filling-in of panels or arches, let your sketch be as carefully drawn as possible, and do not depend at all upon your two-foot rules for the accuracy of your sketching Pay special attention to such points in construction as the jointing of stonework, the design of mouldings meant to meet special wants, as, *e g.* the slopes of buttresses and of other members intended to throw off water, the adaptation of architectural features to their situation, as, for example, the details used near the eye and far from it, and the modes adopted for making them both properly visible and at the same time strong enough for their place and work Finally, in whatever style it is that you are most interested, never fail to draw with the utmost care, and to store up in your mind the effect of all the best mouldings you see There is no part of your studies more important than this Never believe any one who speaks lightly of the science or art of moulding I call it by both terms, because it embraces both By no test can you separate good work from bad more surely than by the comparison of the mouldings. A good moulding grows out of the necessities of the occasion It gives us the power of accentuating our lines or proportions in the most positive manner if we choose, or of softening them off so delicately as almost to conceal the transition from one feature to another. Without their aid there is a rudeness—a coarseness, one may almost say—which is offensive , whilst with their aid that refinement of line which, as I have told you, it should be your great aim to achieve, is made more perfect, and carried to greater perfection than in any other way. In drawing mouldings, I advise you always to sketch them with as much accuracy as possible, and to a good size, and on no account to depend upon correcting your indifferent sketches by a multitude of dimensions   Your eye, your hand, and your memory will be misled.   You will look again and again at your . sketches, and will forget all about your dimensions, and so be led to a permanently false impression of their real contour.

Remember always that sketches of mouldings alone, without equally accurate sketches of the features to which they belong, or with which they are connected, are useless.   One of the most accurate works on the subject is utterly valueless, owing to an omission of this kind.   Arch mouldings are drawn without any plan of the capitals, or of the jambs below the capitals   The relation of one of these to the other is of the very essence of the matter, and unless both are drawn it is really of little use to draw either.   In the same way the relation of the mouldings of a window to its tracery, of a column to its capital and base, and of both to the entablature, ought always to be recorded in a sketch

From the drawing of mouldings you will go on to that of sculptured or carved members, and in these it is the effect which was intended to be produced of which you must be thinking.   So, for this purpose, I attach but little importance, save as a test of mere draughtmanship, to the work which you have to do in our schools from casts.   All architectural features in which carving is introduced ought to be looked at and drawn in the very place for which they were intended   If a cap appear perfectly well hung against a wall, on a level with the eye, it can hardly be suitable for its real position in the building some fifty feet above the spectator , and a great difference in treatment ought to exist between a piece of carving which is made to appear to do hard service, and another which evidently has no such serious work to do, and is rather the evidence of the artist's pleasure in his work.   There is no subject for study more important than the relation of carved ornament to architecture.   You know how in all times it·has formed a leading feature.   The repetition of definite ornaments at regular intervals is one of the easiest modes of securing due attention to the member on which it occurs.   The moulding adorned with carving is always more noticed than any other, and the lines which require special emphasis are those to which such work ought to be confined.   You will soon find that these carvings, as well as the mouldings, are modified to suit their positions, near or at a distance from the eye You will notice also certain contrasts between the ornament in good and bad work   In the former it is never aggressive or too prominent , in the latter it is almost always so   In the former it is used with due deference to the common sense of construction , in the latter it disregards the construction entirely   I cannot give you a better example of this than is afforded by the division of such an enrichment as the so-called dog-tooth flower.   In good work this is always divided to suit the joints of the stonework ; in bad work it is set out with absolute uniformity all round an arch without any reference to the joints, which thus, instead of coming always between the flowers, occur in the worst possible places.   I mention these points because, if you once notice them for yourselves, you will see how important they are, and how certainly they indicate the quality of the work in which they are found   As there is no sort of training for an architect equal to that of the study of buildings, so it is absolutely impossible for you to learn your art only from the lessons which we are able to teach you here, or which you learn in the routine of architects' practice.   At all costs, then, you must spend a certain proportion of every year in travelling and examining buildings for yourselves, and the only special advice I can give you now is, not to try to cover too much ground at first.   It is wiser to study a few good works well, and to make yourselves thoroughly masters of them   Having done this for some time you will find your power of seizing the best points in the buildings you visit increase rapidly, and you may then make your journeys more rapid and less exhaustive and particular.   These very general suggestions may seem almost unnecessary ; but unfortunately I know from experience how few of us spend enough time in sketching and measuring existing works , and how few manage to make clean, clear, decided sketches of what they see   Observe that it is generally impossible to improve a sketch after it is once made , whatever it is, pray leave it with all its first freshness about it.   There is a virtue in that which will never be increased by after-work.   If you have any feeling of the artist in your composition it will be impossible for you to go on for long drawing the good work of other men or other times without gradually finding yourselves distinguishing clearly between good, inferior, and bad work

In this country it so happens that you all have, within reach, examples of a national architecture perhaps as noble, and certainly as universal in its developments, as that of any other land.   Some of you, as you pass through our schools, give painful evidence of the fact that you wholly ignore this great—indeed untold—advantage   Compare your own chances of education with that of the student whose fate has ordained that he shall learn all that he knows in new countries, where not a fragment remains of an older art than that of his own time, and you will see how immense your advantages are compared to his, and how far in advance of him you ought to be in real taste and culture   But I am told, sometimes, that you have no time, no opportunity, no means to avail yourselves of your advantages , and when I ask one who excuses himself in this way whether he has drawn much of Westminster Abbey, or of the cathedral nearest to the town from which he comes, I find that he has deferred this duty to some future day, or that he thinks the advice too impossible to be practicable   Others among you, too, may believe what you are often told, that what you ought to aim at is an original style, and that the constant study of already executed work is not likely to assist you in this   Well, this is too long a question for this evening, but if the nineteenth century is to distinguish itself by not caring for what has gone before, I can only say that it will distinguish itself in a quite unique fashion.   I shall have to speak to you more at length on this point in my third lecture, and need, therefore, only say here that we know of no period in our art in which architects were not studying the work of men who had gone before.   They studied them wisely, so that they might improve them   The variations which they made were sometimes so slight and so slowly made as hardly to amount to variations at all, and if there ever was a people more prone to such a course than another, it was that Greek nation to whose art we all look up as among the most inspired results of the highest training.

I would never have you draw and sketch existing examples with a view to copying or reproducing them   That is wholly contrary to right principles   What I wish is that you should draw so much of them as to find yourselves penetrated with the feeling for architectural form and perfection which, as the results of centuries of development, have been discovered to be the best   This study is, in truth, analogous to that of the sculptor, as illustrated by the exquisite work of that great man Flaxman, which just now you have an opportunity of studying within these walls   You see him drawing from the life until he has mastered all the motions and attitudes, outlines and muscles of the human form.   Then, possessed to the full of this knowledge, he lavishes his poetical spirit on combinations of figures, which illustrate at every turn his power, his knowledge, and the perfection of his sentiment   The commonest subject in his hands becomes endued with a beauty and a grace which are so natural as to seem inherent   What the human form was to him, the complete study of the accumulated experience of ages in existing buildings is to you.   And you are to use them not that you may steal from them, but that you may be able to deal with the problems that come before you with the same spirit and power that they show, whilst you avoid with care the failures and mistakes which you can discover in them

You may well ask me here how far such a due study of ancient examples as I have been advising must be carried in the direction of purely archæological inquiries, and I think some advice on this point will not be thrown away   It is quite true that archæology is not architecture ; but one-half at least of the studies of any architect who cares for anything beyond the work of his own hands has its antiquarian side, and what is important is, that this alternative side to your studies, far from diminishing your interest in them, is sure to enhance them.   In the history of the development of styles, you have matter for endless interest.   The buildings you admire and examine are the work of men of whom you know nothing, and who lived ages ago, perhaps.   Unless you can put them in their proper places in relation to each other, in their proper sequence, you will never be able to understand their gradual developments ; and accurate knowledge on such a point is, beyond everything, useful to men who have any hope of making any further developments in their art   There is a fruitful sort of antiquarianism, and a dry and fruitless sort, and it is with the former only that I care to advise you to interest yourselves   You may well leave the rest to the men who are antiquaries and nothing else, and with whom art counts for no more than antiquity   But you cannot leave to them those analyses of the progress of art in each man's work, from one man and one age to another, or from one country to another, without most serious loss to yourselves   I know nothing more useful than such studies and such accomplishments as these   They will prevent your being drawn into the downward current which sets strongly in the direction of business as against art, for the man who has once devoted himself to them will never lose that interest in the higher developments of his art which it ought to be, above all, your ambition to have and maintain

There is much more to be said as to the direction your studies should take, but before I touch on this I must get you, if I can, to realise that you must devote some at least of your time to the sister arts of painting and sculpture ; and this not with any idea of excelling in the practice of all the arts—that is a happiness reserved for a few heaven-born and greatly gifted mortals,—but rather with the thought that unless you know enough about other arts to be convinced that their highest development is in connection with architecture, you will be, like so many of your predecessors, unable or unwilling to recognise that in the harmonious combination of all the arts is the greatest future for each of them separately, and it is from among the ranks of you who are now growing up that we hope the men will come who will have the happiness of seeing what will really be a resurrection of art in this land.   The practical divorce of the arts has ended in the gravest loss to all   The architect has become too much of a mere builder, the painter lives to make pictures, to be lived with and loved by a few, instead of the many, and the sculptor's life is too often spent on work for which he cannot care much, because it is of no general interest, men having too often forgotten that his work is beyond all other that which completes and beautifies and ennobles the work of the architect On some other occasion I shall hope to be able to speak to some of you at length on this point, for I am persuaded that there is nothing by which both arts will gain so much as by the more-frequent combination of the two. For your own share in such a consummation in the future, you will not find so much opportunity for study in England as elsewhere, but you should lose no opportunity of familiarising yourselves with examples of mural decoration, whether by sculpture or painting, in books, of which, as you know, we have access to a goodly store in the library of this Academy; and for acquainting yourselves with sculpture there is nothing more to be desired than that you should give up some of your time to drawing and modelling from ancient examples, a very large proportion of the finest works of all times being the sculptured decorations of buildings of the Classical, the Mediæval, and the Early Renaissance schools

No small advantage will those gain who devote some of their time to learning to model In my opinion, all the decorative sculpture or carving in a building ought to be modelled in the first instance by the architect. This is the only way in which that harmony throughout the work can be secured which is essential to good effect. It is impossible to direct another man properly merely by giving drawings for such work, and you must learn to give your instructions in the round The day, I hope, may not be far distant when all sculptors will agree with me—if, indeed, they do not so already—in thinking that the best of their work would be even better than before if it showed a thorough appreciation of, and fitness for, the requirements of the building in which it is placed. I know nothing more fascinating than the evidence in most ancient work of the same feeling as to detail being common to the architect and the sculptor. You do not see where the work of one ends and of the other begins The sculptor seems to know all about architecture, and the architect to be quite conversant with sculpture; and I much wish that in the architectural school here we may occasionally—or even, I may say, regularly—find some students of sculpture laying aside their modelling tools and their chisels, and coming to us for some instruction in the art, a good knowledge of which is essential to their own complete success. In future lectures in this course I shall have repeatedly to refer to the works of sculptors and architects, in which it is difficult to say which of the two arts can most rightly claim the artist But if this is again to be the case, the young sculptor must understand that he has to master something more than the rudiments of architectural styles, and that, when he condescends to think of work which is half architectural and half sculptural, it must be with a complete sense of the equality of the two arts, if his work is to live with that of the great masters of all old and true schools.

If the sculptor ought to learn so much of architecture, how far ought the architect to go in the study of the human figure? It is a question surrounded with difficulty. A great building may be built which shall not include any representation of the human figure. Either by accident or by robbery of their sculpture, some buildings which once had figure sculpture have none now, and yet are hardly less evidently beautiful in their effect. The practical difficulty about drawing from the life is that if it is carried a very little way it is of no service, whilst if it is persevered in very far it is almost certain to be at the expense of other accomplishments which are even more essential, and there is a risk that the student may end by being both a bad figure-painter and a worse architect than he would otherwise have been. It is only, therefore, in those cases in which an architectural student feels a complete conviction that he has the unusual and rarely-given power of combining the two arts that he should venture to avail himself, to any great extent, of the privilege which is conceded to him in this Academy, though he should never lose any opportunity of studying the history of the combination of painting with architecture, and of making himself fairly learned in the theory of such work. This he may do, whether he can draw the human figure or not, and unless he has done it he will never be able to associate himself with a painter in counsels as to the completion of his own work.[1]

In addition to improving your skill as artists, on which I have been saying so much, you are bound to spend a great deal of time on other studies, without which you can hardly hope to rise to real eminence. There is, first of all, a long course of practical study, which will show its results in your work with certainty. All the visitors of our Architectural School feel, I am sure, as I do, that there is much to be desired in this respect in the work of the majority of the students. You ought never to make serious mistakes about simple matters of construction, or simple details of arrangement. Many of them are the result simply of a want of a little common sense—a quality which the artist of every sort ought to cultivate very sedulously, and the architect most of all. And as, perhaps, it is when you make a ground plan that this failure is most evident, a few words on this, which is the foundation of all good architectural work, will not be out of place. In making a

---

[1] I should perhaps qualify the statement in the Memoir that my father regarded the drawing of the figure as an unexceptionable training for an architect by saying that, except in some few cases, he looked upon it rather as the best means of becoming a good draughtsman than a good architect pure and simple.

plan there are two things to consider first, the convenience of
the building for its purpose ; and next, its suitability for its position
All good artists welcome with pleasure what is called a difficult site
In truth, there is no site so easy to deal with.   It is when the site
has no marked features of its own that the architect must make those
of his own work prominent   The Acropolis of Athens and the
Forum Romanum of Rome are, in one sense, difficult sites   That is,
they are so picturesque, so irregular in their levels, that everything
has to grow out of the necessities of its situation   There are no
lessons more useful than those which you may learn from such examples as these.   The Greek added one building to another in an
almost picturesque confusion, and in a mode in which, if we believed
some of our teachers of a few years back, it is impossible for any but
the most erratic Gothic architect to take any pleasure   The
Roman made a winding and irregular descent from the Capitol, with
buildings of wholly dissimilar style on either hand as he descended,
and then, when he had passed through the arch of Septimus Severus,
and found himself in face of a straight road for a short distance, he
took care that it should be occupied by a succession of irregularly-
placed and designed columns, monumental pedestals, and buildings
whose beauty was that which came from the individual character of
each, as well as from the gradual growth of the whole, and the
evidence it afforded of the historical continuity of the community and
its arts   Nor when the Forum was left behind, and but a short
distance separated the Roman from the Coliseum, was there any care
to secure a straight road from one to the other.   The paved road-
way meandered on under the arch of Titus, suiting itself to whatever
conditions existed, in the easiest fashion possible, and without any
thought whatever of those necessities for formal setting out of cities
which are only reasonable when, as in many Transatlantic examples,
there is no history whatever to be recorded, and a whole town
is laid out at one time, and completed almost as soon as laid
out

There are cases in which, however, the wise architect endeavours
not only to build to suit his site, but to make the peculiarities of
his site suit some sumptuous and scenic laying out of his whole
building   Time will not admit, however, to give more than a passing reference to a subject which in itself affords materials for
many a lecture   Nor is it at the outset of your life that you are
likely to have such opportunities as would enable you to realise the
advantages of the study

I have told you that you must study convenience of plan   This
you may do, not to the exclusion of architectural effect and character,
but always with a strict eye to it.   In designing the plan of a house,
for instance, it does not do to make the external design first and

then to make the interior fit it somehow or other. It is necessary to keep both in your mind, but it is the interior that ought to be supreme. The best exterior in the world would not atone for a faulty internal plan. And observe that a good interior is not simply one planned upon some everyday scheme, but one which does more than make life merely go on smoothly and without hindrance; to merit the epithet, it should have much suggestiveness and special adaptation as to make it in every way interesting to live in or to use. To accomplish this you must realise how every part is to be used, and so contrive as to give every one pleasure in using it. It is this harmonious and reasonable variation of plan that gives the greatest value and charm not only to the interior, but, as a natural consequence, to the exterior also.

The same rule applies to all other buildings. If they are well contrived for their special use, depend upon it you will be just as well able to make their elevations good as if they are carelessly contrived. A church requires by custom, by law, or by sentiment, a generally similar arrangement of the plan. At least, it requires the same component parts—a nave, a chancel, a porch, a steeple, a vestry. How differently may not these be grouped and designed! The variations in the provisions for the given wants in this case are, as you know, innumerable. And how much more various may not the plans for a house be?

If you realise that the real value of architecture, as of all the arts, is its human and personal interest, you will see how impossible it is that any art can be worth anything in which this is wholly ignored. The only justification of endless rows and groups of houses all arranged on the same lines, down to the pattern of the scraper and the design of the area railings or of the balconies, is, that the people who are to inhabit them are so identical in all their wants, wishes, and modes of life, that one pattern of house will do for all. Fortunately this is no more true of this age than of past ages. And now, as then, the best planned buildings will be those which take account of the existence of a diversity of men, with endless varieties of tastes, and wants, and circumstances. It is here that the study of ancient art is so invaluable. In former days, with much less facility for intercourse and movement, we see how many are the adaptations which architects had to make when they went from one part of Europe to another. In our own times this is of everyday occurrence. An English architect may be called on at any time, at the very outset of his career, to go to some foreign dependency where every condition of life and climate are wholly different from what they are in England. The plans as well as the architectural forms which are suitable in England are wholly out of place in a tropical country. In one, just as much as in the other, the same first principles will have to be observed, but the resulting forms will be wholly dis-similar, and the man who begins life with some knowledge of how such differences have been successfully dealt with before, has an un-told advantage over the man who treats all countries and all climates alike, as if the satisfaction of local requirements were not, in truth, the very first condition of a good piece of architecture

Before I conclude, there are two points only on which I must say a few words. One is the necessity for study of much that we cannot teach you here, and much that you will never learn in the workshop of an architect Such, for instance, is the study of language and the study of books. I cannot too strongly insist on the former. Without a knowledge of modern languages you cannot travel with complete pleasure, and you cannot know anything of the largest half of the literature of your art, and unless you have travelled, and un-less you have read a good deal of what architects and critics in other countries teach and think, you have deliberately shut yourselves out from a large portion of the education which is indispensable to an accomplished architect As students, you have access in this Academy to a most admirable artistic library, year by year becoming more and more complete, and where you may do more to cultivate your own taste by acquaintance with the best examples of all times than I can do for you by any number of lectures or addresses And, in the second place, I wish to say but a few words on the way in which you avail yourselves of the instruction offered you in the schools I have no desire whatever to exaggerate its importance. Most of you, I hope, are at work day after day on the drawings and designs of the architects under whom you are studying. Nothing, I believe, is a better training than such work as this. If you have the original drawing, be it general design, or detail of a part to a large scale, and are condemned to complete it either by putting the pencil lines into ink, or by the slower process of copying it, you are learning in the best way all that it can teach you But you are in one groove, and affected only by one mind; and by coming here you find yourselves brought face to face with new ideas and views, inasmuch as you have to work under the direction of the Visitors assisted by the Master.

But, to make any good use of such opportunities, it is not enough to come here occasionally, and only and so often as is absolutely necessary, but with regularity, punctuality, and prepared-ness The one regret that I feel in connection with our architectural school is that the students do not, as a rule, appear to wish to attend once more than is absolutely necessary; and when one sees any-thing short of the highest zeal, one is led to anticipate something very far short of the highest success. It is this absence of enthusiasm for his work which is fatal to an artist. If you have it, you will think no hours too long for work, and labour, instead of being toilsome, will be your greatest pleasure. Unless you have enthusiasm for your art yourselves, how can you expect that others will have any to spare for you and your work? It is a contagious quality. The artist who really has it does his work in such a way as to make others feel for him what he feels for his own work. This is seldom, if ever, worthy of love and admiration, unless it is the outcome of a zeal and a fire which are real and intense. If we have such a zeal, how will it show itself in our works? This is a question which affects what is called the practice of our art as distinguished from the study. I have left myself scant time to speak on this part of my subject, but fortunately there is not much to be said. In art a man who has zeal must almost of necessity have more zeal for some of its forms than for others. The forms which our art has taken are styles in which it is almost impossible for any artist to take an equal interest. And a man who is really an artist will find it natural to practice in one style, impossible to do so in another. Modern practice has tried to convert the world to an opposite view; it has assumed that an architect can design equally well in any style. Of course, if this were true, there would be no art in the work, for an artist must show himself in his work, and it would be impossible to do this in antagonistic things. It is not, in my judgment, necessary or, desirable that I should pronounce positively to you as to which is the best form for the architecture of the present day. That, when you have studied and thought, and worked for a few more years, each of you will have to decide for himself. But this I can tell you, that if you have zeal enough and enthusiasm enough to care for your art for Art's sake, you are far more sure of success by adhering strictly to what you believe to be good, true, honest, and artistic work, than if you attempt to please everybody by doing whatever you are asked to do in whatever style or fashion may be dictated. The man who knows how to do one thing well is more certain of success than he who tries to know a little of everything, and in study and in practice common sense and good art both claim from you that you should at any rate know the style of your own choice well. Beyond all doubt it is a sort of inspiration that is required in the artist who is ever to do any really great work, and this will never come to one who never dreams of perfection, who thinks first of all of gain and worldly interest, who treats his art as a mere matter of business and routine, not as an imperious mistress who must have all his devotion and all his heart. To secure this enthusiasm you must be dreamers in one way only : you may give reins to your imagination—you may dream of beauty, of majesty, of perfection—you may picture to yourself what you would and will accomplish ; but you must be no dreamers about your proper work. That must be constant, steady in purpose, thoughtful, and always in some way bearing on your art either directly or indirectly. The more time you devote to study the more will you become engrossed in your art, and the more you will find that it is delightful and interesting in all its changes and developments, and in the practical application of what you learn from your studies of old work to the art of your own time.   Industry alone will not make a great artist; but if there is one thing more certain than another in art, it is that all great artists have been industrious, and that if you wish to be numbered in their ranks you must follow their example

LECTURE II

PRINCIPLES OF THE ART OF ARCHITECTURE[1]

IN my last lecture I endeavoured—and, I hope, not in vain—to show you what course you ought to take in pursuing the study of architecture as a fine art. I assumed that you were all students, whether of my own branch of art or of others, and that you would all, if you really aimed at success, gladly welcome my advice, even if at times I seemed to demand very much from you in the way of imagination, of zeal, of enthusiasm, and, more than all, of industry. To-night I advance a step farther in an attempt to show you what are the principles of the art to which some of you are devoting yourselves, and in which all of you are interested.

Few, I suppose, can doubt that there are true and false principles in all the arts; but that they are more capable of definition in regard to architecture than to any of the others is certain—and this because the absolute truth or falsehood of an architectural work is capable of demonstration up to a certain point. But by *principles* you must well understand that I do not mean *rules*.[2] These last have often been laid down, with the result that where they have been obeyed implicitly, all life has been most effectually stamped out. Such, *e.g.* is the supposed rule of proportion of columns and their entablatures in Greek and Roman temples. This was derived from the measurement of some one example, and the establishment of that as the model for all others; so that, given the diameter of your column, the rest followed, and, in short, the rule was not one for designing a good column, but one for copying exactly a particular column. There is no pretence for believing that such rules ever affected the original architects; and the particular features to which they are applied are so different in their proportions in ancient examples as to prove that, even in the best days, there was

---

[1] Second lecture, delivered on Thursday, 17th February, to the Students of the Royal Academy.

[2] Rules have been compared to the parapets of a bridge, which prevent your falling into the water but do not help you to cross the river.

great latitude allowed, and that there was none of the insipidity which is the certain consequence of obedience to such arbitrary rules.   If you want to know how far the framers of such rules may try to take you, a few quotations from Scamozzi's *Mirror of Architecture* will suffice   "Here," he says, "is shown how the columns follow one another, and how high every one must be   . . The Doric must be twelve modules and fifty-three minutes and a half high. . . . The Ionic must be thirteen modules high. . .   The Tuscan arch must be three modules and fifty-two minutes wide. . . . The impost is twenty-seven minutes high," and so on, down to every detail of the column, its capital and base, pedestal and impost.   Everything "must be" of an exact and defined height, projection, or distance apart

The principles of the art of architecture are as eternal and reasonable as the so-called "rules" are arbitrary and ephemeral   It is with the former only that we are concerned to-night.   The most indisputable are those which affect construction, and they are of universal application   The construction of a building must be good if it is to be a work deserving of our respect; and by goodness we understand that it must be (1) permanent , (2) exhibited rather than concealed , (3) natural; (4) suitable to its purpose and material; and (5) it must avail itself of the latest discoveries and inventions where it is clear that they are usable under or consistently with the first four conditions.

A few words only will be necessary on each of these divisions. (1) *Construction must be permanent.*   In my last lecture I told you that our respect for old architects was generally in exact proportion to their respect for themselves and their work.   No architect would willingly, I suppose, build a wall that was certain to fall; but he is hardly less to blame who knowingly builds one that is sure not to last very long , who makes it too thin, builds it without sufficient foundations, or uses a bad quality or insufficient quantity of mortar or cement.   And as it is certain that purely temporary building is not architecture at all, so that is most likely to be architectural which is made to last as it were for ever   Now, to be permanent, a wall must be well constructed.   It must not only have good and solid foundations, but its weight must be evenly adjusted and duly provided for, and its various openings must be, as far as possible, no cause of weakness to it   But, according to the second principle, that construction should be exhibited rather than concealed, the coverings of these openings ought to be evident and obviously strong enough for their place   A lintel is a good thing to use if you can be quite sure that it is strong enough not to break in two, but it is not a good thing if it really does no work, but is relieved of all weight by a hidden lintel of iron, or by an arch concealed in the wall above it.   So, also, in good work, the construction of the exterior should, as far as possible, show the arrangement of the interior, and you ought at once to know something about the positions of the floors, the shape of the roofs, and the sizes and uses of the principal rooms, merely by examining the exterior of a building. The next principle that I have laid down is that the design must always be natural, that is, proper to the place, as simple as the case allows, and not strained or eccentric in its character or detail for the mere sake of producing effect. And on this point I cannot do better than quote what Leon Battista Alberti has well said (book 1, chap. ix) :—

"We ought not to lay out our whole study in adorning one part of our building, so as to leave the rest neglected and homely in comparison of it ; but let them bear that proportion among themselves that they may appear to be an entire and perfect body, and not disjointed and unfinished members Moreover, in the forming of these members we ought to imitate the modesty of nature. Let the members, therefore, be modestly proportioned and necessary for your uses. For all building, if you consider it well, owes its birth to necessity, was nursed by convenience, and embellished by use Pleasure was the last thing consulted in it, which is never truly obtained by things that are immoderate Let your building, therefore, be such that it may not want any members which it has not, and that those which it has may not in any respect deserve to be condemned. Nor would I have an edifice terminated with even continued lines void of all manner of variety Variety is, without dispute, a very great beauty in everything when it joins and brings things together in a regular manner,—things different but proportionable to each other. For, as in music, when the bass answers the treble, and the tenor agrees with both, there arises from that variety of sounds a harmonising whole, so the like happens in everything else. Of course things must be executed according to the approved practice of men of skill, but with this caution, that when famous architects seem by their practice to have determined this or that treatment of Doric, Ionic, Composite, or Tuscan to be the most beautiful of any, yet they do not tie us down to follow them so closely as to transcribe their very designs, but only stir us up by their instructions to produce something of our own invention, and to endeavour to acquire equal or greater praise even than they did "

The natural treatment of the general design of a building is, therefore, that which you should always aim at, providing for the requirements of the building without any violent sacrifice for the sake of mere architectural effect. But such a principle as this has, of course, its limits There is a sort of scenic effect which is not to be obtained so easily in any other way as by elaborately symmetrical

arrangements of plan and building   Few finer examples of this can
be pointed to than Greenwich Hospital, where, save for the blank
absence of any central object to which the rest may lead up, the
effect is unquestionably stately and impressive in a very high degree.
Another example of the same class is Bernini's really grand quadrupled curved colonnade, leading up with a vast sweep to the front
of St Peter's at Rome   Its scale is grand, and its extent magnificent; but it overwhelms the building to which it leads, and, grand
as the idea is, the effect is not perfect, simply, as at Greenwich,
because the central object is dwarfed by the magnificent scale of the
approach.   In the late Genoese palaces you will find good illustrations of the same sort of scenic architecture, dependent for its effect
on stately arcades leading from terrace to terrace, and in many of
the French and English houses of the Renaissance there are somewhat similar arrangements.   One wing corresponds with another,
there is a central porch, and the garden is arranged in regular
terraces, with pavilions or summer-houses at proper intervals.   But
if you compare one of the finer buildings of this class—as, for
instance, Montacute House or Barrington Court—with the design
of, say, Haddon Hall or Magdalen College, Oxford, where every
portion of the building tells its own story, and is differently treated
accordingly, it is impossible to deny that the love of stately balance
and symmetry may be satisfied at too great a cost, and that a far
better artist is generally revealed in the less formal work of the two.
However much one may appreciate scenic architecture, it is necessary here to be rather discouraging as to its common introduction.
For a long time the student has been taught that the only possible
good arrangement of a large building is one founded on this principle.   It has been assumed that all buildings must have a centre
and wings corresponding exactly.   If the stables are built in the
guise of a wing connected with the mansion by a colonnade, then
some use must be found, at all risks, for a corresponding colonnade
and wing on the opposite side   So, a chapel and kitchen having
to balance each other, neither can be allowed to tell its true story
on its face, and, in the end, the scenic effect is the one thing that
seems to be thought of   This is not convenient building, and is
consequently not good art, and the cases in which it can be ventured
on must always be rare and exceptional in their opportunities.

The next rule is that the design should be suitable for the
material which has to be used   This is a practical rule which
involves the wise adjustment of the means to the end.   No architect
should ever quarrel with his materials as long as he can ensure their
being the best of their kind.   His sole business is to take care that
his design is suitable to the material, and, as a general rule, to that
which is nearest to his hand.   Where means are unlimited, or the

object to be attained is one of monumental character, then it is right to go far afield at any cost to obtain the best and most magnificent material, for the first step to be taken, if a building is to be sumptuous, is to see that the material is worthy of the labour that is to be expended on it And to some extent the material that is to be used settles the design of the work. A quarry which produces enormous blocks of granite has scant justice done to it if the architect who uses it confines himself to small blocks of stone It leads almost naturally to the use of great monoliths, than which nothing is more impressive, though there may be no art in the mere magnificence of size. Again, a design suitable for a stone country would be wholly unfit for one in which brick alone could be used; and wherever many marbles could be obtained, the design, to be natural, must be in every respect quite unlike anything that could be built in a country where nothing but a fine and easily worked oolite existed, or in one where the only material was a hard and untractable limestone. Natural use of his material is, indeed, one of the first aims of a good architect, and this not only in the selection of the stone to begin with, but equally in the way in which it is worked. If you use a fine marble for the face of a wall, it must be wrought very finely everywhere, and polished for the best part of the work If, on the other hand, you use a freestone, you may confine yourself to working the elaborated architectural features only, leaving the body of the wall rough, but you must remember that if your architecture is to be good or elaborate, you must begin by working the face of the wall, so that the whole may be of one harmonious texture. The size of the stones and their jointing is equally to be thought of As a rule, large stones are only to be used in large buildings, for the apparent scale of a wall depends much on the size of the stones that are used in it The same is true if the available materials are brick or timber With either of these the whole structure, every moulding and every detail of ornament, ought to be different from what they are in stone. Every material has its own capabilities, and the architect is bound to use each in its proper fashion. And here, on this point of making the best possible use of common materials, I may give you a quotation from Sir Henry Wotton, in the conclusion of which I think we may all very heartily agree .—

"It will, perchance, be said that this doctrine" [which he had been laying down] "touching the five orders were fitter for the quarries of Asia, which yielded 127 columns 60 feet high to the Ephesian Temple, than for the Spirits of England, who must be contented with more ignoble materials. To this I answer that this need not discourage us. For I have often at Venice viewed with much pleasure an anti-porch after the Greek manner raised by

Andrea Palladio upon eight columns, the Basis of Stone without pedestal, the Shafts of meer brick foot and half thick and consequently thirty-five foot high, than which mine eye hath never seen more stately of stone or marble"

He then describes how the bricks were made, and concludes "Which short description I could not omit, that thereby it may appear how in truth we want rather art than stuff to satisfy our greatest fancies"

Finally, the architect must avail himself of the best as well as of the latest discoveries and inventions in construction. It cannot be right to build one day with arches everywhere throughout his work, and on the next to assume that no such convenient servant as the arch had ever been discovered   Nor is it reasonable to say, "I will use a round arch because I like it, but though I know that a pointed arch is more convenient, and, in some positions, far stronger, I dislike it so much that nothing shall persuade me ever to adopt it "—a sentiment expressed with the honest frankness of his time by the old writer just quoted, in the following passage ·—

"As for those arches which our artisans call of the third and fourth point, I say these, both for the natural imbecility of the sharp angle itself, and likewise for their very uncomeliness, ought to be exiled from judicious eyes, and left to their first inventors, the Goths or Lumbards, amongst other reliques of that barbarous age."

The Pompeian architect who carried the entablature above his columns on a concealed log of timber was trying to imitate the work of men who had been dealing with blocks of stone large enough to bridge the space from column to column, and there was laudable ingenuity in the Pompeian's device, who, having no stone to use, invented a substitute for it.   But to us who know that such a substitute is not permanent in its nature, and that there is now a mode of carrying the wall above by arches over such spaces which may be absolutely permanent, there is no justification whatever for the imitation of the Pompeian mode of building

In modern buildings the greater part of the construction is concealed, and there is a consequent temptation—only too often acquiesced in—to make it subservient entirely to supposed convenience A common instance of this is the free use of iron as a concealed support in place of masonry   Our forefathers knew nothing of such aids to easy planning.   When they made the plan of one floor they involved themselves in accepting the same plan for the floors above and below.   Walls came above walls, and no little skill was required, therefore, so to plan the various floors as to make all the arrangements convenient, and yet subject to good and sound structural conditions.   In our own time the temptation to carry walls on iron girders over voids is too often accepted as a matter of course; the ingenuity exercised in planning is diminished, and the structure is less permanent, for a flaw in the iron, its decay, or the accident of a fire, may involve the ruin of a whole building, where, under the old conditions, the walls might have stood unharmed by such catastrophes. I do not, therefore, recognise such aids to construction as these as being real and genuine. They are rather temptations than anything else, and ought only to be adopted when it is clear that their use is not opposed to the principles already laid down. The architect who attempts by concealed construction to imitate a wholly different sort of work must inevitably fail, for sincerity is of the essence of good art, and the detection of insincerity is certain. Even untutored men will surely perceive that a deception has been practised, and will resent it. If you have such magnificent material that you can obtain it in masses of sufficient bulk, I can conceive no reason for objecting to the employment of trabeated systems of architecture. The vast bulk of the horizontal block or lintel is in itself impressive; and if it rests upon blocks of corresponding magnificence, in the shape of monolithic columns, there are few modes by which the imagination can be more surely excited. But the same sort of design, executed with small stones or with bricks covered with plaster, never impresses us in the same way, because the slightest attention discloses the fact that some unseen mode of holding the work together has been adopted, without which the whole must certainly at once collapse. The mediæval architect was, like the Greek, a frank and sincere constructor. There was no disguise about his work. In his hands each stone may be said to have had its office and to have performed its duty. And there are few examples more illustrative of his feeling than those monuments and open porches which are so common a feature in Italian buildings. Here there are four arches carried on four single shafts—a sort of construction which is really impossible. The architect frankly announces the fact that it is so by the exhibition of an iron tie across the base of the arch which ties the whole together, and makes the whole work not only possible, but secure. The modern mode of doing the same thing would be to continue the columns up above the caps to support concealed girders. In this way the evidence of the tie is got rid of, and the eye is distracted by a feat of construction which, to those who are not in the secret, is wholly incomprehensible. In good work the external form is always a translation of the internal structure, a building, if it is perfect, being as complete an organism as the human frame.

So far I think you will see that the principles which are necessary in all good architecture are almost beyond dispute. It may be said by some of you that they are mere truisms. Would that they were always so accepted and acted on ! It is not too much to say that if they were absolutely accepted and always acted on little more would need to be taught. The man who never consented to break one of them would, depend upon it, have so much character as to make it certain that the ornaments of his construction, which convert building into architecture, would at least have that great force which comes from simplicity and fitness for their place and work   His ornament would be that of the construction, and would not be merely applied in front of it and without reference to it   His work would be so complete in itself and in its details that even as a ruin it would be beautiful   The ruins of the consummate works of the Greek architects are hardly less beautiful in their decay than they were in their perfection.   Two thousand years of neglect have left the Temple of Neptune at Pæstum as grand and dignified, and wellnigh as beautiful, as on the day of its completion, whilst the Gothic ruin is equally worth studying, and just as provocative of admiration as the Greek.   Every part of its construction was useful as well as ornamental, and the destruction or decay of parts still leaves what remains instinct with power and beauty   How different may the case be !   In a Roman building you may too often remove the whole *appliqué* face of the architecture, and the building will still stand, but in such a guise as to give you no sense of permanent beauty , whilst in a modern building it is sufficient to let it fall into decay to see how loathsome it has been from the first, for that "calm decay" which seems to give so many added charms to the Greek or Gothic fragment, discloses in it nothing whatever that is good, or pleasant to the eye, or in any sense venerable

We have next to consider how far, out of the vast array of facts which the student finds in the history of his art, some may be selected which involve the establishment of abstract truths.   And to accomplish this we must examine the works of all times rather than of one period only, confident of this, that as all good developments in art have proceeded from the realisation of good principles dormant before, so the more these practices are traced home to the causes or theories out of which they rose, the more likely are we to perceive their true bearing.

The first essential of a building is, as we have seen, that it shall be well built   This is not architecture.   Architecture is the art of giving "style" to building, and, after this, some or all of the other abstract qualities of rhythm, breadth, scale, light and shade, mystery, repose   What, you may ask, is "style"?   I will answer you in the words of one of the most distinguished of my brethren (M Viollet-le-Duc) ·—

"Style resides in distinction of form, and is one of the elements of beauty, though it does not itself constitute beauty.   Our sense of style is instinctive. In the midst of an assembly you distinguish one man among all others. It is not beauty which attracts you in him, and yet, moved by a mysterious influence, your eyes follow him. If you have any power of observation, you find yourself arriving at some sort of explanation of the power he exercises. It is something in his frame, as well as in his contour, in his movements, and the *rapport* which exists between them and his features and expressions. By degrees you have fixed ideas as to his habits, his tastes, his character. It is the first time you have ever seen him, and you know him not; but you build upon what you see a whole romance. It is only those who possess style who exercise this singular fascination. Mankind is so spoilt by false education, by infirmities moral and physical, that it is not common to find any who really have this quality. But look at animals, and you will find that they all possess it. There is never a false gesture, never a movement which does not follow on a want, a desire, or a fear. Animals are never affected, mannered, vulgar. Whether plain or handsome, they have style, because they have none but simple sentiments, and seek their ends by the simplest and most direct means. Man, and above all the most civilised man, being a very complicated animal, transformed by an education which teaches him to fight against his instincts, it is almost necessary for him to get out of himself, so to speak, in order to find 'style.'"

Style in architecture is the perfect harmony between the means and the end, which is found in all the ideas and desires of the highest type of man. Refinement of detail is indispensable; largeness and breadth are its natural forms of expression; but in certain places it may give greater grace to the most intricate and delicate work. It is this noble quality which is essential in good art, and it is as possible to have it in a building as in a man or a beast. The essential condition, you see, is that your style should be a true and sensible expression of simple and abstract principles or requirements. It has nothing whatever to do with styles of architecture, as we call them, for it is possible that every one of these in succession may afford examples of incontestable style. This, at least, is clear, I suppose, to all of you—that a vast chasm exists between architectural designs; that some are vulgar, affected, mannered; whilst others are natural, simple, and dignified; and that whilst the only admiration ever extorted for the former is that ignorant love of a new thing which is so evanescent and so little to be respected, the admiration of the latter increases as they grow older, and year by year becomes more certain and universal. The popular voice, which finds something to praise after an age has passed since the construction of a building, is as certain to be correct as the supposed approval of a new work is fallible, and to be mistrusted.

The next quality at which we must aim is, like the former, one which is common to our own and other arts   The poet cannot afford to neglect style in his work any more than he can venture to trifle with its rhythm, and a perfect building has its rhythm as well as its style   It is a quality very difficult to describe in words, but in architecture it is an art depending on numbers and proportions. Some expression caught up, repeated, balanced, emphasised in succeeding passages, at intervals which are either regular or regulated, constitutes usually the rhythmical beauty of a work of architecture   No doubt it is sometimes secured by direct application of geometrical figures, at other times by that instinct for the beautiful which makes a trained eye go so near to the figures or proportions which might be drawn by rule, but to which the charm is added of something which is fresh, human, and suggestive in its very departure from exactness.   Take the simplest case conceivable, that of a Greek portico.   Arrange the columns with perfect regularity and without any thought, and there is no rhythm ; but arrange them so that a dominant point in the base shall be placed in a certain relation to another, as, *e.g.* the centre in one of the columns or capitals, or in the pediment, and that the line which connects these two points be one which, if repeated again, connects other marked features, and you at once have a simple and admirable sort of rhythm.   Or take another case, to prove the point by a negative.   Design a tower, 300 feet in height, and divide it into twelve equal stages, and you will have an erection which will have no more rhythm than the empty sheet has before the poet has covered it with his rhythmical lines. Yet such a tower may possess all the qualities which I have up to this point included in the conditions precedent of a good piece of architecture   It may be solid, simple, suitable for its purpose, and may even have a certain style, but not having rhythm, it is not architecture at all in any good sense   If we wish to see how the opposite effect may be produced, let us see how Giotto planned the proportions of his tower or campanile at Florence.   My drawing shows you this design in elevation   You will perceive that it is divided into seven principal stages in height.   Of these the six lower are grouped in pairs, and so arranged by lines of dark marble and string-courses as to increase in height as they leave the ground.   In the two lower stages, the panels, being very near the eye, are of the same height   In the next coupled stages the upper windows are one-seventh larger than those below them ; the fifth and sixth stages are nearly equal, but the upper one has panels marked with an outline of serpentine one-tenth longer than those below   Finally, the single story of the upper stage is equal to two of those below, and crowns with rare grace this succession of coupled stages which have gradually led up to it.   The diameter of the tower is the dimension which appears to regulate the whole scheme, being one-sixth of the whole height. The gables over the windows are of the angle whose base is as 3 to a perpendicular of 4 and hypotenuse of 5—according to the ancients the perfect triangle, the square of the hypotenuse being equal to the united squares of the two sides. But the square or circle seems to have been the figure mainly used by Giotto in arranging the lines of his work. In Giotto's tower I have given you an example which shows, I think, how conscious one of the greatest artists was of the use of some definite system of proportion. It is not possible to give you an incidental treatise on so large a subject, in the midst of a lecture which has to embrace so much in so short a time. But in a few words I may direct your attention to it, with a view to inducing you to follow the subject up for yourselves as you have the opportunity. I will take one only out of many figures which has been made much of in old times, and this is the equilateral triangle. There can, I think, be but little doubt that the proportions of the Pyramids were decided by it. Take four equilateral triangles and incline them to each other to a common centre, and you have, as nearly as may be, the outline of the finest among them. The equilateral triangle has always been one of the most favourite forms, but especially was it so in the Middle Ages. Westminster Abbey and Stone Church are both designed with its aid, and M. Viollet-le-Duc has given several French examples—Nôtre Dâme, Chalons, if I remember rightly, among others. Old writers frequently enlarge on the virtues of this and other such figures to the architect, and though in the use of many of them there seems to be something rather empirical, it is not possible to doubt that they have influenced architects in almost all ages.

It is obvious that in all systems of proportion, the parts or divisions of a building which are treated in relation to each other must be either really connected with each other, or so visible together at one time as to be naturally looked at as united members. There need, therefore, be no connection between the lines which settle the proportions of the interior and exterior of a building. What is intelligible is that there should be a distinct relation or system of proportion between features which the eye is certain to compare together—as, e.g. the height of a column to that of its entablature, the dimensions of a metope to those of a triglyph, and the proportions of both to the diameter of the column and the width of the intercolumniation. Another mode of deciding the proportions has been ingeniously formulated by Mr. Watkiss Lloyd in his calculations as to the system of proportion adopted in the Parthenon. It is impossible to deny that his discovery appears to be a real, and, if so, an important one, though the system adopted seems on the face of it to be wholly arbitrary. He shows that the proportions are all derived from a system of figures standing in the ratio of 1 to 6 , that is, separated by the number five—as, for instance, 1-6, 2-7, 3-8, 4-9, 5-10, and so on.   Thus the breadth of the top step is to its length as 4 to 9, the height and width of the front as 9 to 14, and the height of the front to the length of the building as 2 to 7, and so on. What is not clear is whether such a system was peculiar to this one building ; and even then I fail to see why it should produce a good result.   Vitruvius, speaking of rules for proportion, says that "the ancients have directed these to be observed in all works, but more particularly should they be attended to in the temples of the gods, in which the faults as well as the beauties remain to the end of time."   And for the last two centuries or more men have been endeavouring to discover what these rules are.   They have succeeded in ascertaining many facts of the highest interest   And there is evidence that in mediæval times similar rules were observed to those which Vitruvius laid down.   To mention one only, in 1521 Cesare Cesariano published a book on the subject.   Cesariano, in his Commentary, gives a plan, section, and elevation of Milan Cathedral, which, after Vitruvius, he calls the "Ichnography,' "Orthography," and "Scenography."   "*A Trigono as Pariquadrato perstructa Germanico more,*" and "*secundum Germanicam Symetriam*"

Professor Cockerell took much pains, many years ago, to show that William of Wykeham planned the chapels of his colleges at Winchester and Oxford by the aid of geometrical figures, and there is, no doubt, something fascinating in the suggestion of any scheme which shall involve as a certainty a well-proportioned work.   Whether laws can be laid down which can be generally applied is open to grave doubt , but Cockerell's words are, in any case, true, and worth quoting —

"The perception of proportion, the fundamental element of the beautiful in architecture, seems to be the last acquirement of the student instead of the first   We begin by admiring ornaments, details, and forms , but it is at a more advanced stage only that we make all these subordinate to that sense of rhythmical proportion and that harmony of quantities which affect the mind like a mathematical truth, and, like a concord of musical sounds on the ear, are perceived and confessed by the eye as obvious and unalterable."

The only fear in such investigations as these is, that any of you should be led to suppose that any system can stand in place of the genius of an artist.   The utmost that you will arrive at by such a process is the avoidance of errors of general proportion, it being very manifest that this is possible

But it would be a calamity if you were led to suppose for an instant that the use of a mathematical formula could or ought ever to be substituted for the cultivation of the eye; that is, of the natural sense of good proportion or rhythm in architecture. It is by the careful observation of cultivated eyes that some of the most delicate, and at the same time most important, rules have been arrived at for our guidance. A few of these may shortly be referred to here. There is, first, the entasis of the Greek column. The column, first of all, was made to taper, so as to give it the greatest possible appearance of stability, and then it was perceived that there was some appearance of the outer lines being very slightly concave. This is an effect which you will find constantly in absolutely straight lines. A ceiling, the side of a spire, a long line of steps, will all of them, if absolutely straight, appear to be concave. The Greek artist remedied this by the most delicate increase of dimensions, giving his column an almost imperceptibly convex outline,—no more than was enough to correct the ocular deception which the straight line produces. In old examples this entasis appears sometimes to be exaggerated, owing to the decay of the stone or marble at the junction of the column with the capital. And it is important to notice, also, that the entasis was not given where good reason existed for omitting it. Thus, in the two ranges of columns forming the *cella*, the columns of the upper range are continuations of those below them, with an entablature inserted between them. In this case, if the upper and lower columns had had any entasis, there would have been a disagreeable conflict of curves, and so these columns are all formed with straight outlines. Another practice was to make the columns slope slightly inwards, so as to give a greater appearance of strength; another, the placing of the outside columns nearer to each other than the rest; another, the giving a slight curve to the architrave, for the same reason as the entasis was given to the column; and another, the making the whole tread of the line of steps on which the temples were placed slightly higher in the centre than at the ends. In Gothic architecture you will find the same delicate modifications to meet various optical effects. Spires undoubtedly sometimes had an entasis. It was usually so delicate as not to offend; and, indeed, it may almost be said that directly the entasis is obvious it is offensive. The spire-lights and pinnacles of spires were also so contrived as to produce the same effect. Then columns were often banded, not in the centre, but slightly above the centre. The reason is that if you band a column in the exact centre the upper half of the column is certain to look longer than the lower half. Then just as the Greek column was inclined, so are the walls of many steeples. Good examples of this are seen in some of the best of the beautiful group of Normandy steeples which make the neighbourhood of Caen such delightful ground to an architect. Another delicate adjustment is constantly adopted in old traceries, but seldom, I fear, noticed   This is the change in the dimensions of mouldings where the tracery becomes intricate, and where the moulding proper for the large lower lights of a window would, if carried throughout in a mechanical way, entirely block all the smaller lights and spandrels of the tracery and cusps   Another is the stilting of arches slightly, in order to make the curved line sit with sufficient quietness and dignity on the cap , another, the modification of the curved lines of cusps to give the same effect.   These, indeed, were often drawn by hand , no other way allows of their curves showing such delicate growth   At Lincoln the cusped arcades are all so drawn   In the Italian arched canopies to porches and monuments, where the arches are so constructed as not to be able to stand without iron ties at the base, the arch was weighted on the under side with a somewhat heavy trefoil, the effect of which was to give an appearance of stability.   These illustrations will be sufficient to show you how universal has been the desire of architects in all ages to adopt the most subtle variations for the sake of securing the best possible effect in their work, and how important, it is, therefore, to remember that the training of the eye is far more necessary to the architect than the closest adherence to the precepts of Vitruvius, and those who have followed in his steps, interesting and valuable though these precepts may often be, and full of suggestions well worth following out.

The other elements that I have named are what we look for in the best work , but they are not so indispensable as those already mentioned, and for this reason—they are elements which may be aimed at, more or less, according to the choice of the architect.   He may aim, if he chooses, at breadth of effect , and he will always do well to do so.   But he may equally aim at a picturesqueness which sacrifices breadth, and which, if it arises naturally out of the conditions of the case, is by no means to be despised.   In all cases, also, the treatment of the design with the object of impressing the eye with a real idea of its scale is important   It hardly admits of discussion whether or no the artist is skilful who makes the scale of his building look smaller than it really is, for it requires much skill so to dispose and proportion the various members as to make each appear to be of the right size for its place, and yet to add to, rather than diminish, the apparent size of the whole   But I think all these points will be more easily dealt with if we go on now to consider, as far as time will admit, the evidences we have in ancient buildings of the close attention which was paid by their designers to subtle principles which it is necessary to master if we are to produce work at all comparable to theirs

In one point all ancient work agrees   This is, that all parts of a building must be equally well designed   No good work is ever

done which is done solely for show. If you really love your work
you will make it good all round—as simple as you like ; for it would
be absurd to make work which can hardly be seen as elaborate as
that which is meant for the delight of the eye of every passer-by,
but still good in its proportions, and in its detail wherever any is
introduced. To how many buildings of the first half of this century
would it be possible to go with this impression of an architectural
sine quâ non ? The truth is that only too often men seem to have
thought that one elevation of a building would be all that would
ever be seen. They have satisfied themselves with handsome
geometrical elevations of the principal front, and have assumed that
every one would be polite enough not to look at the work in perspective. So you see grand cornices in front, none at all at the ends ;
stone on one side, compo on the other, and other similar mistakes.
It must not be thought that the discovery that old architects often
indulged in sham fronts to their buildings justifies their erection now.
From some point of view the deception is quite sure to be detected,
and when found out produces the worst possible effect. Moreover,
it is hardly possible to design a sham front which does not at once
condemn itself, because it almost always happens that the features,
which are used merely because they are pretty, having no corresponding structure behind them, have no structural effect, and thus
prove themselves to be unnecessary impostors.

A sham feature is often introduced for the sake of symmetry,
and it is worth while to consider how far the symmetry which depends on uniformity is a necessary feature. The uniformity which
arises from an absolutely similar requirement throughout a building
is natural and defensible. Examples of it may be seen in the repetition of the columns round a Greek temple ; in the uniform design of the outside wall of a Roman amphitheatre, where each bay,
having similar requirements, is almost identical with the rest ; and
in the bays of a Gothic cathedral nave, all of which are almost of
necessity alike, because each follows exactly from the same construction. Nevertheless, uniformity may easily ruin the effect of a
work in which, in the right place, the principle has been admitted
to the full. Imagine, for an instant, such a work as Nôtre Dâme,
Paris, altered for uniformity's sake by the erection of a choir exactly
like the nave, with two eastern steeples corresponding with the grand
examples at the other end, and you will see at once how entirely
ruinous this sort of symmetry may be.

Repetition of similar features where the requirements are the
same seems to me to be the true sort of symmetry to aim at. In
this way you gain the required effect without sacrificing convenience
or truth. Then, if the site is not symmetrical, or if the building is
the result of a series of erections at different periods by way of

additions to something older, it is far better to give up the idea altogether, and to let the building tell its story   This is the way in which the Greeks acted on the Acropolis at Athens.   Nothing can be more deliberately unsymmetrical than the planning of the matchless buildings on this sacred spot   The temple called the Erechtheium is an example of the most singular interest in this way. The Greek artist not only disdained the attempt to make all the buildings agree with each other, but may rather be said to have been bent on making them all as different as possible.   He then placed them at all sorts of angles with each other, knowing that the picturesque effect of which he was so fond would thus be secured, so that, in truth, the whole group may rather be said to be too deliberately picturesque if it has a fault at all   The houses, temples, forum, and other buildings at Pompeii are examples of precisely the same feeling   They all bear distinctly the marks of their history.   Each house had its own character and its own arrangements. There was no pretence anywhere to accommodate the architecture of a whole street to what might be deemed to be the average wants of the inhabitants.   And in the street which above all others has architectural character—that of the tombs—you walk now, as men did from the first, between a succession of more or less stately monuments and monumental chapels, none of which have been made with any reference to the effect of their neighbours, but solely with reference to the wishes, the pride, or the wealth of the men who put them up.   In the same way the forum is regular, but the temples which surround it are quite irregularly arranged, and upon altogether different designs , and the laying out of the streets not being regular or rectangular, just the same irregularities occur that we find as a result of natural growth in our own old towns   In mediæval times precisely the same view was taken as by the Greeks.   Historical truth and lifelike character in the design were preferred to uniformity as an almost invariable rule   And in all good work you will find, even where there is apparent symmetry, that considerable differences exist.   At Nôtre Dâme, Paris, the two western steeples are essentially symmetrical, and were probably erected at the same time ; but there are important differences of detail in them, which give a charm and life to the work which it would not have had if each had been a mere repetition of the other.   And in earlier times, in the façades of St. Mark's at Venice, and of the Cathedral at Pisa, you will find that the apparently corresponding dimensions of doorways and arches do not really tally at all, and have evidently been deliberately varied, in order that the eye might be unconsciously saved from the weariness produced by too great uniformity

The mediæval architects have left some most remarkable examples of the extremely small effect that the desire for uniformity had upon them. Of this there is, perhaps, no more convincing example than the façade of Chartres Cathedral. This had a west front, flanked by two steeples, one of which only was completed by the end of the twelfth century with a spire, which, for beauty of design, is not far behind the very best of its period. It was no sooner built than the whole church, save the west front, was rebuilt after a fire, and on a grander scale, so that the new nave roof, reaching to the base of the spire, very much spoilt its effect. Then, in the fifteenth century, one of the greatest men of his time, Jean Texier, was employed to build on the ancient north-west tower a second spire to complete the front. What course do you suppose he adopted? The nineteenth-century answer is, of course, in favour of a steeple exactly like the first, so that, though both would then be too low for the roof, there might nevertheless be that uniformity which is now usually supposed to be the right thing to strive for. Texier did nothing of the sort. He boldly declined to look at the early spire, and simply set himself to work to build the loveliest spire he could design. And his work is a success from every point of view. It is exquisite in itself, properly proportioned for the height of the church, and, though so unlike it, groups well with the other spire, and the result is that we have the pleasure of seeing two *chefs d'œuvre* where otherwise we should have had only one design to admire.

Some of you may perhaps ask whether, after you have done your best to attend to all the principles which I have been insisting on, your work could be worthy of being called really one of architecture, in the absence of all sculpture and painting. Some writers —and they are men of the greatest authority—deny by implication that it can be. But though in my last lecture I told you how strongly I desire to see the three arts employed together, I am not disposed to allow this, and I shall insist upon it now, because I think that for young men the habit of designing without the aid of figure sculpture is very important. A drawing of a poor design may sometimes be made to pass muster by a daintily drawn representation of sculpture, but this is not what is first wanted. At the same time, though it is necessary to be able to dispense with the aid of the sister arts, it is equally necessary that you should know how to avail yourselves of their assistance. The best work is that, as I have before told you, in which all the arts are combined. And no form of architecture can be pronounced to be contemptible in which these accessory arts have been highly developed. The grandest architecture can, however, exist without such aid. It is not absolutely necessary ; and if circumstances compel the architect to dispense with it, he is in no degree whatever relieved from the necessity of doing the very best work. Certainly we have only to think of some of the buildings which are amongst the noblest works remaining to perceive that they never depended entirely upon sculpture for their effect.   Little, if any, is left on the remains of Greek art.   The sculpture is now in museums, and the architecture, unadorned by it, often still remains.   No one can say that the buildings have obviously suffered by its removal, for in some it can hardly be said whether there ever was any sculpture or not ; and yet in such cases, of which the Temple at Bassæ and the Temple of Neptune at Pæstum are typical examples, it is impossible not to feel impressed in the highest degree by the art exhibited.   The same feeling is excited by the monasteries built by the Cistercian order.   They were built under a rule which prohibited all use of sculptures or paintings ; and yet, I suppose by common consent, they are among the most precious relics of old times that remain in the world, and their most enduring charm is the delicate grace of all their architectural lines and details.   Even in the case of a building such as Chartres Cathedral, in which sculpture and painting play a most important part, it is not in their presence or in thinking of them that the imagination is most impressed.   It is probably on the exterior, in some general view of the building, that this happens.   And in the interior it is when, looking down the mighty nave, we see the great columns, the vast clerestory, and the vaulted roof high above, that we feel the impressiveness of the building, and the power of the man who built it.   An impression created in this way is, indeed, one of the advantages which our art possesses.   She can satisfy the critical eye with beauty of detail, skill in construction, and harmony of proportions, but at the same time she appeals to a much wider world than that of connoisseurs by her ability to stir the imagination and touch the feelings of the humblest.   The means by which this is accomplished are the management of masses of light and shade, and the intricacy or mystery of the composition.   Each of these may be done in a variety of ways, and the same treatment is not available in all countries alike.   In Italy and Greece, for instance, under the influence of a brilliant climate, the wall is to the architect like a canvas to the painter, on which every line may be made to tell with precision, and where even the slightest line has its proper force.   In the North it is almost necessary to break this wall in order to produce the shadows.   For the same reason, the more you can deal with deeply-cut mouldings the more certain you are in this climate of your effect.   The primary use of them is to give the architect the power of manipulating and managing the lines of light and shade. A moulding well designed produces the required effect even when there is no sun to light it up, and it is not a little curious that England, having less sunshine probably than any other part of Europe, is the country in which the moulding of architectural features has been carried to the greatest perfection. But one of the results of having to depend on lines for effect is that with us the line is everything, whereas in Italy the wall is all in all. In the best Greek art the line and the wall surface were equally cared for. The Greek delighted above all things in making his work as distinct and clear as possible. The delicate lines of his fluted columns, the ornamented mouldings, and the clear bold relief of the statuary all show this. But the Egyptian, and after him the Italian in the Middle Ages, were happiest when the sun could play on the long unbroken front of a building as it does on the upper stage of the Ducal Palace at Venice, or on the vast and almost unbroken walls of the greater palaces and town halls in Siena, Verona, Pisa, Florence, or Perugia.

The mystery which is so dear to the Northern mind has comparatively little power in the South. But it is a power which the English architect must know how to use. Nowhere is one more visibly impressed by this than in some of our own cathedrals, where the vast length, aided by intricacy of line, variety of detail, and skilful manipulation of light and shade, produce often most exquisite effects. A building in which the light is all equal is that in which the architectural effect is the smallest. That in which the variety of light and shade is greatest, though divided in broad and well-accentuated groups, is that in which it is best, even if its detail is not always perfect. Closely allied to the light and shade is the composition of the outline. As long as this follows a convenience or a necessity in the plan, it is more than merely justifiable; but the determination to obtain an irregular and picturesque outline at all cost is not to be commended. All good buildings teach us the importance of dominating horizontal lines. Without them there is no repose. Contrast the effect of the steep roof of a Gothic cathedral with that of a building where pinnacles rise up against the sky, and you will see how superior the former is. Westminster Abbey and Henry VII.'s Chapel are good illustrations of this. In one the vertical lines are strong as they can be; but they are controlled by the quiet horizontal line of the roof, which in the other is not allowed to produce any effect upon the design.

I have now, I think, touched on most of the principles, strictly so called, by which the good architect is bound. You see that they are many in number, but that they all resolve themselves into an observation and obedience to certain and very few first principles. The best Greek architects and sculptors were the best by universal consent that the world has ever seen, and with a few words upon their work I may well conclude this lecture. Observe, then, that their one object was to secure the utmost refinement, satisfying, at the same time, all the requirements of the best construction. They had the blessing of a sunshine which gave effect to the most delicate lines, and which allowed of their buildings being decorated with a brilliancy of colour almost past belief. Nothing so well proves their extraordinary delicacy of observation as their matchless sculpture of the nude. This was the effect of study of life in active motion by the eye, rather than of simple anatomical knowledge. And all the details of Greek art seem to prove that they result from an extraordinarily patient and delicate observation of the influence and effect of light, as well as of the true necessities of construction. If the same men had had to build in Northern Europe, of course they would have modified their style in endless respects to suit so different a climate. But wherever they built, it would have been as worthy of admiration as in Greece, because their work would still have been done with all their heart and all their power, and because they realised (as all of us must, if we are to be good architects) by their actions, if not consciously, that all noble ornament and all good work are an expression of man's delight in God's work, and that without the refinement which we see everywhere in Nature no work of our hands is worthy to be called a work of art.

LECTURE III

THE DEVELOPMENT OF STYLES OF ARCHITECTURE[1]

TO-NIGHT I propose to speak to you on the development of styles in architecture It is a subject which every one is bound to study who wishes to know anything at all about the meaning and history, not only of the various orders or styles of architecture, but, one may almost say, of every detail of their ornament. In art, it is true, there are periods of progression and retrogression We see a style gradually and patiently developed to perfection, and then, after a more or less prolonged reign, we see it deteriorate, either in the hand of the very nation by which it had been perfected, or, more commonly, by the influence of another nation, who, by right of conquest, have become masters, and have destroyed or modified the style which they found existing

The modes in which styles are developed one out of the other are numerous There is, first, the gradual progress towards perfection There is the change caused by transplanting a style invented in one country to another, whose religious, political, and, more than all, whose climatic conditions are different There is, again, the influence of new processes or new modes of construction, of new materials, or the absence of the materials by the use of which advance has hitherto been secured There is the potent influence of religion ; the influence, again, of individuals, either of great sovereigns or of skilful architects , and—greatest of all—that of military conquests, and the intercourse of traders with foreign countries. All these and many minor causes have contributed to the changes which have from time to time occurred in the history of our art, and to understand them all thoroughly some acquaintance is required with the history of various countries, with the growth and consolidation of states, and the connection which has existed between them at various periods. But, even without this knowledge, it is possible

[1] Third lecture, delivered on Monday, 21st February, to the Students of the Royal Academy

to derive great gain from a merely general and summary study of
the question, and it is in this that I wish to guide you to some
extent to-night.

For our purpose it will be sufficient to go back so far only as
the most perfect period of Greek art With few and minor modifications, all existing European art may be traced back directly to
Greece The more ancient civilisations acted upon Greece, and,
through Greece, upon Europe. Almost all Greek forms are derived
from Assyria and Egypt; and, great as is the antiquity of Greek art,
it is almost to be regarded as modern by the side of that of the
East. We begin, therefore, with Grecian art after it had formed
itself into a well-defined style, some six or seven centuries before
the Christian era. At this date we find the Doric order in so well-
defined and perfected a state in, *e g.*, the Temple of Corinth, that
for many centuries the variations from the type then established are
only slight alterations from time to time in the proportions of the
various parts, with a determined adherence to the general form and
design as it was first seen. Some examples, as, for instance, the
Lycian tomb in the British Museum, are, beyond all question,
imitations of a wooden construction; but the question whether the
design of the Doric order is or is not so also, has always been open
to much discussion The evidence of the entablature with the
triglyphs above it is strongly in favour of a wooden origin , but, on
the other hand, it is in the earliest examples that the columns are
most clumsy, and as unlike as possible to wooden posts. On the
whole, however, this seems a not unlikely fault to have been committed in using a new material, whilst it is at least possible that the
original wooden construction was confined to the roof resting upon
stone or brick piers And if the development of wooden construction into stone resulted in some of the grandest buildings for ages,
showing the same adherence to the primitive type from first to last,
it would be impossible to conceive a more singular survival of
features, some of which had nothing whatever to do with the construction of the building. The Temple of Corinth, and probably
the Temple at Assos in Asia Minor, date from the seventh century
B C. The Theatre at Girgenti was begun *circa* 480 B C , the Temple
of Theseus in 469, whilst the Parthenon was finished in 438. In a
comparatively short period all the best examples of Doric were
erected, but for two hundred years before the Parthenon was built, if
not for more, architects had been building in the same way , whilst
for centuries later the style was still persevered in, until we see one
of its latest examples in the Forum at Pompeii—probably a work
executed under Greek influence—within a few years of the birth
of our Lord.

At the same time, we have the interesting fact that other styles coexisted with the Doric during the greater part of the period referred to. The Ionic Erechtheium on the Acropolis was built in about 420 B.C., and is, therefore, as nearly as possible of the same date as the Parthenon. The Corinthian is a later order, and was used generally under Roman influence, but even this coexisted with Doric and Ionic. We have here, therefore, the remarkable fact that in Greece at the same time three styles of architecture were deliberately practised, and that the only alterations were modifications of proportion. There was absolutely no development of a new style, no combination of the features of the three styles, and the Doric never, as time went on, underwent any modification or improvement from contact with the Ionic, or the Ionic from the Doric. Indeed, it is probable that architects confined themselves each to one style, even if the adoption of the style did not depend—as it did later, in the times of Guelph and Ghibelline in Italy, and of the Moors and Christians in Spain—upon the politics or the blood and the race of those who built.

The Greek mode of construction was so dependent upon the use of single blocks of stone, that it was all but impossible to attempt the erection of buildings of vast size. A remarkable evidence of this is afforded by the Temple of Jupiter at Girgenti. Here the dimensions are vastly in excess of anything ordinarily built by them, the height being absolutely more than twice that of the Parthenon, and the architect ventured on the device of building up his columns with small stones and attaching them to the wall in a way which shows how limited the application of the style of architecture was, and with a result which must have been as unpleasing as it was, happily, unusual. But even such an example as this has its interest, showing as it does that among the Greeks there was no such thing as impatience and fretfulness because new things were not perpetually being invented. A beautiful thing once done could not be too often repeated. Men never tired of seeing it.

The handmaid of Architecture—Sculpture,—in the same way, was just as deliberate, and when a really beautiful work had been done there was no hesitation as to repeating it over and over again. The Venus of Praxiteles is said to have been repeated at least a hundred times; and the same thing may be said of many of the finest works of the greatest Greek sculptors.

The great virtue of the Greek artist was his appreciation of refinement of line, and his intense admiration for the noblest possible representations of man and beast. Compare Greek sculpture with Assyrian or Egyptian, and you see the gap which separates a perhaps dignified but always conventional figure from one in which the fire of the living soul is made to light up the well-wrought stone; and it was this temper which made him—possessor as he was of almost unmatched skill—content to labour on from one century to another in the reproduction of what he had once for all found to be very good.

From the Greek we turn naturally to the Roman, who was influenced by the magnificent remains of the Greek buildings in
Southern Italy and in Sicily on the one hand, and by the even older
work of the Etruscans on the other   He never realised the necessity
of development in architecture, but the introduction of the arch,
which he used freely in all his constructions, soon modified, and
then completely changed, the whole character of his art.   He must
be said, I fear, to have spoilt what he borrowed from the Greek,
having little of his acute sense of beauty.   He never observed that
all Greek art was a reasonable adornment of a reasonable construction, and proceeded to treat the orders as mere ornaments to be
added to the face of a wall, without any serious consideration of the
purposes of the wall itself.   He put the three orders one above
another, three or four in height, pierced arches between them—
having discovered the value of the arch without discovering how it
ought to be used,—and retained to each order and each stage of his
building the heavy cornice which had its *raison d'être* only in being
the finish of a wall   In his larger works it is the brute force of the
work, the vast thickness of the walls, the immense span of the arches
and vaults, the trusting to size and solidity rather than to refinement
or grace for the result to be achieved, that strike us, and not the
beauty, imagination, or architectural fitness of the work.   The architecture and the building were, to a great extent, wholly independent
the one of the other.   In some of the vastest Roman works—as, *e g.*,
the Basilica of Constantine and the Baths of Caracalla—the architecture has disappeared, and yet the walls remain   The architecture
was *appliqué*, like a garment which had little to do with the body it
covered, save to follow, in a general way, its outlines.   The development (if it may be so called) which is seen in great orders piled one
on another in the Flavian Amphitheatre, may well be compared with
the Greek mode of treating a two-storied erection, as we see it in the
cella of the Temple of Neptune at Pæstum, where the upper range of
columns is simply a prolongation of those below, without entasis [1]
(for that would have been fatal to the continuity which was the
essence of the design), and divided not by a cornice aping the top of
a wall, but by blocks of stone forming a string-course and binding
the whole together—a construction strictly analogous to that of Gothic
buildings, and wholly opposed to the Roman succession of orders
   I have said that the Roman used the arch without showing that
he knew at all how it ought to be used   But it is in his capacity as
artist, not as constructor, that I mean to make this statement.   As a
constructor he certainly had advanced far beyond the Greek, but his
constructions are remarkable mainly for their vastness, and for the
impression they convey of being the work of men who regarded the

[1] Cf. p. 348, *ante.*

labour of hordes of untutored workmen with as much satisfaction as the work which could only be wrought by skilful hands. Or rather, I should perhaps say, they regarded the two things as entirely distinct—built their walls, their arches, and their vaults first, and then brought their columns, their mouldings, and their statuary to adorn them. So that—to take a good example—the Villa of Hadrian, near Tivoli, is in its ruin a mass of rough brickwork, with hardly one single evidence of art in its design, whilst the museums of Rome have been richly endowed with statues and sculptures which existed in it without being architecturally part of it. The arch was used as a servant to do good work, and no more, for the Roman never perceived that if it were to be a feature in the building it must, almost of necessity, be the chief feature. His one development was to construct his arch in a wall which was divided into panels by imitations, more or less exact, of columns, with their entablatures and cornices. His endeavour was evidently to make it seem still as if the column and the entablature had something to do with the construction, though, in point of fact, they were absolutely independent of it, and were decorations of the face of the wall, regulated in their position, and in no other way, by the size of the arch required. Then the column, with all its belongings, being found to be an ornament and no more, it was natural to see it at last placed away from the wall, connected with it by a returned plinth and cornice, and at last carrying on its summit a statue or group which, by an afterthought, gave a kind of excuse—and a very lame one it is—for a piece of architectural feebleness which is almost unique. The development of the Roman upon what the Greek had given him was, therefore, nothing less than the destruction of the whole virtue of the original. That had been accurately constructed and well designed, whilst this was constructed with reference to design, and treated as no good architecture can possibly be—as though the wall and its decoration were two wholly distinct and separable entities.

For the first three centuries of the Christian era I see no evidence of anything that can properly be called an architectural development, or that even seemed to pave the way for one—with one notable exception. This is the fondness of the Roman builders for circular arrangements either of rooms or of alcoves in angles of rooms, and of alcoves placed *dos-à-dos*. Of all these, good specimens are seen in the Palace of the Cæsars on the Palatine Hill, and in the double Temple of Venus and Rome hard by, where the two temples are identical in plan, each finishing in an apse placed back to back. In the Pantheon, the enormously thick wall is planned with recesses, some coved and some square on plan, and with detached columns carrying the entablature above them—an arrangement which we shall see somewhat later, distinctly suggesting the design of the circular recesses under the dome of SS Sergius and Bacchus at Constantinople, and San Vitale at Ravenna, whilst in the so-called Temple of Minerva Medica, a circular domed central space is surrounded by a series of ten recesses, nine of which are circular The Greeks had shown their sense of the beauty of circular buildings, and the Romans followed in their steps, as we see in this example in the Pantheon at Rome, the Little Temple at Tivoli, and in the Temple of Vesta at Rome. But the necessity for enormous supports to their skilfully constructed domical roofs led the Roman architects to make these recesses in the walls where they could safely be introduced, and thus to pave the way for the introduction of buttresses, and of the apsidal terminations and circular chapels around them, which played so large a part in much later developments.

It was in about 289 A.D. that the great step in advance was made in the building of Diocletian's Palace at Spalato, on the eastern shore of the Adriatic. Here a range of arches was carried—probably for the first time—on the capitals of columns, without the interposition of any sort of entablature. The same sort of construction had, it is true, been suggested long before in such erections as the portico of the Pantheon, where semicircular arches are turned over the lintels above the columns in order to take the whole weight to the capitals instead of on to the entablature This apparently simple change was one which at once revolutionised all existing architectural laws. The column was no longer a mere ornament. It became at once the most useful, the most conspicuous, and in every way the most important, as it had always been the most beautiful, feature in a building. And from that time forward it was impossible ever again to construct a building as before with the post and lintel only, without deliberately ignoring the most useful and convenient discovery which has ever been made in the art of building From that time the arch became master of the position, just as before the beam had been The old system had lasted one can hardly say how many centuries, and it is needless to declare that nothing can ever make the use of the arch, round or pointed, obsolete in the same real sense as the use of the lintel or beam has become

The Greeks, who, if they did not invent, at least perfected the orders, never in later times seem to have sympathised at all with the Roman modifications of them, most of which were consequent on the use of the arch Their Byzantine art owes but little to Rome. It was, in truth, a genuine invention of a style developed out of Greek, but one in which the arch was an essential feature, and in which the cornices and mouldings, the columns and their capitals, were all modified to suit it. Their decoration was almost entirely Eastern, both in its *motif* and in its mode of execution Their development was a radical one ; for in place of the old Roman and old Greek

construction of plain walls and columns carrying only a dead weight,
Byzantine art is remarkable for the extent to which it treated construction in a new fashion as an affair of weight and counterpoise.
This was provided for in the arch and pier, in the dome and its
supports.   The Roman basilica required no great scientific skill for
its erection, whilst the Byzantine buildings dealt with some of the
most difficult problems of construction, and really foreshadowed the
triumphs achieved in the scientific and delicate constructions of the
Middle Ages.   During this period, *i.e.* between the time of Constantine and that of Charles the Great, the Roman buildings were
not undergoing any development.   The long series of popes, from
the beginning down to 774, the time of Charles's conquest, had done
more in the way of conversion of existing buildings, or reusing
old materials, than in attempting to erect new buildings.   The
basilica, with its long ranges of columns, ending with a throne or an
apse, afforded just the accommodation that was needed for Christian
worship, and the multitude of old fragments available led for ages
to the construction of buildings in which the whole of the details are
antique, and in which the general form is founded also on an ancient
one.   The long ranges of columns of all sizes and sorts are often
very imposing, but the interest of the churches is rather archæological than architectural.   The interest of the fragments of which they
are constructed is great.   They afford evidence of the slovenly execution of much Roman work, but at the same time of the freedom
from all rule as to the exact dimensions, proportions, and decorations
of the various orders.   It is hardly too much to say that no two
capitals in one of these buildings are alike, whilst the remains are,
with few exceptions, of Ionic, Corinthian, and Composite, and not of
Doric.   Not the less were these buildings important links in the
chain of development.   The long lines of columns ; the simple wall
pierced with a clerestory above ; the apse at the east end projected
from a cross nave or transept, out of which other and smaller apses
were formed on either side of the central one, formed a model
which, as we shall see, was one of the principal foundations for the
complete Romanesque buildings of the eleventh and twelfth centuries.
And the buildings (which still remain substantially on the old lines,
as St. Paul without the walls of Rome, San Lorenzo, and St. John
Lateran) were repeated with more or less closeness at Ravenna, in
the two churches dedicated to St. Apollinare, at Aquileia, in San
Miniato, Florence, San Zenone, Verona, and, last of all, in the
ground-plan of Pisa.

But if Rome was thus, as before, uninventive, this cannot be
said of the city of Constantinople, where Constantine the Great
established the seat of Government in 330 A.D., *i.e.* about fifty years
after the erection of Diocletian's palace.   Here the Romans were

going back again to the East, and with an architectural result which has been one of the most remarkable in the whole history of development. Greek art had now for some centuries been all but completely thrust on one side by Roman, after the latter people had become the conquerors, and it was not until the foundation of Constantinople that it once more raised its head. The Greeks again exhibited their powers of invention in the Byzantine style, in which we see so many evidences of acquaintance with the architecture of Palestine. The churches (now converted into mosques) still existing in Constantinople are of various dates and of various stages of development. Constantine's first church was a Roman building, like the old Basilica of St. Peter at Rome—a long building, with wooden roofs, an eastern apse, and probably an atrium. All the ornamentation was internal, in place of external. It was burnt down in 531 A.D., in the time of Justinian, and so vigorous was the architect of the new church (Anthemius) that in forty days from the fire he laid the first stone of the new basilica, and completed the whole church in five years and ten months. The cupola is about 104 feet across, about a fourth less than the Pantheon, but, then, it is carried on arches instead of on a continuous wall, and in constructive skill its architect was far before the man who built the Pantheon. At the same time (*arca* 530 A.D.), SS. Sergius and Bacchus was built, and this has special interest, seeing that San Vitale at Ravenna, consecrated in 547, is on exactly the same plan and design; whilst in the somewhat late church of St Theodore we have a plan copied almost exactly in Sta. Fosca Torcello. And here, though it is a little out of place, you must notice how completely Constantinople gave her art to Venice, not only in these early days, but down, at least, to the thirteenth century, when the Venetians attacked and sacked the city, and carried off as spoil most of the exquisite decorative work which we now see there, and, not least among this, the four antique Greek horses which stand over the portico of St Mark's. Indeed, it is impossible to look at any part of the original work of St Mark's without realising that scarcely a feature is indigenous, and that all is absolutely and wholly Byzantine in plan, in elevation, in detail, and in coloured ornament and decoration.

The construction of these Constantinopolitan domes is as interesting as their design. The cupolas are ingeniously buttressed and strengthened by semidomes below the tambour, by cross arches and vaults and domes in the enclosing aisle. And the domes, instead of being constructed of heavy stonework, were built usually of hollow pots, and in the case of SS Sergius and Bacchus, with eight great vaulting ribs rising from the centres of the arches to the centre of the dome, the spaces between the ribs being filled in with waggon-vaulting resting on them. This extreme constructive skill would alone deserve our highest respect, even if the decorative details had not been, as they invariably are, of a very refined character. No merely architectural carving of conventional foliage has ever excelled in effect or in technical skill the best works of this school, in which for some four or five centuries the same detail is very closely adhered to

Another parallel stream of art must also be noticed—in Syria The examples of this, dating from the first to the seventh century of our era, are numerous, very perfect, and of the profoundest interest to the student. You will find a full and admirably illustrated description of them in Count de Vogué's *Syrie Centrale,* and I advise you to consult it in our library. Here, in part owing to the climate, in part to great solidity of construction, which was wholly of stone, and in part to the absolutely deserted state of most of the sites, time has laid a very gentle hand on the work, and an astonishing number of examples of this most interesting period remain all but perfect in most of their details. The earliest are, as might be expected in a Roman province, generally imitations of Roman work. But by the fourth century the influence of the native Eastern art, closely allied to that which is found in Constantinople soon after, is seen in a well-defined system of design and ornament which prevails in a large number of buildings, and which has so much in common with much later European work as to make one at first almost incredulous as to their great antiquity This is, however, indubitable The most interesting and typical examples for my present purpose are the church at Ezra, the cathedral at Bosra, in the south of Syria, and the vast convent at Kalat Sem'an in the north, between Aleppo and Antioch. An inscription still remaining on the walls of Ezra shows that it was completed in 515 A.D , or about sixteen years before St. Sophia's was begun. Its plan is remarkable, as so many of these Syrian plans are, for its admirable arrangement. It is a square building on the outside and octangular inside, the angles being relieved by semicircular recesses covered with semidomes. A small chancel is projected on one side, and within the octagonal nave eight columns and arches carry a quasi-dome or eight-sided vault of very pointed section, with the important feature of a tambour below it pierced with windows. Here, therefore, we have, though on a small scale, a construction which suggests, in a very definite way, the most advanced constructions of the European builders some centuries later. The plan, simple as it is, is very beautiful, and shows how extremely skilful these Syrian architects were Even more striking is the cathedral at Bosra. This is on a far larger scale than the church at Ezra , but, unhappily, the central dome and the arcades which supported it have disappeared, and we are left to conjecture that it was the experience obtained in such works as this that led to the more stable construction of the domes in Constantinople. Here you must notice the remarkable love of the plan of a circle enclosed within a square, with a number of sunk semicircular recesses in the walls The treatment of these, with columns carrying the wall above them, seems to be the connecting link between the recesses in the walls of the Pantheon, and the management of the semicircular recesses under the tambours of the domes of Sta Sophia and SS Sergius and Bacchus Even more remarkable than these churches is the vast convent at Kalat Sem'an, erected in the fifth century. Here, among a vast number of ruins of buildings attached to it, is still left so much of the grand church as enables us to form a fair idea of its general design The plan is cruciform, with an octagonal centre, the walls of which are buttressed by cross arches contrived with extreme skill so as to be themselves supported by apsidal chapels in the four angles made by the junction of the four arms of the cross. The central octagon stands on eight arches,' and there was no central dome, the church here being, in fact, an hypæthral building, built round the column of St. Simeon Stylites, which stood in the centre of the octagon There is no building of which the date is more certain St Simeon died in 459. The base of the column on which he spent thirty-seven years of his life is still in its position. In 560 Evagrius visited the convent, and has left a most exact account of the building, which had been erected directly on St. Simeon's death, and his account agrees in every detail with the existing building I can hardly express too strongly my sense of the singular excellence of this plan Even with the recollections of Arnolfo's work under the dome in the cathedral at Florence, and of our own Alan of Walsingham's octagon at Ely, it is a very open question whether this far earlier treatment of the same problem is not more excellent than either. At Kalat Sem'an there are but few evidences of Roman influence The long arcades of the four arms of the cross can hardly be said to be certainly derived from the basilica, and the great entrance at the end of the transept, three grand arches each with its own pediment, has no prototype, and is itself more than likely to have suggested the design of the very best French Romanesque, such as we see at St. Trophime at Arles Then we find here a very regular system of window decoration, of mouldings well adapted to their exact position ; and outside the central apse we have a design which might almost be pronounced to be a work of the eleventh century, if we saw it on some so-called Lombard church in the north of Italy or on the borders of the Rhine It is divided on plan into regular bays by attached columns placed one over the other in two tiers, and in height by a cornice which is already treated as a mere string-course. At the summit arches, springing from the caps of the columns, support a cornice. These arches are somewhat large, but otherwise there is little to distinguish them from the Lombard corbel tables of Pavia. Nothing more deserves notice than the really beautiful carved stonework of these buildings. It is truly Byzantine in character. The acanthus leaf plays still a large part, but is treated with great variety of arrangement, and is supplemented by many charming designs of running ornaments, carved mouldings, and patterns in low relief, which speak well for the skill and taste of their designers. Not less noticeable is the fact that these buildings are almost wholly of stone. Stones of large size were obtainable, and floors are constructed by throwing arches across at intervals of a few feet, and bridging the spaces by long horizontal blocks of stone exactly fitted together. It is about the most undying mode of construction ever seen in arched buildings. Nor are there any buildings in which the semicircular arch is more freely, more honestly used than it is in these.

It is not very difficult to connect this school with buildings in other parts of Europe. It is improbable that a flourishing province of the empire should keep entirely to itself such remarkable powers. M. de Vogüé gives some examples of construction with parallel arches covered with flagstones, such as the baths of Diana at Nismes, an arch of the bridge at Narni, and a corridor in the arena of Arles. He asserts also that the tomb of Theodoric at Ravenna, built about 500 A.D., is really so akin to them in all its details of ornament and construction, that to him it seemed to be almost a Syrian work. And it certainly seems possible to trace a distinct influence of these Syrian buildings on not a few of the Romanesque buildings of the eleventh and twelfth centuries in the south of France, throughout the Rhine provinces, and in the east of Spain. The Syrian buildings, dating mainly from the fifth, sixth, and seventh centuries, must at that time have been seen by many in a perfect condition, and were so far in advance of European works of the same age as to make it certain that they would find imitators, who, however, with none but Roman works and traditions before them in their own country, would be likely, as a rule, to graft some of the new features on to their own buildings, rather than to wholly abandon the style of the latter. Doubtless the influence of these Syrian Byzantine architects was largely felt in the Holy Land; and it is incontestable that the influence of the Holy Land—and particularly of the buildings in Jerusalem—on European art was equally great, and too remarkable to be passed over. It was of a twofold kind. Crusaders and pilgrims visited the holy places, and returned knowing somewhat of an art different from their own. Then wherever they formed communities or carried on trade in the East, they erected churches and other buildings for their own use and in their own style, modified by that of the country.

The church of the Holy Sepulchre has been, as I daresay you all know, a subject of much contention. But hardly any one now believes that there is any room for doubt as to its authenticity and antiquity; and to-night, at any rate, I must speak to you as though there were none. The church, as we now see it, is a collection of additions made from time to time to the original church built by Constantine. This was probably a great basilica, with a long nave and double aisles and transepts; west of these a circular building, open to the air in the centre—very much as in the church of Kalat Sem'an—where was a shrine over the sepulchre. This central space was divided from the surrounding aisle by a range of piers and columns. In the outer wall of the aisle were three circular projections or chapels. Here we have a most interesting plan, and one of which the outer wall still remains. At the latest the work can hardly be put after the sixth century, but I see no reason for doubting that it is really the work of Constantine; and though the arrangement is unlike anything that we know of in his time, it is just such a shape as might naturally grow out of the special requirements of the case. Unhappily, in a restoration after a fire in the early part of this century, so much damage was done to this part of the building that it is now a little difficult to realise how venerable it is. The alterations made at various times have been great. First of all the nave was burnt, and in its place was erected, in 1130 A.D., a choir with an eastern chevet and a dome over the crossing. The western side of the transepts then abutted on the circular church round the sepulchre. The architecture of the whole of this later work was thoroughly European. It was the work either of French or Spanish architects, and it is most interesting to see the exterior of its apse giving back to Jerusalem exactly the same outline as had first of all been there devised. The outline is a specially common one in the centre of France— a great circular apse, with three chapels, and spaces between them for windows.

Close to the church of the Sepulchre are other churches—St. Helena, St. Mary, and St. Mary of the Latins, all of them evidently built by Europeans in the twelfth and beginning of the thirteenth centuries. At Bethlehem is a church which is probably also of the date of Constantine. It is a great basilica, with transepts, double aisles, and wooden roofs, above a clerestory. The transepts and choir all end in apses, and may well be compared with the little tri-apsal church at the cemetery of St. Calixtus in Rome, of about the same date. The interest of this church is that it shows us the plan of a Christian church founded upon the Roman basilica before the Greeks had developed the construction of the dome. The Christians, when they had to choose between the form of a basilica and that of the ancient heathen temples, naturally chose the former. The old *cella* of the temple was narrow, dark, and meant only for the functions of the priest; whereas the Christian church had to be large, well lighted, and open to the multitude, and this church at Bethlehem shows so clearly the way in which it was adapted to the purpose as to be well worth study. There is, indeed, a story of the ninth century which attributes the church to Justinian. It goes that when the architect who had been sent by him to build it returned to Constantinople, the emperor was so disgusted with his description of his work that he charged him first of all with malversation, and then finished by having him decapitated. This punishment has been suggested in our own day as a better mode of promoting good art than any other, and perhaps not very undeservedly. I fear, however, that there is no truth in the Justinian story, which only does credit to the originality of the narrator Eutychius. Justinian's principal works are known by contemporary description. They were Sta. Sophia, St. John at Damascus, and the Church of the Presentation at Jerusalem. They were all varied in design. In the first, everything was sacrificed to the dome; in the second and third, the dome and the basilica had been combined very much in the form in which they are seen throughout Germany and France down to the end of the twelfth century.

I have already told you how much Eastern art affected the art of the rest of Europe. But the Holy Sepulchre buildings had a singular influence. The religious interest in the site and history of the spot led men to wish to copy the elevation of the church, and, accordingly, we find a number of buildings avowedly intended to be repetitions of it. Perhaps the most curious of all these is the group of six churches founded at Bologna in 430, avowedly in imitation of the Holy Sepulchre. They are very small, and it is now difficult to see how they can be called copies, save in the one fact common to both of the cluster of churches in one group. A much closer imitation is the crypt of St. Benigne at Dijon. Here the outline was evidently most closely copied, and there was above it a similarly planned church with a double aisle round the centre, which was open to the sky. The people in the triforium galleries and on the floor were thus able to look down into the crypt, and in this way a vast number of pilgrims were able to be present at one time.

The various churches of the Templars all over Europe were, in the same way, rough copies of the Holy Sepulchre Church. The Temple Church, and the round churches at Cambridge, Northampton, and Maplestead—all have a round church at the west end, corresponding with Constantine's circular church, and the choir projecting to the east, just as the later choir did at Jerusalem So also have the Templars' Church at Segovia, and the fine church (not connected with the Templars) of St. Gereon at Koln In France the church of Neuvy St Sepulchre, built by Geoffrey, Viscount of Bourges, after a pilgrimage to the Holy Land, is not the only example of the same influence. The destroyed church of the Temple in Paris, with its circular nave and long chancel, was probably the most beautiful there ; though, on the whole, none can be found that excels our own Temple Church in this city, with which I hope all of you are well acquainted.

In Constantinople, at Jerusalem, and in Syria, we have had the work mainly of the period from the fourth to the eighth century The next great epoch at which we might pause if time allowed is that which followed the coronation of Charles the Great, in the old and completely Romanesque basilica of St. Peter, in the year 800. But it must suffice to say that constant, though generally hostile and warlike, intercourse with Italy was leading the Northern people to a more thorough realisation of what Roman art was than would have been possible from the study of the works which had been executed during the Roman occupation of their own countries And it is clear that from this time began that stream of mixed Byzantine and Romanesque art which so steadily flowed for some two hundred years from the south northwards, and mainly on the two parallel lines of the Rhone to the centre of France and the Rhine from the Alps through the centre of Germany.

The various influences which I have been describing had been gradually forming a style which was well defined, greatly advanced in constructive art, and full of variety At times, as you will have gathered, it was swayed by the Byzantine influence of Venice and the East, at times by more distinctly Roman influence, and some-times by that of Arab art But, on the whole, I incline to give much more weight to the Byzantine share in the work than it is usually the fashion to give Charles the Great evidently copied San Vitale and SS Sergius and Bacchus in his minster at Aachen, and after its erection there grew up a series of magnificent churches in the Rhine country which had far more connection with the East in their plan and general design than with Rome. In England and in Normandy, on the other hand, the style is more properly called Romanesque than anywhere, for from beginning to end our build-ings of the earliest period show no knowledge whatever of Byzantine art, and when compared with the coeval buildings of Italy, of Germany, or of the south and west of France, they illustrate an entirely different phase of development It can hardly be denied

2 B

that far more skill and science was shown in those days in the South than in the North. We have grand buildings, but their decorations are coarse and their plans rude compared to those which are seen at Arles, at St. Gilles, at Poitiers, and elsewhere in countless French examples.

Undoubtedly there was an architectural influence at work in Great Britain which was but little connected with Rome. The early British Church was closely connected with that of Ireland. There we still see remains of extremely early churches or oratories, wholly distinct in style from either English or French Romanesque, and the architectural origin of which it is most difficult to account for. One feature, which is perhaps the most remarkable, is the construction of doors and windows with their jambs inclined towards the head, in classic fashion. This is never seen in England, nor, I believe, in France, and certainly suggests a separate knowledge of Egyptian and Greek detail. It is not a little remarkable that this feature is carried on as late as the thirteenth century, and, as we shall see when we have to discuss our English architecture, it is from Ireland, probably, that we obtained our love for the square-ended churches which are so marked a feature in really English architecture, and so opposed to all the traditions of Roman and Byzantine art.

There is still something to be said about another potent foreign influence, which is seen in almost all early Italian buildings south of Rome. Few countries are blessed with a sea-coast so extended in proportion to the population; and it is no matter for wonder, therefore, if the people were good sailors and good traders. No one can travel in those parts without finding features which are entirely new and unlike those in any other part of Europe. There is so great an infusion of an Arabic, combined with a Greek, element in both design and construction, that it is impossible to class the buildings with those erected under simply Roman influence. To the present day you may travel among villages and towns in Southern Italy whose houses are all covered with flat roofs, out of which small domes occasionally rise, and when you come to a church you will find that it has features entirely unlike any seen elsewhere in Europe. It may have a central dome adorned with intersecting arcades placed slightly in advance of the face of the wall; a tower pierced with lofty round-arched windows, with the openings either extremely stilted, or of horseshoe shape; walls panelled with small pilasters at intervals, with lozenge-shaped panels of ornamental carving or inlaying placed below the arches which connect them. Arches are used for ornament only, as at Sta Maria Ancona, where the whole façade is covered with arcades whose arches avowedly have nothing to do with the construction. It is difficult to explain in words the *bizarre* effect of these buildings. Their authors are to be looked for on the other side of the Mediterranean, but they affected in some respects the whole architecture of Italy, as, to mention one instance, the construction of pointed arches, in vast numbers of which the arch stones or bricks are not made to radiate from the centre of the arch, but are built with the same kind of feeling as in the Moorish arches in Spain, as, *e.g* in an arch at the Puerta del Sol, Toledo, which is for the greater part of its extent not an arch at all—a feature which is of constant occurrence in all Spanish buildings erected under Moorish influence   The decoration, which is profuse, is wholly unlike real Romanesque work ; and, as is usual in Arab work, it always has the look of being used simply and solely for the sake of its beauty, and not for its utility, or as an ornament of the construction   Many of these features are found in the Greek churches of the same period, and it is natural, when we regard some passages in the history of the country, that such marks of foreign intercourse and influence should be seen.   Down to the eleventh century the Greek Emperor had his lieutenant or capitan at Bari   The country was in turn occupied by Normans, by Saracens, and by the German Emperors   But at heart the population seems to have sympathised with Byzantine and Arab art far more than with Roman.

Down to the twelfth century, and even later, the whole south of Italy, and a considerable portion of Spain, were more or less identified with Arab art, either by reason of conquests by the Arabs or by the importation of Saracen mercenaries.   To give an instance.   I remember seeing at Lucera a magnificent castle, in which, even so late as 1230 A.D , Frederick II. kept his Saracen soldiers.   He was not a very Christian king, for, as his troops wanted a mosque, he converted the cathedral at Lucera into a mosque, turning the bishop out, and installing his Saracen mercenaries in his place !—a feat which made Dante condemn him to purgatory

The influence of the Moors upon the course of art in Spain is as remarkable as, but much better known than, the corresponding effect of the southern side of the Mediterranean on Italy.   Here, in the earliest times, it was a point of honour with both Moor and Spaniard to build in his own style.   As time wore on, the Spaniard freed himself from the dominion which the Moors had exercised, but the Moorish architects still remained in the country practising their national art until the time of the Inquisition, and each nation influenced the other.   In the later Moorish work we see constantly a number of completely Gothic details introduced in a very picturesque fashion ; and in the Christian buildings, from the end of the twelfth century, we meet equally frequently with pretty bits of distinctly Moorish detail in the midst of what is otherwise the purest Gothic. And wherever the Spaniards used brick, as they did in a large part of the country from Toledo to Guadalajara, Saragoza, Calatayud, and Tarazona, the whole of it is a most interesting mixture of Moorish and Gothic, both in general design and detail.

Nowhere do we see more instances of the way in which architectural styles spread from one country to another than in the history of the Italian Republics As an example, take the case of Genoa, which is a typical one, for their politics and trade, foreign conquest, mercenary warfare, and foreign travel, are features which meet us at every turn   The Crusades were utilised by its people for purposes of trade.   The Genoese were among the greatest traders to the East from the time of the first Crusade to the fall of Acre in 1291. They had in many Eastern cities their own streets, their own warehouses , and the riches of the East came, to a great extent, through their hands to Europe.   They despatched vessels against the Saracens in the Balearic Isles and on the mainland of Spain, and obtained in return not only shiploads of booty, but also an annual Spanish tribute to the Cathedral of San Lorenzo.   Then, again, they had treaties with, and kept consuls at Narbonne, Montpelier, Aiguemorte, and other Provençal towns   They went as far north as the great fairs in Champagne, where they exchanged their goods with those of the manufacturers of Ypres, Bruges, and other northern towns ; and they built larger ships expressly that they might carry their goods to the Hanse Towns, and even as far north as that singularly interesting trading depôt at Wisby in the Isle of Gothland   In the East they had consuls and warehouses at Trebizond and Kars, in Persia, and, above all, in Constantinople , and one result of their foreign connections is seen in a singular episode of the joint Venetian and Genoese occupation of Eastern cities in the thirteenth century.   We are told that two marble columns from St. Sabbas, at Acre, were sent to Venice, and erected in front of St Mark's in the Piazzetta, after the Venetians, in a hand-to-hand fight with the Genoese in the church, had burnt their warehouses, and compelled them to take refuge in Tyre   Such fighting as this was only too common an incident in Italian history, for, as you know, the Italian republics showed no mercy to each other   Pisa fought with and ruined Amalfi as early as the twelfth century   In the thirteenth century the Genoese, led by Oberto d'Oria, conquered Pisa in the great sea-fight at Meloria, and after destroying the chains which guarded the mouth of the Arno, brought them home in triumph, and hung them over their gateways, where, until our own day, they have remained   A hundred years later Venice fought a duel to the death with Genoa, and what little power was left to the latter was ultimately destroyed by the Visconti of Milan.   Each one of these contests ended in something added to the artistic possessions or developments of both conquered and conqueror.

In France the most fruitful source of development must, no
doubt, be looked for in the Crusades, in which she had so large a
share. An illustration of the effect of the intercourse which these
wars promoted is seen in the case of Eudes de Montreuil, a famous
architect of the thirteenth century, who went to the Holy Land with
St Louis, and built the fortifications of Jaffa. Another French architect, Jousselin de Corvault, also went to the East with St Louis, but
the only record of his work there is that he invented divers instruments of war. But upon the origin and development of French
architecture I shall have so much to say in another lecture, that I
need not detain you upon it now. My object has been this evening
to show you how possible it is to follow the growth of styles of
architecture, and I hope I have also shown you how much interest
there is in such investigations. Unless we make them we shall
always be ignorant of the real history of old buildings, and unable
to follow the course of their developments.

We have traced the progress of our art in the South and East,
where in those days all the progress was being made. We are ready
to go more into detail now as regards the rest of Europe, where in its
later stages the developments of architecture left the South far behind.
We have seen the growth of the art up to the time of Charlemagne
From his time until the fall of the Holy Roman Empire with Frederick II 450 years elapsed, and during all that time Germany and
Italy had been practically one country under one sovereign. Hence
evidence of their union meets us at every turn in the early churches
of the two countries At Pavia and in Milan we are in presence of
the same art as at Mainz, Coblentz, and Koln One illustration,
and this of a singular kind, will suffice The apse of such a building as the baptistery at Gravidona, close to the southern slopes of
the Alps, is distinctly founded on the apse of St. Mark's at Venice.
You will see by the plan the ingenious creation of three little apses
in the thickness of the wall of the principal apse To any one who
had planned, or seen the plan of such an apse, it might occur that
a piercing for a window should be made of the same outline, and
just such windows we do find in the early churches on the Rhine. .

The minor changes and varieties in German round-arched buildings are too many and too great to allow of my mentioning them
now, though not so great as they were in the various parts of France.
In those days France was formed by a number of provinces, each
practically distinct from the other, and consequently we see as many
styles as there are provinces The whole South is fairly uniform, but
if you compare Normandy with Poitou, or either with Aquitaine,
Alsace, the Ile de France, Champagne, or Burgundy, you will find,
in fact, that the one thing common to all was the round arch, and a
perfect freedom of developing whatever was required for convenience,

for good construction, or for the demands of a different climate.   I
have left myself no time to show how this last requirement affected
art.   But when you consider that in the south of Europe a flat roof
is the best covering, whilst in the north a steep one is a necessity;
and that in the south a very small window is necessary, whilst in the
north it can hardly be too large, you have two particulars which
alone would account for an enormous change in style.   The builders
of those days proceeded to modify and develop in a mode which was
everywhere founded on common sense, and varied, therefore, in its
developments in every country   This, indeed, is one of the great accomplishments in the architects of the twelfth and thirteenth centuries.
The Greek architect had been, above all things, a worshipper of
beauty for its own sake   A lovely line lost none of its loveliness for
him by constant repetition   The Roman recognised the skill and
taste of the Greek, and tried to copy his orders and his columns, forgetting that they were always the decorated features of a real construction.   He treated architecture as an art which had nothing to do with
building, and failed conspicuously in leaving anything that was very
original, or much that was beautiful, behind him.   The Byzantines took
up the work, and to a great extent transformed it, but they inherited
the old Greek idea of perfection, and spent ages in developing their
designs.   And then, in the eleventh century, came this new spirit,
which made men suddenly conscious of the exceeding charm of
variety, and of the power which the freest use of the arch gave them
for securing it.   Their art was that of men who were devising everything that they did with a reason   They adapted themselves to the
requirements of convenience with a novelty of resource and invention which is astonishing the more it is looked into.   They tried to
build so that their work should last for ever   Mortals themselves,
they never dreamt of making any work temporary and weak.   By the
middle of the twelfth century, therefore, it need not surprise us to find
that their work was bearing its proper fruit, and that, after having discovered the practical use and convenience of the pointed arch, they
soon invented and perfected a new style consequent upon its use,
which, in rapidity of development, variety of resource, and real beauty,
soon eclipsed all that had gone before.   But this style lies outside my
proper subject to-night, and in my next lecture I shall hope to show
you how it affected Italian art   In that country one of the com-
pletest of the round-arched buildings was the cathedral at Pisa   If
anywhere Roman influence should be felt, one would have supposed
it would be there.   But the Pisans were like their contemporaries
the men of Genoa, of Amalfi, and of Venice—resolute adventurers,
who went far afield—and in 1050 A.D they had made an expedition
to Sicily.   They had captured at sea a prize of extraordinary value,
and they had taken Palermo from the Saracens who held it   Then,

returning laden with their booty, their first and very pious idea was to build a magnificent cathedral, and so cosmopolitan were they that they employed a Greek, Boschetto by name, as their architect. He built them a magnificent church certainly But it was not Roman or Italian. It had the long ranges of columns of the basilica, but it had the Eastern dome, and in every detail throughout the work it is the Greek whose hand you see, and Byzantine architecture, not Romanesque, with some of the same flavour of Arabian art which we have been noticing in the more southern part of Italy. And it was under the shadow of its arcaded walls that the greatest architect of the thirteenth century was born and educated in his art.

It has been difficult to say anything like enough on my subject this evening. In all directions lines might be followed out far beyond what I have been able to attempt But I am in hopes that I may have said enough to induce some of you at least to follow out these interesting subjects for yourselves The course of art is like a stream with endless back currents and eddies, which interrupt us on our way. It takes us from Egypt to Greece, from Greece to Rome, thence to Grecian art again at Byzantium, to Syria and the Holy Land. Then it crosses again to Europe, taking possession of the south and west of France, and, joining two streams, one of mixed Byzantine and Roman from Ravenna and Venice, and the other of pure Romanesque from Rome, flows northward to the German Ocean. There these streams of art, rich in their combined developments, find another art establishing itself, founded upon an independent use of Roman work. At the same time, Moor and Christian are fighting for dear life in Spain, and wherever either plants his foot he builds in his own style, either in the most complete Moorish or in the severest Romanesque borrowed from his neighbours on the other side of the Pyrenees, but each showing occasional evidence in some part of the work of the influence of his enemy In this progress of art it is difficult to say which has done most, the Church or the Sword There had been a pause before what was supposed to be a fatal date, the year 1000. But when that was passed and the world had not come to an end, men breathed again, and began to build with renewed energy and enthusiasm The circumstances of the age were all really in favour of the arts. For it is in countries which are establishing themselves, making their laws, cementing their politics, bringing their communities into order, that public spirit is at its highest point, and that art has its greatest opportunities, and exercises the most fascination In a highly civilised state, where every one is satisfied, and there are no wars or rumours of wars, where life is easy, and men lazy and luxurious, it has a comparatively feeble influence.

In my succeeding lectures—having brought you, as it were, to the threshold of the thirteenth century—I hope to show you somewhat more in detail how the development worked out its course in Italy, in France, and in our own country. If we know so much we shall know almost enough, for in Germany and in Spain the distinctive art of the thirteenth century hardly ever existed. In Germany men were so proud of their early style that they troubled themselves as little as possible about any new one until the magnificence of an Amiens and a Beauvais forced them to an attempt at rivalry, only just completed, at Koln. And in Spain there was much the same enthusiasm for the earlier style, and when it was thought well to follow the new fashion, it was for the most part by the hands of a Frenchman, and not of a Spaniard, that the work was done.

LECTURE IV

THIRTEENTH-CENTURY ARCHITECTURE—ITALY [1]

I HAVE brought-you so far on the path of development in my last lecture, that we find ourselves at the end of the reign of the round-arched styles It is natural, even in treating of pointed architecture, to take Italy before any other country, not because the history of Gothic architecture is seen and studied better there than elsewhere, but because it was from that time for many centuries a sort of central region in all questions of art We shall find, indeed, as we go into the question, that, so far from taking a leading part in the development of pointed art, Italy was always lagging behind—that she produced no very good or original work, and that for some of her best buildings she was indebted to foreigners. Nevertheless, in few countries is there more to interest us. The state of art was not unlike what it is with us. No one style held undisputed sway. There were foreign influences at work which introduced strange novelties into a large part of the country The extensive seaboard , the mercantile character of the people, and their unmatched situation at the centre of all commerce and of the then chief lines of traffic ; the independent and warlike character of the republics— among which Venice, Amalfi, Genoa, Pisa, and Florence were the most active ; the habit inherited from their ancestors of borrowing rather than inventing—all added to the varieties of style seen in their buildings, and to the gradual development of local peculiarities.

Just before the period we are dealing with, Italy had been torn and distracted from one end to the other by foreign princes or foreign invaders, by intestine troubles and constant wars In the eleventh century the Greek Emperor still had his capitan at Bari on the east coast. The country was harassed by Saracen inroads, and was relieved and then occupied by adventurous Normans ; and the German Emperors were ruling a great part of the land. The era

[1] Fourth lecture, delivered on Thursday, 24th February, to the Students of the Royal Academy

itself is as distinguished for the personages it produced as for the troubles among which they led their lives   The Swabian, Frederick II, stands out as a central figure in the history of the times, and is equally prominent as one of the most lavish promoters of building of palaces, of castles, of churches, and even of mosques.   And the artists by whom the time was glorified are, as we shall see, innumerable, whilst their status was much more like what it is with us than it was elsewhere at the same time.   On all sides from the earliest period we meet with the names of the architects and sculptors whose works still remain, and are able to trace them working, now here, now there. Their names are recorded in countless inscriptions—not only in documents, in which Italy is so rich, but on churches, over their doorways, on pulpits, on friezes, on monuments, on columns, and on baldachins   The architecture, instead of being that of the country or the province, seems, as we study it, to become that rather of the individual architects and their followers.   Thus we have at a very early period the Maestri Comacine, freemasons with curious charters and privileges, whose headquarters on the Island of Comacina, on Lake Como, gave them their name ; the Campionesi of Campione, opposite Lugano, who from 1244—when Anselmo da Campione contracted to work at Modena *in perpetuo* for six lire a day in summer, and five in winter—reigned, as it were, until the fifteenth century, having among them Enrico I. and II., and Giovanni I. and II ; the Antelami of Parma, one of whom built the baptistery in 1196, the Cosmati family, of Rome, who succeeded each other for about one hundred and fifty years from 1150 A.D. ; and, finally, the clan of Masuccio, of Naples, among whom, as among the Campionesi, we have Masuccio I., II., and III, always spoken of as if they were a sort of succession of monarchs.   The personal element, which always adds so much to the interest of artistic studies, is seldom absent, and it is because it is all but entirely so at the same period in most other countries that the study of Italian art in the thirteenth century is so interesting.

I brought my last lecture to a close with the erection of the Cathedral of Pisa by a Greek architect, Buschetto.   His work has been too often talked of as if it were in a true sense Romanesque It is, in fact, almost exactly what we might expect from a Greek, or from an Italian brought up in Greek traditions, who wished to conciliate popular taste by conforming to some extent to Italian customs. His plan is evidently founded upon the early Roman churches, it is cruciform, has transepts of great projection, and apsidal terminations to them as well as to the choir.   But with the love of a Greek for the dome, he insists on retaining it, though he is bound by his basilican plan to carry his ranges of columns on from east to west, without any internal mark of the intersection of the transepts.   It is in the plan only that any deference for Roman precedents is seen. His walls are all arcaded externally, the arches in the true Byzantine fashion, very thin and flat, and for ornament only. Under every arch there is a lozenge-shaped panel of coloured stone or marble. The spandrels over the arches are all inlaid with patterns of extremely elaborate character, and the sculpture of the foliage has everywhere the excellence of execution, the conventional symbols, and the variety of design so invariably seen in Byzantine work. This great church was finished at the end of the twelfth century. At the same time, all over the south and east of Italy, the same sort of style, produced by the same Eastern influence, was almost universally adopted. Observe also that it is one of the most singular facts in the story of our art, that over the whole of this district hardly any real or active influence was exercised by the pointed arch. It was used, it is true, but not universally, *e g.* at St. Maria, Aquila, in 1315 A.D., and at Bitonto, so late as 1335, we have buildings mainly constructed with circular arches, a fact hardly to be paralleled in any other part of Europe, though in Southern Italy any number of similar examples exist.

I have said thus much about Pisan art in the twelfth century because it was in Pisa that one of the central figures of the time was born and trained. This was Niccola Pisano, born about 1205. Not very much is known of him or of his origin; but that little is somewhat wonderful, if we are to credit the statement that already, when he was only about fifteen years old, Frederick II. made him his architect, and took him to Naples, where he was employed on the castle which Frederick was building there. Thence, at twenty-six, we find him going to Padua to build the great church of Sant' Antonio, then to Arezzo, to build San Domenico. Then we find him developing his skill as a sculptor, executing pulpits for Pisa and Siena, and designing and, with the powerful aid of his son Giovanni, executing the great fountain at Perugia. I might fill in this chronicle of his work with many more details; but, short though it be, how interesting it is to us! He has been brought up, as we see, in Pisa, in the presence of the Cathedral and of the Baptistery, and of the circular tower begun in 1174 and completed probably before his eyes. He studies it, and then, after a few years at Naples (where he was surrounded on all sides by art of the same sort, as at Benevento, at Salerno, Amalfi, and Caserta Vecchia), he goes to the north of Italy. He visits Venice; for his first great work, the Church of Sant' Antonio, is evidently founded on a study of St. Mark's. But he is a thoroughly eclectic artist, picking up ideas where he can, and adapting them to his own purpose. He thinks the group of domes at St. Mark's might be improved if they were loftier, and if one was in some way more striking than the rest. Then he recollects the

great cone which covers the central portion of the circular Baptistery
at Pisa, and, with striking effect, places it in the centre of his group
of domes   Then he hears, no doubt, of the wonderful effect the
French architects were producing by the beautiful plans of their
chevets—apses surrounded by aisles and chapels—and determines
to imitate them. I say he "hears," for it is inconceivable that, after
having seen any of them, he should have planned anything so clumsy
and ill-conceived as the chevet of Sant' Antonio, a succession of square
chapels as badly designed as they well can be, which, nevertheless,
in the following century, seem to have been the model on which the
never completed choir of San Petronio, Bologna, was to have been
founded   Then, on the exterior, the façade recalls the outlines of
the Greek churches in the south with which he was familiar , whilst
on either side of the choir he builds with most picturesque effect
octagonal towers or turrets, unlike anything in the south, and sur-
passing any of those which had been erected somewhat on the same
lines before his time in Lombardy and along the course of the Rhine
The whole effect of this great church is singularly Eastern—more so,
even, than that of its prototype   Thus grew this great church—still
perfect, but, in spite of all its interest, lacking somewhat of the impress of a really great architect's hand, and not fit to be compared
for an instant with the far more refined and scientific churches which
the French architects had been building during the fifty years before
its foundation ; but, nevertheless, remarkable for the beautiful grouping of the external outline—a point seldom regarded by the early
Italian architects   It was after the design had been made for this
church that his best works as a sculptor were executed   And here,
again, we find him distinctly incorporating figures and ideas which
he derived from Roman sculptures preserved in Pisa. To these he
added, no doubt, so much and such intelligent study from the life
as to give great interest and pathos to his work, when compared with
most of the Italian work that had immediately preceded it, though
I am quite unable to admit that he was so much superior, as is
commonly asserted, to the French sculptors of the same time, of
whose names, and story, and training we know so little   His two
great works, in which he shows us the skill of the architect and
sculptor combined, are the pulpit in the Baptistery at Pisa and the
fountain at Perugia , and of about the same period is the purely
architectural work of Santa Caterina at Pisa.

The Italian pulpits of this century are among the most magnificent relics left to us   The examples which led up to Niccola
Pisano's work are of the type of Guido da Como's at Pistoia, a square
erection supported on columns resting on beasts, and with its sides
covered with sculpture   Niccola followed the idea, but improved
upon it.   He made his pulpit hexagonal, and carried it on trefoiled

arches resting on shafts supported on lions' backs. In this way he gave far more architectural character to his work than Guido da Como had done ; and not only is his sculpture better, but it is the combination of the two arts that most strikes us, whilst the delicate taste with which coloured marbles are used to enhance the beauty of the design is remarkable   The sculpture itself you can study, I believe, at South Kensington.   It shows a sense of the value of grouping, and of the natural treatment of emotions and action, which under his Italian predecessors had been almost wholly neglected or despised.   The type of figure which most affected him was not beautiful, and he always greatly exaggerated the size of his heads   But with any such criticisms as these one must admit, nevertheless that his work paved the way for all that was most excellent in the men who came after him.   He learnt something, no doubt, from such a man as Giunta da Pisa, who was flourishing when he was young, and Cimabue and his successors were aiding with equal power and zeal the work that he was doing.

Niccola Pisano died in 1278, and to the six years before his death two of his most exquisite works are to be attributed.   At Padua he had erected a great false front to Sant' Antonio, in which he sacrificed everything to breadth of effect   At Santa Caterina, Pisa, in 1272, he has left us a façade which is still false, as being a great gable which has no sort of relation to the shape of the building behind it, but the beauty of which is incontestable   Its simple, unbroken outline gives the breadth of which Niccola was so fond. Its lower stage is very quietly arcaded , above this is an arcade of trefoiled pointed arches, carried on detached shafts, standing so free from the wall as to give most 'vigorous light and shade , and above this again a circular window in the gable, flanked and surmounted by arcades like those below.   For an architectural composition, taken by itself, I know few more charming works than this   The steep gable looks like the effort of a man who had seen the steep gables of Northern Gothic, and wished to vie with them in this respect, as well as in the light and shade that northern climates require, but with which Italian architects generally seem not to have concerned themselves   Here, as in other works, we can trace the influence under which he worked   The Leaning Tower stood within a few hundred yards of the spot on which he was building, and his arcaded front is a very simple development of the effect which he admired in the arcaded walls of the Campanile—Niccola's arches being pointed and cusped where those of the Campanile are round, but otherwise being practically of precisely the same order of construction.   Niccola's other great and crowning work is the great fountain at Perugia   It is hardly possible to imagine a more charming work in every respect than this   It stands in an irregular piazza, midway between a cathedral of fair architectural interest, and the vastest Gothic palace after the Ducal Palace, Venice, that I know This, I suppose, was rising about the time that the fountain was erected, and at the same time the cathedral walls were being encrusted with a gay diaper of coloured marbles   The fountain consists of two enormous basins, the upper one supported by an apparently countless group of columns standing in the water which fills the lower one.   The capitals and columns are of various shapes The upper basin has figures at intervals all round, whilst the lower basin has a long series of square panels, separated from each other by clusters of moulded, chevroned, or spiral shafts.   Out of the centre of the upper basin rises a smaller one of metal, out of which the fountain plays.   The whole of the panels in this elaborate work are square, surrounded by mouldings, and Niccola Pisano showed his sculptor's sense in avoiding the common snare of introducing pointed arches for decoration where none are required.   Covered as his work is with elaborate sculpture, what is most felt is the extreme order and simplicity of the whole ; and when you go on to look in detail at the charming sculpture of saints and heroes and tutelars of the Church on the upper basin, and of the labours of the months, the signs of the zodiac, the arts and sciences, Romulus and Remus, and I know not who beside, on the lower basin, and notice how refined are the attitudes of the figures, how delicate the features, and how completely the whole are wrought into one perfect piece of architecture, you must be blind indeed if you do not recognise the grand character of the art of this central figure of the century.   It is true that the design is mainly what we owe to him, and that the execution of most of the sculpture was probably entrusted to his son Giovanni, and some possibly to Arnolfo di Lapo, but not the less is it a crowning work both of his life and of the century that he adorned.

I cannot leave Niccola Pisano without a few words about his son Giovanni.   He, too, was a great artist.   To my mind, it is in his work as a sculptor that there is most to admire, but like his father he was both architect and sculptor   His two most important architectural works are the Spina Chapel and the Campo Santo at Pisa ; and I suppose there is little doubt that it was he who, with singular skill, converted the exterior of the Romanesque Baptistery in the same city into a most picturesque and graceful Gothic work by the addition of a crowd of traceries, of pinnacles, and niches all round the base of its sombre dome.   I suppose that all of you know the Spina chapel.   Before its too wholesale restoration it was impossible not to love it for its eccentric beauty , but it was a beauty obtained in defiance of every law that, in my former lectures, I have told you to observe.   There is hardly a stone in its exterior that can be said to be structurally true. The steepest gables ever seen are put up at the east end of a building, with a roof of very moderate pitch; behind them are three spires, and then all along the side walls, to conceal the flat roof, a whole range of niches, surmounted by pinnacles of a fashion dear to Italian architects, and very pretty, where a statue is placed between four detached shafts, which carry the crocketed finials of the canopy. In all the work of the Pisani mistakes are made such as are never seen out of Italy. There is a most singular confusion of round and pointed arches. Their traceries, as we see them in the Campo Santo, are by no means well designed. They are indifferent about the subordination of orders in the tracery, and pack circles together as if they were entirely separate parts of the work, instead of combining them as the Northern architects did in perfect order, by means of continuous intersecting mouldings. Then their capitals seem always to be made with hardly any reference to the work they have to do. You have a large capital carrying a shrunken and insignificant archivolt And this is the more remarkable because elsewhere, at the same time, one of the most marked features is the way in which every capital had its exact and separate function, to which its size was accurately adjusted. In good architecture this must be the case, and I am obliged to sum up the work of the Pisani by saying that, with all their merits as sculptors, they were not equally good architects, and that in planning, in construction, and in obedience to the prime law of making their ornament grow out of their structure they sinned only too often; though at the same time the decided way in which Niccola at once threw aside the traditions in which he had been nursed is as remarkable as it is honourable to his artistic zeal and insight

I have said so much about the Pisani because they so exactly fill the canvas in this century, but, widespread as their work was, it would be a mistake to suppose that a description of it has at all exhausted what has to be said on the subject of Italian Gothic. A most remarkable fact, indeed, is that, whilst they were building in the way I have described, there were rising three churches of quite different but most admirable character in every respect, one at Vercelli (1219-22), another at Assisi (1228-53), and, lastly, Genoa Cathedral, of which the date is not certain

Vercelli was built, according to the tradition, by an English architect I do not quite believe this, though undoubtedly its details suggest a foreign hand, and are admirably good It is built of brick and stone coursed, all the sections of piers and mouldings and the details of the vaulting are admirable, and none of the faults are committed of which the Pisani were guilty every day. The ground plan is, in most respects, wholly unlike an Italian architect's work. The vaulting compartments of the aisles are square and those of the nave oblong, north and south, contrary to the Italian rule. The choir is square-ended, but the chapels of the transepts are apsidal. The detail of the clustered columns with their capitals and bases, of the groining, of the windows, is all completely like French work, and very admirable, and the Eastern triplet reminds me of England. It is only on the exterior, in fact, that any Italian character is given to the design; but even here there is far more attempt than is usually made to secure a picturesque *tout ensemble.* The west front is flanked by two lofty Italian towers or turrets. There is an octagonal central lantern, and, on the south side of the transept, a campanile placed at an eccentric angle with the rest of the work. A fine cloister and a chapter-house make this church very complete. Its builder was a Cardinal Guala, who had been for some years legate in England; he erected this church on his return, having evidently a wish to emulate some of the work he had learnt to admire in England and France.

San Francesco, at Assisi, is even more remarkable. The architect here is said to have been a German; but the evidence of the mouldings is, on the whole, more in favour of his having been a Frenchman. The singular fact, however, is that, as at Vercelli, this influence did not affect the exterior, which is designed completely in the local style, of which I shall have more to say.

At Genoa, again, we have a work of extraordinary beauty, and so skilfully planned and designed that it is almost impossible to suppose that it can have been wholly invented by its architect. It is evidently a work which is the outcome of a series of developments, and yet not one of the steps which could lead up to such a work are to be found in the neighbourhood or in Italy. It is, again, the work of a man who, if not a French architect, had at least been trained in France, and is so good that it cannot be dismissed without a somewhat careful notice. In the first place, it is to be observed that it is entirely built of black and white marble, the black, a limestone from Lavagna, which is well bonded into the wall, and, indeed, forms its substance; whilst the white is from Carrara, and is used in thin slabs, $3\frac{1}{2}$ inches thick, between the more solid courses of black. The system of using alternate courses of these two materials is carried here to the extremest point. This fashion was obtained, I have no doubt, by the Genoese from the East. You recollect what I told you in my last lecture about their wars and their commerce with Arabia and the East. And there is no fashion more noteworthy among the Arabian architects than this of the use of coloured materials in the way we see adopted at Genoa. Niccola Pisano and his followers had used a different system, and one which to me seems preferable. They used the two materials, but usually the black was in narrow bands on a field of white, placed where it aided by an emphatic line some architectural feature. This plan was adopted at Pisa, Lucca, and Siena. The Genoese adopted the more Eastern system of nearly equal courses of black and white. All their churches are built in this way, and from the simplest designs, such as that of San Matteo, Genoa, up to the extremely elaborate treatment of the detail in the cathedral, all agree in this ; and so prized was the system that in course of time it became an aristocratic privilege in Genoa to build in this fashion, the four great families of the Fieschi, Doria, Spinola, and Grimaldi alone sharing it with the municipality. No doubt the churches were under the protection of some one of them, and the cathedral probably of the governing corporation of the city. Cathedrals in those days were sometimes strangely used. At Genoa general assemblies of the people were held in the nave. Questions of peace and war were there settled by popular vote, and religious and political purposes seem equally to have been served by it. The nave was "renewed" in 1307, as an inscription tells us, but, I have no doubt, on the old lines. The west front and the western arch of the nave, with a groined gallery, are all of the first half of the thirteenth century. The architect—whoever he was—was bound by the black and white system of decorative construction. That, as we have seen, was a point of honour with his clients. He not only adopted the system of construction, but carried it on throughout his work by covering all the plain spaces between the shafts of his doorways with black patterns inlaid on white, and white on black, and in his arch mouldings he counterchanges the colours. The design for the front had three doorways, separated by buttresses. In order to show his decoration, the architect makes the jambs of his doorways simple splays, against which are set marble shafts—three large and four small—on each jamb. He leaves a good space between them, and on these spaces inlays an infinity of elaborate patterns. His bases are beautifully moulded with foliage carved under them, and in the carving of the capitals, and of a tree of Jesse on the jamb of the great doorway, we see the hand of a skilful sculptor, whose work is entirely different from anything that the Pisani were doing at the same time. The arch mouldings are all finely drawn, carved, and chevroned, and some of the marble shafts are spiral, and some carved. Above the central doorway there was the invariable Italian feature, a rose window, and the design included apparently the equally characteristic French feature of two western steeples, of which one only was in part built. Had the whole been completed as it was begun, we should have had in it one of the most exquisite works of the century, and interesting, as it seems to me, beyond measure, from the evidence it affords of the natural fusion of two systems of architecture—French and Eastern or Arabian—in a perfectly fine work. Whenever any of you have

the opportunity of studying this work on the spot, I counsel you first
of all to make yourselves acquainted with the two earliest doorways
in the west front of Rouen Cathedral.   There, in the most perfect
French work, you will see how the Northern architect, having only
one material—and that stone—nevertheless contrived to obtain the
same effect of black patterns on a white ground by deeply-cut patterns in the stonework.   And there is so much analogy between the
two works that I am disposed to think that the architect of Genoa
had seen the work at Rouen before he designed, in a somewhat
similar spirit, his great work at Genoa.   I ought to have added that
his nave arcades are carried upon circular columns, which, with the
arches above, are all built of alternate courses of black and white ;
and that a second arcade, opening to the aisle, takes the place of a
triforium.   Perhaps it is too ingenious to suggest that the architect
of the nave of Rouen had adopted the same singular device ; and
though his work was later in date than the two doors, it was no
doubt earlier than the nave of Genoa

Another very decorative front of about the same period, which
ought not to be forgotten, for it is equally unique in its way, is that
of the cathedral at Ferrara.   I have been unable to learn anything
as to its history.   It is an alteration of and an addition to an older
façade, carried up high above the roofs in three great equal gables,
arcaded and enriched with great boldness and beauty on every portion.   In the central division an elaborate porch of two stages in
height projects boldly from the front   This is gabled on three sides,
and has a sculpture of the Last Judgment scattered about in its
upper compartments.   I hardly know any front in Europe on which
so much work has been lavished.   And though it can hardly be
regarded as otherwise than very striking and interesting, it is impossible to look upon it as a piece of genuine work or construction.   It
is a front put on against the church, with no sort of connection with
it in outline or design.   It depends not on good proportions, but on
extraordinary richness of detail for its effect.   Its architect was not
satisfied to leave a stone unadorned throughout the whole upper part
of the building   His windows and arcades are crowded with shafts;
the mouldings are rich and effective ; and yet, beautiful as the work
is, it has the character of an imported design, and there are no other
buildings in the country which lead up naturally to it.

I hardly like to omit all mention of the cathedral at Ancona.
Here, on the very edge of a country almost given up to Byzantine
work, Margharitone, of Arezzo, is said to have built the front of the
cathedral—a charming composition, with a projecting porch carried
on detached shafts, a rose window above, and a very steep gable to
the porch and to the front   This is soon seen to be altogether a
false arrangement.   The design is made to be looked at only in

elevation; seen in that way it is very beautiful and well-proportioned. The gables have all stepped corbel tables, and the whole effect is surprisingly unlike any common Italian work; and yet the masonry was done by an Italian hand and no other. The doorway has an array of eight detached shafts set against a splay, as at Genoa. The shafts are alternately large and small; some of red marble, some of white, some spiral, and some octagonal; and the base is made of red and white marble and gray granite. The section of this jamb is like that of the west doorway at Genoa. All these works have some features in common which are not usually met with in Italian Gothic. These are the use of clustered columns, as at Vercelli and Genoa; clustered piers, as in the doorways at Ancona and Genoa, each shaft in which carries on its own capital a well-defined member of the arch; the use of buttresses, which at Vercelli are of considerable dimensions, and at Genoa are marked features—a rare occurrence, the Italian buttress being usually a mere pilaster round which a heavy cornice at the top of the wall is returned. Finally, the mouldings are good in the sense in which the best French mouldings are good. They are well drawn, have good light and shade, and are accurately fitted to their places. In all these respects these buildings are entirely unlike the work of Niccola Pisano, and in my opinion far more refined than it is. Moreover, there is no flavour whatever of the revived classicalism which was always evident in his work, and the effect of light and shade, which is striven for and obtained, is quite refreshing in the midst of the platitudes (if I may so call them) of the Italians.

The conclusion at which you may arrive from what I have been saying will be, perhaps, that the less indigenous Gothic architecture is in Italy the more beautiful it is. To a certain extent this is true, but to a certain extent only. There are other effects obtained by the Italians which well deserve admiration, and in every one of the buildings just mentioned it is to a part only, not to the whole, that it is possible to refer in terms of unmixed praise.

Before saying anything more, it is necessary that I should return again to the country which I referred to when speaking of the so-called "Greek" architect, Buschetto, at Pisa. The architects of the east and south of Italy, of whom he was one, were, in fact, practising an art which, even after their own time, was never really supplanted by Gothic work. And I know few parts of Europe which are more interesting. The work we see there is almost as unlike the contemporary work of France, England, Germany, or the north of Italy, as is that of the Moors executed at the same time in Spain. The churches are usually cruciform in plan, with a central and two smaller apses, all projecting from the east wall of the transept; and in this one respect they appear to owe more to the earliest Roman churches than to any others. But the whole of their decoration is wholly unlike Roman or Romanesque work. The arches are constantly used for ornament only, without being in any degree whatever constructional. Santa Maria, Ancona, is a good example of this. Here the whole front is covered with arches one above the other, literally carrying nothing. The intrados and extrados of the arches are commonly struck from different centres The arches are, indifferently, round and pointed The walls are divided into panels by small pilasters at short intervals, generally six or eight feet. These have heavy sculptured capitals, which carry arcades; and these, where there are no windows, are filled in either with circular or lozenge shaped panels of carved or inlaid work. The arches are frequently of horseshoe shape, as in the example shown of a window from Foggia, and some wall arcading from the same church. This is thoroughly Moorish work, and that it should be so is not much to be wondered at, for it is a few miles only from Lucera, where, as I told you in my last lecture, in the thirteenth century Frederick II. built one of the largest castles in Europe for his army of Saracen mercenaries, and gave them the cathedral for use as a mosque—a somewhat strong measure for one for whose character his contemporary, St. Louis, is said to have had great esteem. It is singular that this cathedral at Lucera should have some more than usually Northern features. The nave and transept have pointed arches and a small clerestory. But the three eastern apses are remarkable for having well-designed buttresses and good Gothic windows, with no trace whatever of the usual Eastern influence. The fronts of these South Italian churches are very uniform in arrangement, and their influence is felt all over the north of Italy down to the end of the fourteenth century. They are generally finished with a flat gable in the centre, and all the roofs are of the same pitch when there are aisles Even those gables which seem to follow the lines of the structure are often false. The windows in the fronts are almost invariably wheel windows, filled with delicate tracery, or sometimes with Moresque patterns, and always surrounded by a moulding or carved member, which seems entirely to separate them from the wall, on which they become ornamental panels There are usually flat pedimental canopies over the doors. At Aquila there are round-arched doorways, whose joints are covered with Gothic arcades and gabled and crocketed canopies, with three rose windows above and a wall diapered all over This front was really not finished till 1315, and yet at first sight it looks like a work of the twelfth century.

More to the west, and within reach of Naples, we see the same sort of influence rampant at Amalfi, at Minuto, Scala, Scaletta, Ravello, and Salerno. At Ravello, indeed, the Palace of the Rufolo family is a complete Moorish house, with its *patio* of two stories in height, its great gateway covered with a Moorish dome, and its enclosing walls adorned in true Moorish fashion. And the churches in its neighbourhood, though they are not Moorish in the same frank completeness, are full of evidence of the same influence. The Palazzo Rufolo was, I believe, built in the thirteenth century. The steeple of Amalfi Cathedral is of the same date—1276. Its lower stages have extremely stilted round-arched openings, and the upper stage is circular, with four circular turrets at the angles, the centre circle and the turrets being all covered with interlacing pointed arches. A central dome, similarly arcaded, rises over the church of Santa Maria, Ravello. The cloisters, which lend such a charm to Amalfi, are all similarly adorned, and you must note that the arcades project slightly from the face of the wall in all cases, so as to advertise the fact that they have nothing to do with its support ; whilst the very design equally shows that most of the apparently arcuated work is false and unnecessary. And they are without mouldings.'

My limits only allow me to speak of one other feature in these churches—the pulpits. I take one of those in the cathedral at Ravello as my text.[1] Its date is 1272, written on the marble by the " marmorarius "—as he called himself—of Foggia, who executed it. It is of white marble, inlaid with *opus Alexandrinum* in the richest possible manner. The six shafts which carry it are spirally moulded and inlaid with mosaic, and rest on lions' backs. The mosaic is all let into panels surrounded with carving of most delicate character. The brilliancy of the marble, the delicacy and bright colours of the endlessly varied patterns of glass mosaic, and the richness of the carving, make this certainly one of the most exquisite works with which I am acquainted. Nor is it less remarkable for some of its sculpture. The approach to it is by a staircase guarded at the foot by a doorway, over which is a bust of a queen, executed with considerable technical skill, and of a fair and stately presence. The size of this pulpit is very considerable, and it is one of many. Ravello alone has two others, a second in the cathedral, and one in San Giovanni of earlier date, Salerno two, Benevento two, Sessa one (of 1224 A.D., with round arches), Moscufo one (with horseshoe arches), and there are many more which it is needless to name. Here I must finish this episode. The art of Italy cannot be understood unless you realise thoroughly how completely different its history and development are from those of the rest of Europe at the same time. Few books put you *au fait* with this phase of architectural development, and I advise you to consult the only authority to whom I can send you—Von Quast and Schulz's great German

---

[1] For the possible influence of this pulpit on Niccola Pisano cf. Appendix I. vol. iii. Symonds's *Renaissance in Italy*.

work on the Architecture of South Italy. But it is by sketching and noting the peculiarities of these works for yourselves on the spot that you will alone really understand them.

From this group I turn now to the North, where at this time many churches were built, conceived much more in the spirit of the early Gothic style than the former were. Of these the best examples for our purpose are those of the Frari and SS Giovanni è Paolo, Venice, Santa Corona and some others at Vicenza, Santa Anastasia at Verona, and at quite the end of the century the churches of Santa Maria Novella and Santa Croce in Florence. Some Roman examples existed, but these have been so much altered and modified that it is a little difficult to refer to them. The Church of the Ara Cœli and Santa Maria sopra Minerva are the best preserved. In all these the plan is very similar. They have the usual Italian peculiarity of a transept, out of which a large apse in the centre and smaller ones on each side are projected. Their naves are generally divided into bays, which are absolutely square, whilst the aisle compartments are oblong in the direction of the length of the building. This is exactly opposed to the usual French and English system. It gives arches of great span, and columns placed very far apart, and one of the results of such an arrangement is that the buildings in which it occurs always look smaller than they really are. The columns are usually plain—circular or octagonal—of great size; there is hardly any moulding on the arches, and the clerestory consists usually of a series of small circular windows, one to each bay. The walls have deep cornices. At Santa Anastasia, Verona, and at the Frari, Venice, the apsidal chapels have the rare peculiarity of being planned with an angle in the centre, with a by no means bad effect. Most of these examples are built of brick, and many have timber roofs to the naves and transepts, and groining to the apses and aisles only. They are thoroughly fine and useful buildings, and though nowhere to be classed in the first rank of architectural works, are yet, I think, the group of buildings which best deserve study of all that I have mentioned. In them as elsewhere I see much to condemn as well as to admire. Their window traceries are seldom agreeable, and never really skilful. Usually they appear to be pieces of tracery wrought in a single stone, and then cut off to fit the arch under which they are placed. But, on the other hand, there are many features of extreme beauty. Among these are the porches and monuments. These are commonly built with arches springing from single shafts, with flat gables and canopies over them. Of course, such erections could not stand for an hour without assistance, and this is at once given by an iron tie-bar connecting the capitals. But, with this assistance, there was still felt to be an air of instability in the arch, and this was ingeniously overcome by the addition of a heavy cusp on the under side of the arch, which gave the required effect by appearing to bring the weight within the line of the columns.[1]   So much depended on this cusp that it is generally drawn with the greatest care, and this detail shows as much as any the real artistic skill of the architect.   Nowhere in Europe is there a more exquisite architectural group than in the little burial-ground of the Scaliger family at Verona.   The larger monuments are all of this type, with the addition of a heavy pyramid crowned by a figure on horseback rising from behind the gables.   The sculpture which adorns these works is also excellent—very flat, and in low relief, but full of evidence of careful study of natural forms.   In almost all of these churches the use of coloured materials is more or less common.   Unfortunately, few of the marble fronts with which they were intended to be finished were ever completed.   The lower part of Sta. Anastasia, Verona, where the soft and delicate mouldings of the door-jambs are built in alternate courses of red, white, and gray marble, is of exquisite beauty.   Such a construction, I need hardly say, brings out with great distinctness the most delicate shades of difference in the mouldings.   It led the way naturally, also, to the final example of the most perfect arrangement of colour in construction, seen in such a work as Giotto's tower at Florence, which, it can hardly be doubted, was the result of his acquaintance with this beautiful work at Verona, for only a short time before, in 1294, Arnolfo had faced the Baptistery hard by with black and white marble in equal courses, after the fashion of the Genoese builders and of the architect of the tower at Siena.   Unfortunately, the custom was to build a blank brick wall at the west ends of the Italian churches, with the idea of completing the work at some future time by the erection of a magnificent marble front, and in a number of instances we find the lower part of this, at the most, existing.   The Cathedral and Sta. Croce, Florence, and San Petronio, Bologna, are illustrations of this habit, in addition to the church just mentioned at Verona.

In all accounts of architectural progress it is the religious architecture of the country that first of all attracts our attention.   It is there that we see men's greatest efforts, executed in the most permanent fashion, and usually the examples of them which are still to be seen are manifold more numerous, and have a history much more accurately recorded, than have the other buildings erected for secular purposes at the same time.   But in Italy the life of the people in the cities, with which the land is so richly studded, was so active, so prosperous often, and so self-reliant, that it may almost be said, in many cases, that the secular buildings are of as much

[1] Cf. what Ruskin says of the monument standing over the small cemetery gate at Sta. Anastasia, Verona, *Stones of Venice*, vol. i. p. 137 (edit. 1851).

importance as the ecclesiastical. Every important city had its
public building—Broletto, Palazzo Publico, or Comunale, or della
Ragione—in which its affairs were transacted, and where the courts
of justice sat. In addition to these there were an infinite number of
palaces built by the wealthy citizens whose families formed everywhere the aristocracy, and generally went on from century to century
in the same city, either governing it or taking an active concern in its
affairs. Very many of these buildings are as perfect now as they were
when first built; and in Volterra, Siena, Florence, Perugia, Pisa,
Lucca, Orvieto, Piacenza, Bologna, Como, Milan, and above all in
Venice (but of a later date), so many remain that we are able to
form an accurate and fairly complete idea of what these great buildings were. Most of them were founded in the thirteenth century,
but enlarged and altered greatly in the fourteenth. Volterra has its
palace, built between 1208 and 1257—a large simple unbuttressed
building, without any sort of break in its simple outline. It was of
four stories in height. Its windows, placed irregularly to suit the
rooms, are of trefoiled lights under an enclosing arch, and the lights
are divided by a delicate column in place of a mullion. At the
back rises a tower intended to carry the city bell. The doorways
are simple pointed arches, without any sort of moulding. In this
case, as in most buildings of the period, we find a regular series of
holes in the wall above and below the windows. There can be no
doubt that these were intended for the timber supports of wooden
balconies, and that so far from the effect having ever been intended
to be what it now is, absolutely without shadow, the building in its
original state was as picturesquely varied as was possible by the deep
shadows of these balconies, through which the still darker openings of
the windows were dimly seen. Not far from Volterra is San Gemi-
gnano, where there are not only old houses, but, still standing almost
perfect, a group of lofty towers, which gives the city the strangest possible appearance. Each family erected as part of its home one of
these towers. They are very lofty, almost without openings, and with
no attempt at architectural decoration. Probably this was confined to
an overhanging parapet supported on machicolations at the top, and
two great coats of arms emblazoned on the parapets or walls. They
have but little architectural interest, but as they were universal in
Central Italy I cannot omit to mention them. In Florence the
most important work of the period is the Palace of the Podestà—a
good deal altered, and now turned into a museum. This was built
round a courtyard, on the walls of which the Florentines, who were
always desperately fond of heraldry, have inserted in all parts their
coats of arms. Open arcades are built on three sides of the court.
A great uncovered staircase leads up to a corresponding gallery with
open arcades on the principal floor, and access is gained to the

various halls and chambers from this. The arches used are sometimes round, sometimes pointed, and the details are all of the severest and simplest type. Here, as at Volterra, wooden balconies, with roofs on the topmost, were carried along in front of the upper floor, so as to give access independent of that through the rooms themselves. The walls were crowned with an immense overhanging battlement, and a tower rose out of one angle. In the plan, the site being somewhat irregular, no care was shown to make the rooms or corridors or courtyard rectangular. Yet probably not one in a thousand of those who annually go to admire this really splendid building notices the irregularity.

Of other buildings of the same class and date, I shall mention only two or three. The Palazzo della Ragione, Milan (1228), is one of the best. This has an open arcade on the ground story; above this a double string-course forming a range of panels with coats of arms, and breaking forward in the centre as a balcony or ringhiera—a common and beautiful feature. The principal floor has also its open arcade on a grand scale, and above this, under the eaves, is a smaller continuous arcade, occupied at intervals by grouped figures in three divisions. The elements of such a composition are extremely simple; none, I think, can fail to be charmed with the effect, and it teaches us a lesson as to the results to be obtained by delicately designed elevations, depending entirely upon good proportion and light and shade. Coming from Tuscany to such a building as this, or to the Broletto at Como, one is much struck by the wholly different temper shown in them. The Florentines and their neighbours seem always to have built in a severely, almost savagely simple fashion. You feel as if ornament were proscribed—as if strong and lofty walls, tall unbroken towers, frowning parapets, sparsely lighted chambers, were required by their laws or their temper. The gateways and walls of Florence were grand examples of a savage sort of simplicity—enormous in size and extent, simple to a degree in detail, but executed with an amount of care and solidity which is very admirable. Sad it is to use the past tense of such works as these. Unhappily Florence for a short period dreamed that she was to be the capital of United Italy, and in order to fit herself for the position set to work to demolish her walls, and to leave her gateways standing out alone in the midst of new boulevards, with the sole result of almost ruining herself financially as well as from an artistic point of view. The works at Milan and Como affect one as do the slightly later arcades of the Ducal palace—one feels that life was meant to be pleasant and enjoyed, and that the architect's first thought was how to make it more and more enjoyable.

Another important domestic work, begun in 1281, is the Palazzo

Publico of Piacenza   This has its lower stage entirely supported on open arches, giving on to the piazza in front, and to the usual enclosed court in the centre.   The whole of the lofty lower stage is of white and red marble, whilst the upper is of red brick, with a marble cornice supporting a Ghibelline battlement   All the detail is extremely elaborate, and the brickwork especially is designed with extreme care.   The supporting arches are pointed, the decorative arches semicircular, and all the windows have coupled shafts in place of mullions   Recesses are formed in the wall for paintings, of which traces still remain.   The great advantage which the study of these Italian domestic buildings affords to us is that to a very great extent they show us a noble class of work, dignified, grave, and often very beautiful in detail, and in almost all respects capable of being used consistently with our own notions of comfort and convenience   They are of great extent, and their chambers are lofty and large.   The treatment of their windows is particularly worth notice   The stonework is complete in itself, shafts take the place of our mullions, and balconies are often provided in front of the windows   The glass is fixed in a wooden frame set behind the window shafts, so as not to interfere with their effect.   In the larger houses there is generally a courtyard, in the centre of which is the well.   The ground story is either supported on open arches or appropriated for cellars, stores, etc, and the staircase leads up at once and often from the courtyard of the house to the Piano Nobile. Here the rooms are of fine dimensions, some of the more important being vaulted, and, if we picture them to ourselves as they once were, we may imagine no reasonable amount of comfort as wanting They were the abodes of civilised people, much larger and more stately altogether than we are in the habit of making our homes, and full of suggestiveness for us   On the other hand, there were peculiarities which fortunately we do not want to imitate.   The more important houses had towers attached to them, erected for purposes of defence.   They have no openings beyond those required for the discharge of missiles   Their battlements were swallow-tailed if the owner belonged to the Ghibelline party, square if to the Guelphs.   From their walls were bracketed forward timber platforms, by means of which the approach to the doorway could be commanded.   They are almost invariably plain square buildings, without break or buttress of any sort, and though sometimes of great size nearly always extremely simple in design and detail, and really more like large square chimneys than anything else.   Would that I could tell you more on this head! but the time is too short, and I have left much unnoticed that I ought to have touched upon. There are, for instance, those vast Halls of Assembly at Padua and Vicenza, the former no less than 90 feet wide and 280 feet long;

the latter smaller, but still 72 feet wide. They have simple arched wooden roofs of dark timber, and the walls at Padua are covered with paintings, which have been well described in the *Annales Archéologiques* by my friend Mr. William Burges. Then there are the cloisters, which are so numerous and so beautiful. Many of them are of two stages in height, and their long series of arches in each stage are carried on coupled marble shafts. Some of the best are at Verona and Genoa, and of a more elaborate kind are those of St. John Lateran and St. Paul without the walls at Rome. These last are carried on coupled or quadrupled shafts, plain, moulded, or spiral; their arches are semicircular; they have rich and rather classical cornices, and are filled in wherever there is a plain space, and round the arches, with lovely decoration in glass mosaic. These were probably executed by one of the Cosmati family, who, in the convent of Sta. Scholastica, at Subiaco, in the wild glen which leads to the mountain sacred to St. Benedict and St. Francis, built a simpler cloister of the same sort, and left his name inscribed on the cornice. Beautiful as many of our English cloisters are, I think they never quite equal these Italian examples. One is charmed by the grace and simplicity of the design, by the beautiful proportion of the arcades, and by the evident skill of the men who contrived to carry their walls upon such delicate couples or clusters of columns, without any appearance of their being too weak for their work. I ought also to tell you of the baptisteries, beginning with the austere examples at Parma and Lucca, and going on to Pistoia, Cremona, Asti, Florence, and many more. They are almost all polygonal or circular buildings, Lucca being the only exception, and many of them delightful, not only in design, but in the decorations which have been added to them. I ought also to speak to you of the domes of this period, which we see at Ancona, at Sta. Maria, Arezzo, and elsewhere. Not less does the Italian treatment of towers demand notice. They are either entirely without buttresses, or with small pilasters at the angles, and repeated once or twice on each face. Each stage is similarly adorned, and usually they are repetitions one of the other. A good example is the campanile of the cathedral at Viterbo. For some fifty feet in height it is a plain mass of masonry. Above this, four stages of coursed black and white stone, each stage having two two-light windows, and divided from the next by decided string cornices, complete the elevation of the tower, above which is a very low spire, a feature constantly introduced. This sort of design is of common occurrence. Evidently it is taken directly from the early Roman campaniles, of which so many still remain. I ought to say much more about these towers, which are so striking a feature of Italian buildings; but not less ought I to say something as to the monuments which everywhere adorn the walls of the cathedrals and churches, both inside and out, and oftentimes the piazza by their side. But time fails me, I have detained you long, and my only fear is, having had so many things to speak of, that I may not have dwelt long enough or with sufficient thoroughness on the many points which I wish to impress on your memory. My hope is that if any of you have not concerned yourselves with the subject hitherto, I may have induced you to take an interest in what really contains matter for study of equal importance to all of you, whether painters, sculptors, or architects

To sum up shortly what the study of Italian art teaches us in the thirteenth century, I think it may be said that, unlike the nations of the north of Europe, the Italians never completely or heartily accepted or worked out the changes which came naturally from the use of the pointed arch. They never really realised what its use led to. Their system of groining, for instance, is from first to last simple to a degree. No difficult problems were ever faced or solved in its construction. Ground-plans were never carefully studied; there is little ingenuity or skill displayed in them, and hardly any improvement on those which the earliest Roman church builders had left them in such churches as St. Paul without the walls or the Basilica at Aquileia. This is the more strange because some of the early Italian plans are extremely good, and the fondness shown for the circular form in so many baptisteries might have been expected to produce the same effect as it certainly did in Rome. The plan for the small baptistery at Albenga, with its alternate circular and square recesses and its central dome, ought naturally to have led to something far better than Niccola Pisano's apse at Padua. And it is very strange, seeing that the Italians almost always used the apsidal east end, that they should so very rarely have built an aisle and chapels round it, though they must have been aware of the singularly fine effects that their neighbours in France were achieving at the same time. Their sole care was, in fact, to make their ornament beautiful. It never occurred to them that the proper work of an architect is first of all to make his plan as beautiful, as economic in its use of material, and as light and elegant, as is consistent with stability. They were extremely careless about the general outlines of their buildings. On the exterior, sham gables and false constructions of all sorts abound, and the proportions are seldom agreeable, and any attempt to produce fine effects by combinations of the steeples with the buildings to which they are attached is extremely rare, even if it was ever attempted. The mouldings used are not good in themselves, or drawn with any real feeling for the light and shade to be produced by them, and when they are used for an archivolt, they are usually set upon the capital which receives them in so careless and ignorant a manner as

to produce the worst possible effect. The Italians never seem to
have cared much whether they used a pointed or a round arch ;
indeed, they hardly realised that one gave them more power than
the other, and consequently the sort of constructions to which they
confined themselves were nearly always such as could just as well be
contrived with a round as with a pointed arch. The feature which
more than any other distinguishes true Gothic work—the buttress
—is rarely used.[1] If it is, this is generally for ornament only, and
I do not recollect an instance of a flying buttress. The Italians
never discovered that the proper disposal of buttresses, so as to meet
thrusts and weights at given points, was far more economical than
the persevering use of thick walls without buttresses. Another
difference is that almost all real Italian ornament is applied, and
does not in the least belong to the structure. An Italian window is
ordinarily surrounded by a moulding, which makes a sort of frame
for it. The English window of the same age has a moulding above
it to throw off rain, but elsewhere its mouldings are really cut in the
wall itself, so that the window appears to be what it is—a necessary
part of the fabric. In addition to these peculiarities the treatment
of windows was never very good. The best examples are the
domestic windows in which shafts take the place of monials with
very beautiful effect, but these seldom led to the execution of anything like our Northern traceries ; the spandrels between the centres
of the window lights and the enclosing arches being seldom pierced,
and often left with no relief—perfectly plain. The circular windows
in the west fronts are innumerable. Their tracery, when it remains,
is generally of the fourteenth rather than of the thirteenth century.
One of the very best examples of the latter period anywhere is in
the west front of the Church of Sta. Maria, Toscanella, in which
the doorways, and the arcade between them and the window, are
carved profusely with well-executed dog-tooth enrichments. This
window is rightly called a wheel. It consists of three circles, each
divided into panels by columns, which take the place of spokes, and
between these sharply pierced cusped circles give a brilliant effect
of light and shade to this beautiful design. One goes to Toscanella
to see Etruscan walls and remains, and I confess to a real sensation
of delight when in this sad and forlorn old church standing with the
cathedral outside the walls, and unused apparently, save by a hermit,
who divides his time between them, I came upon so thoroughly
charming a feature as this window and front.

The Italians, as we have seen, were always very open to accept
fragments of work from other lands, it mattered not in what style.
They employed Greeks, Moors, Frenchmen, Germans, Catalonians,

[1] Ruskin speaks of the absence of buttresses as being one of the best features
of Italian campanili.

side by side, at the same time. (They are also said to have examples of Norman and Angevine art, but of this I have never seen any evidence whatever.) The architecture of Italy admits less than that of the rest of Europe of regular classification It was very eclectic. There was no passion for any one style all over the country. The architects rather than architecture ruled; and each had his own fashion and way of working. Then, again, the architects were usually sculptors, and as their taste for the sister art increased, they seem to me somewhat to have sacrificed the elder to her younger sister With so much that is disappointing, uncertain, and unprogressive, there are, however, redeeming features which will always render the study of early Italian art not only most instructive, but, at the same time, most fascinating. The beauty of many of the features in detail is as great as it well can be; and the taste with which coloured materials are used in construction is far in advance of anything that the rest of Europe can show, either then or afterwards The Italians inherited an admiration for, and a due sense of the charm of, detached columns These, being used for their own beauty, were constantly made to taper slightly, and were used frequently to carry heavy weights, though with the closest approach to insecurity In no country is the use of these delicate shafts brought to such perfection. The shaft is used by itself, coupled with another, and in groups of four and of five. Sometimes a precious block of marble is cut into four shafts, apparently knotted together in the centre. It is spiral, fluted, moulded, and carved. It is used with great constructive skill, an arcade carried on small coupled shafts carrying, as at Genoa, a second cloister above. The arches of these cloisters are as simple as they can be, but the shafts are so delicate, and their caps and bases so well proportioned, that I doubt whether any cloisters are more beautiful.

In spite of all such architectural shortcomings, it must be said that in the combination of painting and architecture all other architectural schools were hopelessly distanced by the Italians. All that is beautiful in their work struck root in the thirteenth century; and it is in the magnificent Church of St. Francis, on the steep lower slopes of the Apennines, that we see already in perfection the combination of the two arts. There are here three churches, one above the other, built round the tomb of St. Francis. One enters the middle church by a pointed doorway between walls panelled with the red marble of Perugia, in a lovely diaper of cusped circles. A dark and sombre collection of chapels, decorated on all sides by the painters of the thirteenth and fourteenth centuries, leads one on to the altar Here cunningly wrought screens of iron between marble columns guard the sacred central spot, and as the eye becomes by degrees accustomed to the half-light, one sees and understands the subjects and colours which Giotto and others have left on vault and pillar and wall. The upper church was meant to be entered by a fine western doorway, but this is seldom open now ; and after drinking in this strange and mystic effect of the crypt, access is gained by a small newel staircase to the upper church. The change is one of the most startling that I know. From the darkest of sanctuaries you find yourself in a minute transferred to the brightest, the most beautiful, the most joyous. The architecture of the upper church is light and graceful, the windows are large, and the walls from the floor to the centre of the vaulted roof are covered with paintings, the whole of which are bright in tone, beautiful in arrangement, and, as it seems to me, full of the most exquisite sentiment, if the draughtsmanship is imperfect. Cimabue commenced his works at Assisi in 1265 A.D. The roof and walls of the nave were then ready for him and entirely undecorated. The former, at least, is either his work or that of his immediate followers. The nave is of four bays in length. He painted the first bay with figures of the Four Doctors of the Church, and the third with the Virgin, St. Francis, and St. John the Baptist. The intermediate bays he covered with mere decorative colour—blue studded with stars—the grounds of the subjects being gorgeous with yellow or gold. Borders of exquisite design and variety follow all the leading lines of the construction. The figures show, it is true, no few traces of Greek or Byzantine teaching and influence, but the simple dignity of their attitudes and draperies, the charm of the general system of colour, and the grand decorative effect produced by the alternated bays of subject and ornament, leave little to be desired. Nowhere, indeed, in the whole realm of art can one put one's hand on a work in which the triumph of the Italian school of the thirteenth century is more certainly seen or more universally acknowledged than it is here. And if I have been critical to-night as to what appear to me to be the shortcomings of Italian architects, you will perceive by the terms in which I conclude that the criticism comes from one who appreciates with enthusiasm what he holds to be the real and undying beauty and interest of this great period in the history of Italian art.

LECTURE V

THIRTEENTH-CENTURY ARCHITECTURE—FRANCE [1]

OUR subject to-night is one of inexhaustible interest and extent.
You have gathered from what I said to you about Italy, in my
last lecture, how worthy the art of this age is of our deepest and
most reverent study; and there is no branch of it which is more
worthy of respect than that which had so active, and indeed
extraordinary a growth in France, from the middle of the twelfth
down to the end of the thirteenth century.   You are all aware, no
doubt, that France, as we now know it, is a country gradually com-
pacted out of a number of states or divisions, and that it was in the
thirteenth century, under two distinguished sovereigns, the saintly
Louis and the warlike Philip Augustus, that the greatest strides
were made in welding together the kingdom of which then, as now,
the Ile de France, with Paris as its capital, was both the political
and the artistic centre.   The various provinces preserved, however,
so much of their own traditions and tastes, that each presents its
own local variation of style, which was rather intensified than otherwise during the thirteenth and fourteenth centuries   The buildings
of Burgundy, of Anjou and Poitou, of Normandy, of Picardy, and
of Champagne, are so different in their character, that in the thirteenth century a man might almost have known where he was by
the aspect of the architecture   The same sort of difference that existed between the north and south of Italy is visible in the north
and south of France   But in the latter, the art of the north is again
separated into a number of divisions answering to the provinces
To attempt in one evening to describe all these variations would be
absurd, and I shall confine myself, therefore, merely to the architecture of Paris and its neighbourhood.   It is necessary, before I
do this, to take you back to the twelfth century, in order that you
may see what the state of French art was then, and what promise it

[1] Fifth lecture, delivered on Monday, 28th February, to the Students of the
Royal Academy.

gave of the fruit which was brought to such great perfection so soon afterwards.

The great burst of enthusiasm for building which occurred in the eleventh century has left traces in all directions; and for a century before 1150 the works still remaining are conspicuous for their admirable workmanship, skilful planning, and finished detail. Without dwelling on all these points, it will be sufficient to confine ourselves to a study of their ground-plans. Here there is vast variety; but the plan which, on the whole, is evidently the most favoured, occurring in various stages of development in almost all parts of the country, is worth examining, because it evidently contained the germs of the great thirteenth-century cathedrals. In this the chevet, or east end, is founded on the Roman and Byzantine plans, finishing with a circle around which are set at intervals small circular chapels—three, four, or five in number—which give great variety to the plan both inside and out. As an example of these, I may mention a church of the early part of the twelfth century—Nôtre Dame du Port, Clermont-Ferrand—where the covering of the aisle is a continuous barrel vault; those of the chapels, semi-domes; whilst the central portion has a barrel vault finished at the end in a semi-dome. The construction here is extremely ingenious. The builder had resolved that his work should last for ever; he roofed every part with stone vaults, covered outside with stone roofs, using no timber whatever in their construction. He accomplished this by giving his aisles quadrant vaults, so as to have a continuous flying buttress supporting the continuous thrust of the central vault.

What strikes one in these early churches is the resolve of their builders to make them imperishable, and the scientific disposition of their vaulted roofs, which, in the chevet, owing to the combination of the aisle-chapels with the vaulted aisle, is extremely effective in perspective. The outside is mainly remarkable in this case for the use of coloured materials; but the exteriors do not affect my argument, so I omit all notice of them. One evidence of the scientific character of these buildings is that they are generally designed upon some regular system of proportion. At Nôtre Dame du Port the height and width of the church are equal; and if these are divided by four, two parts give the width of the nave, two the height of the main arcades, three that of the triforium arcade, and four the total. From first to last we cannot but be struck by the scientific and regular way in which the work is done. The same plan is seen in a number of examples, most of which—as St. Etienne, Nevers—have the improved arrangement of three chapels to the apse, in place of the four at Nôtre Dame du Port. The Church of the Holy Sepulchre is the venerable original of such plans as these, and its example is

of special interest, inasmuch as the eastern part of the church, built
by the Crusaders, gives us the Auvergnat plan almost without modification, *vis-à-vis* to the apse of Constantine, which had precisely
the same sort of outline at the western end of the building

This common French plan of the apse is, we have seen, a development from a Byzantine original. The section of the vaults
suggests the use of a flying buttress, and is, indeed, so nearly being
one, that it was not a great step to develop a construction which
should bring all the weight and thrust to one point, instead of
equally along the whole length of the wall. This was done in the
quadripartite aisle vaults, and it was only necessary to repeat them
in the central vault to make the quadrant vault or continuous flying
buttress over the aisles quite unnecessary. And so gloomy is the
interior of churches constructed in this way, that the absence of the
clerestory, so long used in earlier unvaulted buildings, must have
seemed even to the men who were building them a most serious de-
fect; and it is not surprising, therefore, that the combination of this
with a stone vault was, above all things, what men soon strove for.
At the same time, in the west of France, churches were being built
on plans even more obviously derived either directly from the east,
or indirectly thence through Venice. Of the latter class the most
remarkable was the well-known example of St. Front, Perigueux.
Here, whatever the origin of the design, we have domes carried on
pointed arches springing from piers which, at their base, recall completely the planning of St. Mark's, Venice, and Sta. Fosca, Torcello ,
and the story of a Venetian colony settled at Perigueux is not required in order to prove that the example, if not of Venice, at any
rate of countries from which the Venetians derived St. Mark's, was
followed there.

At Cahors, in a church founded in 1100, we see a nave covered
with domes, one to each bay, finished with an apse, and three chapels
of the Auvergnat type ; whilst at Angoulême, at the same date, there
is a nave covered with three domes, and a choir with four chapels as
at Nôtre Dame du Port, Clermont, though in these two examples
there are no aisles, the chapels opening out of the central apse, after
the fashion of Constantinople and Venice

The churches in which domes or semi-domes may be found in
the centre, south, and west of France are numberless And it is
very remarkable that, after having been so popular a feature in the
eleventh and twelfth centuries, the dome should have been so entirely abandoned in all later buildings The reasons for this are
obvious Admirable as the effect of a dome is, long experience has
proved that there is no form of construction which entails so much
waste of material, or such massive supports and buttresses. The
French architects set themselves the task of making their buildings

as light in their construction as was possible, consistently with endurance. They desired, too, to make them useful for large congregations, and they had discovered by experience how difficult it was to control the acoustic properties of a domed building. Even if they confined themselves to a central dome, the points of support were enormous masses of masonry just at the places where their inconvenience was most felt. Their common sense led them to desire the admission of light in their comparatively gloomy climate, in place of the sombre effects which are almost a necessity when the domes are solidly built of stone or brick.

As regards architectural detail in France at this early period, it is to be noticed that in a great number of buildings it was of extraordinary delicacy and beauty of execution. The three western doorways of Chartres, a doorway in St. Benigne, Dijon, the south door of the nave of Le Mans, and the north and south doorways of Bourges Cathedral, all date from about 1150. They are remarkable not only for the really astounding skill of the mechanics who wrought the curious sculptures with which their columns and other members are covered, but for the remarkable fact that among the branches of foliage, in which the utmost skill of Byzantine artists is rivalled, nude figures and animals are represented, with a feeling for nature which is all the more surprising when compared with the stiff and conventional representations of life-size human figures in the same work. Not long after these works a cathedral was built, evidently by French artists, at Santiago in Spain. It was a close copy of St. Sernin at Toulouse—a vast church on the same plan as the Auvergnat examples—and in its south transept doorways are columns carved with just the same desire to represent the nude figure accurately as in the case just mentioned, and so well executed that if done before our eyes now, they would extort admiration from all. One other building must also be named as an example of delicacy in purely architectural work, the chapter-house of St. George de Boscherville, near Rouen. Here there is no sculpture of figures, and what is chiefly to be noticed is the beauty of execution, which is quite consummate. The century closes with an example of still greater excellence in the two earliest of the western doorways of Rouen Cathedral, in which the beauty of design and the perfection of the work leave nothing to be desired. I know no detail more worthy of study, and the wonder is that more work conceived in the same spirit was not executed. The only parallel work with which I am acquainted is that of the western doors of Genoa Cathedral, to which I have before referred, and in which the ornamentation is obtained by the use of black and white marble, while, in the Rouen examples, it is produced by deep cuttings in the stone. This, however, is a somewhat later work. The end of the twelfth century sees France,

then, covered with buildings, mainly churches (though all the others
show the same art), built with great skill on well-defined plans, and
adorned with details of really exquisite beauty   So far the work had
been done with zeal, but under considerable hindrances.   At first the
grandest buildings were those of the great monasteries.   Their designers were, no doubt, ecclesiastics, and the laity were comparatively
unconcerned   But now there is a great change.   The people take
the matter out of the hands of the Church   The architects are no
longer clergy, and, supported by the suddenly awakened zeal of the
people, laymen form themselves at once into a body with the most
scientific aims and methods, and are every day found trying some new
device for the development and improvement of their work.   In a
few years they had changed everything; they had discovered how
to utilise the pointed arch, and this discovery seems to have been
like a revelation to them   The arch itself was known long before
its utility was realised.   It had been used constantly for some fifty
years   The arches which had to carry most weight, and whose
thrust it was desirable to limit, were the first to be built in this
shape   The French builders had found, no doubt, how easily a
round arch becomes weakened, and how serious the results are of
the least giving way of the supports.   But at first they saw no special
beauty in the pointed arch, and adhered to the round arch for beauty
and to the pointed for strength   This fact is a good illustration of
the very practical character of the French architects.   They loved
and admired the old form, but in face of a practical advantage it
was at once abandoned in favour of the new one   When once the
pointed arch had been well used, and had come to be understood,
their eyes were suddenly opened to perceive the powers its use conferred on them.   In a few years, from being carvers they became
sculptors, and at almost a single bound, from being very moderate
because very conventional artists, they became the best and most
skilful designers and constructors the world has ever seen.   And
the artist was so careless of everything but the perfection of his
work, that it is rare indeed that we know his name, or anything
about the way of his life, or the manner in which he set to work at
the development of his plans

The French architects at this time had emancipated themselves
thoroughly and once for all from old traditions.   They found that
the use of the pointed arch gave them a power in construction such
as had never before been wielded   Before their time it was the vast
mass of building or of wall, the great size of the single stones which
composed it, no less than the art which decorated them, which had
impressed the mind.   Now it was seen that this was not the best
way of securing the desired result.   Every day attempts were made
to improve the construction by making it more delicate and graceful.

The size of the piers was reduced ; windows were enlarged, and raised high up in the walls ; the construction was of a most permanent kind, and yet it was all provided for with the least waste of material, so that the comparison between the voids and the points of support is made always largely to the credit of the Gothic architects, whenever it is made at all between their buildings and the works of the schools which preceded and succeeded them.

The names of the architects whose works are so familiar to all students are, I repeat, either unknown, or, if we know them, that is usually about all that can be said. In my last lecture we had a great deal of personal matter, for, in Italy, you are able sometimes to follow the architect about from one work to another, and you see him now architect, now sculptor, and sometimes even painter also. In France we know much less of the life of the artist. We have the names of a good many ; among them of four architects in succession at Amiens—of Robert de Coucy, the architect of Rheims, whose design was faithfully carried out by his four successors ; of Eudes de Montreuil, who went to the Holy Land with St. Louis ; and of many more. But were it not for the fortunate preservation of the sketch-book of one of them—a friend, probably, of Robert de Coucy —we should know but little of their mode of life, or thought, or work. This sketch-book or album was the property of Willars de Honecort, and it brings before us an architect in the early years of the thirteenth century wandering about on business or pleasure, visiting cathedrals, making notes and sketches of them, and evidently studying how best to improve himself. He interests himself in the best way of cutting stones, of lifting them into place, of setting out lines for work, and so forth. He sees a lion, and forthwith sketches him, putting on his sketch (a note which may be freely translated), " Mind you, this lion was alive." He draws figures and designs for sculpture ; he goes to Laon and makes a sketch of one of the western steeples, and writes below it, what most of us who have looked at and sketched it, as he did, would have agreed with : " I have been in many countries, as you may see by this book, but in no place have I seen a tower equal to that of Laon." And then, after a description of its plan, he adds, somewhat oracularly, " Meditate upon these things, for if you desire to build such great angle towers you must choose a form of sufficient projection. Proceed carefully, and you will do as a wise and careful man ought to do." Then he goes to see Rheims Cathedral, which is in course of building, and sketches carefully the chapels of the apse, with notes of their details. He evidently thought very well of them, and having about this time to build the cathedral at Cambrai (now unfortunately destroyed), he gives a plan of it, in which he seems to have repeated very closely the plan and design of his favourite apse of Rheims. On another page he gives a sketch of a plan of a chevet or apse which he and his friend Peter de Corbie contrived together ; and, strangely enough, of so novel a plan is this apse, surrounded by alternately square and circular chapels, that no example of it exists in France.   If he had travelled south he might have seen his suggestions anticipated in the baptistery at Albenga, on the Riviera, whilst at Toledo some French-man did, at about the same time, build the chevet of the largest thirteenth-century church in Europe on precisely this very plan.   In another he gives a plan of a square-ended church, almost identical with our own abbeys at Beaulieu and Byland, on which he writes · "This is a square church, which was designed for the Cistercian order."   Again, he gives a variety of designs for drawing the human figure enclosed within triangles.   He designs foliage, animals, a lectern, a clock-case, and so on.   Then he travels, visits Hungary on business, goes to Chartres, to Lausanne, to Meaux, as well as to Laon and Rheims—everywhere note-book in hand, and making sketches of all that strikes him most   Curiously enough, he makes not a single suggestion in any of his sketches of any geometrical mode of arriving at the proportions of the buildings—a very note-worthy fact, seeing that most of those he visited were either just built or in course of being built.

I have been thus particular in describing this book because it gives us a glimpse behind the scenes of extraordinary interest.   We see just how it was that these French buildings grew, multiplied, and developed as they did.   The men who built them were as keen about their art as it was possible to be.   They were disputing with each other as to possible new plans, new combinations, and repeat-ing work the effect of which they thought perfect , and it is this sort of spirit which we see so actively at work in developing the French architecture on all hands, from the point to which it had slowly attained at the end of the twelfth century.

I believe that in the time at my disposal this evening I cannot do better, first of all, than show you how this improvement and development was effected in the ground-plan of a French church   In most cases a good ground-plan involves the architectural design of a great part of the superstructure.   In the best French churches it may almost be said that it involves the whole design.   In those days every one gave his building a stone roof if it was possible   And nothing so certainly necessitates a scientific arrangement of the ground-plan as the provision for carrying safely a stone vault.   You will observe, then, that the men who had built such a church as that of Nôtre Dame du Port at Clermont, or as St Front at Peri-gueux, had succeeded in covering their buildings with stone, but in a way which left much to be desired.   And the object of each sub-sequent architect was to make the construction safer, or at least as safe, but with much more lightness of effect, and with much less waste of material. The idea of the early churches had been derived from countries in which the climate required that windows should be neither numerous nor large ; and it was not until the period with which we are dealing that architects began to realise how unreasonable such windows were in their comparatively gloomy and cold climate. The cross vault once introduced soon led to the discovery that the use of a pointed arch was almost essential if vaults were to be strong, and adjusted to other than regular compartments. Even in the simple vault of a building whose plan is a parallelogram, the thrust of a semi-circular vault is too great, and the slightest giving way of the walls on which it rests is fatal. With a pointed vault this is not the case. The thrust outwards is comparatively small, and it was soon found that it might be counteracted not only by a buttress in the form of a pier, but by a section only of the old quadrant vault which held up the continuous vaults of Nôtre Dame du Port and its class. The flying buttress adopted in this way rendered it comparatively easy to bring all the thrust to one point on the wall, because it was possible so to fortify this point as to make it certain that it would not give way. Then, when this was accomplished, it became quite unnecessary to erect thick and heavy walls between the piers and buttresses, and in course of time the construction is reduced here to a mere thin screen of tracery, throwing as little weight as need be on the piers, and only sufficient to keep the weather out of the building. In France the whole of the early buildings were, as I have told you, finished with circular east ends. And it is possible almost to count on one's fingers the examples of large churches in the thirteenth century in which a square east end is seen. The most important are the cathedrals at Laon, at Poitiers, at Dol, the church of St. Serge, Angers, and the churches of some religious orders, as, *e.g.*, the Cistercians. Such exceptions emphatically prove the rule. Then, when it became necessary to vault these circular ends, all sorts of problems had to be met, and each man's work presents some mode of solving them different from that of his neighbour or predecessor.

The great difficulty to be overcome arose from the extremely irregular shape of every division or bay of vaulting around a circular building. In the square compartment you have an arrangement in which the arches need not be of the same height, and yet may perfectly well be vaulted with cross ribs, the ridges of the vaulting cells rising or falling to meet the arches, or being level with them. Where a succession of these vaults is required the ribs are usually semicircles, because in this way it was found that the perspective was most continuous and effective. But this was by no means always the case. Sometimes these ribs are made of such curves as will allow of the filling in of the cells being square with the cross arches, and sometimes, as in the Angevine and Poitierine churches, these diagonal arches are pointed arches rising high above the centre of the cross arches. In this case the perspective half of each vault is lost behind the cross vault. It is really a most unsatisfactory sort of vaulting, and though it was persevered in for the best part of the century in the districts named, it was rarely adopted in other parts of France, and not at all, I think, in the Ile de France. In the aisle round an apse the first solution was a continuous barrel vault. This was very easy, but certainly not beautiful; nor was it improved when cross vaulting was introduced corresponding to the openings to the chapels or arcades on either side. But when it was attempted to divide this aisle for vaulting bays the problem was found to be very difficult. Treated like the square bays, with vaulting ribs going straight from angle to angle, the effect is obviously very bad, so the diagonal ribs were usually planned so as to meet in the real centre of the compartment, though this involved a disagreeable broken line in the perspective, and was not so popular as to be accepted without protest. It was probably after seeing such vaults constructed that the chevet of Nôtre Dame, Paris, was planned. Here, certainly, great ingenuity is shown. The apse is divided from its aisle by five arches, and this again from the outer aislé by ten, and the vaulting compartments are all as nearly as possible equal triangles on plan. You will find this form of vault used alternately with square compartments in the aisle round the circular church at the Temple, where the same problem is solved with even greater skill. In these triangular compartments of Nôtre Dame there is a continuous ridge of level triangular spaces, and though a single such compartment is deficient in the light and shade of ordinary vaulting, approaching, in truth, too nearly in principle to a cradle or waggon vault, of which half of each compartment is a portion, yet in so intricate a plan as that of Nôtre Dame no such fault can be found, for the whole plan is full of variety and light and shade. Nôtre Dame was completed in 1208, but the whole exterior of the chevet was greatly modified in 1296 by the addition of a series of chapels between the buttresses. I have myself very little doubt that in Bourges Cathedral we have a chevet which illustrates the probable treatment of the original chapels of Nôtre Dame, all of which were destroyed in 1296. Here, as at Nôtre Dame, the outer wall of the second aisle has three compartments for every one in the central apse, and from the centre division of each of these a small circular chapel projects. This treatment is very beautiful. It retains the windows between the chapels, which was so marked and fine a feature of the early chevets, and relieves what would be the baldness of a chevet consisting, as M. Viollet le Duc assumes to have been the case at Nôtre Dame, Paris, of two aisles, without any excrescences all round the chevet. The architect of Bourges made another important modification. At Nôtre Dame the plan involved the placing of a column in the second series of columns opposite the centres of the arches of the first series. The Bourges architect, however, abandoned the attempt to make all the vaulting compartments equal, accepted the irregular plan for the first aisle, making his intercolumniations wider than in the apse, and then showed that he knew and appreciated the Nôtre Dame arrangement by dividing the outer wall into three, and making one bay of quadripartite vaulting, which is an exact counterpart of that in the first aisle, only reversed, and two bays of triangular shape. Below, in the crypt, the similarity to the Nôtre Dame vaulting is even greater. At Bourges the chevet is a semicircle divided into five exactly equal portions, and these prolonged by twelve bays westward from the church. The architect, having resolved on immensity of scale, confined himself to the simplest possible plan, but gave great originality to his design by raising the intermediate aisle to such a height as to admit of its having a secondary clerestory and triforium. Nôtre Dame was completed in its first form in 1208; of Bourges the date is uncertain, but it is probably safe to put it at about 1220. And in 1226 the plan of another cathedral, almost the vastest in Christendom, was made, and evidently by a Frenchman, for Toledo. Here the plan of the chevet shows a double aisle, with compartments alternately square and triangular in both aisles. In this way all difficulties were overcome. The central column opposite the arches of the apse was avoided. The vaulting has no sameness, the compartments being alternately triangular and square, and the surrounding chapels are of the Bourges type, *i.e.* very small, but alternately circular and square. The whole plan is one of the most beautiful ever devised, and it is strange indeed that the most magnificent development of the French plan should be in the ecclesiastical capital of Spain. Here, too, to complete the likeness to Bourges, the intermediate aisles have a triforium and clerestory, and the ungainliness which is certainly the fault of Bourges is exchanged for a design in which the most captious critic can find little to complain of. The sketching architect, Willars de Honecort, when he devised a plan for a chevet in company with Peter de Corbie, made, you will remember, one almost identical with that of Toledo.

It is impossible to do more than just touch on this branch of my subject to-night. In some future year I may, perhaps, be able to deal with it more exhaustively. The varieties of the modifications of the plan of the chapels round the chevet are very great; but the main point to be observed is that at the beginning of the

century they were all planned on circular lines, and that by the end
of it they were all but invariably polygonal   In Robert de Coucy's
work at Rheims, we see them begun on the first plan, and finished
on the other , and after his time his example was generally followed
His work was planned in 1211, Amiens in 1220, Beauvais in 1225,
Le Mans in 1230, Clermont in 1248, and then all follow on the
lines which he laid down, and which, in a few words, had the effect
of abolishing the wall and throwing all the weight on to the buttresses,
so as the better to enable them to resist the thrust of the vaults
To know what French architecture was in the thirteenth century, it
is, of course, requisite to know a good deal more than the story of
the development of the ground-plan, though it is true that, unless
you study this part first, you will never understand the rest of your
subject   Now no way, I believe, is so good for to-night's purpose
as to take some two or three churches for examination, and, so to
speak, dissect them   Probably, of all the French churches, there
are none in which such dissection is more profitable than it is
in the case of Nôtre Dame, Paris, Rheims Cathedral, Amiens, and
Chartres.   And if I take the last first, it is mainly because it is so
perfect in all its parts, and so completely the work of one period
and the effort of one man's skill and genius, that it presents an
admirable subject for your study.

The original cathedral at Chartres was built in the eleventh century, and a vast crypt still remains of this period   Then, in 1115,
a west front was commenced, and in 1194 the whole church was destroyed by fire.   The new cathedral was at once commenced, but
upon the old foundations   The contrivance of the new architect,
who desired to plan a church suitable for the epoch, and therefore
did not choose to follow strictly the lines of the early church, is well
worth our consideration.   At first sight, the church of Chartres has
the look of being extremely original   It is, in fact, unlike any
other that I know.   The chapels round the outer aisle are alternately polygonal and segments of circles   This variation seems to
me to be in itself very beautiful as well as original , but when we
descend to the crypt we find out at once how it has come to be contrived, and that it was, in fact, the happy result of a necessity turned
to good use · The original church was burnt, but the crypt sustained no damage.   It extended the whole length of the church, and
the architect was compelled, therefore, to build on the old lines.
Compare the crypt as it was, and the church as it is, and you will
say that the compulsion did not amount to much, so different are
the two.   But compare the two plans, and you will see how ingenious the adaptation was   Examining the crypt, we see that the old
church had an apse, a single aisle round it, and three deep chapels
with spaces between them, of the same general outline as those other

Early French churches which I have already described. The architect of the church saw that by making a slight corbelling forward from the old base it would be possible to build a choir with two aisles instead of one, with moderate chapels over the old chapels, and shallow ones in the spaces between them. All this could be done, and was done, without any additions to the old foundations, and certainly with the happiest result, and it would be difficult to give any better evidence of the skill of the architect. The groining of the new chevet is somewhat complicated; the inner aisle is all quadripartite; the outer one has quadripartite vaults opposite the large chapels, and vaults of five divisions opposite and including the small intermediate chapels, whilst the three principal chapels are vaulted separately from the aisle. In some respects this plan is similar to many of later date, as may be seen at St. Pierre, Bourges, and St. Omer Cathedral; but I think the plan of Chartres is far finer than either of these, giving as it does a beautifully curved and varied outline to every part of the apse. I am the more particular in claiming this merit for Chartres, because no less an authority than M. Viollet le Duc speaks rather slightingly of it, evidently forgetting that the great merit of the plan is that the conditions were unfavourable, and that an amazingly good result was obtained in spite of this fact. Nor am I, much as I admire the plan, able to praise everything without reserve in this great church. No doubt there were many difficulties to be surmounted; not only in the plan of the old church, but in the people who had to be employed on the new one. Chartres had a great religious reputation. It had then, I believe, as it has now, a black Virgin, whose power of working miracles was supposed to be extraordinary. It was the epoch of the Crusades. Men were told that to work at Nôtre Dame, Chartres, was as good as to go to the Holy Land. And from distant places—from Rouen among others—crowds of people of all sorts went to aid the work at Chartres with their hands. Such is the story; and I am bound to say that there is much in the fabric which seems to confirm it. The whole scheme was a grand one. But the material—a very coarse, calcareous limestone, full of holes—did not admit of any delicate work, and nothing can well be rougher than the workmanship of all but certain delicate portions, as, *e.g.*, the two transept porches. The stones are put together in a clumsy and unworkmanlike manner. Things which are meant to fit do not do so. The cornices and galleries outside are so carelessly planned as to have to be fitted to their places by taking off and curving angles, or filling them up. All the work has the air of having been executed by men who were in a great hurry, who were not used to such work, and who were entirely careless as to the goodness of the execution as long as they could manage just to put it firmly together. This sort

of execution happens also to tally with the architectural details of
the general design. These are comparatively few, and not too
skilful The main columns are needlessly heavy, being about 8 6 in
diameter, though the intercolumniations are only 11.7. The capitals
are not well planned to receive the groining piers and main arches
All the members are rude in their section, and the flying buttresses
are not only very irregular in their design, but far in excess of what
such a vault as they support ought to require. In the columns
the very common French plan of four shafts surrounding a central
drum is adopted ; but the shafts are all alternately circular and
octagonal, and agreeably varied by being made into clusters of
small columns both at the crossing and at the responds. It must be
noted also that the columns are alternately circular with four octagonal, and octagonal with four circular, shafts surrounding them.
The mouldings are very few and very simple, and the capitals very
plain and rather coarsely carved. The windows, too, are very large
and very plain (the great clerestory windows are no less than eight feet
five inches wide in the clear, and their only moulding is a chamfer)
Finally, there is very little variety The same design is carried on
all round the church, almost without any change. But you must
understand that this was all done designedly The architect had
determined to make his work depend for its effect upon a magnificent
tout ensemble, which should be above and beyond all questions of
detail He could not but know what good work was, for the old
west end and the south-west steeple had escaped the fire, and each
in its way was admirable in design and detail. The three western
doorways have seldom been excelled for the finished beauty of their
workmanship, and the steeple is a perfect example of delicate planning
and design ; and he shows his own sense of what was good, for his
work depended for its effect partly upon the porches of the north
and south transepts, in which he has shown such a mastery over
delicate detail as has seldom been seen, and this with an originality
of design and a fertility of invention which cannot be too much
praised. Both porches are generally similar in outline, but extremely
different in the detail of their planning, which in the case of the
northern one is very varied and beautiful. Nowhere can be seen
better than here the love of variety which so much marks Gothic
work It is as if the architect had felt himself tied and bound in
his scheme for the church, and found himself breathing freely again
when he had to complete the porches There is so charming and
endless a variety of canopies, of shafts, of clusters of them, of figures,
of subjects, that I am at a loss to find terms warm enough for my
sense of their beauty. But this will, I hope, be illustrated more
fully if I am ever able, as I hope, to lecture to you on the connection
of architecture and sculpture, nowhere better seen than at Chartres.

So far I have spoken of this typical cathedral of the thirteenth century without a word about its colour. This was not only internal. There is still evidence in the northern porch that, six centuries ago, the whole was covered with rich colour. Nothing more at variance with our present ideas of what is suitable can be conceived. Yet we must always remember that the thirteenth-century architect agreed herein intuitively with the Greek before him, and that both felt that the best architecture could not be the best possible until it had been beautifully coloured. But it is the profusion of colour in stained glass which is the most striking feature of the church. It is that by which almost all must be most struck, and by which, after all, they must remember Chartres. Evidently it formed part of the original scheme. The windows are all of vast size; and, in spite of this, and of their great number, they are absolutely filled with glass of extremely rich and solid colour, all of the same age as the church, and all arranged in a generally uniform scheme, though it is varied in detail in every part. The architectural features of this portion of the work which most deserve to be noted are (1) the general arrangement in the upper windows of large figures under canopies, and in the lower windows of subjects in panels; (2) the beauty of all the drawing of foliage and ornament; and (3) the fact that all the windows, rich as they are in colour, have their leading lines marked with a white line, so that if you are in the church when light is failing, you find all the openings filled with geometrical figures or tracery. The architect of Chartres was not far from using regular tracery. In the porch he does it in a small degree, and in the great circles over the clerestory he leads the way naturally for similar figures in the glass, and finally he culminates in a magnificent rose window of geometrical tracery in the west front. His work as it stands is perhaps the most perfect and least altered great French work of the period. It was begun, as we have seen, in 1194, and finished in 1260, and there is no evidence anywhere of a change from the first scheme during the long progress of the work. Time has dealt very tenderly with it. Few alterations, and those generally unimportant, have been made since the dedication of the church. The whole scheme was carried out exactly on the lines dictated at the first, and nothing was left for a subsequent age to do. Compared with the puny architectural works of our own time, such an effort is simply amazing. During the same period the cathedrals of Paris, Troyes, Soissons, Rheims, Amiens, Auxerre, Mantes, Beauvais, Le Mans, Bourges, Clermont, Limoges, Laon, Bayeux, Coutances, Seez, and Rouen, together with an endless array of abbeys, of castles, of churches, of hospitals, were being built. Each great cathedral must have been built by its own diocese or district, for every diocese was engaged on the same work. Yet at Chartres there is no evidence of economy or straitened means.

Too great haste, indeed, is the only fault of which I find evidence in the execution of the work   But it was the venial fault of a city which refused to see its cathedral in ruins a day longer than was absolutely necessary

At Nôtre Dame, Paris, we see the work of a very different artist, and are able to trace distinctly the great changes which have been made in the work since its first commencement.   I have told you of the ground-plan already   After this, the most interesting feature is the triforium.   Here, in order to resist the thrust of the main vault, the first architect constructed it with pointed barrel vaults, at right angles to the length of the church , and it is difficult to suggest a stronger form of construction   It was in this way that the twelfth-century builders of the cathedral at Tourmes had vaulted their aisles, and their example was copied in one church in England, *i.e* by the Cistercians at Fountains.   At Nôtre Dame it was soon destroyed in favour of flying buttresses, but at Mantes Cathedral, said to have been designed by Eudes de Montreuil, not far from Paris, much of the similar construction is still perfect.   It was convenient enough, and very strong in the nave, but singularly inconvenient in its application to the irregular bays of an apse , it was probably bad for sound, and expensive and troublesome in construction.   It is not to be wondered at that it was soon abandoned in favour of cross vaults spanned by light flying buttresses   There was an immediate temptation also to reduce its strength by making openings between the vaults to a dangerous extent.   At Mantes these cross vaults are carried on slight columns, on which a flat lintel is placed, from which the cross vaults spring The failure of one of these columns might, therefore, involve the ruin of the clerestory which the vaults buttressed.   Eudes de Montreuil, 1 suppose, introduced this mode of supporting the central vault ; and if he was also the first architect of Nôtre Dame, Paris, he combined it there with a second triforium arrangement, the circular windows to light which still remain here and there   This second triforium was almost necessary when the main gallery was used by the congregation, as it still is in Nôtre Dame   The flying buttresses at Nôtre Dame are of enormous projection, sloping very slightly on the upper side, and, seen in perspective, give an extremely ungainly outline to this otherwise noble work   At San Remi, Rheims, at a slightly earlier date, the same fault is seen, but it was at once felt to be a fault ; and, as we see, both in Rheims Cathedral and at Amiens, was immediately corrected.   At Nôtre Dame the error committed at Chartres, of making them enormously heavy, was carefully avoided.   In many respects Nôtre Dame affords a singularly good subject for study.   It shows us as completely as any one building the vast strides made during the century   The church generally dates from quite the commencement of the century; the west front from 1214, south transept from 1257, the alteration of the choir by the addition of chapels from 1294. In this period the style had become greatly changed. In the earliest work, as in the columns of the nave, we have a stately simplicity which imparts singular grandeur to the interior. The capitals are very large, and beautifully carved with foliage arranged in architectural forms, but largely composed of natural leafage conventionalised. All the work is admirably executed. If you compare it with Chartres, you will see how admirably. The aisles are still, after the manner of Auvergne, covered with stone pavement for roofs, and the whole work has the air of being strong enough to last for ever, without being clumsy. There is nothing frittered away or small, and the western towers, each with an array of shafts in the belfry stage of unusual splendour, are, so far as complete, the finest works of the age. The change in the transepts and the chapels round the apse is great. The architect is not one jot less clever; perhaps he is even more so. His work is beautiful and beautifully executed. But the grand feeling for simplicity which had reigned supreme is no longer so evident. The mouldings have become too fine and delicate; the carving is too much a mere imitation of natural forms; and there is a sensible want of substance in the look of all the larger features, as, *e.g.*, the windows of the transepts, which look too weak to stand.

The cathedral at Rheims is the next in order of date of those which I can touch upon, and is altogether, for our purpose this evening, of very singular value. Its architect was Robert de Coucy, who began it 1211 A.D., after a fire had nearly destroyed the older cathedral, leaving only portions of the two transept fronts in such a state as to allow of their being kept in the new work. The new cathedral was consecrated in 1241, but works were in progress during the whole century under a succession of architects, who must have been singularly loyal to the original design. When De Coucy began his work he had before him the great abbey church of San Remi, still standing at the other end of the town very much in the same state as it was then. It is necessary to say something about this great church, for a comparison of it with the cathedral shows extremely well the process by which developments of design are ordinarily achieved. San Remi was consecrated in 1049, and in its original state was of the severest and simplest Romanesque. In plan it had a nave about fifty feet wide, of twelve bays in length, with a clerestory, and over the groined aisles an enormous triforium gallery for the use of worshippers. The nave, doubtless, had a wooden ceiling, and though the plan of the eastern portion had the same general arrangement as the Auvergne churches, with apsidal chapels to the transepts, the whole church seems to me to have

rather more connection with German buildings than with French.
Its two western steeples illustrate this, being, in fact, lofty turrets on
each side of the west front.   Rheims still retains a grand fragment
of a Roman gateway.   This has three arches, and between them
three-quarter engaged columns, fluted.   The San Remi builders
evidently imitated this work · they regarded the columns as buttresses,
and placed similar buttresses to mark the bays of their church, and
at the west end they fluted them   At St. Jacques, Rheims, they
repeated the same feature, and it is a very interesting example of
the way in which Roman buildings on the spot led to mediæval
adaptation of their features   In 1182 the east end of San Remi
was taken down, rebuilt, and completed in 1198, on a plan which
is nearly identical with that of a church at Chalons-sur-Marne, which
was finished fifteen years earlier.   An extended choir was built, with
five eastern chapels, and outer aisles to the west of them as far as
the transepts   The great triforium galleries of the nave were
repeated, and lighted with large windows, so as to produce a very
fine internal effect   Above the triforium is a simple arcade, which
answers to the ordinary Gothic triforium, and above this a clerestory.
There are thus four divisions in height, instead of the usual three,
though this additional stage is a common feature in this part of
France, as we see still at Laon and Soissons, and one which, I have
told you, exists at Nôtre Dame, Paris.   By far the most beautiful
feature in the building is the plan of the eastern extension, and particularly the way in which the difficulty of the aisle-groining bays in
the apse has been surmounted by opening the chapels to the aisle with
three arches of unequal width resting on detached shafts   This plan
enabled the architect to make the vaulting of the aisle very regular
in its arrangement—a square compartment and two triangular ones
to each bay, the vaulting of the chapels being octagonal, though the
sides of the octagon are not all equal   The columns of the choir
are all plain cylinders, with square capitals, very finely carved in a
bold development from the lines of a Corinthian capital.   The
arches are all pointed.   The choir, in spite of its vast width, is
groined, as, too, are the triforium galleries   The exterior has been
a good deal tampered with   But it is doubtful whether it can ever
have been a really beautiful work   The proportions are low and
ungainly, and the great width of the old church was a stumbling-
block to the builder of the new choir.   He got over the difficulties
ingeniously, and in some respects, especially in the plan, certainly
shows the hand of an accomplished architect

Robert de Coucy, when he began the cathedral, had this building to study.   It had been only finished thirteen years, and it is
extremely interesting to see how much it affected him, and yet how
immensely he improved upon it.   Evidently he fully realised the

beauty of the ground-plan, for his is almost an exact repetition of all its general lines—the same number of bays in the choir and apse, the same number of chapels, and the same outer aisles between the chevet and the transepts.   But he dismissed at once the triforium galleries, and then gave up the fourfold division in height, and increased immensely the proportions both of the main arcade and of the clerestory; though, unfortunately, as I think, he repeated the upper triforium arcade of San Remi without much alteration.   The only great departure from the original ground-plan was in the arches to the chapels, in which he gave up altogether the beautiful San Remi arrangement.   He could not well help himself.   His dimensions in width were the same, those of height more than twice those of San Remi (124 feet as compared with 53 feet), and the three arches, which are well-proportioned in the one case, would have looked absurdly narrow and ill-proportioned in the other.   On the exterior his scheme was entirely his own.   The buttresses are admirably designed, and, in spite of their magnificent scale do not seem, as too often happens, to overwhelm the whole building. In short, though it is clear, if his work is attentively looked at, that he had carefully studied San Remi, it is equally clear that the alterations which he made in the proportions, in the external elevations, and in the details, were so great that few would ever be likely to discover the underlying evidence of similarity.   It is this which seems to me to be so worthy of your notice.   The great and accomplished architect of the cathedral had none of the conceit which prevented his seeing the good in what had been done before; but rather, with admirable skill, seized on the really fine points of the work before him, and showed how much more splendid the scheme might be made.   This is the true spirit for an architect.   It is the spirit in which you must work if you want to be regarded in the way in which we all think of Robert de Coucy and his work.   This is the real lesson which a study of Rheims Cathedral teaches.   To tell you in detail anything about the cathedral would take much time. Its great virtue is its admirable simplicity throughout, save at the west end, where by the end of the century another architect showed in all its glory the latest development of the thirteenth century. Three enormous portals, covered in every portion with sculpture, above them a splendid rose window, and on either side two steeples of rare beauty of design,—these have an interest of the same kind as the rest of the church.   The neighbouring cathedral of Laon is still famous for the six steeples of its three fronts, and the exquisite treatment of their angles, which have open arrangements of arcades and shafts, square in some and circular in others.   Rheims was to have had six steeples also; those to the transepts were begun before De Coucy's design was made, and were evidently to have been of the same type as those at Laon. But at the end of the century the architect had come to dislike the Laon system in which the open pinnacles were built up by a succession of columns and arches, piled one on another   He thought long continuous lines of moulding more effective, and though he retained the idea of open pinnacles, he constructed their piers entirely of clusters of mouldings corresponding with those of his belfry windows.   I think the architect of Laon has the best of it in the result.   But it is impossible not to see the influence he exercised, any more than it is not to admire the beautiful design of the Rheims steeples.   As in most great French churches, the mouldings are few and simple.   There are two features to which I take exception   these are the absence of a sufficient base moulding, and the overwhelming size of the great niches which crown the buttresses of the aisles, and almost conceal the clerestory from the exterior.   The solidity of the whole church is much in excess of that of many later buildings ; but its justification is its perfect condition structurally, and I may almost say the absence of a crack or settlement throughout its vast extent   I wish to see no finer sight than such an interior, as I saw it only yesterday, hung all round with precious tapestries of the fifteenth century, which set off and adorned its superb and dignified architecture in the very best way.

Fine as are such churches as Chartres, Nôtre Dame, Paris, and the cathedral at Rheims, I suppose that Amiens Cathedral is by common consent the greatest achievement of the century.   It is difficult to say precisely why ; for, not to mention others, the slightly earlier cathedral which I have just been speaking of, at Rheims, is even more complete and more exactly what its first architect intended it to be   And for perfect beauty of plan and poetical inspiration of design I think Rouen goes near to excelling all.   Probably the dimensions and the beautiful proportions of Amiens give it the position it has.   Its columns are about 49 feet from centre to centre across the nave, and its total height is above 140 feet, as against corresponding dimensions at Rheims of 54 feet and 124 feet.   It is distinguished for its airy lightness of effect   Its proportions appear to have been regulated by the equilateral triangle   The church was for some time in progress, and the design was much modified during the erection, notably in the triforium and clerestory.   What strikes one most here is the supreme constructive skill of the architect.   No part of the building appears to be unduly heavy or unduly weighted All the details are well designed and admirably fitted together.   The glazed triforium, which is perhaps first seen here in a large church, is very conspicuous for its beauty and lightness, whilst the flying buttresses and pinnacles are beautiful in their outline, and contrast admirably with the heaviness of those at Chartres, the ungainliness of those at Paris, and the apparently overwhelming size and number

of those at Le Mans and Köln.   The vaulting at Amiens is unlike
the common French mode.   In order to get as much light and
shade as possible, the horizontal section is everywhere very square,
and to secure this, the diagonal vaulting ribs are not semicircles, as
is commonly the case in France at this time, but compound curves
generated from the transverse arches, and giving a true horizontal
line for all the ridges.   The lines of such vaults near the eye always,
I think, look crippled; but here, at the enormous height they are
above the floor, it is very difficult to follow the lines of these curves,
and, therefore, there is no sense of their not being exactly true
curves, whilst the best possible effect of light and shade is secured.
The effect of the original scheme of the nave has been much spoilt
by the addition of chapels between the buttresses of the aisles.   The
effect of these is to remove the windows so far back between solid
walls that in the internal perspective they are not seen at all, and so
the lantern-like effect, which was everywhere the aim of the architect, has been lost.   At Amiens, as at Chartres, Paris, and Rheims,
sculpture has its share in the success of the work.   The three great
western doorways are covered with it; and many of the small subjects illustrating the labours of the Months and the signs of the
Zodiac, as well as subjects from the Bible, are full of interest, though
not executed by quite so good a sculptor as those who worked on the
porches at Chartres and the doorways at Paris.   Here, too, let me say
that the whole of the masonry of this great church is finished with
a claw tool, which gave it from the first a texture far superior to the
smooth surface which we all affect so much now.   I mention it to you
in order to direct your attention to what may seem, but is not really,
a very minor point.   At the time Amiens was nearing completion, the
effect produced by its magnificent scale and beautiful proportions
was remarkable.   At Beauvais, not much more than thirty miles
distant, the bishop and people were so jealous that they resolved to
erect a church the glories of which should completely eclipse those
of their rival.   Their architect lent himself to the scheme with as
much zest as any of us would now.   His dimensions were considerably in excess of those of Robert de Luzarches at Amiens, but his
ambitious schemes were too great for safety, and had to be, to a
great extent, altered, after a portion had given way, so that the
building, as it now stands, does not fairly represent the impossible
lightness of the first scheme.   In addition to an imitator at Beauvais, Amiens undoubtedly gave all his lines and plans to the German
architect of Köln Cathedral, as it did to men so far off as the architects of Clermont-Ferrand and Narbonne—perhaps, too, of Leon,
in Spain.   The later variations of the type are certainly no improvement on the original.   We see the art gradually losing its freshness
and force, and becoming perhaps more scientific, but certainly more

scholastic, and consequently far less artistic and interesting   The change can nowhere be seen better than at Köln, where, though the architect took his general scheme and his proportions from Amiens, he gave all his details so essentially hard and violent German a character as to destroy to a great extent the evidence of the parent-age, without, I think, improving the effect

I must now sum up in a few words the general characteristics of the thirteenth-century architecture of France   It was a style which was going through a most rapid stage of transition and development   The century begins with vast, noble, and solid erections, heavy in construction, very similar in general plan and design, and ends with works in which, though the construction was still solid, it was so scientific, so delicate in its adaptation to its requirements in every part, that it had become light and airy almost past belief.   In these respects it has never been excelled before or since.   In complete works of this period there is always a strict relation in every part of the plan to the work to be done   The thing to be supported dictated absolutely the shape of the support, and the nature of the material decided the character of the design   The details had all been developed and improved, the windows, from being plain and rude lancets, had become richly moulded and splendidly designed compositions of geometrical traceries, all arranged with careful adaptation to the proper subordination of parts, the mouldings and traceries following each other in their relations to the primary, secondary, and tertiary importance of the parts.   The buttresses had come to be treated as the real framework of the building.   To them all weights were conveyed, and by them on to the ground.   The panels enclosed between them showed no waste of wall   They were reduced to mere screens to keep out the weather, which was indeed their main if not their sole office   The proportions of height to width were much greater and much better adjusted, and the study of perspective effect, both inside and outside, was carried to the greatest perfection.   The same attention to what one may fairly term a brilliant beauty of detail was exhibited in every part of the work   In sculpture, the study of Nature and of life had taken the place of a steady respect for ancient and conventional representations   Foliage came to be copied directly from Nature, but with an instinctive sense of the necessity of adapting it to structural purposes which is very remarkable.   In a capital, for instance, though the detail was natural, the arrangement of the natural forms was strictly architectural   In a spandrel, where it was simply meant for ornament, an absolute imitation of Nature is allowable, and was freely indulged in   A string-course, as we see at Amiens, was made like a garland of gay flowers carried all round a building.   In the representation of the human figure still greater progress was made.   Compare the west doors of

Chartres with the southern doors, and the change is made very clear. The later sculptors evidently studied from the life. They represented men in the fashion of the day, and in their faces, their attitudes, and their grouping, there is a gay and tender sentiment, which seems to me to be absolutely enchanting. You are impressed, whether you will or no, with a sense of an age unlike our own, where there is no misery, no misfortune, nothing to mar the charm of the pleasantest and purest life ; and though, of course, some men's work is infinitely in advance of others, a general high level is reached and sustained in a striking manner. Everywhere the work of the sculptor is called in to adorn the work of the architect, and so harmoniously is this done that no one can tell where the office of either began or ended. Then in all the subsidiary arts the same excellence is seen—whether it is in the decoration of a manuscript, the painting of glass, the execution of elaborate work in all the metals, in enamelling, in embroidery— everything was done with careful reference to the requirements of the material and the use to which the article to be manufactured had to be put. And though I am loyal to the art of my own country, I am obliged to admit that of France to be entitled to a sort of supremacy. In the previous century she had given an architect and a design to Canterbury and to Compostella ; in this she covered her own soil, stirred up the Germans to an imitation of her work at Köln, designed the great cathedrals of Toledo and Leon in Spain, and had a con- spicuous influence in Italy at Genoa, Vercelli, and Assisi. In the brief space of a century the French architects had almost shown the limits of what was possible in the way of development, and left com- paratively little, and that matter of detail rather than of principle, to their successors to achieve. They had a grand opportunity, and certainly availed themselves of it in the grandest way. The people seconded their efforts with a supply of means for building so large and extraordinary as to be wellnigh incomprehensible. The draw- backs on their work are, generally, a want of completeness on the exterior, which has at the same time the attractiveness of the unex- pected. If you build a church on the scale of Amiens it is impossible to add steeples to it which shall not either dwarf their mother church or themselves be dwarfed. A central steeple is impossible ; and the examples of such a feature are very rare anywhere in France at this time, and then, generally, as at Coutances, they are an evidence of English influence. A multitude of steeples, two at each front, with a lantern occasionally in the centre, making it six or eight to one church, render it impossible to secure such effective grouping as we see in our English churches. And the enormous height certainly goes far to diminish the apparent length.

It is fortunate for you students that you are within easy reach of such masterpieces of art as are the monuments of French art.

The young architect may, indeed, well be advised to study first of all the art of his own country, to which that of Normandy may be considered simply as supplementary, so closely allied is it to English art. But to the sculptor students I appeal with all my strength not to neglect this vast field for study. Far be it from me ever to advise any one merely to copy what has been done before, but not to avail yourselves of it in your studies is blindly to refuse to make use of one of many of the paths which lead to real knowledge and mastery of your art. Remember what Flaxman told you about Wells, and believe me that if, as he said, you may learn much there, it is as nothing to what you may learn in France, where the examples are manifold more numerous, of all dates, and of even greater value.

This evening I have tried to give you some faint idea of the way in which the thirteenth-century architects regarded and treated their art. This seems to me to be at least as valuable a subject for your study as are mere questions of detail; for I· want to see you all working in the same spirit as those great men, and not merely trying to reproduce exactly what they have already done so well.

LECTURE VI

THIRTEENTH-CENTURY ARCHITECTURE—
ENGLAND [1]

My concluding lecture is to be devoted to our own national architecture in one of its very best periods. No educated Englishman
can be otherwise than proud when he thinks of the work his country-
men did all over England at this time. It was in almost all respects
a truly national work, since its developments were distinct from and
unlike those of all other countries, and, I think, little, if at all,
inferior to the very best of them. We shall find it necessary to
review shortly the state of architecture in England before the thirteenth century, and the changes consequent on the invention of the
pointed arch, just as in dealing with Italy and France we had to
begin with the earlier phases of their art. You know, probably,
that we have in this country a number of buildings (churches)
in various parts of England which have such distinct and marked
characteristics that they perfectly admit of exact classification, and
are in almost every particular unlike any of those which we know to
have been built since the Norman Conquest. Their plans, with the
one exception of the church at Brixworth, have square ends, not
apsidal. Brixworth is probably a Roman work, and has all the evidences in plan and elevation that might be looked for in such a case,
and is not really, therefore, an exception to the rule. These churches
generally have masonry with long and short quoins alternately at the
angles. Their walls have narrow pilaster strips at intervals. Their
doorways are generally enclosed with a narrow projecting line of
stone, which rises from the ground and encloses the whole archway.
Their towers are generally lofty, and have belfry windows divided by
rude baluster-shafts; but where, as at Earls Barton and Barton-on-
Humber, the towers are enriched, it is with a system of arcading or
panelling all over the walls, which is like that which I have described

[1] Concluding lecture, delivered 3d March, to the Students of the Royal
Academy.

to you as existing at Ancona and elsewhere in Southern Italy—a system of unmeaning decorative stonework clapped on against the face of the walls, with no reference of any sort to their construction I show you side by side a drawing of the arcading of Barton-on-Humber Church, and on the front of Sta. Maria, Ancona, and you will see at once that the similarity in the system of decoration is so exact as to deserve special notice. In the same way I have made two parallel elevations of a window from St. Mary Bishophill Junior, at York, and from the Cathedral of Ravello, near Amalfi You will see here, again, that the elements of the design are all but identical. At the same time it is to be observed that in the whole of these buildings there is hardly a trace of distinctly Roman influence on the design. The transept arches of Britford Church, near Salisbury, may perhaps be excepted, though even here, in combination with a singularly good and very perfect decorative panelled arch in stone and tile, the arches have the narrow outside stone border which I have learnt to regard as one of the most distinct marks of Saracenic architecture in the south of Europe, as it is of the pre-Norman architecture of England. One thing at least is clear, viz that English art at this time owed nothing, or next to nothing, to the Romans. At the same time Ireland was rich in saints and in churches, and had the most intimate connection with the British Church before the coming of St Augustine from Rome. And in Ireland, as in England, the churches were small, generally divided into two nearly equal parts, and always finished with square rather than apsidal terminations In Scotland, under the same influence, we see the same effects—with the solitary exception of the circular church at Orphir, in Orkney, where the special circumstances of the case account for the variation.

Before the Norman Conquest England was, therefore, provided with churches which had, so far as we can see now, few marks of any sort of connection in style with those of France or Germany. At the time of the invasion, you know, from what I have already told you, that in almost all parts of France the apsidal east end was all but universally adopted; and what happens after the Conquest is equally significant and interesting. The Normans came over, and evidently, as all conquering people do, brought their art and their architects with them. Then our English monasteries had a most intimate connection with French monasteries, and nothing is more common than to find a monk sent from Cluny, or some other great French convent, to become head of an English house, such as Fountains Abbey, or others of almost equal importance. Each of these men, too, brought the latest fashions, and, as far as the English prejudices would allow, imported them in some degree into the work with which he became connected. In no respect is this more evident than in the substitution by the Norman builders of apsidal east ends for the original English square ones. The examples in which either these apses remain in part or in whole, or in which their foundations have been discovered, are the following among our cathedral churches : Canterbury, an apse with a circular chapel at the east end, built, or rather begun, on very much the same lines as Sens Cathedral, by a French architect, William of Sens ; Winchester, an apse with an aisle and chapels round it ; the cathedral at York, built after the Conquest by its first Norman prelate, Thomas, which had, no doubt, three, or even five, eastern apses, a fragment of the wall of one of these under the transept being still *in situ ;* Lincoln not only had three apses built by its first Norman bishop, Remigius, but, as far as can be made out from the small remains below the stalls and pavement, a second apse erected by St. Hugh, of Avalon, between 1186 and 1200, as well as the still remaining apsidal chapels to the eastern transepts ; Peterborough had an apse and probably aisles finished in the same way ; Gloucester, an apse with an aisle round it, three apsidal chapels, and one to each transept, the whole following exactly on the lines of Nôtre Dame du Port, Clermont-Ferrand, and the numerous similar French chevets ; Worcester, an apse with an aisle around it, and doubtless chapels ; Norwich, an apse with surrounding aisle and chapels, and two to the transepts, on the same lines as Canterbury ; Durham, chapter-house apsidal, and choir in all probability so also ; Chester, a short apsidal choir. With the exception of Canterbury, almost every one of these cathedrals had its eastern end greatly modified or wholly altered in the thirteenth and following centuries ; and everywhere, with the rarest exceptions, the later architects returned to what was the old and well-loved shape of the eastern limb of the cross before the Norman invasion. The apsidal termination to a church in England is, in fact, a distinct mark of foreign influence, and the universal objection to the form—for it is nothing short of this—on the part of the English at subsequent periods is, I believe, entirely due to the reviving national liking for what was consecrated in men's minds as their own national form. This was a perfectly natural thing if you consider for an instant the state of affairs. After the Conquest it is hardly too much to say that every bishopric and every abbey had forthwith imposed on it a French or Norman bishop or abbot. These, together with the foreign laymen entrusted with local commands, were the officers who were to keep the country in due order, and to take care that the Norman supremacy was not disturbed. Many of the bishops and abbots could not speak English. Everywhere they found the churches I have referred to existing. Usually these were insignificant, or, at any rate, far from magnificent buildings. They had wooden roofs and ceilings. Sometimes they were thatched, sometimes built wholly of timber, and sometimes of wicker-work—as in the famous case of the chapel which stood on or close to the site now occupied by St. Joseph's Chapel at Glastonbury —which was a structure of twisted rods or hurdles, covered in the seventh century by Paulinus, Archbishop of York, with boards, on which he laid "lead from the top to the bottom."

The foreign bishops naturally introduced foreign architecture and foreign architects Their churches had nothing whatever to do with those which had existed before, for these were a local development from, though with but little evidence of likeness to, the Roman buildings which had been scattered throughout the country during the Roman occupation, or else rude native copies of the basilicas which the British bishops had learnt to admire and venerate in their visits to Rome The new churches were, in fact, almost complete repetitions of the churches which had come to be built in Normandy as the result of the long course of development in French architecture which had culminated in the art of the eleventh century

In course of time the English began again to assert themselves. English bishops, English abbots, were appointed in place of foreigners, and with them English art made its first real mark in our country. Jocelin, Bishop of Wells and founder of the cathedral, and Hugh, the second bishop of the name, of Lincoln, were Englishmen and brothers, and commonly called Jocelin of Wells and Hugh of Wells, after their birthplace. And it was at the end of the twelfth century, when Englishmen were again asserting themselves in their own country, that the invention of the pointed arch enabled them to throw off the architectural yoke of the Normans, and develop a style for themselves, one of the features of which was, in regard to the ground-plan, a return to our own national form of square-ended church.

Whether I am right or not in my theory, the fact remains that, with one grand exception, the whole of the great English churches of the thirteenth century were square-ended. This exception is, of course, Westminster Abbey Here the evidence of the building itself seems to be conclusive that the king had resolved to build a church after the model of the great French churches, but employed an English architect to plan it, and he made his plan on lines which are distinct and different from those of any French church. Nothing is a more interesting subject for study than the adaptation of a foreign plan and design by an able Englishman devoted to his national art, but it is somewhat outside my subject to-night. All of us are proud of our beautiful minster ; we all feel it is no dry repetition or copy of another building ; but, at the same time, it is impossible to regard it as being a fair example of a purely English church. Some years ago, I believe that I proved to demonstration that the architect of Westminster built also, and at the same time, the beautiful church at Stone, in Kent. The arcades round the eastern portion of both churches, the detail of much of the ornament, and the character of the window tracery and of the clustered columns in the two churches, are to a large extent identical, and where they are not absolutely so, they are so nearly alike as to make it evident that they were designed by the same hand. The proportions of both churches are similarly designed on the equilateral triangle, and the materials used are the same. The interest of this smaller work is great, therefore, as showing that directly the architect of Westminster was free to do as he liked, he built as an Englishman of the strictest kind, with no evidence in any part of his work of foreign leanings, and notably with a square east end in place of his Westminster apse.

The gradual growth of an English church is nowhere to be studied better than at Canterbury, where we are so fortunate as to have the account of the building of the cathedral by two monks, Edmer and Gervase, one of whom described the history of the church in 1130, and the other its burning and rebuilding at the end of the century, and this last saw the work absolutely in progress till it became very much as we now have it. What happened at Canterbury gives us a clear insight into what happened, much in the same way, in other dioceses. The Saxon church was probably one built, as far as outline is concerned, to a considerable extent on the lines of the Basilica of St. Peter's. St. Augustine and his successors were so distinctly identified with Rome that it would have been certain in any case that this would be so, had not Edmer's account led to the same conclusion. Archbishop Lanfranc took this church down and rebuilt it on a larger scale, finishing his work in 1130. His plan included a nave and aisles, transepts with eastern apsidal chapels, and a short choir, probably finished with three eastern apses. The church was enlarged by another archbishop in order to satisfy the desire for a large choir, which involved in so many cases the destruction of our old cathedral choirs ; and in 1174 the enlarged church had arrived almost at the dimensions which it still has. It had a long choir, an eastern transept, in addition to the ordinary central transept, a great apse with an aisle round it, and apsidal chapels on either side of the main apse, and probably to the east of it also. The columns and arches were low, the aisles were vaulted, but the central portion was roofed with a wooden roof ceiled on the under side. This was again burnt in 1174, and the archbishop forthwith called in a French architect, William of Sens, who retained but increased the height of the columns and arches, and covered the whole choir with a stone vault above a triforium and clerestory. His successor, William the Englishman, finished the church by the erection of a second apsidal choir, with an aisle round it, which was built to receive the shrine of St. Thomas à Becket, and east of this a circular chapel, or Corona, as it is called   The whole scheme is now one of the most beautiful in Europe   The gradual narrowing of the choir before the junction of the eastern apse with the apse of Ernulf or Anselm is the result of an ingenious utilisation of the older church foundations still existing in the crypt   The same economical considerations affected the builders of many of the enlarged choirs of our cathedrals, as, *e.g*, Winchester and Gloucester, where the existence of a semicircular crypt compelled the later architect, who could not afford to destroy the whole of the foundations, to adopt some ingenious system of plan to enable himself to combine the two.   At the Abbey of St Denis, near Paris, precisely the same necessity compelled the architect to make the first bay of his choir incline considerably on plan   It is one of the charms of Gothic buildings that wherever such a necessity existed it was honestly met, as a matter of course, by some arrangement which, whilst it explained the fact on its face to every one, at the same time added to the picturesqueness and beauty of the design.

So great a work as this at Canterbury was, so magnificent in its results, would, it might have been supposed, have been followed, if not throughout the whole country, at least in the county and diocese. Strange to say, it had no followers, and seems to have produced no effect.   In most dioceses we find the most general and complete architectural influence exercised by the Mother Church   The men who built this either directed or inspired all the work in the district ; so that variations in design which were at first merely personal—the fancies of some one able man—came in course of time to be local peculiarities in which the original personal influence is no longer seen.   It is difficult to account for this contrary state of affairs in the case of Canterbury.   But probably the insular pride or prejudice —call it which you will—of the English resented the introduction of a style of building which had no connection with and never reminded them of the ancient traditional form of the English Church It is clear that the impetus given after the Norman invasion to the adoption of plans copied from or founded on the Norman churches soon ceased to produce effect   The great churches were most of them rebuilt in the new fashion, but not the less was there a deep dislike to the change, and a steady preference for the plan which was gradually felt to be more distinctly connected with the old times before the invasion and conquest   I am disposed also to lay some stress in this matter on the desire of Northern nations to secure the exact orientation not only of their churches, but of their altars also. The French did not feel this, and their altars arranged round a chevet face all ways. In Germany and in England, at any sacrifice almost, altars were made to face west. A singular instance of this I discovered in the crypt of Christ Church Cathedral, Dublin, where, in spite of the adoption of an apsidal termination to the choir, the three chapels to the east of it are all square-ended, so that all the altars might face the same way ; and in Germany, where an apse is built with a number of altars, you will find that they are placed, without any reference to the slope of the walls of the apse, facing due west. A strong tradition of this sort may easily have been offended by the apsidal form. The subject ought to be gone into more thoroughly than I have ever seen it treated. It is one of extreme interest, and an almost unique example of a national submission to a new type of plan, suddenly changed into a determined return to the older and—with the Conquerors—evidently unpopular plan. Certainly, within one hundred and fifty years of its introduction the use of the apse was abandoned, and almost every church in the thirteenth century in England was built with a square east end. The fact is so important, as bearing on the subsequent progress of English art, that it deserves our careful attention. You will recollect that almost all the problems which the French architects set themselves to solve were connected with the more perfect planning and designing of the chevets of their churches. They have left other magnificent ex-amples of their skill ; but it is to this part of their work that I always find myself most attracted, and in which I am sure that they were themselves most concerned. In England, on the contrary, the pre-judice against the apsidal end left the architects more free to devote themselves to all parts alike, and in the case of small churches, if the English system was less academic and exact than any can be which treats the support of stone vaults as the one great thing to be contrived, at the same time it secured an endless and picturesque variety of plan and design, in this respect excelling, in my judgment, all other countries. Observe, also, that the ingenuity of the French architects was devoted even more and more to the increase of the height and the decrease of the apparent means for supporting their lofty churches, so that by degrees it was of the interior of their churches that they came to think most, leaving the exteriors to some extent to take care of themselves. The English architects, on the other hand, being far less occupied with these particular scientific problems of construction, devoted themselves with all the greater zeal to the developing of the detail of their buildings, and being very practical artists, never lost sight of the importance of making the ex-terior as beautiful as the interior. The vast height of such churches as Amiens, Beauvais, Bourges, or Le Mans, makes it impossible that the exterior should be a complete whole, from whatever point it is viewed.

Canterbury, Lincoln, Wells, Salisbury, Lichfield, and York, not to name others, are all churches in which the height is insignificant when compared with the French examples just mentioned. But they are all complete and beautiful works on the outside as much as inside. Nowhere else in Europe is so good and strict a proportion observed. The moderate height of the roof made it possible to erect towers, or groups of towers, which, without trying to attain impossible dimensions, are nevertheless magnificent works. The towers of the west front of Amiens only look like towers when seen from the west front. When seen from the side in connection with the church, they shrink into mere turrets. Then, English architects had great common sense. They realised that the effect of size is not given by height alone. They knew that the effect of length in an interior was just as impressive, and by making the height of their buildings moderate, they immensely increased their apparent length. I remember spending a day at Amiens once, wrapt in admiration of its magnificent interior, and only wishing occasionally that the limits of the church allowed me to take in the upper part of the work, the clerestory and vaults, without lifting my head to an inconvenient angle. The next day I was at that loveliest of English fourteenth-century churches—Exeter. I went somewhat in dread of what I should feel. But the modest dimensions of the interior—not much more than a third of those of Amiens in height —I found had been so used by the Englishman as to produce the effects of infinite length, of size, of mystery, of beauty, to as great a degree as the work of the Frenchman had produced them [1] It is the modest completeness everywhere, the variety and beauty of the detail, and the judicious adaptation of the means at disposal to the end required, that strike me as the great achievement of the English school of architects of the thirteenth century. I hope I have travelled too much, seen too much, and admired too much the great works of other countries to be a prejudiced or unfair judge of the comparative merits of their respective works. But to me it seems matter for real congratulation that the students of our art have around them in this country on all sides buildings which are in almost all respects as well worthy of study as those of any other country, whilst in some of the highest qualities they are, if not unequalled, at any rate unsurpassed

The preference for the square plan of the east end of our churches was one only of the marked differences between English and French architects. The next in importance was the indifference of the former, save in very important works, to the use of

---

[1] In the Memoir I have mentioned that my father regretted much the want of height in our English cathedrals. The opinion expressed there was that of his earlier years, modified, as this passage shows, by further consideration.

stone-vaulted roofs. This indifference led, no doubt, to far greater facility in the way of changing the form of the ground-plan—and led to a freer and more picturesque if to a less stately and formal mode of design than the French system did.

But even more important than this difference is that which we find in the treatment of the capital by the two schools. In France, in all early architecture, the upper member or abacus of the capital is square on plan. This is the classical outline. It was modified at the end of the twelfth century by first taking off the angles. Then they were made octagonal, and at the end of the century a variety of angular lines were adopted ; and, save in such churches as Bayeux, Coutances, Norrey, and the Castle of Mont St. Michel, the circular capital is rarely seen. These exceptions prove the rule, for the architecture of Normandy in the thirteenth century ran a parallel course with that of England, and shows very nearly the same sort of developments. Broadly speaking, therefore, it is the fact, then, that the abacus of the capital is in French architecture square, in English circular. The results on the character of the architectural details from this small difference were very remarkable. French architects satisfied themselves with few, simple, and very uniform mouldings. The most common of all is the edge-roll, with a hollow on each side of it—a moulding which at no time has very much beauty, and soon satisfies the artist as to its capabilities. The square outline of the capital seems to necessitate an equally well-defined and sharp outline for the section of the arch. Broad, strongly-marked lines prevail, and comparatively little care is shown to vary the mouldings which are used. The effect of the employment of the circular capital was curiously different, and equally well marked. The general lines of the stonework of an arch which is fitted either to one or to a succession of round capitals are much softer and less positively defined than the former. The shadows are less strongly marked. With a succession of capitals which have a square abacus you have of necessity a succession of orders in the arch which have soffits at right angles to the face of the wall, and your mouldings are bound to keep to this outline. With a succession of circular caps all the angles have to be chamfered off, and the general line of the arch is at an angle of 45° to the face of the wall. At first sight this involves much less light and shade, and much less decided effect, and it becomes more than ever necessary to mould the stones in such a way as to produce the decided effects of light and shade which are required to make the effect of the arch perfect. Thus the circular capital leads naturally and insensibly, almost, to the development of the art of moulding, or (where mouldings have to be eschewed) to the soft and delicate chamfer in place of the strong and vigorous effects of the square abacus and square soffit in the arch.   The circular abacus is seen but rarely in Norman work in England   Among the earliest examples that I remember are the cathedral at Gloucester, Tewkesbury Abbey Church, and the fine crypt under the choir of St Mary's, Warwick; and at Canterbury one of William the Englishman's first variations from the work of William of Sens was the introduction of circular moulded capitals into his work.   After his time it is extremely rare to see anything save the circular or the octagonal cap used

Another element in the formation of our English style which has to be borne in mind is the nature of the most available stone. Undoubtedly the Caen stone quarries exercised great influence not only in Normandy, but equally in England, to many parts of which it was cheaper to bring that stone by water than to obtain native stones by land-carriage.   And to some extent, at least, the mason follows the stone.   In France, Caen stone was by no means so much used.   Out of Normandy it is very rarely seen; for, in truth, there it had to compete with local stones in all parts, and, as the land-carriage was a great difficulty, it was not used at any great distance.   The masons who developed a style at Caen had much less effect, therefore, naturally, in France than they had in England Their stone was used in London, in Dublin, all along the south and east coast of England, and, in short, wherever water-carriage was available.   Its texture allowed of the most delicate workmanship being seen to the greatest perfection, and I think I have never seen or used a stone which seems to appeal so forcibly to the mason to exercise his skill, wholly unlike the coarse stones which are so common in other parts of France, and which seem to make the best and most polished workmanship to some extent a waste of labour The thirteenth-century buildings in Normandy, thanks to this stone, are extraordinarily rich in delicate mouldings, undercut with the greatest skill, and producing the most intricate and charming effects of light and shade, and in almost all respects just such as are used in our best English building of the same period   In England not only was Caen stone largely used, as I have said, wherever water-carriage allowed of its being easily landed, but in various districts stone was to be found which admitted of the same kind of workmanship as Caen stone.   Each cathedral grew, and the best buildings were erected, in the neighbourhood of some stone quarry which supplied ample material.   Salisbury was built from Chilmark, Wells from Doulting, Peterborough from Barnack, York from Tadcaster, and so on; and in all these cases the stone was of fine and good quality, and admitted of finished workmanship, nearly equal to that which the masons employed in the Caen district.

English architecture in the thirteenth century was launched on its course with its own national peculiarities in ground-plan, in the shape of the capital, and in the practice of the art of moulding as one of the main modes of decoration to be made use of, and, at the same time, with what I am almost obliged to call an indifference to the sculptor's art. The examples of thirteenth-century sculpture are not such as one can venture to compare for an instant with those grand arrays of figure and subject with which the French churches were so profusely adorned. The west front of Wells Cathedral is the finest example we have, and the execution and design of the subjects and statues here is, in many respects, admirable, justifying Flaxman's statement that "in parts there is a beautiful simplicity, an irresistible sentiment, and sometimes a grace, excelling some modern productions." Close upon Wells followed Salisbury; less fortunate, however, in that a larger proportion of the ancient statues have been destroyed or have decayed. But even in these cases the sculpture plays a remarkably subordinate part. It more or less extends over the whole front, and yet it nowhere overwhelms or interferes with the architectural lines. These are as defined as possible from the base to the summit, and are almost as predominant where there is sculpture as where there is none. Crowland Abbey —now, unfortunately, in ruins—the south transept of York, Dunstable Priory, the west front of Ely, had all of them sculpture introduced in the same fashion. Statues standing on corbels under arcades in the walls, and subjects carved in spandrels or in the tympana over archways, as in the north door at Salisbury and the west doorway of Higham Ferrers, are features in the decoration of all these churches. The south doorway of the choir of Lincoln is almost a solitary example of a doorway with sculptured statues on its piers, its jambs, round the orders of the arch, and in the tympanum between the arches of the doors and the enclosing arch. Even here, if you compare it with French work, you will be struck with the modest proportions of the whole, and with the extremely well-defined character of the architectural lines which enclose and keep in due restraint the exuberance of the sculptor. In what is, perhaps, the most poetical conception in England, the west front of Peterborough, it is not until the three magnificent arches are completed, with all their well-ordered and chastely simple array of shafted jamb and moulded arch, that the sculptor has been allowed to fill the gables and the spandrels with an array of statues in niches, capable, possibly, of some religious interpretation, but not near enough to the eye to be criticised as works of art, and only serving for the general decoration of the gables in company with rose windows and arcades and mouldings. If, however, in sculpture used as a decoration of architecture England is somewhat wanting, this cannot be said of sculpture as applied to monumental effigies, or of the work of the stone-carver in the humbler decoration, such as foliage of the capitals and other members of our buildings. In these English buildings are rich, and the refined and delicate beauty which was so evident in them is equally evident in their decorations. The carving of foliage is perfect in the arrangement of the masses and in the beauty of form and line which marks every part. It has far greater variety than French work of the same date, and trusts more to perfection of treatment throughout than to the somewhat violent, if vigorous, treatment of the usual French capitals. The detail of foliage develops gradually throughout the century, from the transitional carving of St. Joseph's Chapel, Glastonbury, to the beautiful adaptation, in some cases at Wells and St. David's, of Romanesque outlines, or at Salisbury, Ely, Lincoln, and York, till it culminates in such admirable and truly architectural treatment of natural forms as we see towards the end of the century in stone in the chapter-house at Southwell and the passage to the chapter-house at York, and in wood in the stalls of Winchester Cathedral

It is time now to do as I did in speaking of French architecture, and to say something on the way in which the English architects did their work in some two or three typical examples. None, I think, are better for our purpose than Wells and Glastonbury on the one hand, and Salisbury on the other, the two cathedrals being wells of English undefiled, and illustrating two different modes of treatment—decoration of the structure by the shaft and column in the one, and by moulding and masonry in the other.

At Glastonbury, St. Joseph's Chapel is of supreme interest. In the delicate beauty of its detail it is worthy to be compared to the chapter-house of St George's, Boscherville. The excellence of every portion is quite incontestable in both, and there are some points of similarity in the two works which can rather perhaps be felt than described The chapter-house was built by Abbot Victor, who was abbot from 1157 to 1211, and its date is therefore somewhat uncertain. The date of St Joseph's Chapel, on the contrary, is most exactly defined. The wicker church, on the site of which it was built, was burnt down on 25th May 1184, and the new chapel was dedicated on 11th June 1186 At this period, then, we see a building in which the architectural features are in part detached columns with caps and bases, in part mouldings of masonry continuous round jamb and arch. The great north door illustrates this—two of its orders have shafts, with capitals and bases, two, continuous lines of carved ornament. The buttresses all have engaged shafts at their angles, *i e* shafts, worked out of the masonry, and not detached nook-shafts The groining shafts, like those to the buttresses, are all pointed in section, *i.e*, they have a sharp line up the centre of the face, and the same feature is repeated in the mouldings on the western turrets. The great abbey church to the east of this chapel is all but destroyed ; but what remains shows that its designers had advanced in style, but had retained many of the peculiarities of St. Joseph's Chapel. The engaged shafts in the buttresses, with the sharp centre, and the system of continuous moulded columns instead of detached shafts, is carried still further. What is more singular is that the wall-rib of the groining is carried up from the window-sills, and returned round them also. Thus you will see that the whole scheme is one of moulded stonework, as opposed to a system of columns or combinations of detached shafts. At Wells the same system is seen. The cathedral was built during the episcopate of Jocelin Trotman, who was consecrated in 1206, and who died in 1242. From 1208 to 1214 he was in France, having been banished for taking the pope's side against the king. Jocelin the Englishman, as he was called, knew all about the French art of the day. He was present at the laying of the first stone of Rheims Cathedral in 1211, and he saw Nôtre Dame completed, and no doubt many others of the great French churches in progress. But even if he admired them, his English sense forbade him to use them, or else his English architect must have been as averse as any one could be to mere repetition of anything that he saw, with the one doubtful exception that to a certain extent he retained the square capital. The nave piers show us in perfection what we see only in ruins at Glastonbury. They are masses of masonry, built up of eight clusters of triple shafts carrying alternately octagonal and square capitals, and on these arch mouldings of three orders, two of which are planned on the chamfer and one on the square. Above the triforium is a long arcade, three to each bay, of moulded members, continuous round jamb and arch, and above this a clerestory, modernised, it is true, but with no sign of ever having had any inside shafts or any string-course or abacus at the spring of the arches. The groining is carried upon a triple shaft built into the wall. Everywhere the detail of moulding and carving is admirable. And the effect of the modest dimensions of this little church (the nave is only thirty-seven feet wide from centre to centre of the columns, and about sixty-six feet high), insignificant as they are in comparison with those of the great French churches, is nevertheless very beautiful and harmonious in all points of view. The groining is supported by flying buttresses under the roofs of the aisles, but there are none above them. The clerestory wall is, instead, very thick, and only moderately pierced with windows, so that the construction is as unlike that of the examples in France, of which I was speaking in my last lecture, as it well can be. I ought perhaps before this to have said that the north porch and the west front and western steeples are in a wholly different style from the work I have been describing in the nave and transepts. The one is probably of earlier, the other of later, date, but in both the detached shaft is used as freely as possible in opposition to the style of the nave, where its use may almost be said to have been prohibited.

The influence of Glastonbury and Wells, or of the Doulting masons and architects—whichever it was—did not end here . Throughout Somersetshire, when you come upon a piece of thirteenth-century work, it is generally in the same style   The same style is conspicuously visible at Llaudaff and at St. David's, and seeing that St. Patrick was buried in Glastonbury, it would not be unreasonable to look for some evidence of its influence in Ireland.   But it was the course of conquest more probably than that of pilgrims which led to the introduction of Glastonbury art into Ireland   Strongbow's invasion was a South Wales invasion, and everywhere within the Irish Pale we see the architecture suddenly changed from the old Irish style to one which has the most definite evidence everywhere of its Somersetshire origin   In Christ Church Cathedral, Dublin, for instance, we see the same triple shafts, the same combinations of groups of them to form columns, the same alternation of square and octagonal caps, the same fondness for the engaged column with an arris or edge formed up the centre of its face, the same general proportions, the same carving of foliage, and the same love of continuous mouldings   Kilkenny Cathedral, Kildare Cathedral, and others show the same features as Christ Church, Dublin, and at Killaloe, and constantly in Irish examples we see the features seen at Glastonbury and at Wells, and rarely elsewhere—the mouldings of window jambs returned round the sills.

Interesting on all these grounds as the church at Wells is, I have selected it for notice to-night not only because of its specially English character, and of the influence it exercised, but because it presents in a marvellously perfect condition the whole group of attached buildings which makes up the complete English cathedral establishment, and which are so rarely seen remaining and still in use anywhere on the Continent   Among them are the chapter-house, the cloister, the bishop's palace, all containing considerable portions of the thirteenth century, besides a marvellous collection of later mediæval buildings   The chapter-house was begun rather late, and its crypt only can certainly be said to be of our period.   This is of special interest, as showing that though our English architects liked a square east end, they had no sort of dislike to a circular building, and the plan of the crypt, with its central column under that of the chapter-house, the eight detached shafts which surround it, and the planning of the groining with none but triangular bays, will have much interest for those of you who followed me in my remarks on the planning of the chevets of the French churches.   The bishop's palace is not less interesting   It, too, was built by Bishop Jocelin, and agrees in style with the later shafted work of the west front. Its lower stage is mainly a long groined chamber subdivided by walls and partitions, and above this, on the first floor, a long gallery lighted by windows, which illustrate well a favourite development of the men who built the west front. They not only began to make their windows more decorative by joining lights together, but they gave them cusped internal or rere arches. By cusped arches I mean arches which are formed of a series of curves without any enclosing arch; these occur frequently in the west front, in a doorway in the cloister, and in various windows in the palace, wherever one meets with the work of this second school of Wells architects.

From the simple Early Pointed work of the palace one goes on to the slightly later work of the chapel, and thence to the magnificent ruin of the hall, at each step finding the development of the style more advanced, till, in the last, the work of Bishop Burnell, at the end of the century (1274-92), we have the complete change effected to the Middle Pointed style. Nowhere, therefore, can you see better than here the gradual change which the century saw completed. At the beginning we have the work of an architect whose great idea was to make his work solid, and yet as beautiful as possible, by the simple use of well-designed mouldings, of groups of moulded shafts for columns, and by the simplest use of the pointed arch. Then, probably, before the west front was begun, another man came upon the scene. The first man had cared nothing for what was being done at Salisbury. He had been not only English, but Somersetshire to the root. His successor thinks this line a mistaken one. He admires what the Salisbury, the Lincoln, and other English architects were doing, and covers his west front with arcades or arches, all carried on detached shafts, and enclosing the figures and statuary of which all Englishmen are or ought to be so proud. His influence is evident also in the bishop's palace, and to a less degree in the great dining-hall, where the windows have still internal jamb-shafts; but in the end the early system is practically accepted again, and almost all over England in the fourteenth century the system of moulded and clustered solid shafts, and continuous lines of arch and jamb moulding, which had been first brought to perfection in Wells, was accepted as the best and universal rule.

Something must now be said of one of the great examples of the other system, and we can hardly do better than see the effect it produced, where, as at Salisbury, it is carried all through a building, instead of being, as at Wells, confined only to one front. Salisbury Cathedral was built from the ground on a site never before occupied. The first stones were laid on 28th April 1220. In 1225 some altars were consecrated, and in 1229 Bishop Poore, the founder, died, and

In 1258 the cathedral was consecrated By this time, after thirty-eight years' work, we may assume that the church was practically complete. It was later in its foundation, probably, by some half-dozen years than Wells Bishop Poore and his architect—Elias of Dereham, probably—had no sympathy with the system of design pursued in the nave of Wells The Isle of Purbeck was in the diocese, and there was every reason, therefore, for indulging as much as possible in the use of its beautiful marble The introduction of detached shafts wherever possible, and which follows naturally from the use of marble, wholly changes the character of the architecture The effect is admirable , but, on the other hand, the risk in construction was great The variety in the plans of the clustered columns at Salisbury was very great. In the nave the common French section of a circular column surrounded by four smaller shafts is adopted, but here the shafts are detached from the centre column. In the choir the columns are surrounded by eight detached shafts In the doorways and windows shafts are placed in various ways—in clusters and one behind another—so as to produce very deep effects of light and shade, with the advantage that, all the lines being curved, the transition from light to dark is never too abrupt In the lady chapel this system culminates. The width is subdivided into three aisles, and the vaults are carried—one is almost tempted to say appear to be carried—on shafts so long, and so delicate and frail, as to have required the very highest skill to ensure their standing, even during their construction, let alone standing, as they do, 650 years after their erection. The architect throughout the cathedral dispensed, as did the architect of Wells, with visible flying buttresses , he used them only under the roofs of the aisles, but in order to make the thrust on the walls less, he built his vaults with stone ribs, filling in the spaces between them with concrete made of a very light calcareous tufa He used an unnecessary thickness of this material, but as it was extraordinarily light, his construction was generally perfectly secure, as in two or three places only has it been found necessary in later times to add flying buttresses above the aisle roofs. Beautiful as the detail of the cathedral is, there is generally some sense of disappointment in its interior Unfortunately it is a church full of windows, and the grisaille with which these were filled is almost all destroyed. Its roofs and its walls were richly coloured, and the only portion which remained has been restored, and is no longer at all like the old in its effect The painters, as at Chartres, painted the outside work in places, as, *e.g.,* in the west porch and the porch to the chapter-house In other places, as, *e.g*, on the concrete groining of the porch and of the nave and on the walls of the cloister, they coloured the walls and then marked them out in imitation masonry lines of red colour.

The ground-plan of this great church is one of extreme beauty. It has not only the usual transept with an eastern aisle, but to the east of this a second and shorter transept, devised evidently in emulation of the eastern transept of Canterbury, which itself was no doubt derived from the great Benedictine abbey church of Cluny, now destroyed, and before its destruction the only church in France in which this beautiful arrangement was seen. This eastern transept has also its aisle on the east, and is of less width and proportion than the great transept. East of the choir are three lower chapels, in which are the delicate arrangements of clustered and single marble shafts which I have already referred to; and it was in the side walls of the central of these three chapels that, before Wyatt's so-called restoration, there remained an arcade which for perfection of design and execution has never, I am bold to say, been surpassed anywhere in Europe. It is now built into the west wall of the eastern transept, and will ere long, I believe, be seen again in its old place. If it is possible to say so much of the interior, what may we not say of the exterior? With one exception—the destruction of the detached bell-tower which stood in the churchyard till Wyatt's time—the church is now more beautiful than it was when it left its builder's hands. Elias of Dereham might well deplore the changes which men have made in the colour of his interior. But could he see it again, he would be amazed with the beauty which time has given to the exterior. There is, so far as I know, no building in Christendom on so grand a scale, which is so complete, so uniform in style, so good in the proportions of the various parts to the whole, and altogether, and from every point of view, so thoroughly beautiful, as this grand and most English church. Its surroundings are as beautiful. The quiet close—unknown out of England—surrounded by deanery and prebendal houses, by a bishop's palace founded at the same time as the cathedral, the whole group surrounded by its ancient wall, and entered by its old gateways, is in itself a sight for an architect; but out of the greensward which surrounds it on all sides the matchless church rises, with its beautiful cloisters, its splendid polygonal chapter-house, its octagonal vestry on its southern side, in such completeness of grace and beauty as leaves nothing to be desired.

Like Wells, Salisbury is a cathedral well worthy of a young architect's study above most others. For not only will he find there the work of the mason in all its varieties; he will find, too, woodwork of all sorts, moulded, carved, and plain,—roofs, doors, chests, tables, choir stalls, even the great wooden wheel which was used to raise the stone for the steeple; and in every portion he will find evidence of the same sense of the necessity for completeness, which is the true mark of a good architect at all times. The detail everywhere is admirable. The carving of foliage is very different from, though in my opinion generally inferior to, that at Wells, and there is one very singular feature which is seldom seen in England The arcades of the parapets, and in many other places, are carried on quite regardless of the buttresses which intersect and stop them. So that, *e.g.*, in the front of the transepts, there are arcades not regularly divided, but quite accidentally arranged with half or a third of an arch abutting against a buttress, so as to give the appearance of the buttress being an afterthought put on against the arcade

I should have liked to take you on to the other great thirteenth-century churches, to talk to you about Archbishop Walter Grey's magnificent work, the transept of York, and to compare this with his work at Southwell I should have liked to show what St. Hugh, and, after him, Jocelin of Wells's brother, Hugh of Wells, Bishop of Lincoln, did so exquisitely in their glorious minster, and, above all, to have seen what that great Yorkshireman, Henry Murdac, once monk of Clairvaux, then abbot of Vauclair, then of Fountains, and afterwards Archbishop of York, did in the magnificent abbey, so much of which still remains in the beautiful valley of the Skell, how at Fountains he built at first in a French style, and how, as elsewhere, gradually the English art reasserted itself. But, after all, the story is much the same everywhere, and the superlative interest of such an abbey as Fountains is the insight that it gives us into the domestic architecture of the period. The more one sees of it the more does one discover that in those good days there was no such distinction between domestic architecture and ecclesiastical as has sometimes been supposed to exist The same details that were applied to one were thought suitable to the other, it was the best construction and the most suitable arrangement, the most beautiful proportion, the most delicate moulding of stonework, the truest system of carving of foliage, that were everywhere seen, whether the work to be done was for a house or a church, for a monastery or for a castle. The work in the great hall of the castle at Winchester is as good as that of Bishop de Lucy at the same time in the cathedral. The castle at Chepstow is as good, and in the same style, as the abbey at Tintern, and the hall for the layman at Acton Burnell is on the same lines as the hall which Bishop Burnell built at the end of the thirteenth century in the palace at Wells. No more pernicious doctrine has ever been inculcated than that which supposes one sort of art to be sacred and unfit for use for secular purposes The best art is that which is fittest for the first purpose, and I suppose we all agree that we should, if it were possible, like to have it for the other also. This is the lesson of the thirteenth century, on which so much remains to be said that I am distressed to think how inadequately I have been able to say what, with more time, I hope I might have said in detail on the subject. It was impossible in an hour all could be said that might be ; and it seemed to me that there would be more chance of saying something new to you if I took a somewhat similar line on the development of styles in the best periods in Italy, France, and England, than if I tried to show you exactly how they differed one from another in each detail of their work, and exactly what those details were. It is my fault if I have failed to show you how interesting the study may be made if you pursue it with something beyond the mere daily drudgery of attention to business. The other arts hardly afford the young student a tithe of the pleasure or the profit from such studies which everywhere throughout the civilised world attend the earnest student of architecture, and my last words to you for this year are, that you should regard the addresses which I have given as being entirely meant to be suggestive of further lines of study and investigation by yourselves. And I end, as I began, by impressing on you that no one can become a good architect who does not earnestly study what men have done before, who has not enthusiasm for his art to make him long and resolve to do nothing but what is good in its practice, and who is not ready to show that he has enthusiasm by the industry which surely attends it, and without which no study, no lectures, and no schools can be of any real service.

THE END

Printed by R. & R CLARK, *Edinburgh*

The Manners and Customs of the Ancient Egyptians.
Their Private Life, Government, Laws, Arts, Manufactures,
Religion, Agriculture, Early History, etc   By Sir J GARDNER
WILKINSON, F R.S   A New Edition, revised and edited by
SAMUEL BIRCH, LL.D   With Coloured Plates and 500 Illus-
trations   3 vols Medium 8vo   84s

History of Egypt under the Pharaohs.   Derived entirely
from the Monuments   By Dr. HENRY BRUGSCH.   Translated
by PHILIP SMITH, B.A   Second Edition, revised.   With Maps
and Illustrations.   2 vols   8vo.   32s.

The Cities and Cemeteries of Etruria.   By GEORGE DENNIS
A New Edition, revised and enlarged.   With Maps and 200
Illustrations   2 vols.   Medium 8vo.   42s.

A History of Ancient Geography among the Greeks and
Romans, from the Earliest Ages   By E. H. BUNBURY.   With
20 Maps.   2 vols.   8vo.   42s.

England's Chronicle in Stone : Derived from the Cathedrals,
Churches, Abbeys, Monasteries, Castles, and Palaces of the
Imperial Island.   By JAMES F HUNNEWELL   With 60 Illus-
trations   Medium 8vo   24s.

Too Late for Gordon and Khartoum.   The Testimony of
an Independent Eyewitness of the Heroic Efforts for their
Rescue and Relief   By ALEXANDER MACDONALD   Maps and
Plans.   Crown 8vo.   12s

Virgil in English Verse.   Eclogues, and Æneid Books,
I -VI   By Lord Justice Sir CHARLES BOWEN.   Map and
Frontispiece.   Crown 8vo   12s

The Consulting Architect.   Practical Notes on Adminis-
trative Difficulties   By ROBERT KERR, Author of "The
English Gentleman's House," etc.   Crown 8vo.   9s

CONTENTS.—Consultation and Evidence—Arbitration Cases—Question of Structural
Damage—Easements—Ancient Lights—Questions of Support—Sanitary Cases—Lease-
hold Questions—Questions of Valuation—Building Questions—The Building Act—
Architects' Disputes and Etiquette.

Persia and the Persians.   By the Hon S. G. W. BENJAMIN,
late Minister of the United States to the Court of Persia.   With
56 Illustrations.   8vo.   24s.

Old English Plate Ecclesiastical, Decorative, and Domestic ,
its Makers and Marks   By WILFRED J CRIPPS, M.A., F.S.A
Third and Revised Edition.   With 104 Illustrations, and 2000
Facsimiles of Plate Marks.   Medium 8vo   21s.

JOHN MURRAY, ALBEMARLE STREET, LONDON.

Lightning Source UK Ltd.
Milton Keynes UK
UKOW011824270312

189687UK00006B/30/P